William Eustis Russell, Charles Theodore Russell

Speeches and Addresses of William E. Russell

William Eustis Russell, Charles Theodore Russell

Speeches and Addresses of William E. Russell

ISBN/EAN: 9783337168353

Printed in Europe, USA, Canada, Australia, Japan

Cover: Foto ©ninafisch / pixelio.de

More available books at **www.hansebooks.com**

SPEECHES AND ADDRESSES

OF

WILLIAM E. RUSSELL.

SELECTED AND EDITED BY

CHARLES THEODORE RUSSELL, JR.

With an Introduction

BY

THOMAS WENTWORTH HIGGINSON.

BOSTON:
LITTLE, BROWN, AND COMPANY.
1894.

TO

MY FATHER,

TO WHOM I HAVE EVER LOOKED FOR SYMPATHY, ADVICE,
AND AID IN MEETING OFFICIAL DUTIES,
AND NEVER LOOKED IN VAIN,

I DEDICATE THIS VOLUME.

IN editing these SPEECHES AND ADDRESSES of the Hon. WILLIAM E. RUSSELL, the Editor has not attempted to make a complete collection of them, but has endeavored to select such as might have a more than temporary interest as well from their intrinsic merit as from the interest in the general subject.

Many speeches of value in themselves have been omitted, owing to their temporary or local character. In pursuance of this plan, it has been thought best to omit all his municipal addresses and messages.

In making the selection from over two hundred and fifty political speeches, the Editor has endeavored to form a series treating of the tariff in as many different phases as possible, and of its effect upon the various industries of Massachusetts and New England. He has also included some speeches which illustrate the marked personal characteristics and style of Governor Russell's campaign arguments.

Many of the addresses, and substantially all the political speeches as published, have been collected from reports in the newspapers made at the time of delivery, and may to some degree lack the finish which would come from more elaborate preparation and revision.

CHARLES THEODORE RUSSELL, JR.

CAMBRIDGE, Dec. 9, 1893.

CONTENTS.

Speeches on General Occasions.

	PAGE
Address delivered at Union Hall, at the Dedication of the Young Men's Christian Association, Dec. 10, 1885	1
Address at the Two Hundred and Fiftieth Anniversary of the Establishment of the First Church of Cambridge, Feb. 12, 1886	4
Speech on the Question of Constitutional Prohibition, Boston, April, 1889	10
Address at Atlanta, Georgia, Feb. 13, 1890. The New North and the New South	16
Address to the Harvard Alumni, at Cambridge, on Commencement Day, June 24, 1891	29
Address at a Public Reception tendered Ex-President Cleveland at Sandwich, July 25, 1891	35
Address at the Dedication of the Monument commemorating the Battle of Bennington, at Bennington, Aug. 19, 1891	39
Address at the Dinner given by the French Societies of Massachusetts to Hon. Wilfred Laurier, Leader of the Liberal Party of Canada, Nov. 17, 1891	44
Address at the Opening of the New Building of the Boston Chamber of Commerce, Jan. 21, 1892	48
Address to the Harvard Alumni, at Cambridge, on Commencement Day, June 30, 1892	52
Address at the Two Hundred and Fiftieth Anniversary of the Settlement of Woburn, Mass., at Woburn, Sept. 27, 1892	57
Speech at the Opening of the Exhibition of the Charitable Mechanics Association, Oct. 6, 1892	61
Speech at the Dinner of the Irish Charitable Society in Boston, March 19, 1893	64

viii CONTENTS.

        PAGE

Introductory Remarks as Presiding Officer at the Dinner given to Hon. P. A. Collins, in Boston, April 4, 1893, upon his Departure as Consul-General to London 68

Speech at the Dinner of the British Charitable Society, in Boston, May 24, 1893 71

Introductory Remarks as Presiding Officer at the Dinner given by the Massachusetts Delegation to the Officials of the World's Fair, in Chicago, June 15, 1893 74

Address at the Banquet given by the Massachusetts Society of Chicago to the Massachusetts Delegation to the World's Fair, at Chicago, June 17, 1893 76

Speech at the Annual Dinner of the Harvard Alumni, at Cambridge, Commencement Day, June 28, 1893 83

Address at Holy Cross College, Worcester, on Commencement Day, June 29, 1893 89

Speech at the One Hundredth Anniversary of Williams College, Oct. 10, 1893 92

Speech at the Dedication of Trenton Battle Monument, Trenton, Oct. 19, 1893 97

Speeches on Military Occasions.

Address to the Cambridge Posts of the Grand Army of the Republic, Memorial Day, May 30, 1885 101

Address as Presiding Officer at the Memorial Service to General Grant in Union Hall, Cambridge, Aug. 8, 1885 103

Address at the Twenty-fifth Anniversary of the Departure of the First Company of Volunteers to the War, Cambridge, April 17, 1886 . 104

Speech at the Dinner of the Ancient and Honorable Artillery Company, Faneuil Hall, June 1, 1891 107

Speech at the Dinner of the Ancient and Honorable Artillery Company, Faneuil Hall, June 6, 1892 111

Speech at the Annual Encampment of the Grand Army of the Republic, Faneuil Hall, Feb. 9, 1893 116

State Speeches.

	PAGE
Inaugural Address to the Legislature of Massachusetts, Jan. 8, 1891 .	119
Inaugural Address to the Legislature of Massachusetts, Jan. 7, 1892 .	147
Message vetoing an Act to authorize the Connecticut River Railroad Company to increase its Capital Stock, May 9, 1892	177
Message vetoing an Act to promote Temperance by the Suppression of the Liquor Saloon, June 16, 1892	184
Inaugural Address to the Legislature of Massachusetts, Jan. 5, 1893 .	189
Message vetoing an Act relative to Persons employed in the Fire Department of Boston, March 27, 1893	214
Message vetoing the Act to incorporate the Town of East Longmeadow, May 5, 1893	217

Political Speeches.

Speech at Middlesex County Democratic Club, Boston, March 5, 1885   221

Speech at Union Meeting of Democrats and Independents, at Music Hall, Boston, Oct. 25, 1886. The Democratic Party the Party of Progress 224

Speech at Baltimore, Md., July 4, 1888, as Presiding Officer of the Convention of the Democratic Clubs of the United States . . . 232

Speech at Springfield, Mass., July 26, 1888. The Tariff 238

Speech at Tremont Temple, Boston, Oct. 27, 1888. The Tariff . . 258

Speech at the Young Men's Democratic Club Dinner, Boston, Dec. 17, 1888, upon the Lessons of Defeat 266

Speech at the Democratic State Convention, Worcester, Oct. 2, 1889. The Record of the Republican Party 272

Speech at the Bay State Club Dinner, Boston, Oct. 12, 1889. Comparison of the Democratic and Republican Platforms 278

Speech at the Young Men's Democratic Club Dinner, Boston, Dec. 14, 1889. The Difference between the Parties 290

Speech at Norwood, Oct. 11, 1890, upon the Tariff and the Lobby . 297

Speech at Lowell, Oct. 19, 1890. The Tariff 312

Speech at Fall River. Labor Legislation. — The Tariff in its Relation to Wages and to the Cotton Industry 320

CONTENTS.

	PAGE
Speech at Gardner, Mass., Oct. 28, 1890. The Tariff in its Relation to the Farming Industry	338
Speech at the Tariff Reform League Dinner, New York, Dec. 23, 1890	348
Speech at the Democratic State Convention, Worcester, Sept. 29, 1891. State Issues	353
Speech at Music Hall, Boston, Oct. 5, 1891. The Tariff and its Effect upon Massachusetts	364
Speech at Lynn, Oct. 29, 1891. State Issues: The Tariff in its Relation to the Leather Industry	380
Speech at Dedham, Oct. 9, 1892. State Issues: The Meaning of Tariff for Revenue. — The Effect of Tariff upon Prices	393
Speech at Malden, Oct. 10, 1892. The Force Bill	409
Speech at Newburyport, Oct. 14, 1892. The Tariff, especially in its Relation to Trusts	418
Speech at Lawrence, Oct. 26, 1892. State Issues: The Tariff in its Relation to the Woollen Industry	430
Speech at Fitchburg, Oct. 31, 1892. The Tariff in its Relation to the Iron Industry	444
Speech at Haverhill, Oct. 24, 1893. The Political Causes of the Business Depression of 1893	454

INTRODUCTION.

IT was noticeable during our Civil War that there were two kinds of officers who called forth especial enthusiasm among their soldiers. One type was "the old man," commonly a person in middle life, who had a sort of paternal relation to those under him, and had the influence that belongs to civic reputation and mature seniority, even before testing his ability in the new field. The other was the kind of officer described by the men as "our young captain," — perhaps, even, "our little captain," — who was possibly more youthful and delicate in appearance than any of those whom he commanded, and who, for that very reason, if he had the stuff in him, was to them a source of pride in inverse ratio to his years. The mere fact of his not needing the vantage ground of age made him stronger than if he had it; his veteran soldiers exulted in his very youth, and in the surprise which it inspired in strangers. It was like the pride taken by old men-o'-war's men in some favorite midshipman; or like the enthusiasm early called out among Napoleon's soldiers for "the Little Corporal" (*Le Petit Caporal*). Something of this feeling survives in our politics; and though the recent campaigns of the Democratic party have brought many young men to the front, no one has so distinctly exemplified this advantage as William Eustis Russell.

He was born in Cambridge, Mass., Jan. 6, 1857, being the ninth child and fourth and youngest son of Charles Theodore and Sarah Elizabeth (Ballister) Russell. Upon the father's side he is of the ninth generation from William Russell, a Puritan colonist who settled in Cambridge in 1645. On the mother's side he is of French Huguenot extraction. He was educated in the Cambridge public schools, and graduated at Harvard University in 1877. His rank in his class was not high, but fair, and he was elected class secretary, which implied a good standing among his classmates. Two years later he took his degree of Bachelor of Laws at the Boston University Law School, where his father was a professor. There he gained the first *Summa cum laude* conferred by the school, winning the Lawrence Prize for the best legal essay, and delivering the class oration. In 1880 he was admitted to the bar, becoming a member of his father's firm, with which he has always remained connected. In that same year he began political speaking in support of General Hancock, the Democratic nominee for the Presidency, and of his own father, who had been nominated, though unsuccessfully, for Congress. In 1881 he was chosen a member of the Cambridge Common Council; in the two following years served as an alderman; and was mayor for the four years from 1885 to 1888, he being during two of these years the only candidate in the field. In this last year he was first nominated for governor, and made nearly fifty speeches for tariff reform in different parts of the State. For two successive years he was defeated; but he was finally elected in 1890, and again in 1891 and 1892, although Massachusetts in each year proved itself still a Republican State. In the last-named year, for instance (1892), the plurality for the highest Republican presidential elector was 26,001, while Governor Russell's plurality was 2,534. It is very rare in our politics to see such a discrepancy as this.

But the greater the personal triumph, the greater the inconvenience subsequently endured. During his whole three years of office he had to hold his own against a Legislature and a State government politically opposed to him. It is unnecessary to point out that this was a great test of courage and judgment, and that he experienced the benefit of the long official training which he had received. The tact, the energy, the patience which had been developed by four years in the mayor's chair were all needed for his three years of gubernatorial life, and he had cultivated those qualities in a high degree. To retire voluntarily from such a position after three years of service without having made a single serious mistake, and with the respect of his very opponents, was to have endured an ordeal such as is not common in public life.

This showed that his public career, though it came to him early, did not come prematurely. When he became, like his father and grandfather before him, a State official, he was far older in experience and in years than Gladstone when he entered Parliament at twenty-two, or Lord John Russell when he entered it at one-and-twenty. The real truth is that Governor Russell looked much younger than he was; and that, still retaining that aspect, he disarms criticism in advance. To the stranger who sees him for the first time it might appear that a mistake has been made, and that, through some accident, a law student or an undergraduate has been deputed to fill the place of his Excellency. Such an impression gives to a public speaker a vantage ground of cordial and kindly expectancy; and more than this no good speaker needs. Having availed himself of it almost unconsciously, since it is now probably an old story, the orator can afford to cast it utterly aside and proceed to business. In Governor Russell's case there has never been any special affectation of youth, in dress, bearing, or language; he does not trade upon it, but wears this youthful appearance for the simple reason that he cannot help it. His habits of physical activity maintain it whether he will or no, and his great power of work preserves the equilibrium on the intellectual side. It was said of an early Cambridge pastor, who founded the church in which Governor Russell was brought up, the Rev. Thomas Shepard, who died before the meridian of life, that he was "a truly aged young man;" and this would be a good formula to describe the impression made by Governor Russell.

It is always noticed by the hearer that after Governor Russell has once entered on his speech, he enrolls himself instantly among what may be called the business-like orators as distinct from the rhetorical orators. Except President Eliot, I know no public speaker in New England who devotes himself so promptly to the matter in hand, and is so utterly devoid of claptrap. I have often spoken with him on the same platform, and have never known an exception to this general characterization of his manner and method. There is never any digression, rarely any illustration; he simply speaks right on, and holds his audience as he grasps the subject. Theodore Parker used to say that a New England audience pre-eminently required two things, — clearness of arrangement, and a great abundance of facts. It is because audiences have both of these things from Governor Russell that he never fails to hold them. He may be right or wrong, but he shoots straight to the mark. He strikes into his theme from the moment of his rising; he holds to it until he sits down. With all the power of a clear head, an earnest conviction, and a powerful voice, he keeps his hearers to the point. The speech is generally localized, — adapted, that is, to the pursuits and interests of the community where he is. He does not treat the tariff, for instance, as an abstraction, but has mastered its application to the precise town or village where he is speaking. His talk therefore, " comes down into every pew," as used to be said of good preaching. What is usually regarded as the flavoring of oratory he uses in the most sparing way ; rarely illustrates, seldom makes a joke or a repartee ; when he does, it is not a trite one but a good one, yet it is rarely expected. Whether this is intentional or a matter of temperament, it is hard to say ; but experienced political managers often tell us that votes are rarely won by those speakers who tell many stories or make people laugh much.

And as humor does not play a large part in Governor Russell's speeches, so neither does sentiment. There are few appeals to mere feeling, apart from conscience and suggested duty. The chief exception is to be found, where it should be found, in the occasional expression of his emotion towards his native State. No one ever heard him utter the words " the dear old Commonwealth " without discovering that he has what the French call " tears in his voice ; " and no one can know him well without recognizing that those thrilling tones represent in this case a very profound feeling. It cannot be said of him as Whittier says of John Randolph, that his patriotism languishes outside of his own State; but it is certain that there never was a Virginian or a South Carolinian in whom this wholesome local pride — the foundation of all true nationality — was stronger. Perhaps something of the force of this feeling may be due to his education in the public schools. It is very certain that this training has given to his democratic feeling an absolute genuineness which is a vast help to a political speaker. He never yields to the temptation to speak down to his audience, because he never feels such a temptation. When we consider how many of our greatest popular orators — Wendell Phillips conspicuously — have been aristocrats by temperament, and democratic by moral conviction only, we can see the advantage held by a man who can neither patronize nor be patronized, but is simply in his natural attitude.

The speeches which follow in this book are to be interpreted in this spirit. He has acted wisely — and, at any rate, frankly — in giving to the public so many of them, showing himself at his average, as it were, without apology and without flinching, and taking the risk that all his themes may not prove alike interesting. If ever a public man gave himself with utter openness in his book of speeches, that is the case here. Should Mr. Russell ever be called to re-enter public life, his whole platform, up to this time, has been presented without concealment in these pages. Should he ever re-enter it, he has here put on record, not only what he did, but what he would have done, had there been time and opportunity for all his cherished purposes to be accomplished.

THOMAS WENTWORTH HIGGINSON.

CAMBRIDGE, MASS., Dec. 3, 1893.

SPEECHES AND ADDRESSES.

SPEECHES ON GENERAL OCCASIONS.

ADDRESS

DELIVERED AT UNION HALL, AT THE DEDICATION OF THE YOUNG MEN'S CHRISTIAN ASSOCIATION, DEC. 10, 1885.

I AM glad to-night to express the city's gratitude to her generous citizens for this noble institution. It comes to meet a want long felt. I know how richly in the past we have been blessed, how much we have had that has added to the strength, honor, and fame of our city, to the comfort and happiness of her citizens. Education and literature have ever thrived among us. Admirable public schools have taken care that "learning should not be buried in the graves of our forefathers," as the old colonial statute seemed to fear. An honored university has grown up with us and blessed us, forever and honorably associating the names of Harvard and Cambridge. Nor have we lacked in industries, or in the life and vigor which come with business men and business enterprises. Here, as in the little village of which our poet sang, and as merrily, "Labor with its hundred hands has knocked at the golden gates of the morning." Patriotism, too, from early days has distinguished Cambridge. It wrought out in our midst national independence and unity; then gave sons of Cambridge as the first volunteers to defend with their lives the work achieved by the struggles and sacrifices of the fathers. Last, but not least, the prayers and faith, in the spirit of which pious Puritan ancestors founded our little town, have not been forgotten or neglected. With all these blessings gradually, too gradually, have come the "charities that soothe and heal and bless."

But none nor all of these alone make the real strength of Cambridge. Schools and education give her a clear, active brain; labor and industries a strong and vigorous backbone; patriotism warms her heart, ennobles and uplifts her; charities keep ever fresh her sympathies and humanity, — yet the real strength of Cambridge is not in these, but in the character of her citizens. This character your Association, with its faith and hope, its Christian sympathy and "pure religion breathing household laws," tends to mould and strengthen. So moulded and strengthened, it is the corner-stone of civil society, and the cure of all the evils which beset it. "We know," says Burke, "and, what is better, we feel inwardly, that religion is the basis of civil society and the source of all good and of all comfort." "The true reformer," says an old writer, "is he who creates new institutions and gives them life and energy, and trusts to them for throwing off such evil humor as may be lying in the body politic. The true reformer is the seminal reformer, not the radical; and this is the way the sower who went forth to sow his seed did really reform the world, without making any open assault to uproot what was already existing." These words of wisdom show the necessity, the object and field of your labor.

So Cambridge gladly welcomes to the warmest place at her fireside this religious and charitable institution; religious in professing Christian principles, charitable in seeking useful and unselfish ends, and making the faith manifest in good works. She welcomes it as the blessed guest who brings to her household sunshine and happiness, and she extends to it the cordial hospitality it has ever ready for all who enter its doors. May God bless and prosper it! and may its purpose be the thought expressed by the poet, —

> "Whoever thou art, whose need is great,
> In the name of Christ, the compassionate
> And merciful One, for thee I wait."

ADDRESS

AT THE TWO HUNDRED AND FIFTIETH ANNIVERSARY OF THE ESTABLISHMENT OF THE FIRST CHURCH OF CAMBRIDGE, FEB. 12, 1886.

I KNOW that the good city of Cambridge, that for two hundred and fifty years has walked hand in hand with this old church through trials and suffering, wars and pestilence, yet always *forward*, is glad to be present to-day at this anniversary, bearing love to her younger sister, and the respect, reverence, and gratitude of a people deeply indebted for her long life of usefulness.

In 1636 our little town, poor, distressed, its people "straitened for want of land," with food so scarce that "many eate their bread by waight, and had little hope of the earth's fruitfullnesse," deserted by the governor, failing in the purpose of its founders, but filled with "quickening grace and lively affections to this temple worke," rejoiced in the founding of this church, that brought to it prosperity and happiness, and was to be its strength and very life.

"God's glory and the church's good" bound Winthrop, Dudley, and their associates, "in the word of a Christian," to embark for the Plantation of New England. "God's glory and the church's good," sought by Shepard and his little band in the planting of this church, became the strong foundation upon which our town was builded. Others had sought to make here a fortified town, a mart of commerce, the seat of government; but they failed. Perhaps, as Mather says of the early settlements north of Plymouth, "these attempts being aimed no higher than the advancement of some worldly interests, a constant series of disasters confounded them until there was a plantation erected upon the nobler designs of Christianity."

Certainly it is no injustice to our first founders to say that not till this church was gathered was Newtowne permanently established.

Others to-day will tell better than any words of mine the story of the birth and life of the First Church of Cambridge. In the telling they cannot fail to give much of the history of our city. The late venerable pastor of this church[1] has pictured to us, with all the rich beauty of his poetic mind, that Cambridge church gathering of 1636; another pastor[2] has faithfully and ably written its life to the time when he came to watch over and guide it. Surely, it is not for me to glean in fields where all is harvested; rather let me express the deep debt the city owes to the church, and offer her homage and thanks to the old Puritan spirit that has always been the life of both the church and the city.

For years the church and town were one, but the church was that one. Only its members were freemen, and none other had any voice in town affairs. In town-meeting the affairs of the church were settled; there repairs were ordered on the meeting-house, grants of land made to the church, and votes often passed that show how carefully and naturally, while the church was the town, the town looked after the interests of the church. The old chronicles constantly speak of "the people of this church and towne." Ever the church

---

[1] Rev. William Newell, D.D.
[2] Rev. Alexander McKenzie, D.D.

before the town, ever the "spiritual blessings" before the "outward things." So were they true to the purpose of their coming, and so building stronger than they knew. As the years passed on, and the church and town waxed strong, their affairs became more separate and distinct. Yet the church was always ruling and leading the town, and the town loyally following in her footsteps. Age and separation did not lessen the influence of the church. I know full well, sir, that a father's threescore years and ten must separate him a little from the life of his son; yet I venture to say that reverence for the gray hairs and ripe years, the recollection of tender care in childhood's days, filial love and gratitude, make the threescore years and ten a more potent influence over the younger life than when the father's will was the child's action, and he directed every footstep.[1] So was it, so may it ever be, with this church and town, the child whom she nurtured and guided, and always followed with love and blessing.

Let me say a word of the great prosperity that came to the town upon the establishing of this church under "the holy, heavenly, sweet-affecting, and soul-ravishing Mr. Shepard." First came the college, with a grant from the General Court six times as great as had been given for protection against the Indians, planted here because of "the enlightening and powerful ministry of Mr. Shepard." Then to the town, now a seat of learning, was given her present classic name. Soon sprang up, under Master Corlet, the first grammar-school in New England; here Stephen Daye established the first printing-press; here was printed the first Bible printed in America; and here, under John Eliot, was begun

---

[1] The reference is to Mr. Russell's father, who presided over the meeting.

"the first Protestant Mission to the heathen in modern times." The limits of the town were extended till they reached from the Charles to the Merrimac River, — a distance of over thirty miles; or a mile for every twenty cattle and every five ratable persons in 1647. The "great bridge" was built to Brighton, and other signs showed the new life the church had brought. Many of these are perhaps the "outward things" of the town's prosperity. Better for the town were the faith and Puritan spirit that Shepard and his company planted in her people.

Restrained by tyranny of Church, oppressed by authority of State, the Puritans abandoned ease and honors at home to lead serious lives in a wilderness where they might found a "Church without a bishop" and a "State without a king." "I'll be upon your back," said Bishop Laud to Shepard, "and everlastingly disenable you." It was bishops on the backs of Puritans that gave us this commonwealth and nation. "Everlastingly disenable" Shepard! No! but everlastingly enable him to perpetuate his name and virtues in the hearts of a God-fearing, liberty-loving people. The Puritans hated the union of Church and State; but here they founded a more perfect union, — a Church not dependent on the State or sustained by its authority, but a Church that was its very life. We care not so much to-day for the distinctive doctrines of their faith as that they had faith; not so much for the scruples of their conscience as that for conscience' sake they dared to suffer; not so much for their suffering as that in spite of it they never yielded. They came here, brave, determined, serious men, taught in oppression's school to love liberty, firm in the faith they would have died to uphold. That was the stuff from which to make commonwealths that were to last. In prayer and faith they founded our little town; by prayer and faith through this church they kept alive the Puritan spirit.

We smile at the austerity of the old Puritans, their long faces and mournful manners; but we forget that their work was no holiday pastime. They were not seeking how easiest to live, but how best to live for "God's glory and the church's good." They were church-building, nation-building, establishing institutions to last as long as men fear God and love liberty. If such serious work had not made them serious men, it would utterly have failed.

What does Cambridge owe to this Puritan spirit? What does she not owe to it? I fancy that if Shepard, Dudley, Dunster, and Sir Harry Vane could revisit to-day the scene of their labor, they would marvel at the fruit it had brought forth. They would find a university, whose vigor and greatness had exceeded their fondest hopes; a city, whose wealth is counted in millions where they left thousands, and whose people would seem to them in number almost as the sands of the sea. But to them these would be the "outward things." I think they would ask, "Is there here freedom of conscience to worship God? Is there tyranny of Church or oppression of State? Are there fear of God and love of liberty? As life has become to you easier to live, has character grown less sturdy? Are men still ready to suffer for conscience' sake, and die for love of country?"

What answer should we make? I would turn to the records of our town and city. I would show that in 1765, four generations after Sir Harry Vane was urging the largest liberty among the Puritans, our town was leading in the struggle that wrought our independence. October 14 of that year in town-meeting was made the first formal protest against the memorable Stamp Act, and it was ordered to "be recorded in the Town Books, that the children yet unborn may see the desire that their ancestors had for their freedom and happiness." Then came the tax on tea, and instantly the vote of this town that "we can no longer stand idle spectators," but will join Boston in any measures "to deliver ourselves and posterity from slavery." The spirit of Shepard, Vane, and Dudley was speaking through Appleton and Stedman, Adams and Hancock. Yes, and soon under yonder elm were gathered men still ready to suffer for conscience' sake, and die for love of country, — few, ragged, half-armed, united in defying the strongest nation of the world. Yet when Washington found in them the old Puritan spirit he knew that there was a force within his grasp that "could marshal the conscience" of his country to achieve her independence.

A short century more passes. There comes a struggle for human liberty, a call again to patriots and to Puritans. And Cambridge, first in the whole nation, offers her children under the lead of a grandson of a Revolutionary hero; and our old University, charged with being backward in these great agitations, and with being forgetful of the Puritan spirit, — though her accuser is himself an answer to the charge, — sends forth her sons to die for the principles this old church has ever taught.

I have said enough. I hardly think if Shepard were with us to-day he would say that the prayers and faith of our pious founders had been forgotten, or that after eight generations we had proved untrue to the spirit of his ministry.

This is the word the city bids me say to-day. Shepard and Mitchel, Dudley and Dunster, all have passed away, but each, "though dead, yet speaketh."

SPEECH

ON THE QUESTION OF CONSTITUTIONAL PROHIBITION, BOSTON, APRIL, 1889.

THE citizens of this Commonwealth are asked to incorporate into their Constitution this provision: "The manufacture and sale of intoxicating liquors to be used as a beverage are prohibited. The General Court shall enact suitable legislation to enforce the provisions of this article."

It is incumbent upon those who advocate putting into the organic law of the State this prohibition upon a beverage, to establish its necessity, justice, wisdom, and expediency as against all upon whom its restraint is to be imposed without their consent and against their protest. The question is not whether the advocates of this measure have a right to apply it to themselves, but how far they have a right to impose it upon others against their wishes.

In answering this question I propose to consider and discuss, not so much the strong and familiar objections to prohibition, but rather the grounds upon which it is advocated. What are these grounds? They all may be comprehended in a single sentence, whatever of form or detail they assume. It is urged that the use and sale of intoxicating liquors as a beverage is a sin, — not only a sin, but a crime of the greatest magnitude, because the cause of other and great crimes and vice, and a most prolific source of misery and poverty. Observe, it is the use and sale, not merely the abuse, of intoxicants that is thus alleged to be criminal and the source of crime; therefore the absolute prohibition of their manufacture and sale is demanded. Without stopping to controvert this position of the advocates of prohibition, does their position require or justify constitutional prohibition? If the manufacture and sale of intoxicants are thus criminal, why not prohibit and punish them by statute law as we do other and greater crimes? Such law alone can effect prohibition. Constitutional prohibition will not enforce itself. There must be statute law, or it is a dead letter. Then why not begin where we must end? Without such law, constitutional prohibition is useless and hopeless; with it, it is needless.

Both our National and State courts have constantly decided that there is abundant authority under our present Constitution to pass most stringent and imperative legislation to prohibit the manufacture and sale of liquor. If, then, the premises of the prohibitionists are sound, why seek a constitutional amendment? Why not go at once to where they must come at last, — statute enactment?

But, again, it will hardly be contended by the most extreme prohibitionists that the act they seek to prohibit is a greater crime than murder, arson, rape, burglary, highway robbery, embezzlement, etc. I say it will not be so contended, because amid all their exaggeration they do not demand to have like penalties attached to it. No one suggests as a proper penalty for it death, state prison for life or for years. If it is a lesser crime, why put its prohibition into the Constitution, and leave out all the others? Does not such distinction come almost within the Biblical admonition, "Woe unto you, Scribes and Pharisees, hypocrites! for ye pay tithe of mint and anise and cummin, and have omitted the weightier matters of the law"? Is not this especially true when the crimes above stated are universally recognized as crimes, while the act proposed to be made a crime by constitutional enactment is far from being so recognized? The reason for their omission from the Constitution is a plain and proper one. The Constitution was intended for no such purpose. Its purpose here, as in every country, is to establish general principles, and to be itself a frame of government. It provides the proper body to make, construe, and execute the laws, and clothes each with ample power. Its end is to provide proper agencies for governing, but not to do their work. The Legislature is its agency to make laws, and especially to define crimes, just as the judiciary and the executive branches of government are its agencies to construe and enforce laws already made. To enact by the Constitution a law which is wholly within the power and the proper functions of the Legislature, is just as absurd as by the same means to do the detailed work of either of the other branches of government.

But, assuming all their premises, will the advocates of prohibition tell us what is the necessity for constitutional enactment? The answer usually made to this question, and by men thoroughly earnest and conscientious, is, "We want stability of action. A prohibitory law passed to-day might be repealed to-morrow. We want prohibition fixed by organic law." Let us fairly consider this answer. If a prohibitory law is passed, it cannot be repealed or modified, unless a majority of the people wish it and so decide. Is it seriously contended that prohibition can or ought to be maintained, whether by organic law or statute amendment, against the wishes of a majority of the people. Is that the purpose of putting it into the Constitution? Is it in order that a minority may control the will of the majority? Surely not, so long as we are to be a government of the people, by the people, for the people. Yet stability of action on this subject beyond the power of the Legislature can only be secured by sacrificing the will of the majority and the principle that a majority shall rule.

Suppose, however, prohibition is established by constitutional amendment, and a majority of the people are or become opposed to it: what will be the result?

One of two things: either, as in Rhode Island to-day, an utter disregard of the constitutional provision, and a demand for its repeal, or a refusal by the Legislature to enforce its provisions. If there is danger, as its advocates say, in a sentiment so hostile to prohibition that men will each year at the polls raise an issue over statute prohibition, why may we not have the greater danger that they will thus agitate each year constitutional change? Which is the greater evil?

Again, if popular sentiment is hostile to prohibition, what is to hinder the Legislature from utterly nullifying the law, or making it ineffective? This need not be by an absolute refusal to enact any legislation. It may be done quite as easily by inadequate legislation, or with inadequate provision for its enforcement. There is now in our Constitution a tax upon the right of suffrage, — in my opinion unjust and undemocratic. This has become of late years very unpopular; but a minority in the Legislature continues to retain it. But to some extent they meet the popular demand for a change by making the tax smaller, and easier to be borne.

A better illustration still of this point is the provision of the United States Constitution for the rendition of fugitive slaves. This provision was believed before the war by vast numbers of our citizens to be unjust, oppressive, and unchristian. So it was practically annulled by inadequate and hostile legislation, or by refusal to enforce such laws as were enacted. If popular sentiment is behind prohibition, it will at once develop in statute law; if it is not, constitutional enactment will be a dead letter.

Many of our people protest against the failure of others to observe properly the Sabbath day. In deference to this sentiment, would it be wise and useful to put into the Constitution the following provision: "Violation of the Lord's day is prohibited. The General Court shall enact suitable legislation to enforce the provisions of this article." Does any one believe that such an amendment would lead to a better observance of the Sabbath, or accomplish anything else than to make what are now violations of statute law violations of constitutional law, and bring the Constitution into disrespect? In case of a popular sentiment hostile to constitutional prohibition, why may not the General Court, sustained by such sentiment, say that "suitable legislation to enforce such prohibition" is a statute with very mild penalties, and with no provisions specially enacted for enforcement. The Legislature is the judge of what is "suitable legislation." Is not its power practically the same with or without constitutional prohibition?

As prohibition, then, if necessary or desirable, must, to be effective, ultimately rest upon legislation, is it not desirable to try it first by legislation, and see whether or not it is a success?

It is true that it has been tried in this Commonwealth under statute law, and has utterly failed and broken down under a hostile sentiment. Is constitutional prohibition, resting for its entire force upon statute law, likely to be more successful? Its advocates must go further, and put into the organic law, not only prohibition, but the entire details of a law to enforce it. In this way only can it be independent of legislation, and until so independent there is no advance over statute prohibition.

I have tried thus far to look at the matter from the standpoint of the advocates of prohibition. It is not necessary, but only frank, that I should say that I do not believe that general prohibition is the best mode of dealing with the liquor problem. Overlooking the difference in the circumstances, needs, and public opinion of different localities, there is always danger that such prohibition may be in name only, but in fact freedom from all restrictions, plenty of law, with free and untaxed rum. The present local option and high license law, with its severe restrictive features, seems to me much better and more successful, and in the agitation of the Yes and No question in every locality each year to do much for the proper education of the people in the principles of temperance and morality. I am inclined to think that the ultimate solution of the problem lies rather in the field of religion than of law, rather in persuasion than in force. In this field our present law is each year doing a great and successful work. It is, therefore, not only unnecessary, but inexpedient to put into organic law legislation which must be entirely inoperative unless enforced by other legislation, and sustained and demanded by a strong public sentiment.

ADDRESS

AT ATLANTA, GEORGIA, FEB. 13, 1890.

GLADLY I find myself to-night in the land of the sunny South, and under the charm of its warm-hearted hospitality. I come without office or title, yet bearing, I am sure, from the old Bay State greeting and good wishes to a younger of the thirteen sisters, who, joined in sympathy and friendship in days of peril and oppression, now in time of peace, independence, and liberty are united as parts of a great republic, joint-heirs of its glorious heritage, and equal factors in achieving its grand destiny. Your cordial welcome tells me that here I am at home; and as at the old homestead the family long scattered sometimes meet, and around its hallowed hearthstone bind more closely the tenderest ties of life, and then with renewed strength and love share each other's burdens, duties, and blessings, so may we to-night, meeting as fellow-countrymen, pledge anew our love to a common country, and sharing in her glory, consider the duties and perils that confront her. In this spirit there is no South, no North, nor East, nor West; no burden upon one that is not felt by all, — the prosperity of each is the sacred duty of all.

If in speaking of the present there is mingled with it necessarily something of the past, and recalling the latter brings sorrow with it, let us remember that Massachusetts and Georgia both have had their days of sunshine and of darkness, and then comfort ourselves with those lines, written in the little chapel in the Tyrol, that to our greatest poet in his hour of suffering seemed to be the footprint of an angel: "Look not mournfully into the past, it comes not back again. Wisely improve the present. It is thine. Go forth to meet the future without fear and with a manly heart." The past of sectional discord and fraternal strife comes never back again, and for the rest, —

> "No fears to beat away, no strife to heal.
> The past unsighed for, and the future sure."

Mr. President, I speak to-night for a younger generation that, loyal to all that has been, yet dwells not in the past, but in a progressive spirit steps forward to meet the "new occasions and the new duties," unhampered by prejudices that obstruct, and impatient of the spirit that would "attempt the Future's portal with the Past's blood-rusted key." I take for my subject this sentiment: A new South, a new North, a country reunited in love and loyalty, ready and anxious to meet the duties of to-day. It is a patriotic theme, suggested by the words of one whose fervent patriotism made the Nation listen, bound hearts together that were estranged, and earned for his memory the noble tribute of a country in sorrow for his loss. He

> "Climbed the sunlit heights,
> And from all dissonance
> Struck one clear chord
> That seemed to reach the ears of God."

I know the sorrow that pervades this meeting; I feel the thought in every mind. A friend, a leader, statesman, and patriot has gone.[1] He loved the South, but spoke for all. With matchless eloquence and the manly

[1] The reference is to Henry W. Grady.

frankness of a noble soul, he proclaimed the undying loyalty of seventy million people to our common country, to all her institutions, and to all her laws; and then he asked forbearance, sympathy, and aid while the new South adjusted the past to the present, and solved momentous problems, vital to her, vital to all, and gave his life in the discharge of this patriotic duty.

Unbounded hospitality and cordial greetings cannot, shall not, repress those thoughts that permit me to share in your sorrow, and pay to his memory my humble tribute of respect and love: —

> "Statesman, yet friend to truth! Of soul sincere,
> In action faithful, and in honor clear;
> Who broke no promise, served no private end,
> Who gained no title, and who lost no friend;
> Ennobled by himself, by all approved,
> Praised, wept, and honored by the land he loved."

North and South mingle their tears at his loss, gather inspiration from his life, and join hearts and hands in worthily perpetuating his memory. To me has been given the sad yet pleasant duty of bringing here from the Young Men's Democratic Club of Massachusetts its contribution to his monument as its tribute to his memory. His patriotic purpose, political convictions, and progressive spirit represented as truly the six hundred young, progressive Democrats of that club as it did his own beloved State of Georgia. As his loss was national, so were his life and the lesson of his life. "Though dead, he speaketh." From his new-made grave, God grant to-night I may catch the inspiration of his teaching.

Mr. President, war settled, as only war could, an irrepressible conflict between institutions that could not live together. Statesmen might lull a country to repose; compromises might postpone the dreaded day; but the skeleton was ever in the closet, — some generation had an awful duty to face and to perform. It was a sectional difference, involving questions of free institutions, constitutional rights, vested interests, and, over and above all, sentiment and a higher law. With heroism, suffering, and sacrifices, and intense loyalty to honest convictions, each side maintained the conflict. I should be false to myself, false to you, and disloyal to the sentiment both of my State and yours, if I hesitated to say that the issue of that conflict was right. Its great results are beneficial both to North and South, and are now loyally upheld by all our people. One is apt, however, to forget that with all the good accomplished, war brings also in its train evils that only time, patience, and patriotism can cure. It left the South impoverished and exhausted, her fields wasted, her railway systems undeveloped and impaired, and her wealth destroyed. As in a night it swept away institutions that for generations had been her very life, and placed her face to face with race and social problems, novel and hitherto unsolved; with industrial conditions for which she had no inherited aptitude or training; and questions of government, difficult, threatening, of vast importance, that must be answered. A revolution in ideas followed a revolution in institutions. With wonderful courage and energy she entered upon her new life. How well she has lived it, how much, vastly much, she has accomplished, you, gentlemen of Atlanta, from the experience of this great and growing city, can tell better than any words of mine. It has been told from the lips of your eloquent orator in language that caught the ear and won the applause of an admiring country. Many and great industries have been established. Your railway system has been vastly extended. Wealth locked up in your forests and in the depths of the earth has been brought to the use of man. Education has advanced with ever-increasing strides, and with equal pace justice, thrift, morality, and respect for law; and last, but not least, free labor and personal liberty have been demonstrated to be the key to industrial and commercial prosperity. Upon those principles North and South stand now thoroughly reunited, believing in them not only because they are right, in harmony with the theory of our government and the purpose of its founders, but also because they are vital to the welfare, progress, and prosperity of every community. As I believe industrial and commercial prosperity to the South have come from these principles, so, too, I believe from commercial and industrial necessity will come the solution of those serious problems that still confront you. Remembering the conditions with which the South had to deal, the revolutionary change that had come in her whole life, and measuring progress, not only by amount, but by variety, the statement of a distinguished authority [Edward Atkinson] in my own State is true that "she has made progress in material welfare exceeding that made in any section of this country, the West included, in any given number of years corresponding to the period which has elapsed since 1865." This she has done without the protection of any tariff law as against the fiercest competition of other sections of the country that had every advantage in capital, skill, freights, and long-established industries.

NOTE.—The census of 1870 showed a loss of $2,100,000,000 in the assessed value of property in the South as compared with 1860. From 1870 there has been a steady gain. Statistics published in the "Manufacturers' Record" of Dec. 21, 1889, show her marvellous progress in the last ten years:—

	1880	1889 (Partly estimated.)
Assessed value of property	$2,913,436,095	$4,220,166,400
Railroad mileage	19,431	40,250
Cost of railroads	$679,000,000	$1,500,000,000
Yield of cotton, bales	5,755,359	7,250,000
Yield of grain, bushels	431,074,630	675,000,000
Number of farm animals	28,754,243	45,592,536
Value of live stock	$391,412,254	$569,161,550
Value of chief agricultural products	$571,098,454	$850,000,000
Coal mined, tons	6,049,471	22,000,000
Pig iron produced, tons	397,301	1,600,000
Number of cotton mills	161	355
Number of spindles	667,854	2,035,268
Number of looms	14,323	45,000
Number of cotton-seed oil mills	40	213
Capital invested in cotton-seed oil mills	$3,504,000	$20,000,000
Number of national banks	220	472
Capital of national banks	$45,597,730	$76,454,510

What the South has accomplished in the way of new industrial enterprises may be seen from the summary of the number organized between Jan. 1, 1886, and Sept. 30, 1889, a little less than four years, as compiled from the weekly reports of the "Manufacturers' Record":—

Iron furnace companies	107
Machine shops and foundries	416
Agricultural implement factories	62
Flour mills	489
Cotton mills	256
Furniture factories	207
Gas works	101
Water works	313
Carriage and wagon factories	165
Electric light companies	433
Mining and quarrying enterprises	1,623
Lumber mills, including saw and planing mills, sash and door factories, stave factories, etc.	2,795
Ice factories	272
Canning factories	408
Stove foundries	25
Brick works	535
Miscellaneous iron works, rolling mills, pipe works, etc.	157
Cotton compresses	108
Cotton-seed oil mills	143
Miscellaneous enterprises not included in foregoing	4,041
Total	12,656

Add to these figures the new enterprises organized during the last three months of 1889, and the aggregate for the four years will be about 14,000.

Truly she has followed the oft-quoted advice of Governor Andrew, and entered upon "a vigorous prosecution of the pursuits of peace."

But, Sir, the evils that flowed from the war were by no means confined to the South. It is true the rest of the country did not suffer as the South in its material prosperity, nor did it have to meet new conditions of life, and to adapt itself to new institutions. It did experience a great and unwholesome change in its political convictions, in its conception of the purpose, power, and scope of government. Force justified by war was defended and advocated in time of peace. Powers of government, rightly strained to meet the exigencies of a great peril, were used for other purposes. Relations between National and State government, adjusted with almost inspired wisdom by the framers of our Constitution, and upheld with unceasing vigilance for generations, were neglected and disregarded. Undue and injurious weight was given to the influence of wealth in public life. Selfish interests rode on the box of government, and drove it to use its great powers for their selfish purposes. Extravagance and corruption, hitherto almost unknown, stalked abroad in the land, and scandals and jobbery entered the halls of legislation. With them, too, remained as a relic of the war, sectional prejudice and ill-will, — an evil in itself, but breeding other evils and curing none. It blinded the North to a just estimate of the condition of the South, to the difficulties that beset her, and their proper remedy. It used force where neither reason nor law would justify it, and strained the powers of government beyond their constitutional limitations.

Many evils of the war have been cured, and all have been cured that tended to divide the country by sectional prejudice upon sectional lines. Faneuil Hall since the war has uttered her indignant and nonpartisan protest against the improper use of National power in the State of Louisiana. The old Cradle of Liberty spoke then the sentiment of Massachusetts, just as she would speak it to-day against any National invasion of State rights or State duties, whether that power comes bearing gifts or with force of arms. The Supreme Court, with that impartiality and political integrity that have won the respect and confidence of the whole country and all parties, has undone much legislation founded upon sectional prejudice and enacted for sectional and partisan purposes, and it has re-established that proper relation of State to National government which is necessary for the safe working of our political system. Best of all, that bitter sectional feeling expressed by the "Stalwart" of the North and the "Bourbon" of the South has now no weight in determining political action, and has lost its virtue even for party purposes. There may be still some aged non-combatants in Massachusetts, as there may be in Georgia, who cling to old prejudices, and would like now to fight the war. But a new generation has come upon the field, intensely loyal to the results of the war, gathering inspiration from the patriotism and brave deeds of the past, but absolutely uninfluenced by any of its prejudices. They believe rather in the sentiment of Macaulay: "It is now time for us to pay a decent, a rational, a manly reverence to our ancestors, not by superstitiously adhering to what they in other circumstances did, but by doing what they in our circumstances would have done." A very large per cent of the voters in 1892 were too young to have had any part in the war. Enough voters of this year have been born since 1865 to turn more than one-half of the congressional districts of the country. This is a young influence, guided wholly by the present, and not the past, who believe that in and between all sections there should be loyalty, fraternity, and charity. It is too late to speak of sectional feeling when Southern soldiers have placed their garlands on Bunker Hill, and the veterans North and South have met again on the old battlefields in friendship and in love, and exchanged the trophies of war. Other more material things, such as business interests and railroads, have woven the silken ties of mutual interests that have hastened the good work of binding more closely together North and South. We realize and welcome now the fulfilment of the wish expressed by Webster in 1847 at Savannah: "Others may value this Union of Confederated States as a convenience, or an arrangement, or a compromise of interests; but I desire to see an attachment to the Union existing among the people, not as a deduction of political economy nor as a result of philosophical reasoning, but cherished as a heartfelt *sentiment.*" In all of this there has been a new North as well as a new South. Sectionalism as a constant threatening peril and disturbing force has gone forever.

The death of sectional ill-will and the removal of its cause have reawakened the interest of the whole country to the duties and perils of the present, and put her in condition thoroughly to deal with them. Much good has been accomplished, as evidenced by the fact of a new South and a new North. Much is yet to be done by the united effort of that new North and South. The conscience of this Nation must be marshalled to assert its independence of selfish influences and selfish control; to give back to the people the right to govern themselves, and then have their delegated power used for their own, and not for selfish or partisan purposes. I am too young to be a pessimist, too loyal to the integrity, patriotism, and common-sense of our people to doubt for an instant that they will remove present perils, as they have all others that threatened the welfare of our beloved country. I do not believe that the remedy lies in legislation for special interests, in National gifts or bounties for special purposes, in National assumption of the rights or duties of the States, or in National control of the suffrage of a free and self-governing people; nor does it lie in vastly increased expenditure, in extravagance, or in allowing organized wealth selfishly to control political power and the people's law; nor in substituting any man's will for established law; nor in making public office party spoils. Rather, all these are parts of the very thing to be corrected. They rest upon a novel, baleful conception of our government, bred of war, fostered by a great party for its selfish purposes, and now so threatening as to demand immediate, thorough, and unflinching treatment. Stripped, in all its nakedness, that conception is that our government is one of benefits and bounties by a party for it and its beneficiaries rather than "of the people, by the people, for the people."

Where is the remedy? It is in organizing public opinion to enact and sustain laws that will keep the source of political power pure, and its exercise free from partisan and selfish purposes.

Three great political reforms are now before the country, each seeking in itself to accomplish a great good, but all more important in bringing our government back to the spirit, purpose, and wisdom of its founders, and to those principles vital to the welfare, permanence, and progress of our political institutions.

The first is ballot reform, — to correct evils that exist at the very source of political power. It is founded on the democratic principle of the right of every man to cast his ballot independently, conscientiously, intelligently, free from all corrupt or undue influence. It throws about him the protection of law to guard him against evils that exist and have been felt throughout the country, and which, if unchecked, threaten the stability of our institutions. It is the first step in giving back to the people the right to govern themselves. I rejoice that Massachusetts has led in this as she has in many other reforms. It was suggested and supported by both parties, and while no doubt open to improvement in details, was a great success, and is now upheld by all the people. It freed votes that never were free before, destroyed the power of selfish and money influence, and gave us an election as pure as any that ever blessed the old Commonwealth. I doubt not that Georgia and Massachusetts will join hands in advancing this reform as they join now in belief in its principle and purpose.

The second reform is of the civil service, — to make the people's servants represent and serve the people, and not a party, and to prevent the abuse of their trust in using, as an organized army, public office to wage war on the political convictions of half the people, whose interests alone they are sworn to serve. This is another step in giving back to the people their own, and in having their own used for their own purposes.

Georgia has suffered under a merciless proscription that for years not only shut out her citizens from the public service of the Nation, if true to their political convictions, but used that service against those convictions. Georgia has loyally sustained a brave and patriotic President, who in this first led the people out of their bondage, and pointed out the dawn of a new day. Georgia and Massachusetts, a new South and a new North, can and will unite in making this reform an accomplished fact.

The third reform is of the tariff, — a commercial and industrial necessity to broaden the field of our activity; but far and beyond that, it is a political and moral necessity, to limit the power of government to public purposes, to distribute equally its burdens and its benefits, to make law just, equal, respected, *because* free from entangling alliance with selfish interests, and untainted by selfish control. No law is just whose purpose, aim, and end is to take from one to give to another, and make the benefit of a few a burden upon all. Such laws come only from halls of legislation over whose portal is written the words of Bastiat, "Whoever has influence here may have his share of the legalized pillage." Let law be the power that stands beside the humblest individual to protect him in making the most of himself, and in guarding sacredly the fruit of his labor, rather than a power to be invoked to make or to unmake wealth. It is not its function "to take from the worthy the things they have labored for, in order to give to the unworthy the things they have not earned." Because this reform means something more than any question of revenue or taxation, because it involves the fundamental principles of sound democratic government, and seeks to limit its power to public and to proper purposes, it is the most important question of the day, — the hopeful cure of the most threatening evil that has followed in the wake of war. It is the people's cause. Its triumph is death to the control by organized wealth of elections and legislation, a restoration of political power to the people, and a guarantee that the people's law shall be used only for the people's interests.

Mr. President, the war is over in both North and

South. Its benefits are permanent, its evils can be remedied. That is the duty of to-day, — easy to accomplish by a new North and a new South reunited in love and loyalty. Not for generations has there been so little to divide, so much to unite, the North and South, and, reunited, so much for them to do. As our fathers bravely met the duties of their day, so let us, unfettered by the past, bravely meet the duties of our day, seeking only truth, justice, liberty, the welfare, honor, and progress of our beloved country.

ADDRESS

TO THE HARVARD ALUMNI AT CAMBRIDGE ON COMMENCEMENT DAY, JUNE 24, 1891.

IT is a pleasure to hear this cordial welcome which you give the Commonwealth through me, to sit at your hospitable board, and to join in the tribute of praise and love which each year the sons of Harvard bring to Alma Mater. Hitherto I have come only as one of her children, to cherish here in the old homestead the memory of life's young day, with its work and its mischief, its day-dreams and its struggles, when "life's enchanted cup" was "sparkling to the brim," and to recall with equal pleasure how Mother Harvard used to pat our heads or pull our ears.

I am bound to confess, Mr. President, that my class to-day, in its sedate and settled age, is rather proud of the fact that under your vigorous influence it showed activity in many and various directions; that old '77 is still remembered by the ambitious undergraduate as an incentive and a precedent for doing something useful or otherwise. Perhaps its "crowded hour of glorious life was worth an age without a name." There was just enough friction between it and the Faculty to make both active, and enough activity to keep both healthy. So mutually beneficial was this relation that it was hard for both to have a formal and a final parting. The class never would or could agree to have a class day with its sad ceremonies of final leave-taking, nor would the Faculty agree to let us all go, but kept in its lingering, loving embrace a score or more with whom she has parted slowly, sorrowfully, and by degrees. But if '77 worried Alma Mater, and in its closing days tried her patience until she was ready to exclaim, with Lady Macbeth, "Stand not upon the order of your going, but go at once," let me say, in atonement for its mischief, that Harvard has to-day no sons more loyal to her, none more proud of her, nor more grateful for all she is and was to them.

But enough of reminiscence. My class is far within the age when one of its members is delegated to speak for it at this anniversary. I am not called upon to speak for Harvard's children, but for Harvard's mother, the good old Commonwealth of Massachusetts. For Harvard is distinctly the child of the State, born of it in the early days of struggle and of poverty, when pious ancestors were founding great institutions that were to be the strength of unborn generations.

With wonderful foresight, they seemed to know that the fruition of their work was to be the creation of a nation, and that nation was to be the beacon-light to lead a world, awakening to the new thought of self-government, freedom, and the rights of man.

So, with severe labor but remarkable sagacity, they laid its foundations deep and strong in the school-house, the college, the church, and the town-meeting. They knew that an intelligent, independent, God-fearing people were the basis of all free institutions and of a prosperous Commonwealth.

As one of the earliest of their works, and nearly coincident with the first grammar-school and printing-press, they founded this College, with the famous grant of £400 from the General Court. Then, in 1642, speaking through Dunster, her first president, and

Shepard, and in the spirit so successfully followed by her later presidents, she appealed to the united colonies for recognition and support on the ground that "their recognition would be both honorable to the country and in especial manner to those scholars whose various inclinations to all professions might thereby be encouraged," and to the end "that the Commonwealth may be furnished with knowing and understanding men, and the church with an able ministry." This appeal was answered by the promise to give "some yearly help by pecks, half bushels, and bushels of wheat." So they gave from their poverty, as later generations have from their wealth, for the building up of this great university, because of her value and her service to the Commonwealth and to the country.

I need not trace step by step the history of the close relation between the College and the State. It is enough to say that, in her gifts, her exemptions, and her government, Harvard, to the full extent of her needs and her desires, has always had thrown about her the strong protecting arm of the State. If in later years this relation has been less close, it is only because Harvard, in the full maturity of her strength, has not needed this direct support or guidance. The devotion of each to the other has not been lessened in its interest or its loyalty.

I have spoken of Harvard as the child of the State. I know that she is sometimes called the child of the Church. I do not forget the religious character of her origin, nor that Harvard, Shepard, Cotton, and Wilson, with their godly associates, gave her existence and shaped her early destiny. I remember her seal with its "Veritas," and her traditional dedication "Christo et Ecclesiæ;" but only as the Church developed and became the State was Harvard a Church rather than a State institution. For nearly two hundred years after the founding of the College there was a State religion in Massachusetts. In the close alliance of Church and State the College felt its influence, and her first president its effects. The College was necessarily denominational. But when, early in this century, the State religion was stricken out of the Constitution, as naturally denominationalism went out of her constitutional College. Harvard remained purely an institution of learning, the child of the State, consecrated to religion and the best interests of humanity, still true to her motto, "Veritas" on the open book, truth from knowledge leading through religion to God.

How has Harvard met the duties and obligations laid upon her by this her relation to the Commonwealth? It would be easy for us, with the love and pride of children, to recount the merits and services of Alma Mater. We could speak of the long line of distinguished men who, in giving their lives here to the cause of education, have rendered faithful service to the Commonwealth; of the countless numbers who have gone hence to carry the inspiration of Harvard's teaching to the wider life that lies outside her walls; of the glorious part Harvard has always taken in every agitation and struggle to better and uplift humanity, and of her brave sons who, to be true to her, were ready to suffer and die for love of country.

But it is better to let the Commonwealth in its own language answer the question. One hundred and forty-four years after Harvard was founded, the Province of Massachusetts Bay became the free and independent Commonwealth of Massachusetts. There gathered the patriots of the Revolution, — Samuel and John Adams, Hancock, and their distinguished associates, — to frame the Constitution for the new State. Before these grand examiners Harvard College came to take her preliminaries, her final examination to be by the people themselves.

And what was the result? These words in that Constitution: "Whereas our wise and pious ancestors so early as the year 1636 laid the foundation of Harvard College, in which university many persons of great eminence have, by the blessing of God, been instructed in those arts and sciences which qualified them for public employments both in Church and State; and whereas the encouragement of the arts and sciences and all good literature tends to the honor of God, the advantage of the Christian religion, and the great benefit of this and the other United States of America, — it is declared that the President and Fellows of Harvard College" shall forever have and maintain their rights and possessions; and it was expressly made the duty of the legislatures and the magistrates in all future periods of the Commonwealth to "cherish . . . especially the university at Cambridge."

That was the testimony of the Commonwealth, placed in its organic law, to the position, character, patriotism, and influence of Harvard after one hundred and forty-four years of her life. This provision has stood unchanged for more than one hundred years. It has passed through two constitutional conventions and one hundred and ten legislatures of the Commonwealth, and no man yet has suggested the retraction of its sentiment or amendment of its language.

So to-day, better than any words of mine, the good old Commonwealth pronounces her benediction upon her earliest child. These sacred walls, too, erected by loving hands to the memory of Harvard's sons, whom she sent forth to die for country, bear silent witness that in her later life she has not departed from the principles and patriotism that endeared her to the heroes of the Revolution.

I know that Harvard has her critics. I know that dogmatists in religion and dogmatists in politics have attacked her and criticised her teaching. But so long as Memorial Hall shall stand, so long as her record is unforgotten, and the Constitution unchanged, neither her patriotism nor her teaching needs apology or defence. From her highest officer to her humblest graduate she strives to find the truth, then dares to proclaim and defend it. She seems to catch and impart the inspiration of her motto, and to speak in the spirit of the old hymn, —

> "Oh, let all the soul within you,
> For the truth's sake, go abroad;
> Strike! let every nerve and sinew
> Tell on ages, tell for God."

ADDRESS

AT A PUBLIC RECEPTION TENDERED EX-PRESIDENT CLEVELAND AT SANDWICH, JULY 25, 1891.

THE Commonwealth greatly appreciates the kindly greeting given her whenever her children gather together, in work or in pleasure, for service to her, or for social intercourse with each other. I know she loves to answer their welcome by bringing to them her congratulations and her blessing, and by joining them, not only in their labor, but in those gentle charities and courtesies which make life easier and happier. A mother's benediction meets the children's pledge of loyalty, and all of us are drawn closer to the State and to each other by this constant interchange of loving sentiment.

The sturdy citizens of Cape Cod, laying aside for the time all distinctions of party, meet to-day to extend a hearty welcome to our distinguished guest. I know that you are glad to have the Commonwealth, standing as she does above all differences of political opinion, join with you in welcoming to her borders the Ex-President of the United States, whom you gladly greet as a neighbor and a friend. It is hard to express the full significance of our welcome and the sentiment of this great meeting without indulging in eulogy distasteful to our guest; and yet, Sir, on this occasion, when thousands have come hither to pay to you their tribute of respect and honor, it would be harder still not to give some expression to their thought, and to utter the word of praise which you have rightly earned by faithful public service, and by the integrity, courage, and patriotism with which you have discharged the duties of high official position.

Having the full confidence of the people, and keeping ever closely in touch with them and their interests, you have been chosen to important positions of public trust, and finally to the place of highest honor and greatest political power within the gift of man.

It is not fitting, here in the presence of men who have honest differences of opinion on political questions, for those of us who were in close sympathy with your administration to recall and praise the many measures which in the people's interest you promoted; nor is it necessary, for the country has not forgotten them. But, sacrificing no political conviction, we can all meet to-day on the one common ground of recognizing duty well and bravely done, whether by political friend or political opponent.

We recall that throughout your term of arduous service you strove to raise the standard of public life from the low level of personal and selfish ends to the high plane of duty and patriotism. Every man to-day clothed with official responsibility, and striving honestly to meet it, is strengthened in his efforts by the courageous standard which you dared to set. We recall with what singleness of purpose and forgetfulness of self you summoned the conscience and intelligence of the country to an examination and discussion of grave measures of public policy, and, in an earnest effort to serve the people, were willing to sacrifice personal ambition and to give up power. To you a campaign of education for the people seemed more important than personal success.

We do not forget that when self-interest would have whispered to you her timid counsel, you dared to interpose your veto on the abuse of a nation's generosity, and were willing to run the risk of misconstruction that you might rise to the full height of patriotic duty. We do not here discuss the right or the wrong of the measures of your administration. Upon these, men may honestly differ, and do differ; but we gladly join in praising the virtues of the man that were potent in and through official life. Patriotism, courage, and unselfishness gave a character to your administration that won the respect and will remain in the memory of the Nation.

But it is not only the Ex-President, but the man, whom we gladly welcome among us. Out of office, stripped of power, you still come close to the hearts of the people, still hold their respect and their confidence. Still is your voice a powerful influence in moulding and guiding public opinion on the questions of the day. It seems to me not inappropriate, as an illustration of this influence, to refer to a public service you have recently rendered. The time has come when the agricultural interests in great sections of our country feel and justly complain of burdens which weigh heavily upon them. Many of us believe, with you, that these burdens are chiefly due to unequal and unjust taxation, and that the best remedy is to follow the clear path you have pointed out; but in their distress, seeking for relief, they have turned also to other remedies, among them one which is opposed by the conservative opinion of the country and the nearly unanimous sentiment of the people of this Commonwealth.

Massachusetts believes in a sound currency. She will not lend her aid to any movement, whatever may be its source, and however honest may be its purpose, which in its result would debase our currency, unsettle credit, impair values, and give to labor in depreciated money less than its just dues. Her people sincerely believe that such a movement mistakes the remedy for a just grievance, and will but add to the distress it seeks to relieve.

The country, with a confidence in you of which any man in private life might well be proud, listened for the expression of your opinion. It would have been easy to remain silent, or to have given an answer meant to hide rather than declare your views. That was the course pointed out by self-interest and political ambition; but had you followed it, you would have been untrue to the people and untrue to yourself. The patriot and the man of conviction dares to tell the people the truth, and to take the consequences. We mingle with our welcome to-day our admiration for the courage that led you fearlessly and emphatically to state your convictions, and again to lead public opinion to a right conception of an important public question.

Gladly and sincerely, I am sure, the people of the Cape extend to you this hearty welcome. It is a welcome from a sturdy, upright people, simple in their tastes, honest in their convictions, patriotic in their spirit, typical of the virtues that have given strength and prosperity to our beloved Commonwealth. I know that among them you will find that "your lines are fallen in pleasant places," and that you will give to their friendship and esteem a high place among the honors which have been bestowed upon you.

ADDRESS

AT THE DEDICATION OF THE MONUMENT COMMEMORATING THE BATTLE OF BENNINGTON, AT BENNINGTON, AUG. 19, 1891.

IT is always a privilege and a pleasure to give voice to the sentiment of friendship and of love that hallows and glorifies the union of our sisterhood of States in one great, powerful, and permanent Nation. It adds to the pleasure when, as to-day, with this sentiment we can mingle our congratulations in recalling two great epochs in the history of a State when courage, patriotism, and perseverance gave life and independence to her, greater safety and strength to her sister States, and to our common country a bright page in its glorious history.

Gladly I bring to you from the old Bay State her congratulations and her love as the unanimous sentiment of her sturdy and patriotic children. This sentiment is but the natural, spontaneous feeling between States whose relations have always been those of amity, good-will, and support from the early days when these green hills had but begun to develop the life which a century ago matured in a free and independent State.

In her struggle with her nearest neighbors, who loved her quite too much to give her up, Vermont had all the sympathy Massachusetts could give, without herself becoming embarrassed in her family relations. Long before Ethan Allen bore to astonished Ticonderoga "the command of the Continental Congress and the great Jehovah," yes, even before the days of Wolfe and Montcalm, Massachusetts looked to the brave sons of the Green Mountains as an insuperable barrier between her and her foes, — a barrier tried and found true a little later in the victory we justly commemorate as the turning-point in the dark days of our Revolution, and again tried and again true a generation later in McDonough's gallant victory on Lake Champlain.

Shoulder to shoulder stood Massachusetts and Vermont in those days of conflict; hand in hand have they walked since, sharing each other's joys and sorrows through the sunshine and the clouds which have broken over our fair Republic.

Massachusetts has a deep interest in this commemorative monument. It recalls the valor of her sons; the union of all, heart and hand, for the common weal; the sacrifices of the fathers for the liberty of the children; the beginning of a great nation; the courage, patriotism, and struggle that wrought its independence, and founded free institutions that would insure to its people happiness and prosperity, and lead the world to a truer, nobler life.

So the mother States, as together they shared the labor of the struggle, the glory and fruits of the victory, so together, generously, gratefully, they erect this monument, that the struggle and victory may live forever. The acts of States rather than the words of men are the fitting tribute to brave deeds bravely done for love of country.

> "Wut's words to them whose faith an' truth
> On war's red techstone rang true metal;
> Who ventered life an' love an' youth
> For the great prize of death in battle?"

But to-day we commemorate not one event only. A century ago Vermont, first of the great incoming sisterhood, took her place among what the poet calls the "stars of glory." Not large in territory, not significant in population, yet she has ever maintained in our Union a position of stability, influence, patriotism, and power which has made her a potent factor in the wellbeing and progress of our continental Republic.

To-day we think of her not only as the Vermont whom Stark and Allen made famous, not only as the pleasant land of hill and valley, but as the greater Vermont, who has sent her children forth from ocean to ocean to build up the nation, and to stamp upon it the sterling virtues of sturdy New England life.

The statistician will tell us that Vermont is stationary, that her population does not increase. Yes, she is stationary, as the family home is stationary, because those who have been born into it have gone forth from it in obedience to the great law which God gave man, — to subdue and replenish the earth. Her children have made her influence felt throughout the Union, because they have carried forth from the home the mother's teaching, the courage, strength, and character which seem to be bone of her bone and blood of her blood. It is her life rather than her size, her virtues rather than her riches, that have made her prominent and powerful. Here in this rugged, typical New England State have been exemplified the glowing words of our liberty-loving, undying Lowell, —

"Before man made us citizens, great Nature made us men."

So as we stand to-day beside the rushing river of our prosperity, and strive to trace its sources, we find one of its clear and sparkling fountains amid the green hills of Vermont.

In their life and work, their character and virtues, their purpose and influence, Vermont and Massachusetts stand close together with mutual love and esteem, each for the other. Massachusetts has never failed in her interest in Vermont, and especially in Bennington, from the day when Stark sent to our Commonwealth the trophies of his victory (still reverently preserved); and in return she voted him her thanks, a suit of clothes, and a piece of linen, and again a century later made her generous contribution to this his monument.

Our affection for our sister State is none the less if we do not settle within her borders, but cling with filial love to the old Bay State, and there as here enjoy the beauty, simplicity, and vigor of our New England life.

In 1782, when John Adams was minister at the Hague, his wife, in his absence, purchased lands in Vermont, and suggested a removal there at some future time. Our gifted minister, broken in health and worn in mind, wrote in despair: "What is to become of the independent statesman, one who will bow the knee to no idol, who will worship nothing as a divinity but truth, virtue, and his country?" And then he exclaims: "O Peace, when wilt thou permit me to visit Penn's Hill, Milton Hill, and all the Blue Hills? I love every tree and every rock upon all those mountains. Roving among these will be the amusement of my declining years. God willing, I will not go to Vermont; I must be within scent of the sea."

So to-day, as the children of Vermont cherish with special love and reverence their native State, we too cannot forget our native hills and valleys and rock-bound coast, our Greylock, our Wachusett, our Berkshire and our Blue Hills, around which are nestled so much of comfort, prosperity, and happiness, and to which we longingly turn for rest and for peace. Much as we love and honor Vermont, we must say, with John Adams, God willing, we will not go to Vermont; we must be within the scent of the sea. But there it will be our pride and our pleasure, as it is our blessed privilege, to do whatsoever we may to sustain the life and the principles which have made Vermont and Massachusetts alike the home of the happy and the brave.

ADDRESS

AT THE DINNER GIVEN BY THE FRENCH SOCIETIES OF MASSACHUSETTS TO HON. WILFRED LAURIER, LEADER OF THE LIBERAL PARTY OF CANADA, NOV. 17, 1891.

I AM glad, Mr. Chairman, to partake of your generous hospitality, and to join with my fellow-citizens in extending a cordial welcome to your distinguished guest and his friends who to-night honor us with their presence.

We recognize in this compliment to him not only the great influence he, as an orator, statesman, and leader, exerts in the public affairs of his own country, but the wide reputation he has established, far beyond her limits, for distinguished public service.

Speaking for a large and worthy body of our fellow-citizens who are bound to you, our guests, by closest ties and warmest sympathy, and bound to our old Commonwealth as faithful, loyal citizens, devoted to her institutions, active in her progress, earnest in all her work, proud of her history, her honor, and her prosperity, I know I voice their sentiment when I say they feel especial pride and pleasure in welcoming you to our State. But speaking also for all our people, and for the Commonwealth herself, I gladly extend to you this welcome.

We know the ability and merit which have distinguished your public life. We also know to-night you come to us representing a neighboring, friendly country, which has much in common with us, and which each year is coming into closer relations with our Nation and our Commonwealth. To you personally, and to you as a distinguished son of Canada, our welcome is extended.

It is a pleasure, after weeks of earnest party strife, where public questions have divided us on party lines, to-night to touch upon a question, suggested by the presence of our guests, upon which our business interests and our people are substantially agreed, quite clear of party division.

Our country and Canada, separated by only an imaginary line for three thousand miles of contiguous territory, interlocked by railroads and waterways, each blessed with special advantages in producing and selling what the other needs, bound together by many interests in common, — these two great neighbors, I believe, were intended to be friends, and, as friends, to have the closest trade and commercial relations, which cannot but be for their mutual interest.

Notwithstanding the restrictions which in both countries have been imposed by the hand of man as limitations upon natural conditions, still a trade of nearly $100,000,000 annually exists between us, fairly evenly divided into exports and imports.

We purchase of Canada necessaries of life for our people and materials for our industries, and she of us, in return, food, manufactures, and crude materials which add to the comfort of her people and to her own growth and prosperity. In this trade Massachusetts and New England have a great and growing interest. To us in this State it means a benefit God intended for us through our sea-coast location, a greater prosperity for our industries, a larger market for their products, and easier conditions of life for all our people.

It means, as this trade becomes fuller and freer, that we, too, can have natural advantages now enjoyed by other sections of our country, and can offset their competition, which we are beginning to feel, by opening up wider markets on the north for our manufactured products.

With existing restrictions removed, or largely modified, I do not doubt great benefit will come to both countries, and Boston, with her enterprise, her energy and industry, can be the commercial metropolis, not only of New England, but of the great country beyond.

Much of the prosperity of our country is due to that wise provision of our Constitution which compels absolute freedom of trade between all our States. Under it all sections of our country have grown, their resources been developed, and their industries established and diversified.

Such policy established between this and neighboring countries, but wisely modified and limited to meet necessary conditions, I believe would foster a larger trade between us, whose benefits all would reap.

The views I have expressed are but a repetition of the opinion often stated by our Press, our business interests, our people, and by leaders of both parties in every section of our country.

In the fall of 1889, at hearings here before a committee of the United States Senate, the heads of our commercial organizations and leading business men and manufacturers, without distinction of party, were united in their opinion in favor of some policy which should lead to fuller and freer trade with Canada.

There was, and perhaps is, a difference of opinion as to the means by which this shall be accomplished. In view of our experience with Canada under reciprocity, and the evident growth of sentiment in recent years in that direction, for one, I firmly believe that a large and liberal policy of reciprocity would establish those closer commercial relations between our countries, equally desired, I trust, by both, and certain to be for the benefit of both.

Because, Sir, I know the sentiment of this Commonwealth is one of cordial friendship to your country, because I believe it is her earnest wish that this friendship may ripen into closer relations of advantage to both, I extend to you and your associates her heartiest welcome, and her wish that your stay among us may be both pleasant and useful. Massachusetts is always proud to welcome any distinguished stranger, and to extend to him her right hand of fellowship. This welcome you have fully earned. But the welcome is the more cordial because you represent that liberal spirit which would bind nations together in trade and friendship, and so promote the peace of the world and the happiness and prosperity of all its people.

ADDRESS

AT THE OPENING OF THE NEW BUILDING OF THE BOSTON CHAMBER OF COMMERCE, JAN. 21, 1892.

MY part to-night is a simple but a very pleasant one, — to extend the hearty welcome of the Commonwealth to the distinguished guests who honor us with their presence, and our cordial congratulations to the Chamber of Commerce, as to-day, in its new and better quarters, it enters upon a new lease of life, filled with hope and with promise, and then to enjoy with you the words of wit and wisdom of those who follow me.

Most gladly I extend the greeting of the Commonwealth to all our guests. We know they come to rejoice in our rejoicing, to bind still closer the sisterhood of States, not only in trade and commerce, but in friendship and good-will.

As we welcome them, and especially the distinguished gentleman who filled so conspicuous a place in the cabinet of President Cleveland, we regret that we are not able to welcome also his distinguished successor and the President of the United States.

Had their responsible duties permitted them to attend, I know that Massachusetts, with her greeting, would wish me to assure them that whatever measures they deem wise and necessary to sustain our flag and to uphold our national honor will receive the undivided and earnest support of this patriotic old Commonwealth.[1]

---

[1] The reference is to complications then pending with Chili, which threatened war.

It is a great pleasure to-night to express to you, however informally, the deep interest of the Commonwealth in your work, which so earnestly and efficiently is promoting her trade and her commerce. In this you represent one of her greatest and earliest industries.

In the early years of this century, when our commerce was nearly annihilated by the utter disregard of neutral rights by the great belligerent Powers of Europe, and by the passage of defensive embargo and non-intercourse Acts at home, your predecessors felicitously declared that the best and most productive farms in New England were upon the seas, and, most justly, they claimed of their government the defence of these freeholds.

What was true then is equally true now. Commerce now as then is the most legitimate and natural business of a large part of New England. Her situation, the genius, education, and enterprise of her people, naturally adapt her to this pursuit. She has a just claim upon the government, not for special favors, but that she should be left free to follow this pursuit, and to reap its benefits unfettered by restrictive laws.

Our National Constitution gave her unrestricted commerce with the whole sisterhood of States. It also forbade preference, by any regulation of commerce or revenue, to the ports of one State over another. In the spirit of these provisions, which made interstate commerce free from ocean to ocean, and foreign commerce forever exempt from any local privileges, New England asks only for laws which shall be equal and just to all sections of our common country, and which, if equal and just, cannot but lift some of the burdens now upon her, and so increase her industries, her trade, and her commerce.

Commerce and manufactures have ever been allied in mutual support. If at times there has seemed to be apparent diversity of interests between them, I firmly believe we are beginning to see that it is more apparent than real, and that they can and will go hand in hand together with mutual prosperity, commerce leading the way for manufactures to the markets of the world. The merchants of Salem, in 1820, in their celebrated memorial against restrictions on commerce, drafted by Judge Story, declared that commerce and manufactures both were vital to the welfare and prosperity of the Union, and that "It can never be a sound or safe policy to build up the one upon the ruins of the other;" and they laid it down as a "rational doctrine that national wealth is best promoted upon principles of perfect reciprocity." We may differ as to the way, we may call it by different names, but all will agree that the purpose and the end are desirable, and mean greater prosperity both to commerce and manufactures, and so to the welfare of our country. It certainly will be most useful in these matters which affect so vitally the great interests of the country that, as far as practicable, all interests should act in harmony for a favorable result, however much they may differ as to the precise and best mode to reach it.

I am sure that the merchants of Boston will give their earnest support to any action which, in their judgment, will promote the great interests of commerce, foreign and domestic, come such action from whom it may. But remembering the able speakers for whom you are anxiously waiting, I must no longer trespass upon your patience and your courtesy. I bid this distinguished gathering of merchants who have done so much for the welfare and honor of the Commonwealth godspeed in their efforts to advance her commerce and all her interests.

Let me close by again extending the warmest welcome

of the Commonwealth to all our guests, especially to the distinguished representatives from other States, who have come to join us in our rejoicing, to assure us of their fraternal interest, and to prove to us that nowhere in this broad land is the old Bay State forgotten. Welcome to our festivities, welcome to our Commonwealth! May your visit be as pleasant and profitable to you as it surely is to us.

ADDRESS

TO THE HARVARD ALUMNI, AT CAMBRIDGE, ON COMMENCEMENT, JUNE 30, 1892.

FOR the second time it is my privilege to bring to a great university the congratulations of a great State; to reciprocate in her name the cordial welcome which Harvard's sons ever give to her Alma Mater, our Commonwealth; then to speak of the relation of the State to the College, now manifest less in law and government than in their mutual assistance and dependence, which have loyally, lovingly intertwined their lives for more than two hundred and fifty years, each striving to benefit the people and to contribute to their strength, happiness, and prosperity.

In extending these congratulations a year ago, I spoke of the close dependence of the College upon the State from the earliest days, when the common founders of both, recognizing higher education as one of the estates of the realm necessary for the building up of a nation, gave to us Harvard as a commonwealth of learning to be a corner-stone of the greater Commonwealth which was to guide and govern an intelligent, liberty-loving, God-fearing people. Through many a generation this close dependence was shown in gifts and statutes, in the exercise of State control, and even in the fundamental law of our Constitution, in those familiar, solemn phrases, where it declares that wisdom and knowledge diffused generally among the body of the people are necessary for the preservation of their rights and liberties. And so it enjoined upon the future "to cherish the interests of literature and the sciences, and all seminaries of them, especially the university at Cambridge, public schools and grammar-schools in the towns."

But as Harvard has grown strong and self-reliant, the obligation upon the State to foster the first-born of its learned institutions has not been the duty of nursing or of governing it, but rather of releasing it from the restrictions of executive and legislative control, that, under conditions of perfect freedom, in the full power of its manhood, it might render service to the Commonwealth better and more useful, because only the fruit of its own resources. So the true connection of Harvard with the State is found no longer in a dependence which chafes and dwarfs, but in the higher, larger relation of a potent influence entering into the life of the State and of her people, and, in sympathy with their wishes, wants, and aspirations, leading towards the high ideals which an enlightened commonwealth ever sets before a patriotic people.

The Constitution places the university and seminaries of literature and sciences at the head of our public schools and grammar-schools not so much because they are the final blossom and fruit of the schools as their essential outgrowth and necessity; and such education, generally diffused, it declares vital to the preservation of our rights and liberties. The founders of our Commonwealth, the framers of our State and National Constitutions, the draftsmen of the Declaration of Independence, and the many mighty minds who gave us our country, our independence, and our government, meant that education and the scholar should go forth among the people, and exercise a just and powerful influence on public affairs. They were guilty of no such folly as to make it the duty "of magistrates and legislatures to cherish the interests of literature and the sciences," and then to repudiate the legitimate and practical result of such action by sneering at the scholar who brings the light of education into the life of the body politic for the solution of its many and complicated problems.

With this opportunity for great influence open to higher education and expected of it, there rests upon it a corresponding duty. With us it cannot remain the studious monk in his cell, or the recluse in his study, even though it discover new truths and develop great principles of science or of ethics. Its constitutional and its natural place with us is to be the pioneer and missionary, the "schoolmaster abroad," to educate and help a people. Religion, with all its vital and commanding forces, became effective only when through Christ it entered into the lives of men. "Go ye into all the world," is a command to education and its scholars no less than to religion and its missionaries. Education felt the inspiration of its true mission when it gathered the little knot of students behind the historic haystack in Williamstown, where it planned to carry the gospel of Christianity across continent and ocean back to the Old World, there to acomplish its great and glorious purpose. Education which teaches liberty in the songs of a Lowell, which marshals the conscience of a people with the eloquence of a Phillips, which fights for freedom and for country in the grand lives and heroic deaths which this hall commemorates, — this is education, not content to bound its work within the narrow and selfish limits of personal success, but which goes forth into the great fields of humanity and public service, and coming in touch with the life of a people, proves itself a fighting force for good. This is education taking its proper place and doing its perfect work. Where wrongs exist, it preaches the gospel of reform and discontent; where rights are to be defended, it fights with the courage of honest and enlightened conviction. Its mission must be service, not contemplation; and, like religion, it must take to its heart and its mind the weary and the heavy laden, and seek to give them rest. So it steps forth from the student's cloister into the lives and hearts of the people, and the college becomes a power in the commonwealth. So, in the language of our Constitution, "Wisdom and knowledge, as well as virtue, are diffused generally among the body of the people." They feel the quickening touch, and, seeking not to be patronized but uplifted, follow with confidence where education with human sympathy leads the way.

Under our glorious system of free institutions and popular sovereignty there are ever problems of government and politics, of industry and society, which require "campaigns of education" for their just and intelligent solution. It needs no word of mine to tell you what in such campaigns is the place and power of a university. Let not the scholar stand aloof from the people, content to help them only with the cold and rigid rules of reason and of logic, but rather let his life run out into the lives of others, and from the abundance given him, freely give to all about him. And as he gives he also receives, gathering, in his sympathetic touch with the people, knowledge not taught from books but from life, which gives him greater strength and power.

I have ventured to speak of this broader, truer relation of the college to the State, because I know I but repeat the lessons taught me by my Alma Mater, and give expression to the spirit which has marked her long and honorable life. To-day, by the example and precept of her authorities, by the manliness and vigor of her student life, — more vigorous and self-reliant because freed, as Harvard has been, from the restrictions of unnecessary authority, — by the many ways in which her undergraduates and her graduates touch the life of the people, Harvard is fulfilling the hopes of her pious founders, and meeting the constitutional duties enjoined upon her by an anxious, loving mother State.

May the time never come when any Harvard man shall feel that the world is bounded by college walls, and that its whole life is within, or when he shall forget the greater world outside surging against the walls and asking the help and guidance of education to meet its wants and its aspirations.

ADDRESS

AT THE TWO HUNDRED AND FIFTIETH ANNIVERSARY OF THE SETTLEMENT OF WOBURN, MASS., AT WOBURN, SEPT. 27, 1892.

AS this old town and city to-day joyfully, with praise and thanksgiving, celebrates the passing of another milestone in its long and honorable life, it certainly is most fitting that the mother State should come with her love and greeting to join in your festivities and to rejoice in your rejoicing. She recognizes that such celebrations are more than local in their significance, or temporary in their influence. Your history is her history, your strength and growth are part of her prosperity. The celebration to-day recalls the past, — your past, her past. It takes us back to the days of our early beginning; to the settlement of our towns, and the founding of our Commonwealth.

As we note the work and spirit of our early founders, their courage and perseverance, their devotion to religion, education, and freedom, their resistance to unjust and oppressive laws; as we see them in the midst of a wilderness creating a Commonwealth, planting churches, schools, and colleges, — we, the generation of to-day, reaping the fruit of their foresight and labor, from their example gather courage and inspiration to hand down to our posterity the Commonwealth they founded and loved, preserved, broadened, and strengthened by a like devotion and patriotism. So, in the contemplation suggested by these anniversaries come to the State a quickening of public spirit, renewed devotion to her institutions and consecration to her service.

When Lewis and Clark, early in the century, made their celebrated exploration, they followed the great Father of Waters up to its fountain-head, and there reverently knelt and drank of its limpid stream. To-day, standing by the broad river of our prosperity, we trace its ever-widening current up to its fountain-head, and there we reverently kneel in grateful acknowledgment.

Not unlike these explorers, the historians of New England trace its progress and prosperity, its liberties and glory, up to their original source, and find them in that primary unit of New England civilization and government, the town organization. That organization, if not original with us, at least found here its full development and maturity. It grew out of the Church, and at first was limited by its control. But as the stream of our life ran on, ever growing and broadening as other influences flowed into it, there came greater freedom and toleration, and Massachusetts was emancipated from early restrictions and freed from early prejudices. To-day she stands before the world as broad as she is great, as just as she is patriotic, with love for all her children, and with no place in her motherly heart for any spirit of intolerance.

Distinguished and prosperous as has been the progress of your town and city, it is not widely different in its history from its many associates that make up the aggregate life and prosperity of our Commonwealth. Here first came the church in 1642; then followed the incorporation of the town; then in its very infancy we find it making liberal grants for school and college. Hardly a generation old, it showed its hatred of tyranny by defiance of the royal governor, and afterwards by taking a hand in his capture and imprisonment.

In all of the early wars with the Indians and French Woburn did her full duty. But though loyal to king and governor as long as they were just to her, she was more loyal to the liberty and rights of the people. In the great agitation preceding our Revolution, again she uttered her indignant protests against unjust taxation and tyranny. When agitation ripened into revolution, she sent her sons to fight at Lexington and on many a battlefield for liberty and independence. So, three generations later, when there came a glorious struggle again for liberty and for the preservation of the Union our fathers had welded together with labor and with love, again went forth the sons of Woburn, ready to suffer for freedom's sake, and to die for love of country.

So, too, in her later life is found constant evidence of the enterprise, patriotism, and public spirit of her citizens. It is seen in the great industries which have brought fame and prosperity to the town, in its many public improvements, and in the watchful care of the attractions which Nature with lavish hand has given you, and which make Woburn a pleasant place in which to dwell. It is strikingly shown in your magnificent public library, which, as it educates and uplifts the people, tells of the generosity and public spirit of a son of Woburn.

All these things, so creditable and honorable in your history, are also typical of the life of our Commonwealth. As you early planted the church and school, and organized the town-meeting, so she throughout her life has ever been devoted to religion, education, and self-government; and from these have sprung an intelligent, liberty-loving, God-fearing people.

As here there have been resistance to tyranny, struggle for independence, and suffering and sacrifice for union and liberty, so too has Massachusetts, marshalling these forces out of all her towns, stepped forth to lead in every great agitation for the rights of a people, the maintenance of their institutions, and the preservation of their country. With vigor and fidelity she watches over the interests of her citizens; with a strong arm she guards their rights; with a loving heart she relieves their suffering; with wise and progressive legislation she seeks to lessen the toil of labor, and to benefit and uplift the masses of her people.

The power, prosperity, and progress of the Commonwealth rest upon her cities and her towns. In them she lives and moves and has her being. May the time not come when anything is done to destroy their autonomy, infringe their rights, or impair that system which was the foundation of the Commonwealth, has been for two hundred and fifty years the bulwark of our liberties, and is to-day gratefully recognized as the source of our independence, prosperity, and happiness.

SPEECH

AT THE OPENING OF THE EXHIBITION OF THE CHARITABLE MECHANICS ASSOCIATION, OCT. 6, 1892.

I GLADLY answer your cordial welcome to the Commonwealth by extending her congratulations to this society, and her best wishes for the success of this its Exhibition, which is evidence of its continued prosperity and industry, and not less its public spirit.

I am glad, too, as a member of this society, greatly honored by election to it, to express my personal interest in its work and exhibition.

I have been thinking to-day, as perhaps have many of you, of the origin of our Association. I have pictured in my mind that sturdy band of mechanics, " more in number than the stars of heaven," so Paul Revere declared, who gathered with him at the old Green Dragon Tavern, and there conceived and founded the society. I have admired again their public spirit and broad philanthropy, which determined them to put their society closely in touch with the life of the people, and to aid them by gentle charity and useful public service, as well as in their material interests and industries. So they declared its purpose to be to relieve distress, to help the cause of education, as well as to promote useful inventions and industries, and to take part in all matters of public importance. How strange it seems to us now that for the first ten years of its life the Legislature refused to give it a charter, because, as the record shows, of "an apprehension that it was a combination to extort extravagant prices for labor"! Had the timid conservatism of that day prevailed, there would have been lost to Massachusetts one of her great institutions, and to her people the blessings that have followed from its success.

I have thought that if its founders could come back and look over its long and useful life of nearly one hundred years, they would rejoice to see how true it had been to the spirit and purposes of its founders. They would find that it had been quick and generous to relieve poverty and distress; that it had been useful and true to the cause of education; that it had done much to promote industries and inventions,— especially by these great exhibitions, which advance the cause of industry, give instruction and pleasure to a whole community, and mark the growth and development of our material prosperity. By such exhibitions could almost be written the industrial history of our Commonwealth and our country.

They would find, too, that on many a public occasion this Association had borne a conspicuous part, and had rendered useful aid to many a public undertaking. Of the many instances, let me recall one which the Commonwealth will ever remember with gratitude.

When the monument on yonder Bunker Hill paused in its upward movement, and the work seemed destined to fail, this Association remembered and put into action the eloquent words of Webster, spoken at the laying of its corner-stone: "Let it rise to meet the sun in its coming, let the earliest light of day gild it, and let parting day linger and play upon it." It felt at once the touch of a vigorous hand, and rose in its majesty to completion, ever to remind us of the independence and glory of our country. So, too, it will remind us of the public spirit and the public services of this Association.

Gladly I bring to you to-day the gratitude of our Commonwealth, and her earnest wish that this Exhibition, now open in all its completeness and for all its great purposes, may meet with the success its merits richly deserve.

SPEECH

AT THE DINNER OF THE IRISH CHARITABLE SOCIETY IN BOSTON, MARCH 19, 1893.

FOR the third time it is my privilege to come to this Society with the greeting of the Commonwealth, mingled with her congratulations upon its long, useful, and honorable life, and for a third time to note in your welcome and in your loyal toast the love you bear to this grand old State, of which we all are justly proud.

I like the language of your toast to the Commonwealth. It speaks not of her wealth, her population, or her size; nor of her trade, her industries, or her prosperity. It passes by these material things, great as they are, and notes as the potent fact of her life that from her sprang American liberty; that, loyal in her devotion to human rights, with sympathy and help she has been the friend always and everywhere of the needy and oppressed, — and so she has left her impress on the Nation, and so in pride and love we pledge to her our devotion and our service.

I do not need in this presence to recall the facts of her history, which justify the sentiment so well expressed in the toast. Every school-child is familiar with them, and knows that throughout her whole life the love of liberty has prevailed, and made her citizens, not only self-reliant and self-governing, but earnest in their sympathy with any people who enter on the path which we have trodden, and have found to lead to prosperity and happiness.

So, to-night, as ties of blood and kinship carry the thoughts of many across the water to the Green Isle beyond, and your hopes and prayers go forth that success at last may reward a struggle of seven hundred years, I think I express the sentiment of Massachusetts, in accord with her history and traditions, in declaring her sympathy with this cause, and her godspeed to the great statesman who, determined to undo the wrongs of the past with a measure of justice, seeks to give to a liberty-loving people the inestimable blessing of the right to govern themselves.

I am glad to-night to speak a word about Home Rule from a New England standpoint. This principle is thoroughly wrought into every fibre of our Commonwealth. When Governor Winthrop brought here from the shores of England the charter of his company, Home Rule had its inception. When from that commercial charter he and his associates developed a system of government, carrying out the fundamental principles of the "Mayflower" compact, Home Rule received a mighty impetus. From that day to this it has been the fundamental policy of our colony and State. It originated, shaped, and guided all the controversies with the colonial governors. It overthrew Andros. It was felt in every law and influence while Massachusetts, like Ireland to-day, was a constituent part of the British Empire, and until its denial by that government resulted in the independence of the colonies. The beginning and the end of the whole Revolutionary struggle was Home Rule; and the successful development of our National and State life since has been in following its guidance.

As in this, the greatest and best of the old Puritan Commonwealths, we, though of different blood, race, and religion, have lived happily and prospered together under this principle of Home Rule, with a common experience and hopes and purposes, with a union of thought and action, with equal devotion to our Commonwealth and country, and all their great institutions, and an equal willingness to struggle and suffer in their behalf,— so it is natural and fitting that we should stand together in our sympathy with the oppressed in other lands, and in our hope that to them as to us there may come liberty and self-government.

What better answer, too, than our own experience to the evil forebodings of those who fear that self-government cannot safely be given to a people because of differences of religion or of race? Early in our history there followed in the footsteps of our founders men of another nationality and of another religious faith. They came to a Puritan State; they brought with them their religion. Generously they were welcomed to our shores, and gladly, ever in increasing numbers, they cast in their lot with us. If they did not forget their native land and its green flag, yet ever above the green have they proudly carried the Star-Spangled Banner of our country and the Home Rule flag of our State. If in their minds there linger the sweet notes of Erin's harp, yet have they never failed to "keep step to the music of the Union" from the days of Montgomery and through the Revolution, to the time when Shields, Kilpatrick, and their many associates led their Irish ranks into the thickest of the fight for liberty and the Stars and Stripes.

Constantly in our American citizenship there has been this intermingling of nationalities and of religions, and of the new with the old. The descendants of the original emigrants to Plymouth, Salem, and Boston, and the descendants of the later emigrants, have become an integral portion of our Commonwealth, sharing in its government, and helping to mould its measures and its influences. And what has been the result?

A prosperous Commonwealth of a united, loyal, happy people, grounded in the principles of liberty, equality, and Home Rule. We hail her as the mother State who gives to all her protection, and gets from all, without exaction, obedience and love.

INTRODUCTORY REMARKS

AS PRESIDING OFFICER AT THE DINNER GIVEN TO HON. P. A. COLLINS, IN BOSTON, APRIL 4, 1893, UPON HIS DEPARTURE AS CONSUL-GENERAL TO LONDON.

WITH pleasure I ask you now to turn from this generous table to the better things which others have prepared for you, — from feasting to the kindly play of sentiment that will give expression to the one thought, the one feeling, and the one name which bring us together in sympathy and friendship to pay our tribute of respect and honor to our distinguished guest.

What need, however, to give expression to your thought? The character, the number, the enthusiasm of this gathering better than spoken phrase utter their " Well done " to a life well lived, and express their congratulation and their confidence as that life goes forth into fields of greater usefulness.

Massachusetts has a way of commending honorable service and faithful citizenship in the presence and the lifetime of those whom thus she delights to honor. She waits not till death to set her stamp of approval upon a useful, honorable life, but, speaking through a representative company like this, she with her word of praise gives for the past the reward well earned, and for the future " the spur to brave and honest deeds."

But a few nights ago there gathered here distinguished citizens, who, disregarding all political differences, gladly joined in words of just praise to one who had given long and honorable service to his State and to his country. With fidelity and ability, with patriotism and an unblemished character, he had discharged the duties of high public position; and with the respect, the confidence, and the love of his fellow-citizens he sought the rest and peace he had richly earned. To him this commendation was the triumphant ending of his public life, the gentle comforter to bear him up in his declining years.[1]

To-night, in the same generous spirit and on the same broad ground, we meet bearing our commendation and congratulation to one in the full vigor of his activity and in the very prime of his usefulness. Our meeting is but the closing of a chapter in his life, marking its past with our "Well done," and its unwritten future with our "God speed." Into that life I have no wish nor need now to enter, — no wish, because the ties of closest friendship and esteem could not withhold the words of praise which would offend his modesty; no need, because his life has spoken for itself. It is stamped upon the community, and its influence felt in State and Nation. It has gallantly led in many a contest for principle and the right, manfully accepting defeat, and wisely using victory. It has fully met the grave responsibilities of high official position. Faithfully it has served the people, with loyalty and devotion upholding the principles and the institutions of our great Republic. And in and through that life there have ever been a keen sense of justice and of honor, the broad spirit of toleration and the recognition of the gentle charities which bring sunshine into the lives of others.

No wonder, General Collins, that to many of us you have been a trusted leader, a wise counsellor, and a true

[1] The reference is to Senator Dawes.

friend. In achieving this success out of poverty and struggle, in winning an honorable place in the esteem and hearts of this community, you have illustrated the truths that the essence of our democracy is "the supremacy of man over his accidents," and that "each man makes his own stature, builds himself."

May I say, then, to you, it is in recognition of your worth, your character and ability, your self-made success, and to give expression to our belief that you will with distinction discharge the duties of the high post to which you have been called, that we, your friends and fellow-citizens, bring to you our heartiest congratulations and good wishes?

But this company needs no words of mine to express its sentiment. It wishes to do that itself, and will not permit me longer to stand between you and its greeting. "Sir, you are very welcome to our house. It must appear in other ways than words; therefore I scant this breathing courtesy." Gentlemen, a health to General Collins: success, long life to him! As, crowned with honors and high station, he goes back across the water to represent the country of his choice, he carries with him our confidence and our best wishes. If the parting touches a little his heart-strings, may he remember that the farewell is ever behind, but the welcome ever before.

SPEECH

AT THE DINNER OF THE BRITISH CHARITABLE SOCIETY, IN BOSTON, MAY 24, 1893.

IT is always a pleasant duty to represent the Commonwealth at these gatherings of her citizens, bringing to them her congratulations, and receiving the cordial welcome which your loyalty to her suggests.

This is the third Charitable Society whose anniversary I have this year attended, — the Scots', Irish, and British, — all founded in the sweet name of Charity, and through the generations of their lives doing her blessed work. All, too, recall the fact that their members, while loyal in their devotion to the country of their choice and adoption, cherish the remembrance of a land across the water to which their thoughts lovingly turn, just as in mature age one remembers the homestead of childhood. What Bonnie Scotland is to one, and the Green Isle to another, to you is Old England with her long life of great men and great things. With her we claim a common heritage; from her have we sprung; and out of her Isles have we received much that is great in our laws, literature, and institutions. As, to-day, arbitration takes the place of war, as we gather here in peaceful array the great navies of the world, — and, may I add, as England, following in our footsteps, grows more and more democratic in recognition of the people's power and the right of local self-government, — I cannot help feeling that the peoples at least who speak our language are drawing nearer together; and that the time may not be far distant when the prediction of a great English writer of to-day will be verified, that the English-speaking race will dominate the civilized world, and that the seat of their power will be upon the banks of the Hudson and the Mississippi. Your Society and its kindred Societies, with their love of other lands, but greater love for this, seem to be one of the influences to hasten this happy consummation.

One other thought this meeting to-night suggests. Our country is now celebrating a great anniversary, — that of the discovery of a continent, which was the first and necessary step for the foundation of a great republic that should lift the people up to the conception and assertion of their rights. To-day, in honor of this the greatest achievement of the last four centuries, the nations bring hither the evidence of their growth and prosperity, and compare it with our own. It has well been said that our grandest exhibit to the world is a happy people governing themselves. The greatest factor in that work is the individual citizen, for whose education and development have been founded our institutions, and upon whom rests the stability of our government. For the development of an American republic, sustained and perfected by an American citizenship, all nations have made their contributions. As their people have poured in upon us, they have brought with them, of course, their religion and language, their national traits, and often tender memories of their old homes and countries. But with these conditions, here in a land of liberty all joined to make a new country, a new citizenship, and a new government of popular rights. Coming here with pure purposes, to labor and to live with us, to enjoy and adopt our institutions, they are made welcome to our shores. We do not expect them to forget the sweet memories of their mother lands, nor to cease to cherish all that is great and good in them. We do expect that they will become merged in our greater, broader American citizenship, prize its privileges, and hold its institutions and its flag nearest and dearest to their hearts.

Gentlemen, I extend to you, and through you to the gracious sovereign whose seventy-fourth birthday you celebrate, the congratulations of a great Commonwealth, which, resting upon such broad and loyal citizenship, stands pre-eminent in her devotion to liberty, humanity, our country and its institutions.

INTRODUCTORY REMARKS

AS PRESIDING OFFICER AT THE DINNER GIVEN BY THE MASSACHUSETTS DELEGATION TO THE OFFICIALS OF THE WORLD'S FAIR, IN CHICAGO, JUNE 15, 1893.

IT is now my pleasant privilege to call you from the delights of the table to the intellectual feast which will be given by those who follow me, and to the flow of soul which marks the spirit of our gathering and binds us together, hosts and guests, State and State, in comity and friendship.

My part to-night is a very pleasant, yet a very simple one, — I speak but the prologue to the entertainment, with words of welcome. Then it is my duty to ring up the curtain, and present to you these sages and wits, these men of affairs and deeds, who, each in his way, has rendered distinguished public service.

I need not, as in the prologue, ask for them your kind attention. You could not fail to give it if you would. Nor need I ask of you for them a cordial welcome. Massachusetts and her citizens ever gladly extend her greeting and her hospitality to the stranger within her gates. And when she lifts her latch-string, not to welcome the stranger in, but to wander a little from her own hearthstone, she carries with her, I believe, the same generous spirit and warm heart, the same broad sympathies and belief in a common brotherhood, which, making her at home a beloved mother to loyal children, make her, I trust, wherever she may be, a generous friend and a gracious hostess, who is glad and proud to extend her welcome to all who gather in her name.

In this spirit, to-night, I speak for her, giving to you her citizens, and to you her guests, her right hand of fellowship and friendship.

To-night one other thought is uppermost in our minds. We have come here officially to represent a great Commonwealth; to express her deep interest and unbounded pride in this grand exposition, which, drawing hither the products and peoples of the world, is itself the greatest national contribution to the world's entertainment, education, and civilization; and then, in behalf of our Commonwealth, to extend, with a deep sense of gratitude and obligation, her heartiest congratulation to the authorities and officials, whose work, ability, and persistent zeal have been crowned with a superb triumph.

We recognize the broad spirit in which they have planned and labored, the difficulties and obstacles which with indomitable will they have overcome; the generous public spirit, municipal, state, and national, which they have aroused as a power to assure success; and the skill, ability, and ingenuity out of which has been wrought this national masterpiece.

Massachusetts is proud to have contributed something of her talent, ability, and means to the development and progress of this work. With full appreciation that it, as broadly planned and carefully perfected, is the product of the united labor of all, and yet with a proud sense of part proprietorship, she rejoices in its complete success, and gladly pays her tribute of honor and respect to those upon whom have rested the labor and responsibility.

But, gentlemen, I fear your indulgence and patience may tempt me to wander from my prologue to the more substantial intellectual entertainment which I was but to introduce; and so I ring the bell and raise the curtain, and usher in the entertainment.

ADDRESS

AT THE BANQUET GIVEN BY THE MASSACHUSETTS SOCIETY OF CHICAGO TO THE MASSACHUSETTS DELEGATION TO THE WORLD'S FAIR, AT CHICAGO, JUNE 17, 1893.

IT is always a pleasure to receive the welcome of Massachusetts' sons, whether within or without her limits. It is always a privilege to answer that welcome by extending to them her greeting and her blessing.

To-night we meet far away from home to accept the hospitality of her sons; and, with her name upon our lips, and her glorious life in every mind, we greet her with the love and loyalty which neither time nor distance can affect.

Many a time it has been my privilege to speak for her at home at her own fireside. There, where her authority is ever unquestioned, her gentle, uplifting power ever felt, her daily life marked by beneficent laws and helpful deeds, we, her sons, think and speak of her as a constant guiding influence, protecting us with her might, and enriching us with manifold blessings.

Perhaps at times we who have something to do with her laws and the exercise of her authority see a little of the sterner side of her life. We may think of her then as a controlling power, binding us about with numerous restrictions and limitations, exacting from us contributions, interfering with personal liberty, and demanding obedience to her sovereign will. If she seems to us then a taskmaster, ever with the commands upon her lips, "Thou shalt," and "Thou shalt not," she really is but the lawgiver, — upright, just, and beneficent.

But, after all, this is only a small part of her life. To us who gather about her hearthstone she is far less of a governing power than a guiding influence. We think of her long life of great men and great deeds; of the glorious work she has done in the fields of education, religion, and charity; of her public spirit and patriotism, and her sacrifices for independence, liberty, and union; of her contributions to science and letters; of her leadership in every great agitation for personal liberty and human rights; of the valor she has shown in every war and upon every battle-field; of the many sons she has sent forth to die for love of country. Then to us she is less a sovereign power of unbending will than " a mother State," guiding the destiny of loving children who are bound to her, not by her strong right arm, but by her heart and soul.

This is Massachusetts at home in the midst of her contented, prosperous, happy family. But to-night in this great city, whose energy and generosity have gathered here the States of the Union and the nations of the world in friendly competition for the entertainment and instruction of all, we cannot content ourselves with a home-view of any subject; but, broadened by our surroundings, of necessity there enters into our conception even of a mother State a sense of comparison and proportion, and of her place and influence in the greater, grander whole. I speak to-night, therefore, of Massachusetts, not as she is to us, her children, but as she stands before the country and world for what she has done for humanity and the building up of a great Republic.

Grand as this Exposition is, almost beyond the power of words to describe; successful as it is in its architecture and its beauty, and perfect in every detail; proud of it as we are, as the greatest national masterpiece yet contributed for the instruction and entertainment of the civilized world, — I have felt that in this, our anniversary celebration, there was a greater thing we had to show to every nation: a powerful, contented people, in the process of building up an indestructible Republic founded on the principles of liberty, equality, and self-government. Into this work have entered the contributions of all countries, creating and developing an American citizenship as the basis of a great Republic of personal liberty and constitutional government.

It was an Italian under Portuguese instruction, and in a Spanish vessel, who discovered our continent. During the next two centuries English, French, and Spanish vied with each other in their further discoveries and achievements here. Note a few of the early settlements, and see out of what varied material was to come our citizenship and our Republic. Puritan settlers in New England, Cavaliers in Virginia; the Dutch on the banks of the Hudson, and the Swedes on the banks of the Delaware; Quakers in Pennsylvania, Catholics in Maryland, the Huguenots in South Carolina, Spanish and French in Florida and Louisiana, — but all coming to a land of liberty, to breathe the pure air of free institutions, and to be moulded into a new type of American citizenship.

Massachusetts stands before the country and the world to be judged by the part she has taken in this great work for liberty and mankind. What has been her contribution? How much has she added to the strength and glory of our common country? What has she done for independence and liberty? I do not need to-night, in the presence of her citizens, to do more than touch upon a few things that mark a long and honorable life, which has been a potent influence in the creation of our Constitution and a priceless contribution to the progress of our country. First, she has given to the country the sturdiness of character, the courage, and the piety which distinguished her Puritan founders. That was the fibre which was to be wrought into the fabric of our Republic to make it great and permanent. Note their wisdom and foresight, and see how much we owe to them. They seemed to foresee the full result of their work, and to know that out of it was to come a great Nation of intelligent, liberty-loving, and God-fearing people. So in education, religion, and self-government they laid its foundation deep and strong. In the midst of the wilderness they established the public-school system, set up the printing-press, printed the Bible, and, out of their poverty, founded a great university. And this, the work of their day, has come down through the generations and spread throughout the land.

The courage, patriotism, and public spirit of her founders have ever been present and potent in the life of Massachusetts, making her foremost in every great agitation for freedom and humanity. Four generations after her founding she was uttering in town-meetings her formal protests against the tyranny of the mother country, and, under Adams and Hancock, arousing the conscience of her people to assert their rights and declare their independence.

So, too, a short century after, when there came again a struggle for liberty, Massachusetts, foremost in the great agitation which was to wipe out the curse of human slavery, is again ready to do battle for the principles which have distinguished her glorious life.

I have touched upon the heroic, martial side of the

life of Massachusetts. No one questions its value as a powerful factor in achieving our independence, establishing liberty, and making our Republic a permanent and indestructible Union. Had I the time, I should love to follow her life as it has been seen and felt in other fields of usefulness; show her prominence in every religious movement for greater freedom of conscience and liberty of thought; her leadership in education, establishing schools, colleges, and libraries, freely giving her citizens advantages unequalled by any state or nation in the world. Then I would point out how much she has done by wise laws and popular agitation to advance the interests of labor and to benefit the great masses of her people; and then her grand work through noble men and women in the manifold charities; and last, but not least, how she has sent forth her sons to every portion of our country, taking with them her principles and teaching, to build up by their courage and enterprise everywhere centres of activity which should stamp her ideas and influence deep into our national life.

But here in Chicago, in the midst of this great World's Exposition and competition, Massachusetts speaks for herself more forcibly than by any words of mine. She has built here a home characteristic of her life. Its name and history tell of her patriotism and statesmanship. Let the stranger who would know what she has done for the world enter its door and gaze upon its walls. He will find there little of ostentation, little to remind him of her wealth, industries, prosperity, her material life; but as he looks upon the pictures hanging there, he will hear her speaking to him through generations of great men who have moulded the literature, the laws and institutions of our country. Massachusetts speaks there to the world through Lowell and

Longfellow, Whittier and Boyle O'Reilly, Holmes and Lucy Larcom, whose poetry has become household words, and who, singing the songs of liberty, have carried education out into the life of the people to do its great and perfect work. Hawthorne and Emerson, Thoreau, Higginson, and Louisa Alcott, will remind him how much our country, through Massachusetts, has done in the field of letters; while Motley and Prescott, Parkman and Bancroft, testify to her prominence in the field of history; Pierce, Agassiz, Bowditch, Maria Mitchell, and Hitchcock remind us of her triumphs in science; Parsons and Story, Curtis and Shaw, of her leadership in law; Edwards and Channing, Parker and Clarke, Brooks and Peabody, are men who have led great theological movements, whose influence has been felt throughout the land. Horace Mann, a host in himself, represents and personifies more than any American, free education, its growth and development.

Then, if we turn to another phase of her life, and ask what public service Massachusetts has rendered, what a full and glorious answer comes from the walls of our Hancock building, with its long line of orators and reformers, statesmen and soldiers. There are found the men and women who have led the great movements for the uplifting of a people, — Garrison and Phillips, Mann, Sumner, and Parker, — all foremost and of commanding influence in great causes; Julia Ward Howe, whose " Battle Hymn " has become the martial music of the Republic; Everett and Choate, whose classic oratory charmed the Nation, and Webster, whose unrivalled intellect laid the constitutional basis of permanent freedom when through agitation and war came union and liberty; Winthrop, Hancock, Adams, Otis, and Andrew suggest the influence and power which Massachusetts, through many great names and patriotic lives, has wielded in the field of statesmanship; Sumner and Hooker, Shaw and Bartlett, Devens and Miles, — names fresh in the minds of the present generation, — recall how willingly Massachusetts men, when agitation ripened into action, answered their country's summons, and gave themselves to her on the field of battle; while Dorothea Dix, Howe, and Peabody, with scores of noble men and women, will speak forever of Massachusetts' work for charity, humanity, and philanthropy.

These are a few of the faces which speak to us from the walls of our State building. The list is almost endless. As I read in their lives of the power and grandeur of the Commonwealth, and of their influence not only on their day and generation but upon the generations yet unborn, I recall a thought expressed by Phillips in his plea for the preservation of the Old South Meeting-house. True, he said, its form is plain, it is not sightly to the eye; but when the soldiers of Massachusetts went forth in 1861 to fight for freedom and their country, as they passed the homely old building there was something within its walls which spoke to them, and reverently they lifted their caps and passed on, braver, truer men. It was the voice of the fathers and the soul of the Commonwealth which spoke, recalling the grandeur of the past, and inspiring them to meet nobly the duties set before them.

So Massachusetts here, not to her sons only but to the world, is speaking through these lives, which have blessed mankind; and the world is better and nobler because of her work and her message.

A health, then, to the grand old Commonwealth! God save her and bless her, and keep us true to her teaching, steadfast in her service, and constant in our love and loyalty!

SPEECH

AT THE ANNUAL DINNER OF THE HARVARD ALUMNI AT CAMBRIDGE, COMMENCEMENT DAY, JUNE 28, 1893.

WITH picturesque ceremony, and in accordance with an old and worthy custom, the University and Commonwealth meet to-day to interchange their greetings. With a deep sense of personal obligation to both, I welcome the privilege of being the messenger who brings to Alma Mater, with the love of a devoted son, the blessing of her mother State. Hand in hand, in mutual support and confidence, these twain have walked together from the early days of common poverty and suffering till the present full development of their prosperity and power.

If the growing strength of the University has made her less dependent upon the protecting arm of the Commonwealth, it has also made more clear and potent their closer union of heart and thought and action. I will not to-day weary you with the familiar story of their dependent and interwoven lives, both so full of great men and worthy deeds. But upon this last occasion when I may express to you the thought and sentiment of a great people, permit me to speak of the future rather than the past,—not of what Harvard and university education have done, but a little of their opportunity and power in our advancing civilization and prosperity.

I know it is a pleasant fancy but a common error to believe that we are always entering upon a new era of human progress and development. Like Lowell's "Spirit of the Age," our constant New Era may be but a delusion, impressing us only with its imposing capitals. Yet, in spite of this warning of authority and experience, I venture the belief that we are in the midst of great social, economic, and political movements, which will distinguish our age by their blessings, and in which education and the university are essential elements, and may be, if they will, sustaining and decisive influences.

The battle of political freedom is over; its results are substantially accomplished; its benefits are permanent. In every English-speaking nation and almost throughout the civilized world the people are recognized as the source of all political power, with a right to self-government and personal liberty. Here, at least, their power and their rights remain unquestioned. No open foe is in the field. This hall commemorates the last struggle in that great movement; and as it speaks of Harvard's fidelity and leadership, it reminds us that at every step of freedom's progress her influence has been felt in her example, her teaching, and the lives of her patriotic sons. I do not mean, however, to dwell upon the part which Harvard and her sister colleges have taken in this glorious past. I am looking forward, not backward, with the purpose to forecast, if I may, in some measure the impending struggle, and the duty and the place of higher education in it.

We have placed the people on the throne. By inherent right and universal assent, they are the sovereign power beyond all question, or the need of any further act of settlement. We gratefully recognize this truth, and rejoice in established democracy.

We know that out of its supremacy, and perhaps its struggles with the forces of selfish interests, have come social and political problems of world-wide interest.

The conflict, if such it be, is not for political freedom or religious toleration, but rather for the advancement of the people with greater equality of law; for adjustment of the laws of taxation and property, with more just and beneficent distribution; and for the uplifting of the masses, with further recognition of the rights of labor and of its share in the creation of a common prosperity. These are the pressing questions which are everywhere taking possession of the popular mind and entering our political life. They demand for their just and wise solution the light which education can throw upon them.

The past has made the people sovereign. The present must fit them to meet their great responsibilities and duties, that their reign may continue to be of law and justice, peace and progress.

Here, then, is a broad field for university work; here are its opportunity and duty. Let it not limit its influence to the seclusion of the scholar's cloister, but reach out with its uplifting power into the great world beyond our college walls. Let it not waste its energy in vain misgivings and idle complaints of popular sovereignty, or in mistaken efforts to thwart or hamper it, but, with sympathetic, grateful recognition of the just and permanent rule of the people, let education's greatest work be to qualify them to use their power with wisdom, justice, and courage.

In the opening page of his History of our University, Mr. Quincy says: "It was from the first intimately connected with political and religious opinion and events. In every period its destinies have been materially affected by the successive changes which time and intellectual advancement have produced in political relations and religious influences."

Here in her past is the key to her future, and a clear indication of the close contact with the world which our

University was meant to keep. In the problems and conflicts of to-day, as in the earlier ones for political and religious freedom, our universities and colleges have their special duties, from which they cannot escape if they would hold their position as leaders of opinion, and be true to their origin and purpose. To guide a people, their life must go out into the life of the people with the sympathy and aid which win their confidence and challenge their support.

When I hear it said, in a spirit of sneering criticism, that Harvard and the struggling, toiling masses have come together, and I know their union is to aid in the settlement of industrial, social, and political problems which need an intelligent solution, I proudly hail the sneer as proof of Harvard's devotion to her duty, and lift up my heart in gratitude to Alma Mater. Higher education is imperatively required to enter into just such alliance, and to take aggressive leadership for truth and right in the great activities around us. Ignorance can never be the founder of liberty or progress or the governing power of any civilized nation. Firmly insisting that the proper sovereign of a nation is its people, we realize that our safety and prosperity rest upon their intelligence and education. For this end has been established our cherished system of popular education, beginning with the primary public school, and culminating in the university. The need our fathers felt and met in establishing that system is vastly greater now than in their day of simple, uniform life and equality of condition. The many, varied interests of our time, the inequalities of life, the tendency to separation and conflict, the enormous increase of the power of government and of the subjects it controls, — all these place upon education a greater responsibility, and open to it a grander opportunity. If, as Lord Sherbrooke said, it was the duty of the rich "to educate their masters," with us is a like obligation; but here it rests upon the school and college, and not so much now to fix the inherent rights of American citizenship as to make American citizens fully fitted to exercise their rights and their own supreme political power.

The greater the capacity for this work, the greater the responsibility to do it. Higher education can never meet this its obligation to a people in a spirit of exclusiveness or separation from the world. The power of the university for good is not limited to its influence on the life within, but rather is measured by its contact with the world outside. As its work and life flow out into this larger life, as fearlessly yet with sympathetic touch it meets and uplifts the people, it rises to the grandeur of its opportunity, and fulfils the hopes and prayers of its pious founders.

Mr. Quincy, speaking of the early contributions to the College, in the "pathos of its poverty," says, "No rank, no order of men is unrepresented in this great crusade against ignorance and infidelity. None fails to appear at this glorious clan-gathering in favor of learning and religion." Harvard in her manly and honorable life has recognized the obligation this early and broad charity laid upon her. As "no rank and no order of men were unrepresented" in fitting her for her work, or failed to appear at her "gathering for learning and religion," so none have been excluded from her beneficence, or will ever be turned away from her abundant riches. The fiery torch her clans of all ranks and orders early lighted still blazes for truth, for Christ and the Church, and still is held aloft for the enlightenment and progress of the world.

We recognize the truth and beauty of the scholar's ideal of the place and duty of higher education.

"The most precious property of Culture," says Lowell, "and of a college as its trustee, is to maintain higher ideals of life and its purpose; to keep trimmed and burning the lamps of that pharos, built by wiser than we, which warns from the reefs and shallows of popular doctrine." Yet to hold this place, education must grasp the grander thought of the great bishop, Harvard's son, who so well exemplified her teaching. "Every life," he says, "except the greatest, lives in its element, — the partial in the universal, the temporary in the eternal. All things that really live are feeding themselves out of a great atmosphere of larger life which surrounds them, and to which they must forever keep themselves open. The part which knows itself and lives in obedience and receptivity to its great whole is strong. The part which calls itself a whole, and shuts itself up against the inflow of that universal which is 'ever green,' grows dry and barren and desolate, and dies." Then, grandly showing us how Harvard has constantly been opening her life to the great world about her, bursting in her growth all bonds and limitations, that "college thought might participate in the more universal currents which were sweeping through the world," he utters this sentiment, which should live here as long as his undying name. "Alas for the man who is not growing into broader sympathy with men the longer that he does his special work! Alas for the institution that does not feel all life clamorous and profuse about it, the longer that it goes on building its little corner or laying its bit of the foundation of the great structure!"

ADDRESS

AT HOLY CROSS COLLEGE, WORCESTER, ON COMMENCEMENT DAY, JUNE 29, 1893.

REVEREND RECTOR:

I AM deeply touched by your kind words and by the hearty welcome Holy Cross ever gives to the Governor. Coming to you somewhat wearied after a month of visits to schools and colleges, I find in this beautiful summer scene rest and peace, and in the young life around me encouragement and inspiration. I gladly bring you the congratulations of the Commonwealth that another year of prosperity and happiness has blessed this institution, fitly rounding out its half century of useful life.

It is one of the happy coincidences of the Governor's experience that at the close of the college year his final visits are to Harvard and Holy Cross, — the one specially recalling the virtues of the early life of our Commonwealth, the other the larger freedom and toleration of later days, but both essential factors in her development and prosperity. When I visit Harvard, — the broadest, greatest university in the land, as I her son believe her to be, — I reflect less upon her present power and grandeur than upon the days of her early beginning. I think of the heroic work of her Puritan founders, of their courage and character, of the largeness of their vision, of their strength of purpose, of their noble determination to make education the very groundwork of our Nation, and of the schools, the seminaries and colleges which in this spirit they founded and cherished. With respect and reverence I recall their labors, and thank God for the priceless contribution they made to our national life. Then I come to Holy Cross, founded by men of a later generation and of a different religious belief. I find here an institution which our Puritan ancestors hardly would have welcomed, — a Catholic college to which my early predecessors would have brought only with hesitation the congratulations of the Commonwealth. Yet to-day, as she extends as hearty a greeting to Holy Cross as to Harvard, one is impressed by the change which has come in her own life. We see how she has broadened out since the early days, cast aside old prejudices, and, freeing herself from narrow restrictions and limitations, become a mightier State, because tolerant in opinion, broad in thought, and just and generous in her love for all her children. As a Catholic and Irish exile [1] stands upon Plymouth Rock and praises in undying verse the sterling virtues of the Pilgrim fathers, and as many a man with their blood in his veins pays his tribute of love and respect to this Irish poet and patriot, we know that times have changed, and we rejoice that in our emancipated Commonwealth religion is not now a matter between the individual and the State, but only between him and his God. We rejoice that Massachusetts takes to her bosom all her people, without regard to race or creed, or to any accident of birth or fortune.

May I close with a word to these young men who now step forth from Alma Mater to become our fellow-students and workers in the world outside. If my words have not the weight which years and gray hair would give, they come at least from one who has not been so

[1] The reference is to John Boyle O'Reilly.

long away from college life as to have forgotten its activities and pleasures, but long enough, perhaps, to know something of the larger life into which you now enter. Carry into that life the same vigor, courage, and honorable ambition which have marked your college days, and maintain in it the same high standard of character and manliness. Remember, the advantages you have here received are held by you in trust, not to be selfishly enjoyed, but to be used to help your fellowmen, and that, as the world ever needs the light of knowledge, so does the duty rest upon the scholar freely to give what freely he has received. The work, the struggle, the victory in the contests of later life are but the repetition of experiences you have had. Bring to these contests, with your training and education, the zeal and perseverance of your college work and sports, and no man need fear failure; but remember that there is something greater than material success, that more important than making a living is the making a life. So —

> "Grandly begin; though thou hast time
> But for a line, be that sublime.
> Not failure, but low aim is crime."

The valedictory has been spoken, — Holy Cross has said farewell. As her doors close upon you, and with sadness you part from Alma Mater, I give you the salutatory of the Commonwealth, her welcome and godspeed as you take your place of usefulness and honor in her larger life.

SPEECH

AT THE ONE HUNDREDTH ANNIVERSARY OF WILLIAMS COLLEGE, OCT. 10, 1893.

AN honorable, useful life, whether of an individual or institution, is always worth commemorating, not only as our grateful remembrance of worthy things accomplished, but as a duty to make them an influence helpful to the present and the future. And when such life is part of the history of the State, interwoven with her work and fulfilling her high ideals, it is fitting that she should give it her recognition and commendation. So to-day as old Williams gathers her children hither to celebrate her anniversary and to renew their loyalty to her, the Commonwealth of Massachusetts, to us a living, loving personality, gladly comes to rejoice in her rejoicing, and to offer her greetings and congratulations.

I esteem it a privilege to be her representative to bring to you her message: yet not as her representative only have I come; but, greatly honored by this College, I am no longer a stranger within your gates, but permitted, as one of Williams's children, to kneel with you at her feet, and with gratitude and love to call her "Alma Mater." It is true, I am a recent alumnus, born perhaps, in the words of the apostle, "out of due time." It is also true, as sailors say, that I have come in by the cabin window rather than by the hard work of the forecastle and deck. If, because of this, I cannot under your adoption be received into full standing in the family circle, may I hope to be recognized at least as one of her warmest friends, glad to come whenever the children gather at the old homestead.

In this presence, and amid these scenes so full to you of cherished recollections, I hesitate to use the precious minutes in which others will tell of the work and life of this College and, recalling to you familiar faces and old days, give fresh glow to the fraternity and friendship which bind closely college men each to the other, and all to Alma Mater. And yet the presence here of the Commonwealth suggests that a word should be said of the relation of Williams to the State, and of higher education to her people.

I doubt if in all history there is an instance where the founders of a State so distinctly felt and clearly forecast the influence and necessity of the highest education for the success of their grand work as did our Puritan fathers and those who followed in their footsteps when they created and developed our State and National Governments. They seemed to comprehend the importance and result of their labor, to know that they were founding institutions for generations to come, whose happiness and welfare depended upon the fathers' wisdom and foresight. So they determined to make education through public school and college a permanent, permeating influence to strengthen character, promote good citizenship and the prosperity of the Commonwealth.

We all remember the first instance in this Commonwealth of this purpose of the founders, — in the establishment of the college at Cambridge. Out of their poverty they gave it; with struggle and sacrifice sustained it; in prayer and pious faith watched over it; and brought the full power of Church and State to guide and govern it. In the terse and simple language of its founders, in the colonial statute establishing it, in many later laws, and in our Constitution repeatedly, is found the people's recognition of the necessity and place of higher education in the body politic. As Church and State became more distinct, and the latter assumed more fully the practical work of government, she did not fail to cherish the higher institutions of learning as an integral part of our great system of popular education, upon which the security and prosperity of our free institutions must ever rest. As among the first Acts of the Colony was the founding of Harvard College, so its last legislative Act was the charter, Oct. 4, 1780, of Phillips Academy at Andover, based upon the declaration that "the education of youth has ever been considered by the wise and good as an object of the highest consequence to the safety and happiness of a people." In the same year the noble sentiment and purpose of our wise and pious ancestors were incorporated into the State Constitution in those grand provisions of its fifth chapter which have stood unchallenged for more than a century, and will stand as long as that fundamental charter of our State endures. So the wisdom of our ancestors and their devotion to education were vigorously maintained in the laws and by the acts of generations of their children.

One such act, hardly second to any in importance, to-day we celebrate. In the founding of this, the second College of the Commonwealth, in the necessity for its creation, in the generous spirit and lofty sentiment which gave it birth, in its purposes and principles, there was a striking resemblance between the older and the younger sister, between the two great institutions which planted civilization and learning each in the midst of a wilderness. The resemblance marks the continuity of Puritan influence, the development of the work of the founders of our State, and the permanence of their ideas and institutions.

Here in the depths of the primeval forest, in the days of colonial government, and in the very midst of war, a frontier colonel, with armor on, facing his country's foes and standing in the shadow of death, brave and generous, filled with practical Puritan sentiment and the loving spirit and forecast of Harvard and Shepard, anxious that others should have advantages he lacked, — here with this spirit and purpose he founded this College of the wilderness. But two conditions he imposed, — we thank him for both, — one that his infant institution should "fall within the Colony of Massachusetts," the other that it should bear his name. Its location, but not its influence or work, was to be limited to our State. Like the old "Farmers' Almanac" of Bailey Thomas, it is "calculated for the meridian of Massachusetts, but will answer for any of the adjoining States."

So came the second of our great institutions which was to promote and develop that higher element in our public education which, in accord with the dominant and universal sentiment of the people, had found recognition through all our colonial legislation, and become permanently embodied in the organic law of our State.

And now we come to celebrate its hundred years of useful life, to rejoice in its prosperity, and to note how faithfully it has carried out the purpose of its creation. Others will tell its history, of the master minds who have guided its destiny, and of the many men who have gone forth from here, carrying the teaching and influence of Williams into every walk of life. Religion and education have felt its quickening touch, literature, science, and the professions been advanced by its work, and public life in State and Nation uplifted by its high ideals. In all of this its life has gone out into the world's activities.

following the injunction of our Constitution to diffuse wisdom and knowledge generally among the body of the people, and recognizing the duty of education, not only to instruct, but to influence and lead them. Mills and his associates, planning under the historic haystack in yonder meadow to carry religion and civilization, which their missionary ancestors had brought to Plymouth Rock, back across continent and ocean to the Old World for the enlightenment of heathen peoples, rose to a true conception of the duty resting upon education if it would fulfil the purpose of the founders of our colleges and the framers of our Constitution. Many a son of Williams since, feeling the impress of Griffin or Hopkins and their learned, pious associates or successors, has gone forth into other fields of usefulness in the spirit of the divine command, "Freely ye have received, freely also give." So in the lives and work of her children this "Missionary College" has made higher education not a mere preparation for professional life, but a pioneer and leader in great movements to benefit mankind; and in the teaching and example of its authorities has ever followed the high ideals and aspirations of its famous president, who believed the truest education to be " when the spirit of literature and the spirit of science shall minister before the spirit of piety, and pour their oil into the lamp that feeds its waxing flame; when study shall be nerved to its highest efforts by Christian benevolence, and young men shall grow up at the same time into the light of science and the beauty of holiness."

SPEECH

DELIVERED AT TRENTON BATTLE MONUMENT, OCT. 19, 1893.

THE Commonwealth of Massachusetts, which gladly has contributed to this commemorative monument, comes now as gladly to join with her sister State in its dedication, and to renew the ties of friendship and union which, born of struggle and war, of a common experience and patriotism, have ever bound closely together our respective States, and made them powerful factors in creating, preserving, and developing our national Republic and the institutions of a free and prosperous people.

Most fitly and usefully we recall by this monument the heroism and patriotism of the past, and the dark days of a great struggle, when, through suffering and death, men became heroes, and, rising above little things and petty interests, attested their supreme devotion to a great cause and to the freedom and safety of the whole people.

I need not repeat the story to-day recalls,— the wintry crossing of the stormy Delaware, the midnight march, the attack, the victory, which broke away the clouds of despair, and brought to Washington and his country new hope and courage.

"At that awful moment," says one historian, "the whole future of America and of all that America signifies to the world rested upon his single Titanic will."

"Until that hour," says Bancroft, "the life of the United States flickered like a dying flame. . . . That victory turned the shadow of death into morning." Nor need I speak again the praises of brave men who ever have had their country's gratitude for their patriotic service.

Massachusetts rejoices that in those events and upon this historic battle-field she did her full duty. Yonder amid the ice and perils were Colonel John Glover and the men from Marblehead, leading the army with unflinching courage on that fateful Christmas night. Here with him stood eight regiments of Massachusetts troops as her contribution to a great and necessary victory.

Where all were true and brave soldiers, where each of the Thirteen Colonies was doing her utmost for the common weal, one hesitates to make selection or comparison. Yet, speaking for Massachusetts, I may be permitted, with pardonable pride, to quote the words of General Knox, a hero of this battle-field, in his speech to the Massachusetts Legislature. He said, —

"I wish the members of this body knew the people of Marblehead as well as I do. I could wish that they had stood on the banks of the Delaware River in 1776, in that bitter night when the commander-in-chief had drawn up his little army to cross it, and had seen the powerful current bearing onward the floating masses of ice which threatened destruction to whosoever should venture upon its bosom.

"I wish that, when this occurrence threatened to defeat the enterprise, they could have heard that distinguished warrior demand, 'Who will lead us on?' and seen the men of Marblehead, and Marblehead alone, stand forward to lead the army along the perilous path to unfading glories and honors in the achievements at Trenton. There went the fishermen of Marblehead, alike at home upon land or water, alike ardent, patriotic, and unflinching, whenever they unfurled the flag of the country."

The bronze statue of a soldier of that Marblehead regiment, the contribution of Massachusetts to this monument, commemorates their valor.

What they did, others did. All shared in the danger of the struggle and in the glory of the victory. And so we build this monument in grateful recognition of patriotic services.

Yet not for the past only do we build it, but for the present also, and the future. Gratitude it expresses, patriotism it teaches, making of the past an education to us. From these monuments we can catch an inspiration to become braver, broader, and more patriotic, and go hence consecrated to nobler, truer lives. Peace has followed revolution and war. Ah, but peace, too, has its duties, which call for courage and patriotism. Institutions for freedom and self-government have by the blood of the fathers been created, but they require sacrifices by the children, too, for their maintenance and preservation. The Union has been established, but it rests with us ever to make it stronger in the hearts and lives of all our people.

Are there not duties of to-day which can best be met in the spirit and patriotism of 1776? Do we not hear the mutterings of discontent and the strife of selfish interests? Do we not see patriotism yielding to policy, and partisanship more potent than the people's welfare? Have we not heard the right of a majority to rule — a fundamental principle of our Republic — obstructed and called in question? Have we not seen a part made greater than the whole, and the Nation's demand for necessary legislation pass unheeded in the clamor of local interests?

This is not the spirit of 1776 It was not in such conflict and selfishness that our nation had its birth, nor will it in them find safety and prosperity.

To-day we have our leader. We need the wisdom and courage which sustained Washington, the patriotism and self-sacrifice which here, on this battle-field, placed country above everything, and that larger view which, despising petty things, bound the Thirteen Colonies together, hand in hand, heart to heart, for the common welfare. Then shall we, as the fishermen of Marblehead, be "alike ardent, patriotic, and unflinching" in devotion to our country and to its brave and loyal President.

So this monument teaches us its lesson. God grant we may heed it, and meet our duty as bravely as did the fathers theirs!

SPEECHES ON MILITARY OCCASIONS.

ADDRESS

TO THE CAMBRIDGE POSTS OF THE GRAND ARMY OF THE REPUBLIC, MEMORIAL DAY, MAY 30, 1885.

I DO not think, Mr. Commander, I ought to waste the precious minutes of this hour with thoughts too crude to gently touch the sacred memories the day recalls. You will hear from lips much more eloquent than mine of the heroism and sacrifice it commemorates, and of the patriotism and duty its touching ceremonies ever teach. And yet I am glad of the privilege of saying a word in behalf of the city of Cambridge. She gladly joins her honored living to pay her tribute of respect to her honored dead. It is most fitting for her to do so. Their loss was her loss. Generously this old historic city, rich in the memory of brave deeds of brave men, gave of her strength, youth, and manhood that the Nation might live, and live, in fact, the land of freedom. No city did more; Cambridge, if true to her history, could have done no less. The Nation's life was spared, the curse of slavery was abolished; but the graves which to-day we decorate tell how great was the cost, how fearful was the sacrifice of that struggle.

And now, following a most worthy custom, we hush the hum of business, and peacefully, with love and reverence, we deck the graves, and read again the lesson they teach. It is not for me to tell, but rather to listen, to that lesson. Yet, speaking for a younger generation, whose memory hardly reaches back to those grand days when it was glorious to live, there is a word I feel that I must utter. Twenty years have stilled the bitterness of the conflict; its animosities are over. The hands of Southern soldiers have placed their garlands on the tablets yonder. The great heart of the North has gone forth with forgiveness, love, and blessing to the people whom it conquered. But the best of the war remains, — its patriotic education. It was a grand marshalling of a nation's conscience, it was a great outpouring of a nation's patriotism. In the blood that was shed we may consecrate ourselves to nobler, manlier lives. Our government, founded on universal suffrage, needs universal education. More than that, it needs the education which shall touch the hearts and mould the character of its citizens. Such education will build a bulwark for the safety of the Nation, and make the generations yet to come ready and willing, in their turn, to do the duty for which their fathers died. As we younger men look back upon the war, we bless this day, which keeps ever fresh in memory the lessons of patriotism that have outlived the sting of the conflict. Cambridge never has forgotten, and never will, Memorial Day or her veterans. Their love and devotion to her have touched a responsive chord in her heart which answers with equal love and devotion. She gladly joins with you in the celebration of the day; and as the years roll on, and your ranks become thinned, and one by one the veterans linger and fall by the wayside, she, ever young, ever strong, ever patriotic, will rejoice to take up your labor of love and remembrance; and as she scatters her garlands on the graves of her heroic dead, making of the patriotism of the past inspiration for the present, she teaches her children the best lesson that can fall from a mother's lips.

ADDRESS

AS PRESIDING OFFICER AT THE MEMORIAL SERVICE TO GENERAL GRANT IN UNION HALL, CAMBRIDGE, AUGUST 8, 1885.

TO-DAY the Nation, bending over the bier of one whom she has honored, trusted, and loved, humbly bowing to the will of God, pays her tribute of respect to him who is dead, and honor and homage to him who still lives, and ever will live, in the hearts of a grateful people.

She remembers that he was her successful general when success was needed for a Nation's life; her firm and prudent ruler when a firm but gentle hand was needed to bring back the old-time vigor to the new-born Union; and, in his dying days, while suffering bravely and patiently, he — the grim victor of a hundred battles — spoke the words of forgiveness, peace, and love that joined a new patriotism to a new vigor, and welded the States into a more perfect Union.

No wonder the *whole* Nation mourns and misses him; no wonder a Nation, saved, re-born and re-united, to-day, sadly, with tears and universal grief, feels the deep debt she owes to him.

Loyal old Cámbridge, who proudly followed him in his victories, mingles her tears with those of her sister cities. The city government has most fittingly set apart this day as a day of mourning, and has chosen familiar voices to speak her grief.

ADDRESS

AT THE TWENTY-FIFTH ANNIVERSARY OF THE DEPARTURE OF THE FIRST COMPANY OF VOLUNTEERS TO THE WAR, CAMBRIDGE, APRIL 17, 1886.

WHAT means this great outpouring of the people? Why do we hear to-day these strains of martial music in our streets, and march again under the old flag which every patriot proudly follows?

Surely the war is over; its great mission is accomplished, its last trace of bitterness has vanished under the dying benediction of the great commander. There is now "No war or battle's sound," the trumpet speaks "not to the armèd throng," but "peaceful is the night" as when "the Prince of light His reign of peace upon the earth began." There remains a country forever free and forever united as the first-fruit of the struggle and the sacrifice; with that have come contentment, happiness, and prosperity. This is the picture of to-day. How different were the days of '61! Then there was an "irrepressible conflict" that was passing from the forum of debate unsettled to the battle-field. Slavery was in our midst, and about the land rebellion boldly stalked. There came a cry of agony from a Nation in distress, a call to her sons to serve, defend, and save her. Many heard and answered it. But here in old historic Cambridge, whose earliest records attest the patriotism of the fathers for the happiness and freedom of the children, whose soil has been consecrated with blood shed at the Nation's birth, where now —

> "The tall gray shaft on Bunker Hill
> Speaks greetings to Memorial Hall," —

here, first, the citizens heard the call, and volunteered, as you, Sir, requested, "to maintain the integrity and glory of our flag and Union."[1] This is the meaning of our greeting. Cambridge to-night proudly honors her sons who added to her historic record this honorable distinction, who forgot themselves in remembrance of their country. She celebrates not the war, the struggle, nor the victory, but the patriotism, the heroism, and the sacrifice; and by this act she educates her children's children. I call it education, for I hold that there is a soul in brave deeds and patriotic services which lives and speaks to us through their memorials and celebrations, making of the past inspiration for the present. So the Old South Meeting-house spoke to the troops as they cheered her, and then marched with stouter hearts to the front. The soldiers' monument on Cambridge Common, as it will ever commemorate the dead, so will it ever uplift and educate those who remember them. Memorial Day, the saddest and most beautiful of all the year, with its touching remembrance of men who live because "they died to win a lasting name," is the ever-living spring of patriotism, where we may consecrate ourselves to deeds as worthy and to deaths as noble. All such memorials inspire patriotism, strengthen character, and make men. Men so educated are the safety of the State. Better for her protection than standing armies and compulsory service are the patriotism, the love of law and love of liberty, that come

---

[1] Captain James P. Richardson, who organized at Cambridge the first company of volunteers for the war.

from honor and reverence to those who dared much and suffered much for her sake.

> " What constitutes a state? . . .
> Men, high-minded men,
> Men who their duties know,
> But know their rights, and, knowing, dare maintain."

Captain Richardson, you, earlier than the rest, saw gathering the dark cloud of war. You felt the suffering of the Nation before the storm broke over her. You and your gallant company heard her cry almost before it was uttered. For this, to-day, we honor you. Cambridge will ever hold in loving remembrance this act of her loyal children. She bids me tender to you all, her gratitude and greeting; and every one of her sixty thousand people joins in giving you a royal welcome.

Sir, you, as a son of Cambridge, gave of your youth and strength and life to the service of our country. Now, in ripening years, you come back to gladden us with your presence. What can we wish for you as you approach the threescore years and ten? Honor? That you have, and well have earned it. Remembrance? That you shall ever have. What more or better than that Time may deal gently with you, and give you rest and peace and happiness!

SPEECH

AT THE DINNER OF THE ANCIENT AND HONORABLE
ARTILLERY COMPANY, FANEUIL HALL, JUNE 1, 1891.

IT is a pleasant and fitting custom of the Commonwealth each year to extend her greeting to this, her oldest military organization, and to congratulate it upon reaching another milestone in its long and honorable life, with its reputation, its vigor, its numbers, and even its privileges, all fully maintained. Hitherto my military duty has thrown me rather with the younger soldiers, and my active military service has been to receive their generous welcome, to lead them in marches, not against an enemy, but where the only danger seemed to be from the artillery of fair ladies' glances. To-day, with pleasure I face the brave and the venerable, the Ancient and the Honorable.

I am told that an illustrious predecessor of mine, with a taste for genealogy, declared that this company could boast not only of two hundred and fifty-three years of life, but back even to the days of Israel, and that the Prophet Isaiah had it in mind when, in foretelling condemnation on Israel, he said, "The Lord will cut off from Israel head and tail, . . . the ancient and honorable, he is the head." Much as we regret condemnation from so high an authority, we rejoice to find that its life was spared by an all-wise and overruling Providence. But even in his condemnation, the prophet complimented you, not only by placing you at the head, but by placing you far above another class, whom he thus described:

"The prophet that teacheth lies, he is the tail. For the leaders of this people cause them to err; and they that are led of them are destroyed." He evidently refers to the politicians, those reckless men who in peaceful June are alarming the people with dire prophecies of what will happen in November. The loss of the Ancient and Honorable, he says, is cutting off the head of the body politic; the loss of these others, he declares, is merely the docking of its tail.

But, speaking more seriously, the Commonwealth appreciates the value of this organization, and greets it as one of her oldest and most cherished institutions. It may be true that it is not perfect in military tactics, that it does not always set an exact, undeviating standard of military uniform; and yet in its honorable age, in its distinguished membership, in its *esprit de corps*, in its interest in public affairs, it has always rendered valuable service to the Commonwealth. These virtues I count as better than steadiness of step. They quite excuse a raiment as varied as the colors of Joseph's coat. During its life of over two hundred and fifty years it has always had upon its rolls men who have rendered public service honorable to themselves and useful to their fellow-men. Here have been mustered many men distinguished in civic life. Here have been mustered many more who have gone forth to give their blood and even their lives for the defence of their Commonwealth and their country. Through this organization, too, many have been led to take a keen interest in the militia of our State. I count this organization as one of the potent influences that have raised the militia of our Commonwealth up to its present high state of efficiency. Many other influences have had their weight. The men, ambitious, energetic, have done much for themselves; the fostering care of the Commonwealth has done much; the splendid administration of its able and permanent adjutant-general has done much. But to all these things has been added the kindly interest of the older veterans in this organization, who, with undiminished love for it, still take a keen interest in the active and younger soldiers of the State.

But, Mr. Toastmaster, you have asked me to speak for the Commonwealth. Her first word, in courtesy and in justice, is for you; her next, with pride, honorable and just, is for herself. How true is the sentiment of your toast! "Radiant she has been in the annals of war and in the arts of peace, ever at the front in every advance for human rights." I count among the arts of peace, religion, education, self-government, the church, the school-house, and the town-meeting. These, early and ever since, have been established and fostered by the people of our Commonwealth, and have placed her in the very forefront of this sisterhood of States. Our forefathers knew that the first essential for free institutions and a prosperous Commonwealth was to have an intelligent, God-fearing people. So, with great sacrifice but wonderful foresight, they planted the school-house by the church, and at the very birth of this your glorious military organization they founded the university and established our public-school system. From that day to this, generously of her wealth, freely of the best of her ability, has our old Commonwealth given to the cause of education. With like energy and generosity have the people supported religion in all of its denominations. So, too, with skill and industry have they promoted commerce, agriculture, and our manufactures; and then by individual effort and wise laws have sought to bring prosperous capital hand in hand with contented labor, that here, as in the Acadian land of which the poet sang, industry might be described as "the whirr of the wheels, and the songs of the maidens."

Radiant, too, has Massachusetts been in the annals of war, ever in the front for the rights of man. Half-way down the lifetime of your company, when the oppressive laws of the mother-country were infringing upon the rights of the people, here came the indignant protests of the town-meetings, which meant revolution and independence. And later, when there came the clash of arms, here were found the volunteers, ragged, half-armed, but for liberty and independence ready to defy the strongest power in the world. This old hall recalls their deeds as it does many a glorious agitation since, where Massachusetts has led for humanity and freedom. Why, but a few hours ago, with loving hands we were strewing our garlands on the graves of sons of Massachusetts, her patriotic dead who stood true to her when she was summoned to do her full duty to the Nation in its struggle for life and liberty. Proud of her glorious history, rejoicing in her prosperity and leadership, now let us one and all pledge to her again our love and our loyalty, and join in the prayer, "May God save the Commonwealth of Massachusetts!"

SPEECH

AT THE DINNER OF THE ANCIENT AND HONORABLE ARTILLERY COMPANY, FANEUIL HALL, JUNE 6, 1892.

I ESTEEM it one of the high privileges of my official position to meet with this old and honored military organization, and after listening to the stirring words of martial preaching, to enjoy your abundant hospitality and good fellowship, and then to exchange with you the cordial greetings which the mother State ever extends to her children, and which you, her loyal sons, give to her with your whole heart and soul.

For a second time it is my privilege to be with you, bearing to you her hearty congratulations that another year of honorable record has been added to the more than two hundred and fifty years which have distinguished your life, and have kept it, not only in its age, but in its patriotism and public spirit and in the high character and honorable service of its members in war and peace, fully in touch with the grand life of a great Commonwealth. Perhaps the fact that for a second time I address you, and now as old acquaintances and friends, has led you to be a little personal in your toast, and in it to refer to the terrible warlike powers with which the Constitution invests the Governor. I am sorry you have done this. Not that you have incorrectly quoted the Constitution. It is true he is given supreme military power, with authority " to assemble in martial array and put in warlike posture the inhabitants, and to kill, slay, and destroy all and every such person and persons as shall at any time hereafter in a hostile manner attempt or enterprise the destruction, invasion, detriment, or annoyance of this Commonwealth." But I had hoped the fact was little known, and that in these days of dramatic political events and surprises I might avail myself of the power thus given before an alarmed people had awakened to the fact of its existence. My past experience has convinced me that in the fall of the year there are certain persons, in many ways most reputable and eminent, who are accustomed to go from one end of our State to the other in a "hostile manner, invading, conquering, and annoying this Commonwealth," but especially her chief magistrate. I had quite determined that her good and his own required that this warlike power of the Constitution should be invoked, and that the governor should "assemble in martial array and put in warlike posture the inhabitants, and destroy, if necessary, and conquer by all fitting ways, enterprises, and means, whatsoever all and every such person and persons." I was planning to call out this ancient military organization, to urge it to lay aside all political differences, to permit within its ranks opinions varied and picturesque as its many-colored raiment, and, rising to the full gravity of the situation, to rally to the defence of the Commonwealth and the support of her Governor. This I found I could do, even without the advice and consent of the Executive Council. But, Sir, this publicity has defeated my plans and my hopes. Our political campaigns must be conducted in the old way, and the commander-in-chief must abandon the idea of leading the Ancient and Honorable Artillery in martial array and posture against political or other opponents.

But, speaking more seriously, I like the quaint phrases

you have cited, in which the patriot Adams in 1780 defined the power of the Governor in our now venerable Constitution. They speak with an emphasis of authority and a consciousness of freedom. They establish a stringent measure of executive responsibility, and compel in the critical time of war the chief executive of the Commonwealth to take with the high honors of his office the full burden of power and responsibility. When to those phrases there were given life and meaning by the master-mind and patriotic soul of Governor Andrew, under his leadership the whole people of a great Commonwealth were marshalled to brave deeds and glorious sacrifices, and loyally and proudly followed him as he guided, governed, and inspired them; and then in the discharge of his exacting and responsible duties gave his life for his country as truly as any soldier who ever died upon the field of battle.

Everywhere in the great work of the Revolutionary patriots who gave to us our independence and our Constitution will be found the recognition and assertion that the people are the sole, the sovereign power to which is owed allegiance, and that their executive magistrates are their servants, and should be responsible ever to them. So, drafting in the midst of war the fundamental law of the Commonwealth, they gave to their elected Governor extraordinary war power, making him constantly and frequently answerable to them for its exercise, and so retaining sovereign power in the sovereign people. Just as clearly they intended, in time of peace and in civil administration, that the people, through the Governor whom they control, should retain full control of executive power. The modern idea, which has crept in through many statutes, but not through the Constitution, of a system of executive government by commissions and officers beyond the reach of the people, and responsible to no one, is wholly foreign to the views and purposes of our founders, and is at variance with their abiding faith in the people, and in their power to govern themselves.

But, Sir, this discussion of her authority reveals the sterner side of our Commonwealth. We who represent that authority in civil or military life are apt to think only of this. But yet she has a gentler side. She is a mother State, tender and true, sympathetic and human, with a heart and a soul. See how she has planted throughout her limits in every village and community her public school, and beside it there has grown up the church, that education and religion might go hand in hand to benefit and uplift her people. With her institutions of learning are found, too, her institutions for freedom, that liberty and self-government might, with religion and education, be the corner-stones of a great and prosperous Commonwealth. See how, with the gentle hand of a loving mother, she has given to her children her hospitals and asylums and reformatories, and the great charities which bring Christ into the lives of men; how she has ever been foremost in the great agitations for freedom and human rights, and with wise and progressive laws is ever seeking to benefit the great masses of her people, to lighten the toil of labor, and to make life easier and happier. Recall her unflinching loyalty and public spirit through all the generations of her life, from the early days when here were done those brave deeds which this historic hall, Bunker Hill, and the Old South will forever commemorate. The same spirit is seen in her later life. It led forth the children's children to battle for the preservation of the institutions and the country which sturdy ancestors in prayer and faith had founded, and handed down to us as a priceless heritage. Only when we think of these things do we appreciate the true grandeur of our Commonwealth and find in her a mother State, with a heart overflowing with love to her children, and with a soul which will live forever. From her to-day I bring to you and your distinguished guests a cordial greeting.

SPEECH

AT THE ANNUAL ENCAMPMENT OF THE GRAND ARMY OF THE REPUBLIC, FANEUIL HALL, FEB. 9, 1893.

WE meet to-day in what Wordsworth calls

> "That sweet mood when pleasant thoughts
> Bring sad thoughts to the mind."

No gathering of the year is more full of patriotic sentiment touched with tender recollections than the reunion in this historic hall of the veterans who have carried into their lives its influence and its teaching, and have fought and suffered for the principles and institutions it commemorates. Never is the greeting of the Commonwealth more cordially extended than when she adds to the comrade's brotherly welcome the benediction of a grateful State. You meet in the spirit of fraternity to renew old friendships born of battle; to recall the days when together you shared the dangers and hardships of patriotic service; to note with sorrow that as the journey of life lengthens, the ranks grow thinner; then in love and charity to draw more closely each to the other, and all, united, to renew your loyalty to our Commonwealth and country. And Massachusetts, proud of her veterans, grateful for their services, in full sympathy with these their sentiments and principles, comes to rejoice in your rejoicing, and to share with you these blessed memories and patriotic purposes. To understand how closely such an occasion touches the heart of our Commonwealth, how strongly with its patriotic associations it appeals to what is best and truest and oldest in her life, one has only to run back over her history, and see how faithfully she has ever struggled for liberty, self-government, and the interests and institutions of our great Republic.

When, as the poet says,—

"God had sifted three kingdoms to find the wheat for this planting,"

the seeds he sowed here were men, independent, courageous, capable, firm in their faith, strong in their character, who understood well the truth which Webster happily expressed, that "God grants liberty only to those who love it and are always ready to guard and defend it." Out of such seed grew our State and country, with every generation of their life guided by this influence and true to this teaching. So have we advanced in strength and power and usefulness, not by complacent ease, but by struggle and strife which have wrought out our independence, and established liberty here as the hope and the beacon-light of the civilized world. Peace may be the true grandeur of nations, the ideal condition of the ideal State; but peace it must be with liberty, justice and honor established and upheld. So long as wrongs are to be righted and rights defended, so long as liberty and union must be guarded, and the honor of a nation and the supremacy of law asserted, then, not peace, but discontent, agitation and strife mark the real progress and the true prosperity of a country. "Ense petit placidam sub libertate quietam," says the motto of Massachusetts. Peace? Yes, peace, but with the sword for liberty's sake.

This is the spirit which runs through the life of our State from 1620 to 1775, and through every generation since, culminating in the great conflict which in '61 led you forth to fields of battle because conscience and patriotism summoned you to duty as they had the fathers, and bade you fight for liberty and union.

So the past lives again in the present. Patriotic services which founded and created a nation become the inspiration for the sons to defend and save it; and out of their sacrifices and sufferings come the example and the education which make the generation of to-day more fervent in its patriotism and public spirit, and stronger to meet its own duties and responsibilities. Strife and war in a great and righteous cause may lift a people out of petty things up to noble purposes and high ideals, and, purifying and unifying a nation, make it for generations to come better and greater and stronger. Not war as war, but as the mighty struggle of a whole people for the right, as their sacrifice to conscience and to duty, — herein are its glory, its education, and its inspiration. Such was our civil war. It had a righteous purpose and a glorious result. Its good is permanent. Its veterans, its memories and memorials teach now, and will the children yet unborn, the lessons of valor and patriotism which preserve a country, its honor, and its liberties. But the evil of the war is over. Its bitterness, hostility, and passion are gone. No soldier from his honored grave speaks to us of wrath or hatred, but his voice joins with the living veterans, telling of bravery and duty, and of peace, forgiveness and reunion. So let us, as will the coming generations, look back upon the terrible conflict as the sun looks down upon the troubled ocean, to draw up from it all that is pure and sweet and invigorating, while it leaves the salt and the bitter to rest forever in the silent depths. This, I believe, is the sentiment of Massachusetts. These are her words she bids me speak to you. Her gratitude goes out to her veterans. Her blessing rests upon them. May peace and prosperity lighten the weight of their advancing years as the just reward of duty well and bravely done!

STATE SPEECHES.

INAUGURAL ADDRESS

TO THE LEGISLATURE OF MASSACHUSETTS, JAN. 8, 1891.

GENTLEMEN OF THE SENATE AND HOUSE OF REPRESENTATIVES:

ENTRUSTED by the people of the Commonwealth with the management of her affairs for the current year, we meet to-day to begin this responsible and honorable duty.

A usage long established requires me at this time to submit to the two branches of the Legislature suggestions and recommendations that seem to need their consideration and action. It has been usual in such a message briefly to consider the finances of the Commonwealth, the condition of the various departments, their wishes and needs. Necessarily this information is gathered from official reports, all of which are submitted to your consideration. As I can have but little trustworthy knowledge outside of these reports, it seems to me useless and perfunctory to anticipate your careful review of them by stating briefly what they state at length, or by repeating their recommendations. Especially is this true when other matters quite as important, and much more fundamental, demand your attention. I therefore depart from this usage, with full confidence that you will give to the reports and recommendations of the departments the careful consideration to which they are entitled, as the best thought of experienced officials upon subjects with which they are familiar. As experience gives me a more full and accurate knowledge of the work and condition of the departments, I may hereafter call your attention to changes and reforms that may be advisable.

The Constitution of Massachusetts declares: "Government is instituted for the common good; for the protection, safety, prosperity, and happiness of the people, and not for the profit or private interest of any one man, family, or class of men: Therefore the people alone have an incontestable, inalienable, and indefeasible right to institute government; and to reform, alter, or totally change the same, when their protection, safety, prosperity, and happiness require it."

This declared purpose of government and power over it guaranteed to the people make it the imperative duty of their chosen representatives, as their trusted servants, to keep it ever true to their interests, to watch for the expression of their will, and when ascertained, implicitly to obey it. Rarely is such expression directly made in an election or with a partisan voice. Yet by petitions, public meetings, the public Press, and other signs, there is unerring evidence of their will as to the policy of their government. A political revolution may then give emphasis to their discontent, weight to their criticism, and be their mandate, not for partisan legislation, but for heed to their wish. Massachusetts, with her sturdy, intelligent, patriotic people, jealous of their rights and courageous in defending them, has many a time been the fruitful field of agitations meant to be the forerunner of law, and successful in their purpose. This has justly made her a leader in the sisterhood of States. Here have been great agitations for human rights, for upholding the nation in important crises, for reforms that insure purity and independence in elections, efficiency and unselfishness in administration, for retrenchment and economy in State expenditure, for wise and progressive labor legislation, and for other objects, where the voice of the people was heard as distinctly and followed as faithfully as if they had directly passed upon these questions. There was no need of a poll to know the popular will.

Judged by such signs of the people's thought and wish as have controlled in the past, I ask you to consider whether there is not within our Commonwealth and throughout the country a profound and just feeling that there is a growing tendency to divert legislation and government from their true purpose, and to surrender their control to selfish interests for selfish objects, rather than to use them "for the common good;" whether there is not also with this feeling an earnest demand for some changes and reforms, within your power to grant, which will check this tendency, and keep their government well within the control of the people, — to the end that all law may be the free and full expression of the people's will, and its administration just, pure, and honest.

With a strong conviction that such demand exists, that it is just and should be heeded, I submit to your consideration suggestions for legislation in this direction. They are based upon a firm belief that the people can safely be trusted with political power; that legislation should be for their interest, and never controlled against their interest; and that their government, as far as possible, should be made directly and immediately responsible to them. Many of these suggestions deal with matters that have been considered without partisan bias by your predecessors and by the people generally. They are submitted in no partisan spirit, and will be considered by you, I am confident, with the single purpose of faithfully serving the public interests.

THE SUFFRAGE.

As a first and fundamental change necessary to accomplish the reforms suggested, I call your attention to a restriction upon the suffrage, which is based upon a mistrust of the people, is unjust in principle, injurious and corrupting in practice, and which leaves this great primal right of freemen without proper constitutional guaranty, and subject to be controlled, obstructed, and possibly defeated, by legislative action. Massachusetts, almost alone of the States of the Union, requires the payment of a tax as a qualification for voting. Besides certain conditions as to age, sex, residence, and education, our Constitution also prescribes, to qualify a voter in any election, the payment of "any State or County tax which shall within two years next preceding such election have been asssessed upon him in any town or district in this Commonwealth." There is excepted from this provision "every citizen who shall be by law exempted from taxation." Whether or not there shall be any State or County tax, and upon what such tax shall be laid, whether upon polls or property, are matters within the control of the Legislature. When laid, the assessment of the tax upon the citizen requires the action of the local Board of Assessors. The failure of either body to act means the disfranchisement of voters. Thus the suffrage, the very foundation of republican institutions, instead of being protected by constitutional guaranty, is left to the discretion of the Legislature, and is dependent upon its annual action. There have been years in the past when no State tax was required or laid. It may be that other sources of revenue will make it unnecessary at some time in the future to lay either a State or County tax. It is possible that in such a case there would be a wholesale disfranchisement.

Judicial interpretation has declared: "It [the Constitution] confines the power, therefore, in terms to those who shall have paid some tax assessed within a short period preceding the election, and for the sake of exactness fixes that period at two years. If, therefore, the persons in question have been exempted for two entire years, either by being omitted in the assessment or by the abatement of the tax by the assessors, such persons are excluded by the plain terms and manifest intent of the Constitution." By statute law, within the power of any Legislature to change or repeal, a portion of the State and County tax is assessed upon polls; otherwise all except the owners of taxable property would be disfranchised. By statute, too, the person assessed may have the State and County tax separated from the town tax; otherwise he must pay more than the Constitution requires, or be disfranchised. By statute, too, no poll tax can be abated within the year in which it is assessed; otherwise the power to disfranchise every person who pays only a poll tax rests absolutely with a local board, and abating taxes would be a convenient way of abating voters. So it has become necessary by statutes to lay a tax, to separate the tax on polls from the tax on property, to forbid its abatement, that the sacred right of suffrage may be preserved to the freemen of Massachusetts. To repeal any of these statutes in any year puts in jeopardy this right. By a simple change in them, the Legislature may raise the most stringent and odious property qualification, and disfranchise a large majority of the voters in the State. If, for example, a statute was passed abolishing the poll tax, or exempting all polls from any State or County tax, or providing that those taxes should be laid wholly on real estate, at once by legislative act there is raised a new qualification, severe, repulsive, intolerable, and from one-half to three-quarters of the voters are disfranchised. "It is liability to taxation, not want of taxable property," as our Supreme Court has said, "which distinguishes citizens generally from citizens exempted by law from taxation. The exemption by law contemplated by the Constitution is an exemption from all taxation, without any distinction between a poll tax and any other tax. . . . So, if the Legislature were to take off the poll tax altogether, it could not be said that all persons having at any particular time no taxable property would be exempted by law from taxation; therefore to come within the other provision of the Constitution they must actually pay a tax to enable them to vote; and such in the absence of all poll taxes must be a property tax." That no Legislature probably would ever dare to exercise this power to disfranchise, is no reason for allowing the right of suffrage to remain within its control. A right so fundamental and sacred ought to be established, defined, and protected by the Constitution, and so be placed beyond the reach of legislative discretion. Opportunity for the arbitrary use of power in a political emergency, for partisan purposes, is one of the first evils against which a republican form of government should guard.

The maintenance of this qualification seems clearly in conflict with the Fourteenth Amendment of the Constitution of the United States, and renders the State liable, as provided in that amendment, to a reduction of her representation in the National House of Representatives.

There are other reasons quite as important that require the abolition of this tax qualification for voting. It is no test of a man's intelligence, capacity, or honesty, of his interest in public affairs, or even of his contribution for the support of government. Indirectly, in the cost of necessaries of life, especially in rent, does every self-supporting man pay taxes. The real taxpayer is not the one who pays the tax, but the one upon whom it finally rests. This tax deprives a man of his vote because of his poverty only. It forgets that his very poverty makes him the more dependent upon the efficient administration of laws that are wise, just, and honest, and that our democratic idea of government requires that he be given a voice in the making of these laws. In matters which concern the health, safety, education, convenience, and happiness of the community he must often look to law, while wealth can always protect itself. He is required, moreover, to perform all the duties of a citizen, and, if need be, to give himself in defence of his country, to hold his liberty and life subject to her laws, to all of which he is required to render implicit obedience. Why should he not, if of mature age and proved intelligence, have a voice in these matters, which vitally affect him? There were both truth and just sentiment in the touching appeal of Henry Wilson: "Poverty is bitter enough to be borne, without the degradation of disfranchisement. The man of toil who has reared a family, contributed hundreds of dollars by indirect taxation to support the government, who may have given perhaps his blood to the defence of the country, who has paid his tax cheerfully for years, should not, as life begins to cast its shadows over him, as his arm begins to fail, and his step to totter, be degraded because he is, in his old age, compelled to drink the bitter cup of poverty. That constitutional provision which would deny to the poor man, who could not pay his tax bill, the right to vote, should be forever blotted out of the Constitution of a Christian Commonwealth."

Is it wise to deprive men of all share in the government merely because they cannot pay a direct tax? May they not, if deprived of a proper, conservative way of giving force to their opinions or their grievances, in their discontent try other means to make their wishes known, and their power felt? This tax qualification either disfranchises many thousands of men or tends to subject their votes to the control of another's will. It leads to the debasement of our politics, to the collection and expenditure of large sums of money at elections; it tends to make wealth a necessary qualification for candidates, because poverty is a disqualification for voters. In important and exciting contests it is of no effect except to degrade the voter, to burden the candidates, and to suggest and encourage corruption.

Upon such grounds the Constitutional Convention of 1853 voted more than three to one against it. Democrats, Whigs, and the founders of the Republican party stood side by side demanding its abolition, — amongst them such distinguished jurists and statesmen as Marcus Morton, Charles Sumner, Joel Parker, Henry Wilson, Charles Allen, Francis W. Bird, Otis P. Lord, Richard H. Dana, Jr., George S. Boutwell, Amasa Walker, Anson Burlingame, Nathaniel P. Banks, Robert Rantoul, and William Schouler.

There is now the same demand, just as strong and non-partisan. Recognizing it, your predecessors of last year, by a large majority, adopted a resolution to amend the Constitution by annulling so much of it as requires the payment of a tax as a qualification for voting. This resolution now comes up for your consideration. I strongly recommend immediate and favorable action upon it, and its submission to the people, as required by the Constitution, at an early day, — to the end that the suffrage may as soon as possible be made broader, safer, and purer, by removing the injustice, danger, and evil that now surround it.

PROPERTY QUALIFICATION FOR GOVERNOR.

In this connection I submit to your consideration the question whether any useful purpose is now served by the constitutional qualification for Governor that he must "at the time of his election . . . be seised in his own right of a freehold within the Commonwealth of the value of one thousand pounds." The very terms of value point to a time and circumstances vastly different from the present. Is not this, our sole remaining property qualification, out of date?

ELECTION LAWS.

In a government really representative, which would have law the true expression of the people's will, the protection of elections from all improper influences is next in importance and order to a free and pure suffrage. This has been, and should be, peculiarly a matter of State legislation. Much has already been accomplished by the wise and successful reform embodied in our ballot law, which secures to every voter independence and secrecy, and puts upon the State a proper charge and responsibility. Legislation can still do much in the same direction. The expenses attending nominations and elections are great and growing, and are believed by many to be in part unnecessary, and in part injurious. All of them affect public interests. In my judgment, the people have a right to know the amount of such expenses, for what and to whom incurred, and to limit their amount and define their proper objects. Expenditures which cannot bear the light of day ought not to be made.

Your immediate predecessors considered this subject, and passed in one branch of the Legislature "An Act to secure the Publication of Election Expenses," as a first and proper step in this direction. I commend this matter to your favorable consideration, with the suggestion that this Act, to be effectual, must be more stringent, and that it should be followed by further legislation.

THE BALLOT LAW.

The advantages of our present ballot system are so great and universally acknowledged that it should be our aim to strengthen it by removing any just ground of criticism upon it. At present, either through misunderstanding or carelessness, the voter often fails to mark for the full number of candidates. In presidential elections the voter will be required to mark separately the names of at least fourteen electors in order to give full effect to his vote for President. It is probable that in this case the evil of partial voting will be much increased, and may lead to an unintentional division of the electoral vote of the State. I suggest that the law be so amended that a single mark may be a vote for all the electors of a party, with an opportunity for the voter to scratch any name and to insert another. It is desirable to encourage the voter to exercise his full right of franchise, and to make it easy for him to do so, by any means that will not impair the efficiency of our ballot system.

Further and more effectual notice of the names of candidates to be balloted for should be given to the voter before each election, — either by the distribution by the State of sample ballots, or in some other proper way.

I would suggest also for your consideration the expediency of establishing some uniform and accurate system of counting and canvassing the votes, in order to avoid errors now common. Such a system could make the accuracy of the first count so certain as to obviate or restrict the necessity of any recount.

PRECINCT OFFICERS.

By section 75 of chapter 423 of the Acts of 1890, provision is expressly made for the representation among election officers of the voters who do not belong to either of the two leading political parties. Subsequent clauses in the same section conflict with this provision, and defeat the evident intent of the Legislature. The matter deserves your attention and correction.

THE LOBBY.

One thing above all is necessary to make law the true expression of the people's will. Broadening and protecting the suffrage, reforming and purifying elections, will fail of this purpose, unless the law-making power is protected from insidious and corrupting influences, which tend to control legislation against the people's interest, and to impair public confidence in its impartial enactment.

There exists in this State, as in other States, an irresponsible body, known as the lobby, representing or preying upon special interests, which professes and undertakes for hire to influence or control legislation. Its work is wholly distinct and different from the advocacy of one's cause in person, or by counsel or agent, which is the constitutional right of every one. It seeks often to control nominations and elections, and to subject the individual legislator, directly or indirectly, to secret and improper influences. It throws suspicion upon the honest, and temptation in the way of the dishonest. Professing power greater than it has, it frequently extorts money as the price of its silence or unnecessary assistance. It has initiated legislation attacking the interests of its clients, in order to be hired to defend those interests. It has caused the expenditure of large sums of money to obtain or defeat legislation. It cares little for the merits of a measure, or the means employed to make it successful. In my judgment, improper measures have, by its influence, been made law against the public interest, and just measures have been defeated. These criticisms are not based upon rumor or conjecture, but upon facts reported after most thorough investigations by your predecessors, who then denounced in unsparing terms the evil, and diligently sought a remedy.

In 1887 they spoke of the methods thus employed as "a struggle for success without regard to means," causing "a growing demoralization;" and they added, "The venality and corruption which these practices encourage, tending to defeat that right and justice which the State is bound freely and without price to bestow, are a reproach to a free people." In the same year, the Governor, vetoing a measure because of the lobby influence, described the lobby as "a pernicious system," and its methods as "a monstrously bad and corrupting practice." In 1890 a committee of investigation of the House reported, "It is a fact beyond denial that a body of professional lobbyists has for years formed part of the machinery of legislation, . . . and has been growing in numbers and influence," and again they denounced its methods. The evils of the lobby have become so flagrant and disgraceful that for the purity of legislation, the protection of the Legislature, and the fair name of our Commonwealth, they demand your serious consideration, and some stringent and radical remedy. This is a matter which especially concerns the Legislature, and therefore one which the Executive approaches with some embarrassment. Yet I feel I should be derelict in my duty if I failed to do all in my power to aid you in its solution.

It is far easier to state the evil than to suggest the remedy. Clearly it is impossible and improper to prevent a constituent or any other person from having the freest access to a legislator. This constitutional right guaranteed to the people gives opportunity to the lobby to do its work. Prevention by non-intercourse is therefore impossible. Prevention by publicity is possible, and I would suggest for your consideration whether a remedy may not be found in this direction, by making it easier than it now is publicly to investigate the methods used and money spent on pending legislation; and also, by giving power to some proper officer, before a measure finally becomes law, to demand under oath a full and detailed statement as to these matters. The fear of publicity, and through it of defeat, may stop improper practices by making them worse than useless. Your immediate predecessors, with an earnest desire to cure the evil, and believing in the remedy of publicity, passed an Act requiring all counsel and agents employed by any special interest on matters pending before the Legislature to be registered, and a statement under oath of all expenses incurred to be made within thirty days after the adjournment of the Legislature. I believe that good will come from this Act, if fairly and thoroughly enforced, but that it falls short of being a sufficient remedy. It makes public the names of all persons employed, but not the acts of the lobbyist. It makes public the expenses incurred, but too late to affect the legislation for which they were incurred.

I ask you also to consider whether something cannot be done to relieve the Legislature of much work that seems to be onerous and unnecessary, to prolong its sessions, and to give life and strength to the lobby. Recent amendments to your rules have been made, I am informed, with this purpose. You may deem it wise to make further provision for an earlier introduction of business, and for its more systematic conduct. Any steps which would tend to reduce suggested legislation to a specific form, and to give the fullest possible notice to the public of the exact status of any matter pending, would, I am confident, restrict the employment of the lobby. If additional clerical or expert assistance is required for this purpose, the State can well afford to pay for it.

RELIEF FROM SPECIAL LEGISLATION.

As a further and more fundamental remedy, I submit for your consideration whether much of the special legislation which makes a large proportion of the business of every session cannot be avoided by the passage of general laws or by other means. The Constitutions of several States prohibit all special laws. In this State constant applications for charters for banks, railroads, insurance companies, and other corporations, which involved the expenditure of large sums of money and the employment of the lobby, led to the passage of general laws on these and other subjects, which left them, under proper limitations, to be settled as business questions, and at once relieved the Legislature of much disagreeable and onerous work. There seems to be a necessity for further legislation in the same direction. A general law in reference to public water supplies would prevent the frequent and necessary, but often conflicting applications on this subject to the Legislature by cities and towns, and provide for its broad and just treatment. The applications of corporations for further powers and privileges might well be covered by general laws, which, with careful restrictions protecting the rights of the public, might give to some public authority jurisdiction over such applications.

Much special legislation is enacted in behalf of cities and towns, and is made necessary by their limited powers. Twenty-three cities and forty-one towns were the subjects of special Acts at the last Legislature. In my opinion, greater powers might be given to cities and towns with safety and advantage, not only as a relief to the Legislature, but as a just and proper extension of local self-government. I therefore commend to your consideration the subject of enlarging their powers by general laws, especially in matters of taxation, franchises, municipal control of municipal work, and ownership of the instrumentalities for its performance. The exercise of such powers might well be left as a question of expediency for each community to determine for itself.

CONTROL OF MUNICIPAL FRANCHISES.

Upon what terms and conditions a city or town shall grant franchises for the use of its public highways, and what control it shall have over such franchises when granted, are questions of public importance which have been much discussed, and are worthy of your serious consideration. On the one hand, it is urged that special privileges in the public highways, distinct from their public use, ought to be paid for, either by a gross sum or a fixed rental; on the other hand, it is said that such payment, exacted from a corporation whose business is solely with the public, only adds an expense which the public finally pay, either in higher charges or poorer service. Last year an Act, compelling the sale by auction of such franchises in the future, was passed by the House. In my judgment each community is best fitted, has the right, and ought to have the power, to determine this question for itself. I therefore suggest for your consideration the expediency of giving to cities and towns, with such limitations as you deem necessary, the power of selling such franchises in the future, and of fixing the terms and conditions on which they shall be granted. In this and all matters of local administration let us guard jealously the right of local self-government, preserve it when possible, and restore it where necessary.

GENERAL MUNICIPAL LAW.

The constant demand by our cities for charter amendments, the apparent necessity for enlarging their powers, the number of towns that soon will ask for municipal charters, the wisdom of having them uniform and comprehensive, suggest the expediency of framing a general municipal law, under which future cities shall be incorporated, and which can be adopted by present cities if they see fit. Under it towns, upon having the required and ascertained qualifications, might after a proper vote at once organize a municipal government.

Where different local circumstances may require different powers or officers, discretionary power can be given by the law. If the time and research necessary for framing such a law make it impracticable for your consideration, you may deem it expedient to have the matter made the subject of a thorough and independent investigation by able and experienced men. Such an investigation might at least make valuable suggestions on the important and difficult subject of the best form of proper municipal government.

RAILROAD PASSES.

For many years, I am informed, it has been the custom for the railroad corporations of this State to tender free passes over their respective roads to members of the Legislature. Even if this is done without purpose to create an obligation, the custom is open to just criticism. Measures in which these corporations are interested are certain to come before the Legislature. Its action ought to be free, not only from any obligation, conscious or unconscious, but even from a suspicion of such obligation, that the public may have full confidence in its impartiality. The pay now allowed to a member of the Legislature for his services makes it unjust to put upon him any further expense. I believe the giving of such passes ought either to be forbidden or compelled by law, and that any expense involved should be borne by the State. This may be done by a fair and proper mileage system, which seems, however, to require an amendment to the Constitution, mileage being by it limited to "travelling to the General Assembly and returning home once in every session, and no more;" or you may deem it wise for the State to purchase and give such passes; or, if within its power, to require the railroad corporations to give them. They could hardly object to a law which should compel them to do only what they now do voluntarily.

Another custom of the same character, and open to the same criticism, I call to your attention, — the entertainment, often with profuse hospitality, of committees or of other members on behalf of some special interest having legislation pending. Expenses of this nature, properly incurred, ought, in my judgment, to be borne by the State rather than by the special interest, which may thereby gain some advantage. The only remedy seems to be an absolute prohibition of such entertainment.

ADMINISTRATIVE BOARDS AND COMMISSIONS.

The suggestions I have made in reference to the suffrage, elections, and legislation have been with a desire and hope that, if they meet your approval, they will tend to make our government more thoroughly representative, its laws a truer expression of the people's will, and its power more directly within their control. With the same purpose, I commend to your consideration its system of administrative and executive work. With much truth, Massachusetts has been described as a commission-governed State. Its great Departments of Education, Health, Charities, Prisons, Reform Schools, Almshouse and Workhouse, Agriculture, Railroads, Insurance, Fisheries, Harbors and Lands, Savings-Banks, and others, are governed by independent boards practically beyond the control of the people. Besides these there are commissions on Gas, Pharmacy, Dentistry, Civil Service, Arbitration, Cattle, Wrecks, Pilots, State Aid, and others for special and temporary purposes. Almost without exception, the members of these boards are appointed by the Governor, but only with the advice and consent of nine other men. Their tenure of office is usually for a term of several years, often without power of removal by any one, sometimes subject to removal for cause or otherwise by the Governor, with the same consent. The latter power in effect necessitates a trial upon formal charges, which seldom would be made or could be proved, except for flagrant malfeasance in office. The subordinate officials are generally appointed by the boards. These boards and their work are practically beyond the control of the people, or of any one immediately responsible to them, except in the limited power of the Governor occasionally to appoint a single member. The people of the State might have a most decided opinion about the management and work of these departments, and give emphatic expression to that opinion, and yet be unable to control their action. The system gives great power without proper responsibility, and tends to remove the people's government from the people's control. The head of the Executive Departments of the State, elected by the people and directly responsible to them, has but little power and few duties, except social and perfunctory. I make this criticism on the system with full knowledge that, as a rule, the work of these boards has been excellent, and their members have been faithful public servants. But Massachusetts may not always be so fortunate. Is it not far safer to rely upon a sound system than on the chance that a defective system may be made to work well by good officials? I submit that the first essential of sound administration is to couple power with responsibility, by making it subject to the people's control. Speaking of this necessity, one of the ablest and most experienced public officials, Mr. Seth Low, has said, "Power without responsibility is always dangerous; but power with responsibility to a constituency which can readily call it to account, is not dangerous. It is the first requisite of efficient administration."

To accomplish this, I suggest for your favorable consideration, *first*, whether boards and commissions, whose work is wholly executive, ought not to be departments of State, each with a single responsible head; *second*, whether power of removal of their members, for cause stated, ought not to be given to the Governor as the chief executive, thereby compelling him to exercise a supervision of their work, and making him, and so making them, responsible to the people for its administration. Such power has been given to the mayor of our largest city, as the best and safest system of municipal administration. Can it not be safely intrusted to the Governor of the Commonwealth? It makes any man conservative; its selfish use for patronage only is fortunately sure to be both disagreeable and destructive.

EDUCATION.

From the earliest days, Massachusetts has generously provided for the education of her children, and maintained with jealous care her public-school system. She has wisely deemed it essential to the preservation of her institutions and our liberties, and so the concern of all her citizens. It is certainly our desire, and plainly our duty, not only to uphold this system in its full vigor, but also to provide for its progressive development. Its special aim should be to furnish an education beneficial to the many, rather than exceptional privileges to the few; to equalize for all, as far as practicable, the opportunity for education, by providing ampler means in many places now poorly circumstanced, and thus placed at a great comparative disadvantage; to have its course of study practical, adapted to the condition and occupations of our people, recognizing such new methods and courses of instruction as, after thorough trial, have proved to be useful educationally, and of immediate benefit in the work of later life; and to keep its control clear of any spirit of intolerance, which cannot but weaken its influence and limit its work.

In my judgment, industrial education and manual training have been so successful where tried, and are of such practical benefit, that I recommend to your favorable consideration their adoption as part of the system of instruction in our public schools, at least in some communities. At present a large proportion of the children who enter the grammar schools leave before graduation. A still larger proportion do not enter the high school, and comparatively few graduate from it. In Boston, I am informed, only about sixteen per cent of the children who enter the grammar schools reach the high school, and only about five per cent graduate. This is due, no doubt, to the necessity of beginning early to earn a livelihood, or to get the special experience and instruction necessary for this purpose. If such instruction could be had in the public schools in connection with other studies, many children would remain longer. It might then be expedient to increase the maximum age for compulsory attendance at school, and more easy to limit still further the employment of children in manufacturing and other establishments.

There exist in this State a great difference and inequality in the character and efficiency of the public schools in different places; also in the amount spent upon them for each pupil, and in the burden of taxation for such expenditure. Almost invariably the burden is heaviest where the amount raised and spent is least, — due to the vast difference in the wealth and valuation of respective places. In 1889 the average rate of taxation throughout the State for all purposes was $14.68, and for school purposes (estimating it at 25 per cent of the total tax), $3.67 per thousand, or an amount equal to about $20 for each child between the ages of five and fifteen. Yet in different places there was an endless variety in rate, differing, for example, from 64 cents per thousand in Manchester, and $1.06 in Nahant, and $2.28 in Milton, to $7.48 in Holbrook, $8.91 in Wellfleet, and $10.42 in Palmer. Yet the amount spent for each child in the first-named places was nearly twice as much as in the last, and many times as much as in some towns. Necessarily there is a corresponding difference in their educational advantages. The result is a great inequality in the public education of children in the State, and a marked contrast in such education between the wealthy towns with few children, and the poor towns with many children.

How far this condition ought to be and can be remedied by legislation is a matter worthy of your serious consideration. The State has always recognized the education of her children as a matter of State concern. She has compelled the establishment of public schools of various grades, prescribed the courses of study, enforced the attendance of the children, exercised State supervision over the public schools, appropriated money in various ways to assist in their maintenance, and required an educational qualification for the franchise. This she has done while properly recognizing the right of each locality to control the expenditure of its school money, and the right of every parent to determine what school his children shall attend. Her interference is based upon the just assumption that every citizen is interested in the proper education of all her children, and that such education is necessary for her own safety and prosperity. I ask you to consider whether she cannot properly go further, and not only provide for the education of all, but strive for the *equal* education of all to a certain standard, and whether the richer localities ought not to contribute something for the public schools of the poorer, upon the ground that the interest of every locality in public education is not limited to the education of its own children. Such action would do much to equalize educational advantages throughout the State, generally improve the condition of the public schools, do something to correct the gross inequality in general taxation that now exists between different places, and make every taxpayer bear a fairer proportion of the cost of educating all the children in the State.

TAXATION.

The inequality of the burdens of taxation in this State has been known and felt for years, but no adequate remedy for it has yet been found and applied. A subject so complicated in its details and important in its bearings requires most thorough investigation as preliminary to legislative action. I have been unable yet to make investigation sufficiently thorough to warrant me in making suggestions for your consideration, except to commend for your favorable action the recommendation of my immediate predecessor, "of levying, as a duty or excise upon the settlement of estates, a tax upon legacies and successions," with proper exemptions and limitations.

LABOR LEGISLATION.

Though Massachusetts has led the States of the Union in this field for many years, she has not reached the limit of wise and progressive labor legislation. Her course in the past has seemed too slow and conservative to some, too radical to others, but has been approved by the great mass of her citizens, and amply justified by results. I doubt not it commends itself to your judgment, and will be continued with your approval; and that you will give to all labor legislation that discriminating attention which neither accepts everything because asked for in the name of labor, nor rejects everything because opposed in the name of capital.

I recommend to your favorable consideration the reduction of the hours of labor of women and children employed in factories and workshops. Such a law passed the last House of Representatives, and was barely defeated in the Senate. In England, where it is often claimed that the condition of the laboring classes is deplorable, the hours of such labor have long been limited by law to fifty-six a week. While with us the problem is more complicated, because each State has its own legislation, and no uniform statutory regulation of hours for the whole nation is possible under the Constitution, yet it is not desirable to stand still because there are obstacles in the way of progress. Our very dependence upon manufactures requiring skilled labor should lead us to adopt a liberal policy in respect to the hours and conditions of toil, — one which will promote the welfare and increase the utility of our working population.

While a general reduction in the hours of labor must be brought about mainly by the organized action of employees, it is urged, and I believe with justice, that the State should lend its co-operation and the weight of its example in this direction. I therefore commend to your careful consideration the question whether the time has come to reduce still further the hours of labor of public employees engaged in manual work.

A bill to prohibit the imposition of fines or deductions of wages upon factory operatives employed at weaving has been considered by the Legislature for a number of years, and failed to pass last year by a single vote in the Senate. While legislation on this subject is not free from difficulties, it is desirable that the constant friction which this practice causes should be removed by any practicable means. In many factories this practice does not exist, so it cannot be an absolute necessity. I trust that you may find some satisfactory solution of the question.

Three years ago the Employers' Liability Act was passed. It has, I believe, been just to the employers, while it has provided relief for the families of many workmen injured or killed in the performance of their duty. By a recent decision of the Supreme Judicial Court, the operation of this Act, if death ensues, has been limited to cases where death was instantaneous or without conscious suffering. The wording of this Act no doubt fails to express the real purpose of the Legislature. It is manifestly unjust that widows and orphans, otherwise entitled to relief under this Act, should be deprived of it merely because there was an interval of conscious life after the fatal injury was received. I recommend that the Act be restored to its full beneficent purpose by a suitable amendment. Even when so amended it is not so broad in its scope as the law which has long been in force in England.

The railroad employees in this State feel a just grievance that the law passed in 1884, which requires that freight-cars be provided with automatic couplers, and which was intended to give such employees a long-needed protection, has failed of its purpose. The difficulty seems to be in the fact that a large proportion of freight-cars used here come from other States, and National legislation is therefore necessary. I strongly recommend that you petition Congress to take action, and consider whether any further steps can be taken by you for the proper protection of railroad employees against the dangers to which they are exposed.

LIQUOR LEGISLATION.

I call to your attention the well-known variety of opinion as to the meaning of the statute provision which forbids the keeping of a public bar, and the utter lack of agreement in its construction and enforcement. It is inconsistent with sound public policy that a provision of law which is the same for the whole Commonwealth should be open to these objections. In my judgment, this provision, as construed and enforced in the city of Boston, does not tend to promote temperance, is not sustained by public opinion, and ought to be corrected.

RE-APPORTIONMENT OF THE CONGRESSIONAL DISTRICTS.

The passage by Congress of a bill re-apportioning representatives in the House of Representatives, upon the basis of the Census of 1890, which now seems probable, will make it your duty to divide the Commonwealth into new Congressional Districts.

The present political situation and division of political power in this State make this year peculiarly favorable for a fair and honest treatment of this question.

I strongly recommend the passage at the present session of such a re-districting bill, establishing districts of proper geographical shape and contiguous territory, and of such political complexion as to give to each political party, as nearly as possible, the representation to which its numbers entitle it.

OTHER RECOMMENDATIONS.

Greater uniformity in the legislation of the several States upon many subjects, especially upon marriage and divorce, is very desirable, and this requires concert of action between the States. To this end New York has appointed a commission, serving without compensation, and, through this commission, requests like action by this State, which request I commend to your favorable consideration.

A thorough reform in our system of land transfer and registration, upon the lines of legislation which has long been successful in other countries, and intended to make it safer, cheaper, and easier, will, I am informed, be called to your attention. It deserves your serious consideration.

At an early day I shall submit for your consideration such recommendations and suggestions of the departments as seem to be of sufficient importance to be called specially to your attention.

Senators and Representatives,— There is an opportunity for us, by wise and progressive legislation, to meet the just demands of the people and merit their confidence, to strengthen the institutions of our beloved Commonwealth, and to add something to her glory and prosperity. Such inspiring work should lift us above party strife, encourage mutual respect and confidence, and insure cordial co-operation in the fearless and unselfish discharge of our respective duties. Then may the law be the free and true expression of the people's will, and only for their interest.

INAUGURAL ADDRESS

TO THE LEGISLATURE, JAN. 7, 1892.

Gentlemen of the Senate and House of Representatives:

PROFOUNDLY grateful to the people of the Commonwealth for the renewed confidence which has again entrusted me with important public duties, I enter upon their discharge by submitting to you such suggestions and recommendations as seem to merit your consideration and action.

This privilege of addressing the Legislature, accorded the Governor by long-established custom, is not, in my judgment, best used in a perfunctory statement of the recommendations of the various departments of the Commonwealth, all of which are set forth fully in their reports to you. I believe it better to make this the occasion for a broader treatment of public questions, for giving expression to the people's wishes and wants, and for suggestion to the Legislature, and through it to the public, of any policy or reform which seems to the Governor wise and necessary, and for which he is ready to assume responsibility. Department recommendations can be called to your attention in a later message, if necessary, with such indorsement or criticism as they suggest. This course separates more clearly the views of the Executive and of the departments, and gives to both greater emphasis and responsibility. It requires the chosen representative of the people, as his first duty, to submit to you their opinion, indicated by their votes, upon such public matters within your jurisdiction as demand your attention. So will elections mean a choice between principles and measures, rather than between men.

The close dependence of the people upon their State government, the great and immediate control it exercises over them and their liberty, property, and welfare, make the duty imperative of keeping that government efficient and responsible in its work, and of adopting any changes or reforms necessary to this end. With the tendency each year to increase its duties and to multiply its subjects, and thus to enlarge its power over public and individual interests, the greater is the necessity that this power should be restrained by such official responsibility as will keep it well within the control of the people, and make every administrative officer answerable to them. "The first requisite of efficient administration," says an experienced writer, "is power, with responsibility to a constituency which can readily call it to account." Machinery of government which worked easily and well when its duties were comparatively few and simple, may be too cumbersome to meet its many and complicated duties of later days, and entirely inadequate to bring the government, now more and more felt by the people, within their control. Faithful and efficient service may make a bad system work well, or mitigate its lack of responsibility; but sound administration cannot permanently be had under such conditions, nor until the system itself is changed and corrected.

In my judgment, the time has come when the attention of the Legislature ought to be directed to the executive branch of our government, to the great increase of its duties, the lack of uniformity or system in the organization created for their discharge, and its entire absence of responsibility, except in the high character and conscientious service of officials in its various departments. My criticism is not of officials, but of a system; and the test of that system is not the faithful work which they have done, but the unfaithful work others might do without adequate responsibility to call them to account. If danger lurks in the system, if it can permit arbitrary acts without control, misconduct without correction, or official administration without responsibility, it is wrong.

A year ago in my inaugural address I briefly considered this subject. The experience of the year has strengthened my convictions upon the views and recommendations then expressed. As the subject has been constantly before the people in the mean time by executive action, debate in the Legislature, and discussion through the Press and in the last political campaign, and the people may fairly be considered to have formed and expressed their opinion upon it, I deem it my first duty to urge upon you a thorough examination of our methods of executive and administrative work, and the adoption of such changes as will bring into it complete responsibility to the people, and will simplify machinery at present complex, without system or uniformity.

A brief examination of the gradual but large growth of executive work and executive offices in the more than one hundred years of our constitutional government, is necessary for an intelligent consideration of this matter. For some years after the adoption of our constitution, in 1780, there were few administrative officers to be appointed or supervised by the Governor. While the Constitution definitely fixed the appointment and tenure of judicial and military officers, it left to the Legislature the power "to provide by fixed laws for the naming and settling all civil officers within the Commonwealth, the election and constitution of whom are not in this form of government otherwise provided for, and to set forth the several duties, powers, and limits of the several civil and military officers of the Commonwealth." It was not then foreseen, nor has it been at any time since, how great would be the growth of executive work, and how varied and intricate the subjects of public and private interest with which it would deal. Consequently, neither by the Constitution nor by any legislative Act has there been established any uniform system, but as the exigency of the moment demanded, an office has been created, apparently without much thought of its relation to the executive machinery already or thereafter to be established. As in the multiplicity of laws it becomes imperative at last to codify and systematize them, so in the multiplicity of offices the same necessity may exist.

The growth of the Commonwealth, the creation and increase of her penal, reformatory, and charitable institutions, and of new subjects of public supervision or control, have compelled the Legislature, under the authority conferred upon it, to establish numerous offices and departments as the necessary machinery for the administration of this work. Most of these are of comparatively recent date, created with little regard to uniformity of government or direct responsibility. There are to-day in the executive department of the Commonwealth over three hundred officers, commissioners, and trustees, not including clerks and other subordinate officers, participating by statute authority in the administration of our government. There are over twenty-five State commissions (some, however, not purely executive), and more than one hundred trustees of public institutions. Whether this number can be reduced by abolition or consolidation of offices has been considered by a special committee of the last Legislature, who will submit to you the result of its investigation.

In my judgment that question is rather one of detail than of principle, and by no means as important as the question of uniformity and responsibility in the administration of these public trusts. At present there is neither. The tenure of some commissioners and trustees is three years; of others, five; of others, seven; and of one board, eight. This tenure is fixed by law, and gives the occupant a right to hold the office for its full term, in the absence of express statute provision for removal. In many of the statutes there is no such provision, and where it exists there is no uniformity. Members of four commissions and the Medical Examiners can be removed for sufficient cause by the Governor with the consent of the Council; members of eleven commissions can be removed with or without cause by the Governor, but only with the same consent. Only eight officers, outside of the District Police, can be removed by the Governor alone, upon his own responsibility. That is the extent of his effective and responsible executive control. Five boards of trustees are removable "for sufficient cause," but without any provision as to who shall exercise this power. Of the remaining administrative boards and officers appointed for a fixed term, including the Boards of Lunacy and Charity, of Health, of Education, of Prisons, the State members of the Board of Agriculture, and other officers holding important public trusts, there is no power of removal in any body, except by the cumbrous machinery of impeachment. More than one hundred and twenty important executive officers are thus, during a tenure of office varying from three to eight years, beyond the reach and control of any executive power. All of these officers perform public duties, expend public money, and administer public trusts. In some way they should be made responsible to the people; otherwise there is danger of friction and conflict. Arbitrary acts cannot be controlled, misconduct cannot be punished, nor can any one be held directly and properly responsible for official action.

As an illustration of our irresponsible system, I again call the attention of the Legislature to our method of prison management. At present the warden in charge of the prison has no power over his principal subordinates, either in their appointment or removal, except with the concurrence of the Prison Commissioners, with an appeal to the Governor and Council in case of conflict; the commissioners in charge of the institution have no power over the appointment or removal of the warden; and neither the Governor nor any one else has any power over the commissioners. In case of mismanagement, inefficiency, or trouble and insubordination within the prison, such as have occurred in times past, where lies the responsibility or the remedy? In my judgment, the warden should be given power over his subordinate officials, the Prison Commissioners power over him, and the Governor power over them; and for its exercise he should answer to the people. A bill to this effect was reported to the last Legislature by one of its committees. In the House it was amended by a provision that the power of the Governor should be exercised only with the consent of the Council, thus destroying the most important link in the chain of responsibility, and the one which brought this executive power within the control of the people, and its exercise under responsibility to them. The bill as amended was properly defeated in the Senate.

Suppose that some administrative board, within its limited authority in part to administer the people's government, should knowingly adopt a policy against the wish of the people, or against their will as deliberately expressed through their Legislature, — are the people to have no control over such board or its action? Is their government to this extent to be beyond their reach?

All must agree that the safe and democratic form of government is to make these administrative officers in some way responsible to the people. This is in accord with the constitutional intent, as expressed in the Declaration of Rights, that, "All power residing originally in the people, and being derived from them, the several magistrates and officers of government, vested with authority, whether legislative, executive, or judicial, are their substitutes and agents, and are at all times accountable to them." Again it says: "In order to prevent those who are vested with authority from becoming oppressors, the people have a right, at such periods and in such manner as they shall establish by their frame of government, to cause their public officers to return to private life, and to fill up vacant places by certain and regular elections and appointments." In giving to the Legislature authority to create administrative offices, and to fix their tenure, duties, and powers, the Constitution contemplated that such authority would be exercised with due observance of its injunctions to make such officers accountable to the people, and to preserve to the people their power over them.

How can this best be done? It is not practicable to elect them. They must be appointed; and, to be responsible to the people, they should be under the control of the elected servants of the people. They cannot be made responsible directly to the Legislature, for this is expressly forbidden by the Constitution. The Legislature which created the office can abolish it; but responsibility dependent upon such remedy involves destruction of the administrative machinery whenever a particular administrator is inefficient or unfaithful. There remains only its power of impeachment, restricted to cases of "misconduct and maladministration in office." This involves trial and conviction upon formal charges, and requires so much time and effort that it cannot be an effective and constant means of making administrators responsible to the people.

The power of removal, as a necessity for responsible control, must then be vested in the executive department; and I submit that it can best be vested in the head of that department. Our Constitution, in creating his office, declared that he "shall be a supreme executive magistrate;" and, further, "that he should in all cases act with freedom for the benefit of the public." It nowhere limits his executive supervision of executive work, nor suggests that his direct and immediate responsibility to the people should be lessened by statutory creation of departments, boards, and offices beyond his control. If they are not within his control, they are beyond that of the people.

Provisions much like ours in the Constitution of Pennsylvania have been construed by her Supreme Court as vesting in the Governor the absolute power of removal. In its decision the court says: "The powers of the Governor are never suspended. He is at all times authorized to exercise ' the supreme executive power.' The fact that an officer may be removed by the dilatory process of impeachment creates no argument against the summary power of removal by the

Governor. Crime, imbecility, or gross neglect of duty may demand that an officer shall be removed at once. The power to protect the people of the Commonwealth by prompt action is wisely given to the Governor. In giving construction to the Constitution, we cannot assume that he will abuse that high trust."[1]

Our Constitution, framed and adopted in the midst of war, when military powers were uppermost in the minds of the people, and remaining unchanged in this respect through wars and rebellions within and without the Commonwealth, gives to the Governor at such times power almost autocratic. The exercise of this power by a Governor accountable to the people has been ever — but especially during the Civil War, by the great Andrew — efficient, responsible, and to their entire satisfaction. It is hardly conceivable that the Constitution intended that the Governor, thus trusted with great responsibility and power in time of danger, should in civil administration have but little power, and be in name only the "supreme executive magistrate." I think the framers of the Constitution meant that the Governor should be in fact the chief magistrate, and as such should have authority commensurate with his responsibility; and this not for the purpose of giving him power, but of imposing upon him responsibility, and so retaining power in the people. To them he is directly responsible for the exercise of his power, and he hardly begins his duties before he is called upon to account to them. If he cannot justify his acts, he deserves and receives their condemnation.

The Council has its function in the executive government. The Constitution created it "for advising the Governor," not for tying his hands, not for dictating his appointments, nor for exercising co-ordinate and

---

[1] Lane v. Commonwealth, 103 Pa. St. 481.

equal power with him. It creates, not ten, but one "supreme executive magistrate." The jurisdiction of the Council was fully and ably discussed in the Constitutional Convention of 1853. No one in that elaborate debate claimed as part of its power the right to advise in cases of removals from office. Its only powers, as there stated and claimed, were to advise and consent to appointments, to advise in cases of pardon, to audit accounts, and to act as the supreme returning board in the election of State officers. These powers a majority of the Convention deemed of sufficient importance to justify the continued existence of the Council.

In appointments to office there may well be a confirming power. It is approved by an experience of more than a century in National and State government; it affords an opportunity to correct mistakes, and to defeat any improper or personal influences governing an appointment; but it still leaves to the Executive a field for selection practically unlimited. If not abused and made a power to dictate, it does not infringe upon executive responsibility. Whether this power can better be exercised by the Senate, as in the National government and in many States, or by the Council, does not seem to me of the greatest importance; nor does the question whether the Council itself shall remain or be abolished, although in but three of our forty-four States is there an elected executive Council. But whether power to remove shall be shared by the Council is of great importance, and vitally affects executive responsibility. This power is necessary for proper executive control. If not intrusted to one alone, either its efficiency is lost, or greatly impaired by divided responsibility. Such divided responsibility, or no responsibility, is the system of executive management established in this Commonwealth wholly by statute law, mostly of recent enactment. Experience has shown as practical results of such a system —

First. That neither the Governor nor the people through him have any adequate power over the executive departments, of which he is the head, but his power is practically limited to suggestions, advice, and appointments to fill vacancies.

Second. That over many of the departments and executive offices there is no power of control in any one.

Third. That the power of removal, and so of control, usually requires for its exercise a formal trial upon specific charges, and proof of absolute malfeasance in office.

Fourth. That an officer of an important public department, accused of official misconduct which, in the opinion of the Governor, requires his removal, may remain in office without the confidence and against the will of his executive chief.

Fifth. That a member of an important commission may hold his office indefinitely after his term has expired, without appointment and without the approval of the Governor.

Sixth. That nominees of the Governor, beyond criticism and objection, may be refused confirmation for the sole and declared purpose of holding in office men whose term of office has expired.

Seventh. That with the present limitations upon the power of removal, the power to confirm can always be used for this purpose, and successfully in every case of an expired term.

I state these results of our present system, not to discuss here executive action in any particular case, but because I believe all can agree, whatever their opinion in such case, that a system which can produce these results is without proper responsibility, and ought to be so changed as to give to the Chief Executive power that shall fix upon him full executive responsibility.

I am confirmed in this opinion by the established and nearly unbroken practice in the National Government for more than a century, by the full recognition of this principle in modern municipal government, by its adoption in the executive system of other States, and by its indorsement alike by the student of government and by those who have had practical experience in its administration. The Constitution of the United States, vesting in the President the executive power, gives to him the power of appointment "by and with the advice and consent" of the Senate, and is silent as to the power of removal. The same phrase and the same silence are found in the Constitution of our Commonwealth. The first Congress, in establishing executive departments, expressly conferred the power of removal upon the President. In the debate upon that question, Madison, one of the framers and expounders of the National Constitution, declared its purpose as follows: "It is evidently the intention of the Constitution that the first magistrate should be responsible for the executive department. So far, therefore, as we do not make the officers who are to aid him in the duties of that department responsible to him, he is not responsible to his country." The Act conferring this power was carried in the Senate by the casting vote of Vice-President Adams, who gave at length his reasons for his vote. Speaking of these, his grandson, Charles Francis Adams, writes: "These reasons were not committed to paper, and can, therefore, never be known; but in their soundness it is certain that he never had the shadow of a doubt. His decision settled the question of the constitutional power in favor of the President, and consequently established the practice for the country which has continued down to this day." He adds: "All have agreed that no single act of the first Congress has been attended with more important effects upon the working of every part of the government."

The policy thus established remained unchanged down to 1867, and gave to the President unlimited power, directly or indirectly, to remove all subordinate officers, now numbering more than one hundred and twenty thousand. In that year, owing to a conflict between the President and Congress, an attempt was made to restrict his power by the passage of an Act of doubtful constitutionality, requiring the consent of the Senate to removals from office. That Act was greatly modified during the next Administration, and was finally repealed in 1887, after it had long ceased to have any active operation. I do not believe that the people would now permit the hands of their President to be tied, and executive responsibility to be divided and lost between him and the Senate.

The same principle has been successfully applied to municipal government, and is strongly indorsed by municipal administrators. I have already quoted the well-known views of ex-Mayor Low, of Brooklyn, to this effect. Equally emphatic is the opinion of ex-Mayor Hart, of Boston, who says, in a recent publication: "It is not certain that the mayor should have absolute power of appointing his subordinates or any other public officers. The power of removal should be vested in the mayor." An able commission, appointed in Pennsylvania in 1878 to devise a plan for city government, reporting in favor of this principle, said: "It is self-evident that the affairs of government cannot be well conducted unless there is an executive head upon whom responsibility therefor is imposed. It is equally clear that such responsibility cannot be exacted without the grant of corresponding power. . . . It may be said that it is dangerous to clothe him with so much authority. The answer is that such power must be lodged somewhere, if good government is to be attained, and wherever placed, it is essentially executive in its nature. The mayor is the chief executive of the city, and therefore he is the proper officer to exercise it. Without it there can be no efficiency in the performance of his duties."

In the great cities of the country this principle has been fully established as essential for a responsible and efficient system of government. Its soundness has been repeatedly recognized by the Legislature in this Commonwealth in its later treatment of municipal charters, notably in the case of the city of Boston. The principle thus accepted as proper in the executive government of Nation and city prevails in the executive departments of many of our sister States, which vest the removing power in the Governor alone. If undivided responsibility is essential for proper government in Nation, city, and other States, why is it not wise to place such responsibility also upon the Governor of our Commonwealth? If the principle is sound, it obviously applies to all executive power. I believe that it has been thoroughly tested, that it has proved to be sound, and that it best secures what Webster felicitously called, "The people's government, made for the people, made by the people, and answerable to the people." Three hundred or more subordinate public officers, now under divided control or none, would thus be made directly responsible to the Chief Executive, and he by the Constitution is directly and immediately responsible to the sovereign people. These administrative officers, with few exceptions, exercise their jurisdiction over the whole Commonwealth. They should be responsible to a representative of the whole Commonwealth, and not to a body, each of whose members represents and is responsible to only a local constituency. I therefore earnestly commend to your favorable consideration such legislation as will give to the Governor the power to remove all these administrative officers for cause stated, leaving to the Council the power of confirmation of his appointments.

In making this recommendation, my criticism is of a system, and not of officials. I recognize the ability and fidelity which our public servants, with few exceptions, have given to their Commonwealth. Especially do I appreciate the unselfish, patriotic labor freely given her by noble men and women in her great work of education, charity, and reform, and for the health, safety, and prosperity of her people. This recommendation is without personal or selfish motive, and simply in the interest of efficient and responsible government. The record of my administration is proof of this fact. Of the few executive officers wholly under the control of the Governor, not one has been removed during my year of service except the Gypsy Moth Commissioners, and they for admitted cause. Of the many others whose terms have expired, a very large majority, though not of my political faith, have been reappointed. It is far easier and more agreeable for a public officer to have less rather than greater responsibility; and the exercise of power over offices is the most irksome part of executive duty. Such power, I repeat, "makes any man conservative; its selfish use for patronage only is fortunately sure to be both disagreeable and destructive." I am confident that you will receive this recommendation in the spirit in which it is offered, and, seeking only the public good, will give to it your careful consideration.

EXECUTIVE BOARDS AND OFFICES.

Again I call the attention of the Legislature to the subject of executive boards and offices, in the firm belief that some steps can be taken tending to simplify and systematize executive work. In its consideration you will have before you the report of the special committee of the last Legislature, which has made an investigation of the matter during the recess. Apparently in the past some boards and offices have been created to meet an exigency of the moment, without due thought of their proper relation to existing administrative machinery, or to the question whether or not it could do the new work; and there never has been, I believe, a comprehensive consideration of this machinery as a whole, with a view to reduce it to a system, with proper dependence, responsibility, and harmony between its separate parts. I do not believe that the mere consolidation of boards and offices, having distinct fields of work without necessary dependence on each other, is any gain. This was tried without success with the Boards of Health, and of Lunacy and Charity. But greater efficiency and economy can be had by the abolition of some unnecessary offices, where the transfer of their duties can be made to some other authority as well or better fitted to do the work. Without attempting to cover the field or to outline an administrative system, I call to your attention some instances where such changes, in my judgment, can properly be made.

Board of Agriculture. — The State Board of Agriculture is one of the oldest of our boards, and represents an industry most important to our people and our Commonwealth. Its membership consists almost wholly of practical men, thoroughly conversant and in touch with that great industry. With their knowledge, experience, and personal interest in agriculture, they are especially well fitted to deal with all matters and laws relating to it, and to act for the Commonwealth where she touches agricultural interests. Yet from time to time there have been created for such work separate and distinct administrative commissions and boards, such as the Cattle Commission, the Gypsy Moth Commission, and the Board of Control of the Agricultural Experiment Station. Last year your predecessors abolished the Gypsy Moth Commission, and transferred its powers, duties, and appropriation to the Board of Agriculture, — to the great gain of agriculture and of the Commonwealth. They also created out of the Board a Dairy Bureau for the enforcement of the law to protect dairy products, instead of making a distinct commission. Both of those steps were in the right direction, and tended to concentrate executive work in the proper and most competent hands, instead of dividing it among independent, unnecessary, and expensive commissions. I believe, as further steps, that the duties of the Cattle Commission should be transferred to the Board of Agriculture, and the commission abolished; and that the board should also have charge of the Agricultural Experiment Station. With these enlarged executive duties given to it, there should be added to the board necessary specialists for its various departments, and the board itself should be organized into properly paid bureaus for executive work. Among its departments there might well be included one on roads, bridges, and drainage, having attached to it a competent engineer. These subjects are of great importance, and affect seriously the health, comfort, and convenience of all our people. The travel upon our highways, especially for long distances between centres of population, has much increased. The need of improving these highways, and of more uniform and systematic methods in their construction and maintenance, is apparent. Without infringing on any local right or power, such a department could gather and distribute valuable information on this subject, and give experienced advisory assistance on road construction and maintenance. I believe that this would lead to a more comprehensive and scientific treatment of all our highways, and to greater economy and improvement, than by unaided local effort. This subject has been called to the attention of the Legislature by several of my predecessors. I commend it to your careful consideration.

I urge this transfer and grant of executive duties to the Board of Agriculture for the purpose of placing in one responsible and thoroughly representative board all the executive work of the Commonwealth relating to agriculture, and of giving to the farmers themselves the enforcement of all laws in which agriculture is especially interested. The board will then be, as it ought to be, one of the strongest and most important in the Commonwealth.

State Board of Police for Boston. — This board was created in 1885, against strenuous opposition, for the purpose of taking from the city of Boston the control of her police force, and of vesting it in a State board, which was also given the licensing power. Since then the people of Boston have had no power whatever over their police, or over the enforcement within her limits of the laws of the State, or of the municipal ordinances enacted for their safety and benefit. If in their opinion constant and repeated violations of law are permitted, to their injury; if municipal ordinances are not enforced, resulting in detriment to the public health or to the public convenience; if notorious and illegal resorts are allowed to exist, to the scandal and disgrace of the city; or if the control of the police and of the saloons is abused for political purposes,— the citizens of Boston have no power to correct these evils, but must patiently submit to them, while they are taxed for the whole expense of such enforcement of law. Boston is the only community within the Commonwealth which has thus been deprived of the right to govern herself. The declared reason for such legislation was mistrust of her citizens. I do not share that sentiment. On the contrary, I have not only a firm belief in their right to govern themselves, but full confidence in their capacity and ability to do so. The jurisdiction of this State board over both licenses and police is a union of two distinct powers, which, in my judgment, it is not for the public interest to have united in any one board. The power of granting or revoking licenses is judicial in its character; the other is purely executive. The first should be vested in a board of such appointment and tenure as to be judicial in its action; the other in a board responsible to the community over which it exercises executive control. I earnestly recommend a separation of these powers; that the control of her police be restored to the city of Boston; and that you then consider whether the control of licenses should be left in the present board, or placed in another board of such character, appointment, and tenure that it shall be above all political, personal, or selfish influences, and shall command the confidence of the people.

Superintendent of Prisons. — This office, created in 1887, and involving an expense of sixty-five hundred dollars a year, has few and very limited duties, all of which can be and should be performed by the various boards in charge of our penal institutions, or by the heads of such institutions under the direction of such boards. It is independent of the Board of Prison Commissioners and its work, and seems to be out of gear with any existing administrative machinery. Unless you are prepared to follow the plan adopted in New York, which gives to a superintendent of prisons, in place of other boards, practically full charge of the whole prison system, and makes him, and so the administration of the system, responsible to the Governor, I believe the office is not necessary or useful. For these and other reasons, more fully stated in a special message to the Legislature, March 23, 1891, I recommend that it be abolished.

Topographical Survey Commission. — This commission reports that it is now engaged in surveying and delineating the town boundaries of the Commonwealth, and that it will require at least ten years more for the work, of which about one-third is completed. In its opinion this work can best be done under the management of the Board of Harbor and Land Commissioners. It recommends such transfer, which recommendation I submit for your favorable action.

Board of Supervisors of Statistics. — This board, consisting of State officials, was created, in 1877, to have general supervision and control of all matters relating to statistics. It is required to "meet regularly at the State House at least once in each month." I am informed that it has met but once since its creation, and has done nothing. It is responsible to no one. It seems to be useful only as a good illustration of the continued existence of unnecessary boards, and of the need of a thorough overhauling of our administrative machinery.

Building Commissions. — The custom has prevailed in the past, when any important State building was to be erected, of creating a salaried commission, usually of three members, to have charge of the work. These commissions have then employed architects, engineers, superintendents, clerks, or such other assistants as seemed necessary. While this work has been done in some instances with unquestioned fidelity and success, in others there have been delay, unnecessary expense, and great criticism, and in one instance the commission itself was finally legislated out of office. I do not believe this method of construction is the most economical or expeditious, or that the creation of these commissions, with rare exceptions, is necessary. If a building is to be erected for an institution already existing, I believe that the board in control of that institution should have general supervision of the work, having under it a proper person to superintend the construction. If the building is for a new institution, the board which is to manage it should be created at once, and should be given charge of the work. The advantage of this would be greater expedition, less expense, more care, and better results in building, and a better institution when in operation, because of the experience and knowledge acquired by the board in its erection. This was the plan adopted in building the hospital provided for in chapter 412 of the Acts of 1889, — a precedent which I recommend be followed in the future. If the building is not or is not to be in charge of any board, then its erection might be under the direction of the Governor and Council, or other proper officials having under them some one to superintend the work. If this plan, suggested for future building, meets with your approval, it may be wise and necessary to create a State officer to superintend the details of the construction of State buildings, under the control of the respective boards in charge of the work.

The entire absence of responsibility or system in our executive work; the instances suggested of needed change or abolition of offices, and others which may occur to you; the advantage of grouping under proper departments our executive boards and commissions; the expediency of devising some better way of bringing the needs and the information of the executive departments to the attention of the Legislature; and the necessity of reducing to a proper system and control our present cumbersome executive machinery, — all these reasons will, I trust, lead you to make a comprehensive and thorough examination of this branch of our government.

Two other matters connected with executive work deserve your attention.

CLERICAL ASSISTANCE.

Over one hundred thousand dollars are spent each year by executive departments for clerical assistance, under appropriations which give to the head of the department a gross sum to be divided and distributed for this purpose as he deems necessary. For one department sixteen thousand dollars are so appropriated. The head of that department can hire sixteen clerks for one thousand dollars apiece, or one clerk for sixteen thousand dollars, if he wishes. The Civil Service Commissioners have earnestly requested a change in this system, in which request I concur. In my judgment, the clerical force of the departments should be established by law upon a permanent basis, with fixed salaries, and with a small contingent appropriation allowed to the head of the department for such temporary and additional clerical service as may be needed in an emergency.

DEFICIENCY IN APPROPRIATIONS.

Each year in some departments contingent liabilities are incurred beyond their appropriations, which are paid later out of a deficiency appropriation. It is then practically impossible to question the expenditure. While such liabilities are no doubt for necessary and unforeseen expenses, still, as the law absolutely forbids any public officer to make any purchase or incur any liability beyond the amount appropriated, in my judgment when a department finds its appropriation exhausted, and yet there is necessity for further expenditure, it ought, before incurring any expense, to get the sanction of some other proper authority. I suggest that in the contingency stated, the department should be required to report the facts to the Governor and Council, and to receive their assent before incurring any further expense.

THE SUFFRAGE.

It is a pleasure on this occasion to congratulate you upon the ratification and adoption by the people, with great unanimity, of the constitutional amendment submitted to them by your predecessors, abolishing the tax qualification for voting. After a struggle of more than a century, untaxed suffrage in the election of State and National officers has thus been established in our Commonwealth. This amendment may require to some limited extent changes in the law of registration. These should be on the lines of our established policy, without essential modifications. While they should seek to protect the franchise, they should not render its exercise any more onerous and difficult than is necessary for its security As the abuse of the franchise should always be discouraged and severely punished, so its exercise should be encouraged and made as little burdensome as possible, that we may avoid the evils which a failure to vote by large numbers of our fellow-citizens seems at times to threaten.

At present there is a difference in the qualification of voters in State and National elections, and in town and city elections. The tax qualification for the former has been abolished by the recent amendment; it still remains on the latter by statute law. Of course this difference should not continue to exist. As the people have, by an overwhelming majority, abolished the tax qualification as far as it was directly in their power, and as in the past, suffrage has been uniform for all elections, with the single exception of a limited franchise for women, it is now necessary that this tax qualification should be abolished also in town and city elections.

ELECTION AND BALLOT LAWS.

I again recommend the passage of a comprehensive and stringent law to secure the publication of election expenses, and, if practicable, to limit their amount and define their proper objects; and I again urge, and now as a matter of pressing importance, an amendment of the ballot law, so that a single mark may constitute a vote for all the presidential electors of a political party. At present, to give full effect to a vote for President, the voter must mark separately the names of fifteen electors. As these electors are only the constitutional machinery for electing a President, with a single perfunctory duty to perform, and this already determined, and as the voter is not supposed to have any individual preference between them, there seems to be no use in requiring the separate marking of each name. The danger is that, with the present tendency to partial voting, many voters, through carelessness or mistake, will not mark the full list of electors. In a close election, this would almost certainly lead to an unintentional division of the electoral vote of the State.

OTHER RECOMMENDATIONS.

The following recommendations, submitted to the last Legislature in my inaugural, or later messages, and based upon reasons therein fully set forth, I submit to your favorable consideration: —

First. Further legislation, of a stringent and radical character, to remedy the evils of the lobby, and to limit its influence.

Second. The passage of general laws, upon the lines already suggested by me, to relieve the Legislature and the public of the burden of constantly increasing special legislation.

Third. Extension of the powers of cities and towns, and of local self-government, especially in matters of taxation, control and sale of franchises, and extending the limits of municipal work and of municipal ownership.

Fourth. The passage of a general municipal law for the incorporation and government of cities, with the limitations heretofore suggested. This subject was investigated by a special committee of the last Legislature, who will report to you the results of its investigation.

Fifth. Legislation to prevent railroad corporations from giving free passes to members of the Legislature, or to other officials before whom come matters in which these corporations are interested.

Sixth. A thorough reform in our system of land transfer and registration, upon the plan of the Australian, or Torrens, system, so called, to bring about greater freedom, security, and cheapness in the transfer of real estate. You will have, in considering this subject, the benefit of the investigation made by a special committee of the last Legislature.

Seventh. Further consideration of legislation asked for in the interest of the wage-earner, especially the reduction of the hours of labor of women and children employed in factories and workshops; amendment of the Employer's Liability Act, to broaden its scope and make it more efficient and beneficent in its results; and further action for the proper protection of railroad employees against the dangers to which they are exposed. The appalling fact that in the United States, during the year ending June 30, 1890, 369 employees were killed in coupling or uncoupling cars, and 7,841 were injured, makes legislation for the adoption of safety appliances which will prevent such accidents imperative. National legislation is necessary as the only effective remedy. I recommend that, following the precedent of the Legislature of last year, you petition Congress to take action, and that you use every means possible to hasten a remedy.

I call your attention to the fact that chapter 125 of the Acts of 1891, entitled, "An Act to prohibit the Imposition of Fines or Deductions of Wages of Employees engaged at Weaving," has been declared by the Supreme Judicial Court to be unconstitutional. I submit for your consideration whether a proper measure, not open to constitutional objection, cannot be adopted to accomplish the purpose sought by this Act.

I congratulate you upon the success so far attained by the important and popular agitation against the conditions of labor and of health in tenement-houses, especially against the so-called sweating system, and upon the earnest efforts which have been made by the Commonwealth and individuals to improve these conditions, to elevate this labor, to relieve this distress, and to protect the health and welfare of the public. It was my privilege to call the attention of the Legislature last year by special message to this subject. An Act was then passed to regulate the use of tenements as workshops, and providing for the appointment of two additional State inspectors on the district police force. I am informed by the chief of this force that through their efforts many of the evils have been stopped, and the use of tenements as workshops has been largely abandoned. Much still remains to be done. I urge your earnest co-operation in all efforts in this direction, which cannot but be a benefit to the Commonwealth.

Eighth. Again I recommend to the favorable consideration of the Legislature the adoption of industrial education and manual training as part of the system of instruction in our public schools, at least in some communities. This subject is now under thorough investigation by an able and experienced commission, which will later report to you. I believe that such instruction is useful and successful educationally, and of great practical benefit to the people; that it would increase and lengthen the attendance at our public schools, and would raise the maximum age for compulsory attendance, as provided in chapter 361 of the Acts of 1891, and make it proper to limit still further the employment of children in manufacturing and other establishments.

A year ago I called the attention of the Legislature to the great inequality in public education in different places, and to the marked difference in the character and efficiency of their schools, in the amount spent upon them for each pupil, and in the burden of taxation for such expenditure; and I asked your predecessors to consider whether the State, having wisely done so much for the education of her children, as of vital consequence to her safety and prosperity, could not properly go farther, and strive for the equal education of all to a certain standard; and whether such equalization could not justly be based upon the fact that the interest of every locality in public education is not and ought not to be limited to the education of its own children. Something was done in this direction by chapter 177 of the Acts of 1891, which provided for a new distribution of the school fund, for the benefit of the poorer and more heavily taxed towns. I commend the subject to your careful consideration. With most gratifying unanimity the people of the Commonwealth have shown their devotion and loyalty to our public schools. Let us in the same spirit earnestly seek to promote their interests, to maintain them in their full vigor, and to extend their great field of usefulness. Let us keep out of them any spirit of intolerance, which cannot but work them harm. Above all, let us not seek to divide our people politically over this great and cherished institution, when they are and ought to be one in word and thought and act in their devotion to it.

THE WORLD'S COLUMBIAN EXPOSITION.

Last year the Legislature appropriated $75,000 for a proper exhibit at the World's Columbian Exposition of the resources, products, and general development of the Commonwealth, and provided for the appointment of a board of five managers to have charge of this work. This board has since been appointed and organized, and has begun its duties with commendable energy. In its opinion, and in the opinion of others familiar with the matter, the appropriation is not sufficient for such an exhibit as the Commonwealth ought to make, nor does it compare favorably with the appropriations of other States. I recommend that the appropriation be increased. I believe that all our people are determined that this exposition shall be an unqualified success, and are willing to do their full share to this end. It certainly is most important — more important than the question of expense — that Massachusetts should make such an exhibit of her products and resources, of her history and institutions, as shall give her there the proud pre-eminence which she holds throughout the Union.

RAPID TRANSIT.

The Legislature of 1891 created a commission to investigate the important problem of rapid transit for Boston and vicinity, and to consider the many questions connected with this subject. The results of its thorough investigation will be reported to you, and will demand your most careful consideration.

Senators and Representatives: We now begin our respective duties in the government of the Commonwealth. While realizing our responsibility, let us rise to our opportunity. The oath we have taken subordinates all fealty to party to fidelity to the State, and subjects every personal and class interest to the public good. Steadfast to principle, true to conviction, however variant our opinions, let us in all measures be careful and candid in consideration, tolerant, cautious, and conservative in action, that in our legislation we may realize the aphorism of Lord Bacon, that "it be the reformation that draweth on the change, and not the desire of change that pretendeth the reformation." A sense of responsibility to the people, an earnest desire to serve their interests and to merit and receive their confidence, will bring to the discharge of our duties the courage, fidelity, and unselfish purpose which make useful, honorable public servants. Let our only strife be how best to advance the interests of our Commonwealth, and to promote the prosperity and happiness of all her people. As loyally we cling to her, the blessed mother, and lovingly as her children take up her work, "with us as with our fathers, may God be;" and may He enable us to transmit our goodly heritage, enriched by faithful stewardship.

MESSAGE

VETOING AN ACT TO AUTHORIZE THE CONNECTICUT RIVER RAILROAD COMPANY TO INCREASE ITS CAPITAL STOCK.

EXECUTIVE DEPARTMENT, Boston, May 9, 1892.

TO THE HONORABLE HOUSE OF REPRESENTATIVES:

I HEREWITH return, with my objections, a bill entitled "An Act to authorize the Connecticut River Railroad Company to increase its capital stock," which originated in your body.

The bill authorizes an increase of $2,420,000 of said stock, making the total authorized capital $5,000,000, or about double its present amount. In the absence of any restriction in the bill, this additional stock may and no doubt will be divided at its par value of $100 among the stockholders of said company in proportion to their holdings. The present market value of the stock of this company, as fixed by recent sales, is about $235 a share; so that in effect this bill authorizes the distribution to its stockholders of new stock, nearly equal in amount to the present stock, at less than one half its present market value. The difference between its par and market value will be clear profit to each stockholder, and represents the proportion of new stock not necessary for the purposes of the company, and for which the company itself gets no benefit or return. Less than one half of this proposed increase of stock, if sold at this market value, would yield to the company as much money as the whole increase so distributed to the stockholders. The bill, while in form an authorized increase of capital for the purposes of the company, practically gives the authority and sanction of the Commonwealth to the creation of more than double the amount of new capital, estimated at its market value, required for such purposes, and indirectly to the division of the balance among the stockholders as an enormous dividend.

Speaking in round numbers, the two and one-half millions of dollars of proposed new stock at present market value is worth over five and one-half millions of dollars. Of this last amount two and one half millions of dollars will go into the treasury of the company, and more than three millions of dollars into the pockets of the stockholders. To enable them to obtain this bonus, nearly one and one-half millions of dollars of unnecessary stock is added to the capital, the dividend upon which at ten per cent places an unnecessary burden of $150,000 each year upon the business of the railroad, that is, upon the public. Every pound of freight and every passenger carried by this company will contribute to meet this burden. Meanwhile, this unnecessary increase of capital adds nothing to the resources of the railroad, to the facilities for its use, or to the compensation of those who make such use practicable.

So far as this bill provides for any necessary increase of the capital stock of this company, I see no objection to it. But if in the mode of the increase and its distribution it creates an unnecessary amount of stock for the sole benefit of its stockholders, but which is to be a perpetual and needless burden upon the public, then I believe it to be my duty, before giving my approval to such a measure, carefully to consider whether the public cannot properly and justly interfere to prevent such burden. In the trust relation in which this company, under the uniform decisions of all our courts and legislatures, stands to the public, I believe such interference is proper, and that a sound public policy requires its exercise. At least it requires that the Commonwealth shall not actively co-operate in placing the burden upon the public, by grant of the necessary authority.

I recognize and appreciate all the rights of capital and property in our great lines of transportation, and would guard them with most conservative and scrupulous care, and, remembering the great public convenience which they serve, would grant them every just demand. But the rights of the public should be guarded as zealously, and asserted as against the personal wish or benefit of the individual.

Our Supreme Judicial Court has clearly defined the trust relation of a railway company to the public. It has declared that "the establishment of such a great thoroughfare is regarded as a public work, established by public authority, intended for the public use and benefit, the use of which is secured to the whole community, and constitutes, therefore, like a canal, turnpike, or highway, a public easement. The only principle on which the Legislature could have authorized the taking of private property for its construction, without the owner's consent, is that it was for the public use. . . . It is true that the real and personal property necessary to the establishment and management of the railroad is vested in the corporation; but it is in trust for the public. The company have not the general power of disposal incident to the absolute right of property. They are obliged to use it in a particular manner and for the accomplishment of a well-defined public object; they are required to render frequent accounts of their management of this property to the agents of the public; and they are bound ultimately to surrender it to the public at a price and upon terms established."[1]

These principles have been repeatedly recognized and affirmed by all courts, National and State, and by legislation everywhere in our country. They are fundamental law.

This company has a valuable property in its railroad, for which it is entitled to all just protection and consideration. But it is a property to which, in its origin, a public trust is attached. To sustain this trust the property itself was created, and in indissoluble connection with this trust in all legislation it must ever be considered. It cannot divest its property from the trust, nor ought it to do anything which can impair the value of the trust, or hazard its rights and objects. The company cannot sell, lease, or otherwise dispose of this property, deflect it from its purpose, or abandon its use. Because of this public trust, the company is exempt from certain taxation, and is given by law extraordinary powers and privileges, while it is properly allowed, for services rendered, fair and liberal compensation. The company, holding its property thus in trust, while most carefully protected in its every property and personal right and interest, must be rigidly held faithfully and fully to administer the great trust imposed upon it. As with other trustees, it cannot be allowed in any way to depreciate, impair, or unnecessarily to burden its trust, nor in disregard of its obligations and duties, to look exclusively, in the administration of the trust, to its own benefit and profit. Where the beneficiaries of the trust are the public, who

[1] Worcester vs. Western R. R. Co., 4 Met. 566.

constantly depend upon legislative action for the protection of their rights and the redress of any grievances, it is especially incumbent upon us to see that such action is not detrimental to their interests.

The public trust imposed upon a railroad corporation distinguishes it widely from private business or manufacturing companies, which have no such legal obligation, but are established for the holding, use, and control of private property for only personal ends and profit.

The Commonwealth has reserved the right, not only to amend or repeal all railroad charters, but also to purchase the property itself, and to fix the rate of compensation, under certain limitations. The law provides that upon purchase it shall pay the amount of capital stock paid in, with a net profit thereon of ten per cent a year. This seems by law and custom to have been regarded as a fair maximum profit for the supply, management, and risk of the capital necessary for these quasi-public corporations. The Legislature has rarely had occasion or disposition to use the great power thus reserved to it, and the railroad companies have considered it prudent and just to keep within this limit. This is a stronger reason why the Legislature should not sanction a measure which indirectly carries the profit much above this limit.

I know and appreciate the argument that an increase in the value of the stock of a railroad company, caused by its prudent management and extension of business, belongs to the company. But requiring the disposition, at its market value, of any new stock created does not conflict with this right. It gives to the company the whole benefit of such increase. It prevents the issue of stock more in amount than is necessary to raise the sum needed. It saves to the individual stockholder any depreciation of his stock likely to follow from such unnecessary addition to the capital, and to the beneficiary public the burdensome charge of paying a dividend upon it. A needless burden is always an unjust burden, and is the more felt and resented when the occasion out of which it has arisen has been created by the activity, progress, and business of those upon whom it falls. The commercial activity and increased travel of a community give a large business to a railroad. This requires of it permanent additions to and improvements of its property, and so an increase of its capital. This increase ought not to be so made as to be itself an enormous dividend to its stockholders, and an unnecessary burden upon the contributing community.

To a people largely dependent upon the railroads and cheap transportation, not only for their convenience and happiness, but also for their commercial prosperity, such burden comes with greater weight. Against it have been uttered their protests, emphasized by the formal action of the leading commercial bodies of New England.

For these reasons I believe the interests alike of the public, the railroad company, and, in the long run, of its stockholders, require that when the authority of the Commonwealth is asked and given for an increase of the stock of the company, some provision should be made for the disposition of said stock at its market value, where such market value is largely in excess of its par value. If there is objection to its sale by auction, the option might well be given to the stockholders to take it at a fair value, to be determined by the Board of Railroad Commissioners.

While the Commonwealth has not made such provision by general law applicable to all railroad corporations, it has already established a precedent for such a policy in the future. In giving authority last year [1] to the Boston and Lowell Railroad corporation to increase its capital stock, it expressly required that the new stock should be sold at public auction. What was sound public policy then when applied to that railroad seems to me sound public policy now as applied to this railroad. Other great railroad corporations, such as the Old Colony and the West End, have without compulsion of law sold their new stock at auction, and every gas company chartered in this Commonwealth is required by law to do so.

In the light of this practice and these precedents, I can see neither injustice nor hardship in requiring that the increase of capital authorized by this bill shall be upon a similar condition. On the contrary, I believe that both the public interest and a just public sentiment demand that it be done.

I therefore return this bill for your further consideration, with the suggestion that if the views herein expressed meet with your approval, a bill in conformity with them, granting to this company authority to increase its stock, be passed.

[1] Chap. 207, Acts of 1891.

MESSAGE

VETOING AN ACT TO PROMOTE TEMPERANCE BY THE
SUPPRESSION OF THE LIQUOR SALOON.

EXECUTIVE DEPARTMENT, BOSTON, June 16, 1892.

TO THE HONORABLE HOUSE OF REPRESENTATIVES:

I RETURN herewith, with my objections, a bill entitled "An Act to promote temperance by the suppression of the liquor saloon and tippling shop," which originated in your body.

If I believed that this bill would promote the cause of temperance, I would gladly give it my approval. But I do not believe it will have or is expected to have this result; but, on the contrary, that it will lead to evasion, and to the unequal and imperfect application and enforcement of law, as was recently fully illustrated in reference to the public bar law.

This bill in substance merely prohibits the keeping or sale of liquor in any room, building, or place where the sale of liquor is the exclusive or principal business carried on. It therefore requires only that every licensee should provide himself with some other business in addition to the sale of liquors, — such, for example, as the sale of food or of newspapers, providing billiards or some other amusement as a business, or the exhibition of pictures or delivery of lectures, etc., — to which he may claim to make the sale of liquors subordinate, and then leave it to a jury to determine this fact. It is perfectly clear to me that this is only encouraging a repetition of an experience in this Commonwealth which proved to be so much of a farce and scandal as to lead the Legislature last year to repeal the cause of it. It was found then that the provision in reference to a public bar was enforced in only one or two places, that it had not advanced the cause of temperance, that it was not sustained by public sentiment, and that, by constant evasions and non-enforcement, it was an injury to the cause of law and order, and so the provision was repealed.

Under this bill the seller of liquor can go through the farce of establishing a "principal business," and again we shall have an experience with unequal and imperfect attempts at enforcement of law.

I believe it is an unwise policy to enact legislation which, it is almost certain, will open the way to make a farce of law by non-enforcement, when law ought to be thoroughly enforced, with the full support and approbation of the community.

I will gladly give my sanction and aid to every proper measure which will advance the cause of temperance, and to the full extent of my power will have the laws of this Commonwealth thoroughly enforced. Wherever in the past such enforcement has fallen within my official duty, I have sought to make it effective. But I do most earnestly urge on the consideration of the Legislature the mischief of making provisions of law which, in the light of experience, it is believed will lead only to evasions, non-enforcement, and a farce.

Under the wise and well-established policy of this Commonwealth, each locality has full power to determine for itself the question of the sale of liquor within its limits, and, if it desires, can absolutely prohibit such sale.

The annual discussion and decision of this question in our local communities have preserved fully their local rights, and have also been an educational influence of great importance in advancing the cause of temperance. Even if a community votes for license, the local authorities have now absolute power to determine how many licenses, if any, shall be granted, and to what persons and what places and for what purpose.

Everything sought to be accomplished by this bill can now be accomplished by the local authorities of any community. They can limit licenses, if they wish, to apothecaries, hotel-keepers, or grocers, or any other class within their discretion. They cannot now grant a license for sale of liquor to be drunk on the premises except to a common victualler, that is, to one who conducts also the business of furnishing food. If this provision, now existing in law, can be and is enforced, it covers the case sought to be reached by this bill; if it is not enforced, and cannot be, it is not more law, but more enforcement of law, which is needed.

In view of the full powers now given to local communities to establish prohibition or to restrict the persons or places to be licensed, or the purpose for which a license shall be used, and of the many other restrictions and limitations now existing, I do not believe this proposed law is wise or necessary.

If this measure is directed especially to the city of Boston, it should be remembered that for every liquor saloon or tippling shop which now exists there, the responsibility rests directly upon the Board of Police created by the State, and that there is now and has been in their hands full power to prohibit the existence of any and every such saloon or shop.

The conditions and sentiment of different communities vary greatly upon the question of the sale of liquor.

It seems to me wiser to allow for such differences of condition, opinion, and sentiment, by giving discretion upon this question to each community and its properly constituted authorities, than to disregard such differences by general provisions of law; so the law enacted by each community will have behind it the power and public sentiment of that community, and will be, as it ought to be and must be, thoroughly enforced. It is such a policy which has received the repeated approval and indorsement of the people of this Commonwealth. It is in thorough accord with our belief in local self-government, and in my judgment it is constantly advancing the cause of temperance.

This bill does not in any way or form prohibit the sale of liquor or limit the number of places where it may be sold, or tend to promote prohibition. Such sale may be just as open as at present, and as easily accessible to any person desiring to purchase liquor; nor will he be required to order food therewith, or to patronize any other business of the seller.

This Legislature has shown that it does not believe in prohibition, by its refusal to establish it, or to limit further the number of licenses, or to enact any other measures in that direction.

The provision of this bill is solely that some other principal business must be carried on at the place of sale. This is certain to be difficult of construction and enforcement, and may well add to the admitted evils and temptations of the saloon. It certainly is of doubtful public policy to force the association of other business with the sale of liquor.

It is not at all likely that this business, which is notoriously profitable, would by this law be limited in extent or change hands, but only that it would disguise its conduct to meet the formal requirements of the law.

Instead of suppressing the saloon, in my judgment it would add to its evils, and instead of promoting temperance, it would lead to evasions and conditions which would tend to injure this most worthy cause.

As this bill comes to me with fifty or sixty others in the closing hours of your session, I am compelled to express in a hasty and imperfect way the reasons which lead me to believe that the measure is injudicious, and that it is more conservative and wise to withhold my approval of it than to allow it to become a law, especially as it is not to take effect until May 1, 1893, and there is, therefore, ample opportunity for another Legislature to give it consideration.

INAUGURAL ADDRESS

TO THE LEGISLATURE, JAN. 5, 1893.

Gentlemen of the Senate and House of Representatives:

AS I enter upon the duties of Governor for the third time, I gratefully express to the people of the Commonwealth my appreciation of their renewed confidence, and of the honor, dignity, and responsibility of the trust they have committed to my charge. We all are their servants to do their work, and should be ready and anxious faithfully to discharge our obligation to them by unselfish devotion to their interests.

In accordance with well-established custom, it is my duty at this time to submit to you suggestions and recommendations for your consideration and action. This duty I construe to be a privilege to deal with broader matters than the specific recommendations of departments, however important these may be, and to suggest principles of legislation and necessary reforms, rather than perfunctorily to indorse or transmit details of administration, all of which are ably and fully set forth in the reports of State officials made directly to you.

Acting upon this view, it was my privilege in addressing the Legislature of 1891 to recommend important and fundamental reforms in reference to qualifications for the suffrage, protection of elections and legislation from improper influences, relief from special legislation, greater system and responsibility in administration and other matters, — all to the end that law might ever be the free, true expression of the people's will, and its administration just, pure, and honest. In 1892, in my inaugural address and in special messages, I directed the attention of the Legislature to the executive branch of our government, to the great increase of its duties, the lack of uniformity or system in its organization, and its entire absence of responsibility; and I urged such changes as would create complete responsibility to the people, and would remedy these evils.

Some of these recommendations of the past two years have become law. The abolition of a property qualification for the office of Governor has followed the abolition of a tax qualification for the suffrage; and neither restriction, I am glad to say, has any longer a place in the Constitution of our free Commonwealth. Wise laws to guard the purity of elections and of legislation have been passed, but more stringent measures are necessary to accomplish the desired reforms. The use of money in large amounts for campaign purposes without restriction is still a public evil; and the lobby, if not as notorious and scandalous as in the past, still exists as a malignant influence, tainting legislation with its corrupting touch. I recommend legislation to define the objects of expenditure for campaign purposes, and so restrict its amount, and the most stringent treatment by law, on the lines heretofore suggested by me, of the evil of the lobby, so as to obviate its necessity, take away its opportunity, and give publicity to its acts. I also commend to your consideration the justice of giving the same recognition upon the official ballot to any well-established and regularly organized political party as is now given to the leading political parties, and the expediency of repealing the law permitting a recount of ballots. In my judgment, such recount is open to more serious objections and dangers than to make the count at the polls final, as is done generally in other States. If the recount is abolished, every effort should be made by legislation to insure the absolute accuracy and fairness of the original count. Other recommendations heretofore made, and not necessary here to enumerate, have been considered and approved by your predecessors. There are still others of importance not yet adopted which I again submit to your careful and early attention. Of these, I believe the most important is the reform of the existing machinery for the discharge of executive duties, — machinery now without system, and destructive of that executive responsibility and supervision which the Constitution devolves upon the Governor, and for the proper exercise of which it meant to make him at all times amenable to the people. I have heretofore so fully considered this subject, and stated the facts and arguments upon which I based an earnest recommendation for radical changes, that I need now but briefly refer to them.

With the exception of a few elected officers, the administrative work of the Commonwealth is in the hands of boards and commissions composed of hundreds of members. In their creation no fixed principle of appointment, tenure, or removal has been followed, and no uniformity in these respects exists. Some are unnecessary, and should be abolished; others should be systematized into proper departments, or made subordinate to existing departments. Over many there is no power of removal, and so of control, in any authority. As far as this power is given to the chief executive, its use almost without exception requires the concurrence of an executive council of nine, which concurrence, as experience shows, practically involves a trial of an official upon formal charges; so that administration is largely beyond the control of the people, because not subject to any officer immediately responsible to them. Another year's experience has only shown more clearly the danger, friction, and irresponsibility of our present system; the absence of proper power in the Governor, and so of responsible control in the people. Another year of public discussion of this important State question, with past experience as an object lesson, has, on a direct appeal to the people, shown distinctly, I believe, their dissatisfaction and demand for a change. They mean that the executive head of the Commonwealth, their servant, shall be in fact as in name the supreme executive magistrate, always and solely responsible to them, and that he shall have all the powers commensurate with such responsibility. They repudiate a system which devolves executive duties, for which he is and ought to be held responsible, upon bodies over which he has little or no control or influence.

The question of continuing in our executive system an elected council, which exists in but three of our forty-four States, and here has become the subject of serious criticism and opposition, I submit to your consideration. Its constitutional power is not important, and could well be exercised by other existing bodies. The power given it by legislation to control, concurrently with the Governor, some executive boards and departments, is, in its exercise, either perfunctory, and so unimportant, or, if independent, necessarily divides responsibility, and so becomes inconsistent with any sound system of executive management. There are no such peculiar conditions of executive work in this Commonwealth as to require the continued existence of this now anomalous institution. If, however, its power were properly limited to its constitutional duties, it might perhaps remain as a harmless concession to a conservative, antiquarian sentiment. I again renew the suggestions and recommendations I have heretofore made upon this general subject: *first*, that certain unnecessary offices and commissions be abolished; *second*, that proper steps be taken to simplify and systematize the machinery for administrative work; *third*, that administration be placed upon a basis of full responsibility to the people, by vesting in the Governor alone the power to remove, for cause stated, any executive officer appointed by him. I also renew the recommendation thrice made by my experienced predecessor, Governor Long, that the people be given an opportunity to express their opinion upon the need of an elected executive council, by submission to them of a constitutional amendment providing for its abolition. To these suggestions I urge your careful attention, trusting that you will take such wise and patriotic action as shall promote efficiency and responsibility in the discharge of executive duty.

STATE PRISON.

In this connection, and at the risk of tedious repetition, I submit for the third time to the consideration of the Legislature the immediate necessity of a change in our system of prison control. The management of the State Prison has for years attracted the attention and criticism of the public. While I believe that under its present administration there has been improvement in the conduct and discipline of the prison, notwithstanding the serious disadvantages of its crowded condition, and the confusion arising from new construction, yet its management, in my judgment, cannot be entirely successful without important changes in the system. The first requisite for a proper system is power with responsibility, and this at present is lacking. The warden has no power over his principal subordinates, except with the concurrence of the Board of Prison Commissioners. They have no power whatever over him, and the Governor little, if any, over them. The chain of effective responsibility, from the humblest officer up to the people, is broken at every link. I again recommend that the warden be given control of his subordinate officers, the Board of Prison Commissioners control of him, and the Governor control of them. The advantage of such a change, as stated by me nearly two years ago in a special message, will be to "establish a system of prison management which gives to each official the power proper and necessary for the discharge of his duty, and to concentrate responsibility where it properly belongs. Under such a system, if there is lack of discipline, insubordination, or mismanagement at the prison, the subordinate officers are answerable for it to the warden, who has the power and responsibility of correcting the trouble. For the proper exercise of his power the warden is answerable to the Prison Commissioners, they to the Governor, and the Governor to the people of the Commonwealth." I again dwell upon this subject, not merely because it is one of many illustrations which might be given of the inefficiency and irresponsibility of our general system of administration, but also because in this instance, as the evil may lead to serious consequences, its correction is of pressing importance. The people should know the cause of the trouble, that they may place the responsibility for its continuance where it properly belongs.

RIGHT OF LOCAL SELF-GOVERNMENT IN TOWN AND CITY.

The right of self-government is an axiom of our political system. Wherever this right can be exercised directly by the people themselves, such exercise should be carefully conserved. Where representation of the people is necessary, the representative should be directly and immediately responsible to them. In recognition of this principle, I have urged that greater executive power and responsibility be placed upon the Governor, not to establish but to prevent autocratic rule, by giving to the people themselves, through their immediate representative, full control of their own affairs. In further recognition of this principle, and of the steadfast devotion of our people to home rule, as seen in the formation and history of our Commonwealth, I earnestly recommend that whenever and wherever possible the right of local self-government shall be left in or restored to her respective cities and towns.

The concise compact in the cabin of the "Mayflower," creating "a civil body politick," made Plymouth a fully equipped republic. As the population grew, the little bands of people pressed further into the wilderness, each under the lead of its clergyman; and, clustering around its meeting-house and school-house, formed in every settlement a self-supporting, self-governing community. The Puritans followed this example, and so, with the cordial approval and God-speed of the General Court, Massachusetts grew by what one of her most distinguished lawyers[1] happily called a "cellular formation." She grew from her towns quite as much as they from her. In his great work upon "The American Commonwealth," Professor Bryce says: "Each such

[1] The reference is to the late Robert D. Smith, of Boston.

settlement was called a Town, or Township, and was in fact a miniature Commonwealth, exercising a practical sovereignty over the property and persons of its members, — for there was as yet no State, and the distant home government scarcely cared to interfere, — but exercising it on thoroughly democratic principles. . . . And though presently . . . the Legislature and Governor, first of the whole colony, and, after 1776, of the State, began to exert their superior authority, the towns . . . held their ground, and are to this day the true units of political life in New England, the solid foundation of that well-compacted structure of self-government which European philosophers have admired, and the new States of the West have sought to reproduce." [1]

This right of local self-government, jealously asserted by the towns, was ever cheerfully recognized by the State. To the present day, in the establishment of a town government, the Legislature uses almost these identical words of the old colonial statutes: "And that the same town be and hereby is vested with all the powers, privileges, and immunities that any other of the towns in this province do or may by law exercise and enjoy." All towns are placed upon an equality, based upon the right of home rule. Legislative interference with an individual town is a discrimination, and manifestly places such town upon an unequal footing; and just to the extent of such interference is she controlled by her sister towns. If a town desires proper local regulation, she should have the power to make it; if she does not, the other towns, through united action in the Legislature, should not force it upon her, independent of a general policy established by general law.

While the Constitution of 1780 gives the Legislature

[1] Vol. I. p. 562.

power broad enough to control municipalities and their local concerns, it is evident throughout its provisions that the framers regarded the towns as the aggregate constituting the Commonwealth, and assumed that the town right, like the individual right, would be impaired only under circumstances of gravest necessity. The Bill of Rights secures to the people "the sole and exclusive right of governing themselves," and, with the Constitution, recognizes the town as the existing unit of self-government. In 1820, by amendment to the Constitution, authority was given to the General Court to erect and constitute city governments in towns containing twelve thousand inhabitants, but only with the consent and upon the application of a majority thereof. This amendment was necessary in view of the growth of Boston (then having nearly forty thousand inhabitants), which made the continuance of the town system of legislation and administration impracticable and inefficient. Boston, therefore, though with much reluctance and considerable opposition, by the acceptance of a city charter substituted local representative self-government for the democracy of the town meeting. The change was only one in the form of local self-government. It did not alter the relation of the city to the Commonwealth. The Legislature delegated none of its powers to the city, and the city gave to the Legislature no greater control over the municipality. The delegation of power was by her citizens and to the city, not to the State. So the first section of the city charter provided that "The inhabitants of the town of Boston for all purposes for which towns are by law incorporated in this Commonwealth shall continue to be one body politic in fact and name, . . . and as such shall ever exercise and enjoy all the rights, immunities, powers, and privileges, and shall be subject to all the duties and obligations now incumbent upon and appertaining to the said town."

Decisions of our highest court have repeatedly held that this change from town to city government was only one of form and organization of the municipality, and did not affect the extent of legislative control. Chief Justice Shaw, who is understood to have drafted the city charter of Boston, speaking in the Constitutional Convention of 1820 of city as distinguished from town government, declared that "he disclaimed all idea of claiming powers or privileges for one class of citizens which were not equally extended to another; but an act of incorporation is equally enjoyed by all the towns in the Commonwealth. . . . Every town is to all substantial purposes a city. They are towns corporate, having the power of choosing their own officers, and sending members to the General Court, with jurisdiction over all their local and prudential concerns, such as the support of schools and highways, the relief of the poor, the superintendence of licensed houses, and other matters of local police. They have the power of making by-laws and assessing and collecting taxes. They possess all the powers and privileges of municipal corporations in Great Britain or in this country." This language was quoted with approval by Chief Justice Gray in the elaborate opinion in the case of Hill *vs.* Boston, 122 Mass. 355.

Until recent years this division of government, under which the General Court controlled the general concerns of the people, and left to each city or town control of its local concerns, was with us universally recognized and respected, and received the commendation of statesmen, historians, and thinkers. Thomas Jefferson, when studying the best form of government for his native State, turned to New England, and said:

"Those wards called townships in New England are the vital principle of their governments, and have proved themselves the wisest invention ever devised by the wit of man for the perfect exercise of self-government and for its preservation." John Adams, the framer of our Constitution, enumerated "the towns, militia, schools, and churches as the four causes of the growth and defence of New England," and as the place where "the virtues and talents of the people are formed." The great French student of our institutions, De Tocqueville, writes: "The townships are only subordinate to the State in those interests which I shall term social, as they are common to all the citizens. They are independent in all that concerns themselves, and among the inhabitants of New England, I believe that not a man is to be found who would acknowledge that the State has any right to interfere in their local interests." Again he says: "Municipal institutions are to liberty what primary schools are to science: they bring it within reach; they teach men how to use and how to enjoy it. A nation may establish a system of free government, but without the spirit of municipal institutions it cannot have the spirit of liberty." Professor Bryce describes the town-meeting as "the most perfect school of self-government in any modern country." John Fiske, in his "Civil Government in the United States," declares it to be "the form of government most effectively under watch and control." Dr. Palfrey in his History insists that nothing "has had more influence on the condition and the character of the people through the eight generations of their history." Judge Cooley, the learned writer upon "Constitutional Limitations," speaks of it as "almost a part of the very nature of the race to which we belong." In Elliott's "New England" it is said that "The prime strength of

New England and of the whole republic was and is in the municipal governments and in the homes." It would be easy to multiply such authorities. No thoughtful student or reader of our history has questioned the value of municipal self-government, or the necessity of maintaining it in its full integrity.

I have called your attention to this familiar principle upon which our system of government was founded, and has most successfully developed, and the universal commendation of it by jurist, historian, and statesman, because in recent years a tendency has been developed to violate the principle by impairing the right of local self-government, especially in the largest city of the Commonwealth. The belief is held by some of our citizens that if municipal machinery seems for the moment to be out of gear, the proper remedy is not to appeal to their fellow-citizens to repair it, but to the Legislature to take control of it. But State assumption of municipal functions cannot be so wholesome, just, or effective as self-correction of municipal abuses; and the latter is certain, unless our people have lost the capacity and desire for good government and self-government.

While other instances might be given, some of which occasioned vetoes of bills passed by your immediate predecessors, the most striking illustration of this tendency, and the most flagrant violation of this fundamental right, are found in the law of 1885, which took into the keeping of the Commonwealth the control of the police of Boston. Against the wish of a great majority of her citizens and the protest of most of her representatives in the Legislature, other members, representing constituencies under no pecuniary responsibility for its support, and no moral responsibility for its efficiency, placed the police force of Boston in the hands of State commissioners, and authorized them by requisition to compel that city to raise by taxation whatever sum in their sovereign judgment was necessary. Since then the citizens of Boston, representing one-fifth of the population of the Commonwealth, have had no power whatever over this most important executive branch of their government, no voice in the enforcement of law, the preservation of peace, and the protection of life, liberty, and property. Whatever abuses may exist, however inefficient, partisan, and scandalous such administration may be, however coercive or unprincipled in its dealings with the interests under its control, however detrimental to Boston and the welfare of her citizens, they must patiently submit to any wrongs, content to agitate and protest, powerless to remedy or to punish. No self-respecting community in the Commonwealth, after living and prospering under the blessings of liberty and self-government, would permit without emphatic protest such violation of their rights; nor is it easy to see why they should inflict or tolerate it upon their neighbors. Naturally and fortunately, such a wide departure from the spirit of our institutions and the teaching of the fathers has brought only evil results. A law founded on a mistrust of the people, removing government beyond their reach, and officials beyond their control, is certain to lead to grave abuses. Such has been our experience with State control of the police of Boston. The Board of Police by its acts has deservedly lost the confidence of the citizens of Boston and of the people of the Commonwealth. I again earnestly recommend the separation of the powers of this board; that the control of her police, which is a purely administrative function, be restored to the city of Boston; that the control of licenses, which is judicial in its nature, be placed in a board of such character, appointment, and tenure as to be judicial in its action. It is within your power thus to correct a serious evil, do justice to the city of Boston, and a service to the whole community. I shall endeavor by executive action to lift this board out of politics, and to give assurance to the public that the administration of the important interests under its control shall be efficient, upright, and free from partisan perversion.

EXTENSION OF LOCAL SELF-GOVERNMENT AND RELIEF FROM SPECIAL LEGISLATION.

Due regard for the right of local self-government requires, not only non-interference by the State in the purely local affairs of cities and towns, but also the grant to them of greater powers, in order that there may be the most successful treatment and control of the ever-increasing problems of local concern. Such grant would be both a wise and just extension of local self-government, and in harmony with what I believe to be the sound policy of substituting, wherever possible, general laws for special legislation. Something was accomplished last year in this direction. General laws, providing for the establishment of city governments, granting greater powers to local governments in the construction of sewers, pensioning of the police, the raising of money for celebrations, and the control of the streets, were enacted to cover matters which had been the subject of many special laws. A reference to the Acts of last year shows the need of more legislation of this character. Of its four hundred and forty Acts, nearly one-third were special laws passed upon the application of twenty-five cities and eighty-five towns.

Of these Acts, eighteen were to introduce, increase, or improve water supplies, or regulate water rates; sixteen to authorize water debts; nine to refund indebtedness; seven to issue bonds; ten to confirm proceedings of town meetings; nine to take land for public purposes; seven relating to grade crossings, six to rights in bridges, four to fisheries, seven to duties of officials; and there were many others relating to salaries, sewers, celebrations, and other local matters. There were also eighty-seven Acts relating to other corporations, including many Acts to give authority to hold additional property, increase or reduce capital, issue bonds, sell real estate, confirm proceedings, and for the incorporation of trust and water companies. A careful examination will show, I believe, that the authority and proper control of the State can better be exercised over many of these matters through general laws, with wise limitations and official supervision, than by the constant grant of special rights, powers, or favors. The incorporation of safe deposit and trust companies, like savings and co-operative banks, in my judgment should be made by general law, under the scrutiny and authority of the Savings Bank Commissioners, instead of being, as now, a matter of special legislation; and I again recommend the passage of such a law. Other corporate matters, now the subject of numerous special laws, you may find can wisely be covered by general laws. In this connection I ask you to consider the expediency of providing by general law for the sale of new railroad stock by auction, or other disposition of it at its market value, where such value is in excess of par, instead of its distribution to its stockholders at par, as now permitted. My reasons for believing such law to be wise, just, and for the public interest I have fully stated in a special message to the Legislature of May 9, 1892, vetoing

"An Act to authorize the Connecticut River Railroad Company to increase its capital stock."

The passage of a general law in reference to public water supplies, to regulate grants, to establish proper authority to examine and determine the rights of conflicting claimants, and to provide for the broad and just treatment of the whole subject, as well as for the details of water rates and debts, now the subject of special legislation, is each year becoming more urgent. But more fundamental and important are the preservation and extension of the right of local self-government, by the grant under general laws of further powers to cities and towns to deal with franchises, taxation, extension of municipal work, and other matters of a local character, leaving to each community to determine the expediency of availing itself of these enlarged powers.

This principle of home rule, which asserts that the highest efficiency, greatest social happiness, and political contentment are obtained by local control of home affairs, need not and does not conflict with the establishment by the State of a general policy in any field of public work, nor with her creation of such machinery of local government as she deems expedient. It does require that the working of that machinery shall be left to the local authority, and be under the check and control of the local constituency.

METROPOLITAN QUESTIONS.

Nor does this principle overlook the fact that there are public matters, affecting the interests of a number of communities, where necessary union of action can be accomplished only by the interposition of a superior authority. In such cases, in the absence of some comprehensive method of mutual action, State control is necessary. The questions are not local, but metropolitan in their character, and the whole population affected must be considered, and made one community for their successful solution. The tendency of our modern civilization is to build up clusters of communities around a central dominating city, each with its local needs and aspirations, but these often subordinate to its interests as a member of the group to which it belongs. This at present is the relation of Boston to the surrounding cities and towns, and may soon be the position of other fast-growing centres of population in this Comomnwealth. It has led to metropolitan problems of great and pressing importance, which have been recognized and treated as proper subjects for State action, and, therefore, so far as they are still unsolved, will demand your most careful consideration.

METROPOLITAN SEWERAGE.

The problem of proper sewerage for the metropolitan district along the Charles and Mystic rivers has been successfully met by the creation by the State of a metropolitan system now under construction.

METROPOLITAN RAPID TRANSIT.

Of the metropolitan questions still unsettled, none is more important or pressing than that of rapid transit. Recently this subject has been carefully and thoroughly investigated by a commission created by the Legislature of 1891. Its very able and suggestive report, with important plans and recommendations, was made to the Legislature of 1892, but so late in the session that it was deemed best to refer the matter to you. I commend it to your most careful consideration, in the earnest hope that your efforts will result in some solution of a problem which affects most seriously the convenience, happiness, and welfare of many of our people. Cheap and rapid transit for the residents of the metropolitan district of Boston is no less important as a social and sanitary blessing than as an economic and industrial necessity. It would surely and effectively tend to dissipate the crowded centres of sickness, misery, and vice which so readily gather in the hearts of our great cities. Make transit to the suburbs easy, swift, and cheap, and the squalid tenement-houses of the city cannot compete, as experience shows, with the attractions of a country home. Life then will be developed under conditions more favorable to physical health and sound morals, while the central city will be relieved of densely populated areas, where disease and crime may flourish. To the poor this will give more of fresh air and sunshine, cheaper land or rent, and so cheaper cost of living, under healthier and happier conditions. The industrial gain from better transit is too apparent to need extended statement. It means greater facility in the transaction of business, and its consequent extension; and to the whole community a saving of time and labor, with greater comfort and convenience. Street blockades in Boston, slow transit, insufficient accommodations, either in transit or at terminal stations, are quite as much an annoyance and loss to the residents of the suburban cities and towns as to the residents of Boston. Because of this interest of many municipalities in the matter, if not their responsibility for its solution, it requires treatment sufficiently broad to cover the entire field, by an authority which can compel concert of action. Under existing conditions this can spring only from the State, but it should be sustained and enforced by the willing co-operation of all the communities interested. The time has fully come for action. Further delay only complicates the problem, and makes its solution more difficult and expensive.

METROPOLITAN PARKS.

Among other metropolitan questions which may soon demand attention are those of parks, water supply, and highways. Under the provisions of an Act of last year a Metropolitan Park Commission was appointed to consider the advisability of laying out ample open spaces for public use in the towns and cities in the vicinity of Boston. As required by the Act, the commission will early in the present session report a comprehensive plan for laying out, acquiring, and maintaining such open spaces. The subject is one of great and increasing public interest. With the opportunity thus to improve river basins, protect the sources of water-supply from pollution, and guard the public health, as well as to furnish to a crowded population breathing-spaces for exercise and recreation, the subject not merely affects the beauty and comfort of a locality and the happiness of its people, but becomes an essential factor in the well-being and prosperity of a modern city. If anything is to be done, the sooner action is taken by proper authority the better. Ample reservations, such as the Middlesex Fells and the Blue Hill forest, can now be secured at reasonable cost. Unless secured now, these and other like tracts may be lost by occupation for other purposes, or later can be secured only at very great expense.

METROPOLITAN WATER SUPPLY.

The subject of a water supply for the metropolitan district of Boston, including by that term the territory within ten miles of the State House, may in the near future demand serious attention. The present population of the district is about nine hundred thousand. While some places within it have an excellent water supply sufficient for many years, yet I am informed by competent authority that the total available supply of pure water within reasonable distance is probably only enough for the consumption and need of a population of one million five hundred thousand, which number may be reached in fifteen years. In view of future necessities, it may seem to you prudent to make now preliminary investigations to determine the best source of water supply for the entire metropolitan area.

IMPROVEMENT OF HIGHWAYS.

The improvement of our highways is another subject which will require your consideration. This, of course, is largely a matter of local duty, under the control of local authority. But it is also of such general interest and importance that the State last year established a commission to consider the best and most practicable method of construction and maintenance of highways, and what legislation is necessary for their improvement. The commission will report to you the results of its careful, thorough investigation. The evident need and demand for the improvement of our highways, and of more systematic, uniform methods in their construction and maintenance, require careful attention.

EDUCATION, LABOR, AGRICULTURE.

These important interests of the Commonwealth, over which she has ever exercised watchful care, demand and will receive, I am sure, your earnest attention, with every desire to maintain in their full vigor and integrity our great institutions, and by wise, progressive legislation to promote the welfare of the farmer, the wage-earner, and all the people. Without repeating in detail the recommendations heretofore made by me upon these subjects, I refer them to your consideration.

MILITIA.

The militia of the Commonwealth has during the past year been drilled under the new regulations adopted by the general government, and has maintained its efficient condition. It has been proposed during the World's Columbian Exposition this year to mobilize in Chicago the militia of the country for instruction. As yet no definite plan has been formulated, but it is suggested to muster the troops by a call from the President of the United States for a period of fifteen days, under command of officers of the United States Army, the government to furnish transportation and rations. I believe such muster, under careful regulations, with the necessary preparatory drill and discipline, will be of service to our militia, and I urge your co-operation in the matter. Should the troops of Massachusetts be so mustered, I assume that their regular encampment here would be omitted. An addition to the annual appropriation will probably be necessary to carry out the plan.

LAND REGISTRATION AND TRANSFER.

I regret that little or nothing has yet been done to reform our system of land registration and transfer. At present, serious delay and expense, constant re-examination, and then possible insecurity, attend a system where freedom, security, and cheapness are most desirable and for the public interest. I cannot doubt that the ability and ingenuity of our people can devise or adapt some system to remedy these admitted evils. The Torrens system of registration of titles, the general features of which were fully stated by me in a message to the Legislature of 1891, has proved to be a simple, safe, and admirable plan of land transfer in Australia and other countries where it has long been used. I commend it to your consideration, in the belief that further investigation will show that the principles of this system can be adopted here, or at least that important changes can wisely be made in our present cumbersome methods of land transfer. An able commission recently appointed in the State of Illinois has recommended the adoption of this system there.

FAST DAY.

A memorial concerning Fast Day, signed by prominent representatives of religious denominations and colleges within the Commonwealth, was submitted to the last Legislature late in its session, and by it referred to you. It is worthy of your careful consideration. Massachusetts, in her inception, growth, and development, as well as in her Constitution, is emphatically a Christian Commonwealth. The Bill of Rights declares: "It is the right as well as the duty of all men in society publicly and at stated seasons to worship the Supreme Being, the great Creator and Preserver of the Universe." True to the religious character of their origin, and in accordance with the union of Church and State which they established, and which for a half-century in a mild and tolerant form existed under our Constitution, our pious fathers with entire unanimity early instituted the custom of setting apart annually by public authority a day to be observed as "a day of public fasting, humiliation, and prayer to Almighty God." Each year the Governor, with the advice and consent of the Council, appoints this day, and requests its due and appropriate observance by the people, and the statute provides that all public business shall be suspended thereon. But in the progress of time, with its changes of custom and feeling, in the growth of the Commonwealth with diversity of religious sentiment and of race, in the entire separation now of Church and State, or perhaps for the better and higher reason of a more general observance of the great and solemn historic fast of the universal Church, or of others suggested by deep religious sentiment according to the dictates of conscience, — whatever the cause, the fact is clear that the annual State fast has come to be generally disregarded, or deflected from its original and grateful purpose. It has become little else than a holiday. It seems inconsistent with sound public and religious sentiment, and almost irreverent, to require a day to be set apart by public proclamation to a most solemn purpose, when it is well known that it will not be so observed. I therefore suggest whether you may not properly sever the secular duties of the State from the spiritual obligations of the churches and the people by providing another legal holiday in the spring of the year, leaving to voluntary action the recognition and reverent observance either of the religious fast of Good Friday, or of such other day of fasting, humiliation, and prayer as the various churches and religious communities in the Commonwealth may at any time appoint for themselves. To accomplish the change it is only necessary to strike out the words "fast day" from our existing statutes prohibiting or regulating public or other business on holidays. After such legislation the Governor and Council no doubt would assume that they were not required to appoint such day. In its place as a spring holiday I would recommend the selection of the historic 19th of April.

RECIPROCITY WITH CANADA.

The establishment of closer trade relations between the United States and the Dominion of Canada is a matter of much importance to this Commonwealth. On few subjects is there a stronger interest or greater unanimity of sentiment among our citizens. To our manufacturers and merchants it will give the opportunity for a large extension of trade, by opening to them an important and profitable market, and an abundant supply of the raw materials necessary for our various industries. A broad measure of reciprocity with Canada would make Massachusetts, and especially Boston, the industrial and commercial centre of a greatly enlarged territory, add to our prosperity and wealth, and to the welfare of our people. While the settlement of the question is beyond your power, I believe it would be both proper and wise to express to Congress by resolution this opinion of Massachusetts upon it.

Senators and Representatives: We meet at a time of useful agitation, when more than ever the people are discussing political, industrial, and social questions with searching intelligence and fearless independence. Appreciating the importance of these matters to their welfare, and the power of government over them, the people rightly demand that as far as public authority undertakes to act, its power shall be used in their interest, and be kept under "their watch and control."

We, as their representatives, are confronted not only with old and difficult, but with new and unsolved problems. To their consideration, however our opinions may vary, I doubt not we shall bring honest conviction, patriotic purpose, and a sincere desire to promote the public welfare. Under such influences, with due regard for the needs of the present, but also for the conservative principles and practical wisdom of the past, led by the "kindly light" which the Supreme Lawgiver ever vouchsafes to his dependent children, let us step forth into this new year with hope, courage, and enthusiasm to meet the new duties and the new responsibilities.

God save the Commonwealth of Massachusetts, and keep us steadfast in her service!

MESSAGE

VETOING AN ACT RELATIVE TO PERSONS EMPLOYED IN THE FIRE DEPARTMENT OF BOSTON.

EXECUTIVE DEPARTMENT, BOSTON, March 27, 1893.

To the Honorable House of Representatives:

I RETURN herewith with my objections a bill entitled "An Act relative to Persons employed in the Fire Department of the City of Boston," which originated in your body.

This bill applies to a single executive department of a single city of the Commonwealth, and undertakes to regulate therein an important detail of administration, which is at present wholly controlled by the executive authority of said city, and so by her citizens themselves. A general law, enacting the provision of this bill as a general policy for the State, applicable to all her cities, has been defeated by this Legislature.

I fully sympathize with the desire of the Legislature to lessen the hours of labor in this department, but I do not believe in the principle that the State, even to accomplish a desirable end, should interfere with the right of local self-government by the city of Boston or by any other community, or should undertake by special law to control a department thereof, or to regulate its details.

Against such interference I have constantly protested, both by recommendation and veto, frequently declaring that the right of local self-government "should be carefully conserved," and recommending "that whenever and wherever possible this right should be left in or restored to her respective cities and towns," and that "as far as possible every local community should be left to govern itself, and to determine for itself questions of administration and public policy which affect its interests." I have earnestly urged that the control of the police, of which she has been most unjustly and unfortunately deprived, should be restored to the city of Boston. I am quite unwilling to sanction an attempt by the State to direct another of her departments, or to interfere with its control by the proper local authority. I can think of no department in which the citizens of Boston just now have a keener interest, or over which, through their chosen servants, they should have a more direct and unhampered control, than their fire department. They know its needs and its wishes, and are vitally interested in its efficiency. They appreciate, I believe, the labor, danger, and faithful service of the men in this department, and are ready to grant them such relief from constant duty as is consistent with the public interest and safety.

Of these matters they are most competent and responsible to judge. I sincerely trust that their opinion, expressed through their officials, may agree with the opinion expressed by the Legislature in this bill; but I am unwilling, by approving the bill, to say that they shall have no power to control this matter, or that a hard-and-fast rule shall be laid down for them in the administration of this department, which, if adopted, places the matter beyond their discretion and supervision.

Nor does it obviate this objection that the Act does not take effect until approved by the mayor and city council. If this leaves to them the same power they now have, then the Act is wholly unnecessary. If it does not, then it is an interference with the right of local self-government. It is clear, however, that if approved, the control of an important part of this department will not be within the discretion, as now, of the city of Boston, but will be defined by statute, which can only be changed by the Legislature. The amended charter of Boston places this department under the executive of the city, who is immediately responsible to the people, and subject to their control. Without any petition or request from him or the city council, or the department itself, but against the protest of the authorities in charge, this bill has been passed.

I regret to differ from the Legislature in this matter. The end desired commends itself to my sympathy and judgment.

The general tendency to shorten the hours of labor and improve the condition of all wage-earners has constantly received my official recommendation and approval. I shall be glad to co-operate with you in any wise measure or general policy, consistent with public interests, in this direction. But 1 believe it important also, as urged in a former message to the Legislature, "jealously to guard the right of local self-government, preserve it when possible, and restore it where necessary."

MESSAGE

VETOING THE ACT TO INCORPORATE THE TOWN OF EAST LONGMEADOW.

EXECUTIVE DEPARTMENT, BOSTON, May 5, 1893.

TO THE HONORABLE SENATE:

I HEREWITH return, with my objections, the bill entitled "An Act to incorporate the Town of East Longmeadow," which originated in your body. The bill provides for the division of one of the oldest and best of the towns of the Commonwealth, against the earnest protest of the inhabitants thereof twice formally expressed by a very large majority. Amendments to the bill providing that it shall take effect only when accepted by a majority, or even by one-third of the voters of the town, have been rejected. The evident and earnest wish of the town upon the vital question of its continued existence, in my judgment should be decisive in the absence of strong reasons justifiying its forcible division. I have carefully examined, therefore, the reasons urged for such action, the consequences which would result, and the general policy of the Commonwealth upon the subject.

I find that it is the established policy of this Commonwealth, as evidenced by its legislation for many years, to allow each community to decide for itself this question.

Usually the village seeking separate incorporation has come to the Legislature after formal application to the parent town and with its consent. While cases may arise of such injustice and hardship that it is impossible to obtain such consent, and nevertheless inexpedient to deny the application, yet the instances have been very few where the Commonwealth has been willing to overrule the expressed wish of the community interested, and to disregard this right of local self-government.

During the last fifty years, while there have been over one hundred and fifty petitions for town divisions, but five towns have been divided against their will. Forty-six have been divided with their own consent, and one hundred applications have been opposed and defeated. This very town of Longmeadow was set off from Springfield one hundred and ten years ago, with the consent and by the vote of Springfield. During the last thirty years but one town in its county has been divided, and then by vote of the parent town. This almost unbroken record of refusal by the Commonwealth to divide towns against their will makes it necessary, in my judgment, to prove strong reasons to justify such action. I do not find such reasons in this case.

It appears that the town consists of two villages some three and one-half miles apart, and quite distinct in the life and occupation of their inhabitants. But this fact is true of numerous towns; and if sufficient to justify a forcible division of a town, would lead to endless subdivision of communities into small political units, where, if not constant friction, there would be difficulty and embarrassment in proper concert of action, the more necessary as better means of communication and common public interests in schools, institutions, etc., are bringing the people closer together. The town of Falmouth, for example, consists of seven or eight different villages, many of them clearly separated by natural conditions and the life and occupation of their people. This would hardly justify the creation out of it of seven or eight towns, especially against the overwhelming protest of its people. I do not find in the case of Longmeadow any course of conduct by the majority towards the minority which constitutes a grievance and justifies a separation. There appears to have been no unfair division between the two villages of the burdens and benefits of their town government, or of their town officers, no excessive tax-rate or valuation, and no injustice in the holding of their town meetings. On the contrary, its tax-rate has been low, much below the average of the Commonwealth, and the lowest in its county. I am informed that no complaint has ever been made to the assessors, of unequal or unjust valuation, and that the petitioners have asked for no appropriation from the town which has not been granted, and have, through their counsel, admitted at the hearing a year ago that they came to the Legislature without a grievance.

Except upon the question of division, the inhabitants of the town seem to have lived happily and prosperously together for more than a hundred years.

It further appears that if this bill is enacted, among the results which follow will be, —

First, The division of a town at present below the average of the towns of the Commonwealth in population, area, polls, and voters, and below the average population of the nineteen towns of its county.

Second, The creation of a town with a population of only five hundred and seventy, and a little over one hundred voters, and without a single industry, — a town smaller than any in Bristol, Norfolk, and Essex counties, or, with six exceptions, in Plymouth, Worcester, and Middlesex counties.

Third, That there will be great inequality made by the division in the burdens of taxation and town government upon the two villages; that substantially the whole of the bank and corporation tax will go to the smaller village, and will be sufficient to pay for the care of its highways, schools, and poor; that, on the basis of past expenditure, the tax-rate of the smaller village can be reduced from $9.50 per thousand to about $4, while the tax-rate of the larger village would be increased to over $13.

The Commonwealth is asked, therefore, against the emphatic protest of this town, to interpose her superior authority, and forcibly to divide it, with no substantial grievance as the basis of such action, but with the certainty that there will result great inequality in the burdens upon the separated villages.

I believe such action is not only contrary to a sound and well-established policy of the Commonwealth, but also to a just and healthy public sentiment, which seeks to lessen rather than increase the great inequality in taxation and in the public burdens and benefits between different localities.

While the rights of a minority in any community should be carefully protected and upheld, the rights of a majority in such community are also entitled to respect. Among these is the fundamental right, if not forfeited by their own misconduct or controlled by a supreme public necessity, of preserving undivided and unimpaired their town existence, with its history and traditions, its long and honorable life.

POLITICAL SPEECHES.

SPEECH

AT MIDDLESEX COUNTY DEMOCRATIC CLUB, BOSTON,
MARCH 5, 1885.

THE time has come when it is my duty and pleasure to ask your attention to the words of wit and wisdom, of congratulation and counsel, which always flow at Democratic love-feasts to temper the digestion, but which also, by reminding us of the principles, history, and purposes of our party, strengthen our loyalty to it, and make us proud of the faith that is in us. Before I call upon those whose familiar voices are old friends to you, and to the party in its battles are the "bugle blasts" that are "worth a thousand men," will you pardon me if I inflict myself upon you.

For the honor of presiding over this club, I am deeply grateful. Kindly overlooking my many faults, you have chosen me, I presume, because you thought the honor might well be given to ripe old age spent in party service, and you knew of none older in the faith than one who was born a veteran Democrat. I only ask that the same kindness which has chosen me to this office may bear gently with me while I endeavor to discharge its duties.

As to-day our party nationally assumes power and responsibility, passing from opposition and criticism to the duty of legislation and action, it is most fitting that the Democrats of old Middlesex should meet and organize to hold up the hands of the administration. I believe that a "decent respect to the opinions of mankind" requires our party everywhere to declare what it believes to be the principles and policy that will govern its administration. It is no time for a doubting, hesitating, halting policy. There are promises to be kept, professions to be lived up to, grave questions to be met by wise and prudent statesmanship, and the living principles of Democracy to be ordained as law, — all for the honor, peace, and prosperity of a happy, united country. Speaking for the Democrats of Middlesex county, I do not believe that their idea of Democratic administration and statesmanship is to stop by the wayside to gather in the spoils, but rather to march on, under our fearless, honest President, to make a party victory the country's good. I appeal to the patriotism of our party that in 1860, under the lead of Douglass, passed from power rather than extend a National evil; that in 1876, when Tilden was elected President, gave up power rather than disturb a Nation's peace, — I appeal to that patriotism to listen to a just public sentiment that asks for an unselfish administration. I believe our party will serve the country rather than itself, and legislate for the "silent suffering many" rather than devote its whole energy to reward the eager few. There are many offices that shape and execute the policy of an administration that should be filled by its friends, many that have been used for "offensive partisanship" that should be emptied of men who have forgotten to be servants of the people. But to make the whole civil service the spoils of victory is to perpetuate an evil we have fought for years, a principle that obstructs legislation, and a practice that has developed a feudal system of political servitude. Let Massachusetts Democrats still demand, as in 1882, that "fitness, not favor, should be the passport to public service," still demand " a system of civil service established by law, protected by law, that, like government itself, it may be the agent of law, and not of men; to the end that it may be kept free of all corrupting dependence upon political favor and patronage," and again, "favor the principles" of the legislation that seeks to cure this evil by enacting into law the tests that Jefferson first stated and adopted.

Then our grand old party, filled with patriotism and unselfishness, is ready to enforce the ideal of Jefferson, — "a wise and frugal government, which shall restrain men from injuring one another, shall leave them otherwise free to regulate their own pursuits of industry and improvement, and shall not take from the mouth of labor the bread it has earned."

Let us be Bourbons in our love and devotion to Democratic principles, traditions, feelings; but ever remember that our party to-day are, in the words of Macaulay, "legislators, not antiquaries;" that it is time for us to pay a rational and manly reverence to the old founders of our party, not by superstitiously adhering to what they in other circumstances did, but by doing what they in our circumstances would do.

Gentlemen, I propose a health to President Cleveland. May God bless and prosper him, and may the Democracy stand true to him, and he to it, as with honest purpose and unflinching courage he gives to the country the blessing of a Democratic administration.

SPEECH

AT UNION MEETING OF DEMOCRATS AND INDEPENDENTS, AT MUSIC HALL, BOSTON, OCT. 25, 1886.

AS I stand here to-night, a Democrat, speaking to Democrats, and to men whose conscience party could not bind, — men who carry their sovereignty each under his own hat, — there comes vividly back to me the stirring words, Sir, with which you opened a similar meeting on the eve of the great battle of 1884, "This is a union meeting;" and, as you spoke, the minds of your hearers went back to war days, when principle was placed above party, and patriotism above partisanship.

You fought the campaign of '84 upon that basis. All the signs foretell the same crisis, the same necessity for patriotic, unselfish action in '88. It was a crisis made by the personality of the candidates, — a brave, honest, vigorous man, who had been tried and found not wanting, against a scheming, unscrupulous, and dangerous politician. The one has been further tried, and his work proves his fidelity to his principles and his pledges; the other is still actively, and, we fear, successfully scheming. It is time that the voice of this Commonwealth was heard. If she speaks in no uncertain tone, she can to-day remove this issue from the fight of '88. A Democratic victory won in Massachusetts rings the death-knell of Blaine and Blaineism, and gives to President Cleveland the God-speed he richly deserves. Aside from that issue, the campaign in Massachusetts this year is on a broader basis than the personality of the candidates. The candidates fitly represent the position and principles of their parties. I do not speak to-night so much for Andrew[1] as for what he represents. We who are Democrats heart and soul, in thought, belief, and feeling, rejoice that there are many others who, not by personal preferences only, but by political faith, are led along the pleasant paths of Democracy. Our union is not for the triumph of any man, but for the triumph of ideas; for a living faith, a progressive spirit. It is of that to-night I speak.

It has often been said that there was little difference between the two parties. Perhaps that was the criticism of honest men, whose earnest desire for honest candidates led them to look no farther. To-day every intelligent man in Massachusetts knows that there is a wide difference between the parties, — all the difference that there is between standing still and moving forward. I do not believe that this difference is accidental. It is the natural evolution of the history and purpose of the parties. A political prophet of a generation ago, who knew this history, who had studied the Democratic faith, had seen the birth of the Republican party and its purpose, could have predicted the position of the parties to-day. The Democratic party is old enough to have outlived and defeated all other parties, young enough to represent the progressive spirit of to-day. It must be founded on vital principles and have a living faith. Its creed from its first to its thirty-ninth article is an abiding trust in the people, a belief that men, irrespective of the accident of birth or fortune, have a right to a voice in the government that rules them. Its principles are the equality and freedom of all men in affairs of State and before

---

[1] The Democratic candidate for Governor.

the altar of their God, — that there should be allowed the greatest possible personal liberty, that a government least felt is the best, that it should lightly and never unnecessarily impose its burdens of taxation and restriction, that in its administration there should be simplicity, purity, and economy, and in its form it should be closely within the reach and control of the people. It preaches home rule, — home rule that objects to the strong arm of government with its troops reaching into the States to control their elections; — and the voice of Massachusetts, irrespective of party, has been heard to sustain this principle; home rule that objects to the government with its subsidies controlling education in the States, while it saps local energy and industry: a Blair educational Bill or a Blaine retail taxation and wholesale distribution measure is a violation of this principle. So, on principle, we object to State control of local police, or the refusal to allow our cities and towns to settle the liquor question each for itself. Only an overwhelming public necessity can justify a metropolitan police bill or a general prohibitory law.

These, as I understand it, are the principles and faith of my party. They are applicable to every time and to nearly every public question, — living principles, a living faith. Turn now for a moment to the history of the Republican party. It was born of a great and glorious agitation, to perform a great and glorious mission. It had no other purpose. It did its work, and it did it well. It had no other work to do. There gathered about it, as the party in power, selfish, corporate, special interests, demanding, in return for their support, legislation for their benefit. Special interests were protected, the public lands were given away, the civil service was made a Republican machine, and the people were forgotten. It became corrupt, incompetent in administration, aimless in its purpose. It drifted with its mission ended, and with no fixed principle to guide it. It tried reform within the party, and ended by driving its reformers out. Again and again it has tried to lift itself to some higher moral plane, and has succeeded only in driving away its men of conscience. No wonder to-day it is standing still, stock still, and seems dead, stone dead.

Take any question of to-day, State or National, which divides the parties, and see if the issue is not between progress and stagnation. I do not propose to-night to discuss in detail these questions, but only by them to illustrate my proposition. The great National questions to-day before the people are tariff and civil service reform, and possibly, if it be the will of the Republican party, an issue on the South. The great State questions are labor and prohibitory legislation.

Blaine and Sherman, after two severe defeats, are again marching the Republican party under the standard of the bloody shirt. The people have welcomed back the South to the Union, and our sisterhood of States is reunited in unquestioned love and loyalty; but the Republican party would live over again the war, would forget the dying words of peace and union of the great commander, the thousand acts of fraternity, charity, and love that bind the North and South together. The person or party who would, for partisan purposes, disturb that union, is taking a backward and a disloyal step. The cry of a suppression of the vote in the South is only the wail of bitter disappointment. It assumes as a fact that the negro is without independent political convictions or judgment, is bound in servitude to the Republican party, in place of the servitude from which it helped to release him. Here with us to-night is evidence enough that so many colored men do not mean so many Republican votes. The Southern question has been settled on the Democratic principle of home rule. It is time for the Republican party to accept the fact and to move on.

Take as a further illustration of my proposition, reform of the civil service. For many years both parties have known and advocated the necessity for this reform. With our one hundred thousand office-holders it has become of vital importance that the offices should be a public trust, and their occupants not an army to wage war through them on the political convictions of half the people.

The Republican party had the power to accomplish this reform. Instead, it carried on a merciless proscription. It made the great administrative offices of the country hotbeds of political activity to control the will of the people and to corrupt the public service. It established a feudal system of political bosses. Four hundred and ninety-nine of every five hundred people in this country are not and cannot be office-holders. They are interested only in having the offices faithfully, honestly, and economically administered. The country demanded this; the parties promised it. The Democratic party gave to the country Grover Cleveland as its pledge that it meant what it said. He had told the truth. He would live up to the truth if elected. He had been tried and tested, and had stood the test. He has had the courage, the will, and the honesty to enforce the policy of our party. He has redeemed our pledges with an unselfishness and a patriotism equalled only by that of our party in 1876, making the reform a reality, and lifting the many offices of the country out of the sphere of politics. He has made offensive partisanship in office a thing of the past, enforced the Democratic doctrine of fidelity, honesty, and economy in the public service, and immeasurably raised the standard of public life.

Has not Cleveland appointed Democrats to office? Of course he has, and undoubtedly will appoint more. The very stability of the reform depends upon departisanizing the civil service. Has he not made some mistakes in his appointments? Perhaps he has; but he has made a character for his administration that, like the character of an honest man, explains and redeems a mistake.

The Republican party stands criticising, ridiculing, and obstructing. Of what use is it for that party to make fair promises, if it opposes their fulfilment? The Republican party is standing still, while the greatest administrative reform of a generation is moving on.

Take reform of the tariff as another illustration. It is now 1886, and not 1861. There is now no war. A straitened treasury is changed to one overflowing with a hundred millions of surplus. There is no need of war taxation. Infant industries have become full grown and settled. There have come great wealth and grossly unequal distribution of it. Contented labor has become discontented, and justly discontented. There has arisen an earnest protest against legislation for special interests that enrich the few; a demand for legislation for the people that shall relieve the many. The tariff is taxation, — taxation pure and simple. The Democratic party, believing that a government has no right unnecessarily to impose its burdens, demands that this taxation, — which yields an enormous and unused surplus, which bears unjustly and oppressively on the poor, because it taxes men according to their needs and not their property, which, after twenty-six years of trial, finds great inequality in the distribution of wealth, and the laboring man in discontent and almost open revolt, — the Democratic party demands that this taxation shall be reconsidered, and the people relieved of some of its unnecessary burdens. The Republican party stands still, boldly advocating continued and higher taxation. It does not know that the war is over. I never knew a man whose constitution was shattered by whiskey to be benefited by more whiskey; nor do I believe that the discontent and distress of society to-day will be relieved by more taxation.

> But James G.
> Blaine he
> Sez this is his view o' the thing to a T;

and we all know that

> "The world 'll go right ef he hollers out 'gee.'"

There is no interest either of consumer, wage-earner, or manufacturer, as has well been said to-night, that will not be benefited by a reduction of taxation. How long will a patient people submit to unnecessary, unequal, and oppressive taxation?

Turn now to questions nearer home, and show me, if you can, where there is life in the Republican party. What is its position on the question of prohibition? It favors license, and has favored it for ten years; it seems to oppose the licensed places. It favors license by legislation; it seems to favor prohibition by constitution. It could enact prohibition to-day if it wished to and had the courage. It dares not take the responsibility, but postpones the question for three years. It is standing still, straddling, stretching to catch the votes on either side.

There is running through this State to-day a great labor agitation caused by discontent and suffering. The Republican party is not awake to that agitation. It never has been awake to the wants and wishes of working-men. I know there is some labor legislation in the statutes of Massachusetts, legislation suggested and supported by the Democratic party, and obtained grudgingly through the fears of the Republican party. It never has willingly given anything that was opposed, — it has no real remedy to suggest to meet this agitation. And yet, with plain hypocrisy, under the lead of the most adroit vote-catcher of a generation, the Republican party would make a pilgrimage to the working-man to persuade him that taxation taken out of him to benefit the few is the panacea for all his woes. I pity the working-man when he leaves the party of which he is the backbone, and trusts his interests to its and his opponent.

Mr. Chairman, I have spoken longer than I ought. I have preached, I trust, the faith of a progressive Democracy. Progress, merely as progress, is nothing; but progress that sees the changes of a generation, — a blessed, lasting peace in place of the horrors and burdens of civil war, a reunited, loyal country; progress that hears the demand of the people for pure and economic administration, for relief from restrictions and taxation; progress that feels the discontent and suffering of great masses of the people, — this progress, if willing and ready to shape into legislation the new wishes and the new wants, rises to the height of statesmanship.

> "New occasions teach new duties; time makes ancient good uncouth;
> They must upward still and onward who would keep abreast of truth;
> Lo, before us gleam her camp-fires! We ourselves must Pilgrims be,
> Launch our 'Mayflower,' and steer boldly through the desperate winter sea,
> Nor attempt the Future's portal with the Past's blood-rusted key."

SPEECH

AT BALTIMORE, MD., JULY 4, 1888, AS PRESIDING OFFICER OF THE CONVENTION OF THE DEMOCRATIC CLUBS OF THE UNITED STATES.

FOR the honor and privilege of addressing this gathering of Young Democracy I am deeply grateful. With earnestness and enthusiasm, with devotion to the party and its principles, and with unflinching loyalty to its glorious leaders, Young Democracy meets to-day for organization and action. Gladly it volunteers in a campaign where its very faith is at stake; impatiently it awaits the coming of the battle.

We fight for measures, not men; the principles of government, not men's characters, are to be discussed; a nation's policy, not personal ambition, is to be determined.

Thank God, we enter the fight with a living faith, founded upon principles that are just, enduring, as old as the Nation itself, yet ever young, vigorous, and progressive, because there is ever work for them to do. Our party was not founded for a single mission, which accomplished, left it drifting with no fixed star of principle to guide it. It was born and has lived to uphold great truths of government that need always to be enforced. The influence of the past speaks to us in the voice of the present. Jefferson and Jackson still lead us, not because they are glorious reminiscences, but because the philosophy of the one, the courage of the other, the Democracy of both, are potential factors in determining Democracy to-day.

Their faith and ours rests upon an abiding trust in the people, a belief that power can safely be put into their hands, and that the broader the foundation, the safer the structure of our government. We believe in the freedom and equality of all men in the affairs of state and before the altar of their God; in the freedom of the individual from unnecessary restrictions and unnecessary burdens; that taxation, with its enormous power and burdens, is not to be used to take from one to give to another, nor to enrich the few at the expense of the many; that of itself it is not a blessing which excuses and demands a wild extravagance, but a necessary evil, to be lessened by prudence and economy; that it should be levied justly, equally, according to men's means, and not their necessities; upon luxuries that endanger the home and the Republic, and not upon those comforts that make the humblest fireside more cheerful, and in its happiness and strength reflects a nation's prosperity.

We believe that a government which controls the lives, liberties, and property of a people in its administration should be honest, economical, and efficient; and in its form a local self-government kept near to the power that makes and obeys it. To safeguard the rights and liberty of the individual, the Democratic party demands home rule. Democracy stands beside the humblest citizen to protect him from oppressive government; it is the bulwark of the silent people to resist having the power and purpose of government warped by the clamorous demands of selfish interests. Its greatest good, its highest glory, is that it is, and is to be, the people's party. To it government is a power to protect and encourage men to make the most of themselves, and not something for men to make the most out of.

And, lastly, we believe in the success, the glory, and

the splendid destiny of this great Republic. It leaped into life from the hands of Democrats. More than three-quarters of a century it has been nurtured and strengthened by Democratic rule. Under Democratic administrations, in its mighty sweep, it has stretched from ocean to ocean, not as a North and South and East and West, but now as a glorious Union of thirty-eight sovereign States, reunited in love and loyalty, a great Nation of sixty million loyal subjects. And now, under the last and best of Democratic administrations, the courage, fidelity, patriotism, and democracy of Grover Cleveland are holding it true to the principles of its founders. Patriotism is a thing of action, and not of declamation; loyalty and disloyalty are not proved by a sneer.

The faith we profess is distinctly an American faith; the principles we proclaim are distinctly American principles, and have been from their first utterance in the Declaration of Independence to their latest in the platform of the St. Louis Convention; the policy they demand of us as Democrats is emphatically an American policy.

Which is the more American policy, — to welcome with fraternal love the reunion of the whole country in loyalty, happiness, and prosperity, or to stir up sectional hatred for partisan purposes? The one is patriotism, the other steps to the verge of treason.

Which is the more American policy, to follow the path of peace, and endeavor by negotiation, treaty, and arbitration to make a fair settlement of international troubles, or, in a spirit of bravado, to plunge the Nation into war?

Which is the more American policy, to hold fast to the Constitution, or to violate its spirit and its letter by supplanting the rights and duties of the States either by force of arms or gifts from the National Treasury? The one follows the teaching and policy of the past; the other launches us on a sea of doubt and danger. Which is the more American policy, to urge economy, prudence, and restraint in expenditure, or to yield to wild and wilful extravagance, devised and demanded only for the purpose of spending? To relieve the people a little of their burdens, or to set for them an example of riotous living? Neither an individual nor a nation can be a successful profligate. Better sink our surplus in the depths of the sea than raise the standard of expenditure, to exhaust in days of peace the resources needed only — but then how sorely needed! — in time of war.

Which is the more American policy, to take one hundred million dollars, not needed, not used, each year from the hard earnings of an industrious people, or to leave it with those who earn it, and who best can spend it? To use the power of taxation for the interest of the few at the expense of the many, or to restrict its use to a Nation's needs? To give millions of the people's money to a class, trusting to its charity for a just and honest redistribution, or to leave them ungathered in the people's pockets? We believe that legislation should be just, honest, equal to all, and in the interest of all, unawed and uninfluenced by selfish demands that, like prowling wolves, howl about its halls. How well the words of the French philosopher define the issue between the parties. "What is law," he says, "or, at least, what ought it to be? What is its rational and moral mission? Is it not to hold the balance even between all rights, all liberties, and all property? Is it not to cause justice to rule among all? Is it not to prevent and to repress oppression and robbery wherever they are found?" And he might have turned to the Republican party when he added: "Your system has written over the entrance of the legislative halls these words, 'Whoever acquires any influence here can obtain his share of the legalized pillage.' And what has been the result? All classes of society have become demoralized by shouting around the gates of the palace, 'Give me a share of the spoils.' What! the law is no longer the refuge of the oppressed, but the arm of the oppressor! The law is no longer a shield, but a sword. The law no longer holds in her august hands a scale, but false weights and measures. And you wish to have society well regulated!"

Which is the more American policy, to tax luxuries, which are allowed to exist only when bound hand and foot by law, or to tax the great necessities that make life happier in every home in the land?

Economy, low taxes, free wool, free lumber, free salt, free coal, cheaper necessaries of life, and raw materials that quicken industry, we believe to be the true American policy, and that the Republican policy of extravagance, high taxes, free expenditure, free tobacco, and free whiskey, is an insult to American intelligence, even when supplemented by a plank in favor of true goodness and general morality.

Which, finally, is the more American policy, to restrict the inventive genius, the marvellous industry and energy of the American people to a home market, or with free scope to let them place our Nation at the head of the markets of the world, and make her again the mistress of the sea?

Fellow-Democrats, our faith and our policy rest not in declaration, but in action; in the faithful, fearless administration of our glorious President, and in the whole life of the old Roman who stands beside him to lead us on to victory. Cleveland! What a tower of strength there is in that name! His is the firm hand that has maintained the rights and the interests of the people against selfish demands from any and from every quarter. He has defended the Constitution against those who would violate it for selfish purposes. He has upheld the honor and patriotism of the soldier against fraudulent claims made in the soldier's name. He has guarded the people's money against the wild raids of selfish schemers. He has improved and uplifted the civil service after a merciless partisan proscription for a generation, and has immeasurably raised the standard of public life. He has stood for "peace with honor" against the brag and bluster of reckless partisanship. And now, in the name of the people and in their interest, he demands relief from the burden of taxation, and as their champion enters the lists to fight the tremendous power of monopolies and trusts.

We seek not to make an "uncrowned king" the power behind the throne, nor is our talisman to victory "the heart of a dead Bruce," to be followed in childish sentiment. We do not kill our Bruce, and then expect him to lead us. "The soul of our great leader" is in no "golden casket."

He lives in the faith we profess. He speaks in the principles we assert. He leads because we follow Democracy, its faith, its principles, and its policy, and hail him as the foremost Democrat of the Nation. Thus comes victory. Thus victory means something. Thus power and responsibility go together, and the only influence behind him are the wishes, the rights, and the welfare of the great American people. In such a cause, with such a leader, there is no room for failure.

> "To doubt would be disloyalty,
> To falter would be sin."

SPEECH

AT SPRINGFIELD, MASS., JULY 26, 1888.

FOR your cordial welcome I am deeply grateful. I take it not as personal to me, but as evidence of your interest in a campaign where our faith is at stake, and as a sign of your devoted loyalty to our party, its principles, its policy, and its glorious leaders. I have come to-night, not to amuse you with jest and story, nor to argue my case with sneers and declamation, but in a sober, serious way, to discuss the great issue of this campaign, and the question that just now is agitating the whole nation, and is of practical importance to every one of its sixty million citizens. If I speak earnestly and emphatically, it is because I sincerely believe that every principle of the party to which I am proud to give my allegiance is at stake in this campaign. The party has always stood for the liberty of the individual, for his freedom from unnecessary restrictions and burdens, for the equality of all men before the law, insisting that the great power of the government should be used, not for a class interest, not for a sectional purpose, but for the interest of all, and to protect and guard the rights of the humblest citizen.

We are met by a foe that unblushingly says that the greatest power of the government, — its power of taxation, — is to be used, not to meet the necessities of government, but to take from one and give to another, and to enrich the few at the expense of the many, by placing unnecessary burdens and unnecessary restrictions upon all. For a minute let us glance at the history of the two parties, and see how they approach this question. The Democratic party has always been the people's party, founded on an implicit trust in them, and ever ready to defend them, and each of them, against any power that dares to infringe upon their rights. Under its influence, the first great war of this country, after its independence, was undertaken, to assert the right of the sailor against a foreign power that unjustly dared to impress him into its service. Under Jackson the Democratic party waged battle against a great corporation and monopoly that was undertaking to use the immense power of government for its interests against the interests of the people; and that battle, as every such battle when the people are thoroughly aroused to their own rights and interests, was successfully fought through against one of the greatest money powers that this Nation has ever seen. Under Democratic rule a second war was begun and successfully carried on against a power that dared to encroach upon the rights of this Nation; and, as a result, it added to the Nation an almost boundless territory that extended it from ocean to ocean. The Democratic party later met and successfully overcame a great political party which asserted that there was a distinction between our citizens, and that those of foreign birth were not entitled to the rights and privileges of American citizens. Still later, when corruption was stalking abroad in the land, entering the cabinet of a President, with its sinister influence controlling legislation and disgracing legislators, the Democratic party, true to its principles, exposed and fought the great scandals which arose from wealthy corporations seeking to influence the power of government to be corruptly used in their favor. The Crédit Mobilier, the Whiskey frauds, the Star Route frauds, are but instances of a reign of corruption under Republican rule that have made a blot on the history of this Nation. Later still, Democracy, under the lead of glorious old Thurman, for the first time brought the great Pacific railroad corporations to a sense of their obligations and duty to the National Government. Time and again the party has stood for the right of a State in time of peace to govern itself, and against the encroaching power of the National Government. It has resisted and forever defeated the odious rule of carpet-bag government. And last, but not least, under President Cleveland it has again stood for the rights of the people against powerful corporate interests, and restored to the Nation thousands and millions of acres of public lands, to be reserved as homesteads for the people, and not to be seized by grasping selfishness.

In this State the Democratic party has emphatically been the people's party, watchful always of the interests of the humblest citizens, ever ready to lend its mighty influence to help the wage-earners by wise and proper legislation, and finally compelling the Republican party to give to them a small measure of justice. Many a time it has fought hard, and often almost with success, for the abolition of the poll-tax as a qualification for voting, believing that a man's manhood, and no accident of birth or fortune, gave him a right to the exercise of political power. It would be strange indeed if it had not taken this position. The brawn and sinew of the party are the laboring man; and when the party acts, it is the organized action of the plain and humble citizens of this Commonwealth.

For a single minute let us look now at the history of the Republican party. It was born, I admit, for a great and glorious purpose, — to arouse this Nation and to marshal its conscience against the great evil of slavery. But when, by the united action of Democrats and Republicans, that object was accomplished, and the results of the war had been put into the Constitution and legislation, the only mission of the Republican party was ended, and it would have been well for its history if it had then quietly died. As the party in power, it soon became surrounded by selfish interests that demanded, in return for their support, its services. Steadily, year by year, for twenty years, it has been driving out of its ranks its leaders and its conscience. In 1872 Sumner and Trumbull and Greeley and many others who had made the party famous left it, disgusted with the corruption that had followed upon its yielding to selfish interests. In 1876 it was found guilty of the greatest political crime that has ever been perpetrated upon the people of our country. Soon after there began to leave it other men for conscience' sake, who organized the Prohibitory party, because they believed that the day had passed when the old Republican party could carry on any great moral agitation or accomplish any great reform.

At last, in 1884, when the Republican party had the courage of its audacity, and defied a sound public sentiment, there came another great revolt that finally, and I trust permanently, hurled it from power. Year by year, and almost day by day, it has been driving from its ranks men who had no other thought or wish than pure, honest, and unselfish government; and now, controlled by sordid influences, it is violating its promises to the people, repudiating its past platforms, eating its own words, turning its back on the past recommendations of its present leaders, and is best described, perhaps, in the language of a Republican senator from

New England, that was not meant for publication, when he said it had become the "humble servant of those people who have been gathering their millions."

I charge the Republican party in this campaign with hypocrisy, deceit, and a violation of its past promises, and out of its own mouth I believe I can convict it, and at the same time answer the scare it has endeavored to raise by the cry of free-trade. With this as their past history, the two parties approach the great question of tariff reform. Surely the natural inference would be that the people's party would, by its policy, serve the people's interests.

There are certain facts in this discussion that all concede. There is no question that the present tariff is a war tariff, instituted for war purposes, but raised, instead of lowered, when that exigency had passed. There is no question that it is much higher than any tariff this Nation had ever known before the war. There is no question that before the war industries thrived, and great industrial centres like Lowell, Lawrence, and Fall River were founded and prosperous, and that happiness and contentment reigned throughout the whole country. Why, the census shows that from the years 1850 to 1860, under almost the lowest tariff that the Nation ever had, there was an increase of 90 per cent in capital invested in industries, of 60 per cent in wages, and of 85 per cent in products; while the increase from 1870 to 1880, under almost the highest tariff, was but 32 per cent in capital, 22 per cent in wages, and 27 per cent in products. Since the war it is conceded there has been a reduction in taxation, but not in tariff taxation. Those taxes which affected especially the rich, and were paid by them, have been gradually taken off; but the taxes which affected the humble firesides and the poorer citizens have not been lessened, but, on the whole, have been increased. Internal taxes on incomes, corporations, deeds, bank checks, have been abolished, and reduction has been made in postage-stamps; while the taxes upon the necessaries of life, upon raw materials, upon clothing and the things every one must have, have gradually been increased, until, as Mr. Mills said recently in Congress, this monument of unjust discrimination has been capped by taking off the tax on playing-cards, and putting a tariff tax on bibles.

I said that out of its own mouth I would convict the Republican party of hypocrisy and deceit upon this question. I propose to show you that time and again the Republican party itself, through its recognized leaders, has advocated a reduction of the tariff greater and more radical than any reduction now suggested by the Democratic party; and I cite as my authority the last Republican President, the last two Republican Secretaries of the Treasury, the author of the present Republican platform, and the official acts and utterances of Republican conventions and Republican leaders. In 1882 President Arthur in his message to Congress said: "The present tariff system is in many respects unjust. It makes unequal distribution both of its burdens and its benefits. . . . Without entering into minute details, which under present circumstances is quite unnecessary, I recommend an enlargement of the free list so as to include within it the numerous articles which yield considerable revenue, a simplification of the complex and inconsistent schedule of duties upon certain manufactures, particularly those of cotton, iron, and steel, and a substantial reduction of the duties upon those articles and upon sugar, molasses, silk, wool, and woollen goods." Pray tell me in what respect, except in language, does the recommendation of that Republican President differ from the message of President Cleveland when he recommends that the "necessaries of life used and consumed by all the people, the duty upon which adds to the cost of living in every home, should be greatly cheapened"? And he adds: "The radical reduction of the duties imposed on raw material used in manufactures, or its free importation, is of course an important factor in any effort to reduce the price of these necessaries."

The last Republican Secretary of the Treasury, in his report of December, 1884, appreciating what all concede, said that there must be a reduction of the tariff, and he specifically recommended: "First, that the existing duties upon raw materials which are to be used in manufacture should be removed. This can be done in the interest of our foreign trade. Second, that the duties upon the articles used or consumed by those who are the least able to bear the burden of taxation should be reduced; this also can be effected without prejudice to our export trade." And he added: "The tax upon whiskey could not be repealed without a disregard of public sentiment, nor without creating a necessity for higher duties upon imported goods." In other words, he outlined exactly the main features and the policy of the Mills Bill.

Mr. Folger, Republican Secretary of the Treasury under President Arthur, in his message of 1882, demanded "that a reduction should be made in the revenue from customs." "It is believed," he says, "that the time has arrived when a reduction of duties on nearly all the articles in our tariff is demanded and is feasible. A careful revision of the tariff should be made, with a view to placing upon the free list many articles now paying a duty."

Coming now to our own State, let me cite, at the

risk of wearying you, the views of a few of the recognized Republican authorities as they existed up to a very recent date. And first, who could speak for the Republican party with more authority, with more honesty and sincerity, than Henry Wilson, loved and honored by all the people of Massachusetts? Listen to his words: "I think American labor will be best protected by taxing all the necessaries of life lightly, placing the raw materials which enter into our manufactures on the free list, raising revenue to support the government upon articles that come in competition with our manufactures, and upon the luxuries of life which are consumed by the more wealthy classes of society. . . . We want all those articles that enter as raw materials into the manufactures of the country free of duty, so that the country can stand on an equality in the markets of the world with other nations of the world."

And for more recent authority, though not so great, because their opinions seem to vary as the winds of heaven, let me cite our own Henry Cabot Lodge and John D. Long. As recently as 1884, Mr. Lodge, in addressing the Republican State Convention of that year, said: "There is a large, perilous, and increasing surplus in the revenues. It must be removed; not by needless and extravagant expenditures, not by abolishing the proper taxation of whiskey and tobacco, but by freeing entirely those great necessaries of life which enter into the daily consumption of every household, and by wise and discriminating reductions." Not abolish the proper taxation of whiskey and tobacco, Mr. Lodge? Why, your own National Convention has unanimously declared for the abolition of that tax. No needless and extravagant expenditure, Mr. Lodge? Why, your own National Convention has specifically announced ingenious schemes for just such expenditures. Free the necessaries of life, and make wise and discriminating reductions, Mr. Lodge? Why, your own Convention has emphatically turned its back upon that policy, and says that the tariff system must not be touched.

Mr. Long, the president of the Republican State Convention of 1884, said: "There are only two ways to reduce the surplus revenue, — one by raising the tariff to a prohibitory height, which nobody advocates; the other, the free list. The free list is the honest revenue reformer's hope." A prohibitory tariff nobody advocates, Mr. Long? Why, your National Convention declares in favor of raising the tariff to a prohibitory height to check imports and stop revenue. The free list the honest reformer's hope, Mr. Long? Why, your Convention denounces and derides it as free-trade, and says that the Democratic party in wishing to enlarge it is unpatriotic and un-American. That State Convention of 1884 in emphatic language insisted "upon a reduction of customs duties." Were these men honest and sincere in 1884? If so, how have they now the sublime audacity to charge us with free-trade and hostility to American interests and industries, and then to dare to appropriate the American flag as a party emblem, and to pretend that the glorious Stars and Stripes, and what they represent, are not still loved and served by all our sixty million loyal subjects? In 1884, they advocated what every intelligent man knew to be a wise and necessary policy; but now, when the necessity is increased tenfold by an enormous and constantly growing surplus, they have turned right-about-face, and their position to-day is "for politics only."

But I have not quite finished my evidence from the

Republican camp. A shrewd lawyer always saves till the last his strongest bit of testimony gathered from the other side. In 1882, under a Republican administration, the necessity for a reduction of the tariff had become so great, as was generally conceded, that President Arthur not only recommended it, but also recommended the appointment of a Tariff Commission which should, with the utmost deliberation, examine the whole subject, and report to Congress. The appointment of that Commission, suggested for the purpose of tariff reduction by a Republican President, was supported by the Republican party in Congress for the purpose of making such reduction. The Commission as chosen by him was made up almost wholly of Republicans and experts taken from and representing all the great protected industries of the country. It was the best exponent and representative of the protective system of recent times. Its chairman was one of the ablest protectionists in the country and the secretary of the Woollen Manufacturers' Association, and its other members were almost equally prominent in their special interests. For more than seven months it held almost daily sessions, visited nearly every large city of the country, hearing every interest, and collecting a mass of evidence from over six hundred witnesses that made nearly three thousand printed pages, which presented, as the Commission said, "a faithful photograph of the various economical opinions of the great business centres of the country." Surely that was a Commission that would not create free-trade. Surely that was a Commission that would have an eye, though a selfish one, to protected industries, and protected industries only. Now listen while I read a few extracts from its report to Congress, made Dec. 4, 1882. "Early in its deliberations," the report says, "the Commission became convinced that a substantial reduction of tariff duties is demanded, not by a mere indiscreet, popular clamor, but by the best conservative opinion of the country, including that which has in former times been most strenuous for the preservation of our national industrial defences. Such a reduction of the existing tariff the Commission regards not only as a due recognition of public sentiment and a measure of justice to consumers, but one conducive to the general industrial prosperity." And it adds: "Entertaining these views, the Commission has sought to present a scheme of tariff duties in which substantial reduction should be the distinguishing feature." And the reduction advocated was, "Not less on the average than twenty per cent; and it is the opinion of the Commission that the reduction will reach twenty-five per cent." And it suggests that this reduction proposed by the Commission may "benefit consumers to the extent of hundreds of millions of dollars."

Listen for a minute to some specific reductions advocated by this Commission. It says: "It has given special consideration to the tariff on steel rails. The present duty has served its purpose in a protective sense. It is now excessive, and should be reduced." The reduction advocated was from twenty-eight to about seventeen dollars. On copper, old zinc, and other metal it advocated a reduction of the tariff of from fifteen to twenty-five per cent. Prefacing its suggestion in regard to wool and woollens with the remark that "No part of the existing tariff law has been arranged with so much deliberation and care as that relating to the manufactures of wool," it says: "The Commission proposes a reduction, for the great bulk of woollen fabrics, of from eighteen to forty per cent, making it so as to apply most effectually to the cheaper goods of necessary consumption, with a view of benefiting producers as well as consumers; for reasonable prices to the consumer mean increased consumption, and of course corresponding increased stability and lucrative employment to the producers." Certainly the recommendations of that Tariff Commission, appointed by the Republican party in the interest of protected industries, are vastly more radical than the reductions advocated to-day by the Democratic party, and denounced as free-trade by partisan and unscrupulous opponents.

And what became of this Commission's report, do you think? It went into Congress, and there, in the secret deliberations of committee-rooms, selfish interests got control of legislative action, and instead of a reduction of twenty or twenty-five per cent, as advocated, they passed a measure actually increasing the then existing tariff duties.

With these facts in mind, let us now take up the issue of this campaign. Remember, if there was need of tariff reduction in 1884, there is much greater need of tariff reduction in 1888. An overflowing and a dangerous surplus demands that some remedy should be found to stop it. The position of the parties has been clearly defined, not by promises or platitudes, but by their legislative action and by the explicit declarations of their party platforms; and the two parties stand radically and absolutely opposed to each other. The Democratic party, following the lead of its brave President, who himself follows in the footsteps of President Arthur and Republican officials, leaders, and commissions, has brought forward a bill for tariff reduction which advocates, not twenty or twenty-five per cent, but an average reduction of five per cent in the tariff duties. If that is free-trade, for Heaven's sake what is protection? If that is free-trade, for Heaven's sake what was the position of the Republican party in 1882 and 1884? It is simple nonsense to speak of it as free-trade. In their sober moments the Republican leaders have laughed at the idea of describing tariff reduction as free-trade. Senator Sherman, in 1867, in Congress, when not under party pressure, said: "It is simply an absurdity to talk now about a free-trade tariff; and to talk about a protective tariff is unnecessary, because the wit of man could not possibly frame a tariff that would produce $140,000,000 in gold without amply protecting our domestic industries." To-day that tariff is producing more than $212,000,000 in gold. How closely his language comes to the language of our President when in his message he said: "The question of free-trade is absolutely irrelevant; and the persistent claim made in certain quarters that all efforts to relieve the people from unjust and unnecessary taxation are schemes of so-called free-traders is mischievous, and far removed from any consideration for the public good. The simple and plain duty which we owe the people is to reduce taxation to the necessary expenses of an economical operation of the government. . . . These things can and should be done with safety for all our industries, without danger to the opportunity for remunerative labor which our workingmen need, and with benefit to them and all our people by cheapening their means of subsistence and increasing the measure of their comfort."

But the Republicans say that the average reduction shows nothing, and that we should consider the specific features of the Mills Bill, and those features are a reduction of taxation on the necessaries of life and upon raw materials. It advocates free lumber, upon which there is now a tax of two dollars a thousand;

and who is benefited by that reduction? Every one who builds a house, every one who leases or occupies a lodging,— and that includes every person in the whole Union; every industry in the land that uses lumber in its finished product, that has to build its factory, all benefit by this reduction of the tariff. And who, pray, is injured by it? Why, the Algers and those men who have made their millions, gathered by taxation from you and me and every living soul who has in any form to use a bit of lumber. Where lie the interests of the people on that question? There is and can be but one answer. And when the Democratic party demands that that tax be removed, it is true to the people's interests, and it is urging a measure for their benefit.

The Mills Bill provides for free salt. Who is benefited by that provision? First, every consumer in the country; second, every industry in the country that uses salt, — the great meat-packing establishments, the fish-packing establishments, and many others that could be mentioned.

The Mills Bill advocates free wool. Is that for the interest of the people? It means cheaper clothing to every man, woman, and child in the country. It means more than that, — the strengthening, developing, and enlarging of the great woollen industries of the country. That provision, too, is a benefit not only to consumers, but a vast benefit to the industrial interests of the country. What better evidence of this could be found than that honest, straightforward letter of Mr. Lyman, who represents one of the largest industries in the Nation, a Republican who frankly admits that free wool must help the woollen industries, and because of that he denounces and repudiates the Republican party and its platform. Take as an illustration of the benefit that will come to the industries of the country from free wool the result that followed from free hides. I quote, as evidence on this point, from a most unfriendly source. You all know that the "Boston Daily Advertiser" and the "Evening Record" have for weeks and months been scouring around amongst the manufacturers, exciting alarm and endeavoring to scare the people into a belief that industries were to be injured by the policy of the Democratic party. And day by day these papers print interviews with this and that man who is willing to lend his aid to this scheme. On June 21 the "Advertiser" published an interview with a well-known leather dealer who tries to believe that free hides have not been a benefit to his industry; but in that interview he says three things: That wages in it have increased, that prices have diminished, and that at least twenty-five per cent of the leather made in this country is now exported; and adds, in answer to the question if there have been many failures in his business, "No; I have heard of but few failures." That is to say, the results that have followed from free hides, upon the admission of this unfriendly critic, have been higher wages, lower prices, and a large foreign trade. And this is exactly what will also follow to the woollen industries and to other industries if their raw material is given them free, as advocated by the Democratic party. It is impossible that it should not be so. With cheaper raw material, the finished product is cheaper; its cheaper price makes greater demand; the greater demand makes more work and higher wages, and brings that product into the markets of the world. Instead of curbing and restricting our industries to a home market, we advocate a policy that will give to them almost a boundless market, with increased work and increased wages.

The Mills Bill provides for free copper. Let me take

a minute of your time to explain that tax. That tax of two cents a pound was imposed for the benefit of a very few owners of rich copper mines. And what has been its effect? That every man who in his manufactory or in his house is obliged to use a pound of copper, pays nearly two cents a pound more for it because of that tax. Why, that tax has done much to restrict and destroy a great industry along the seacoast in repairing and making vessels. Hundreds of shipwrights and caulkers by it have been thrown out of employment, because the owners of vessels can take them abroad and recopper and repair them there cheaper than by doing it here and paying the higher price for copper. Meanwhile, the copper owners send millions of pounds of our own copper abroad, and sell it cheaper in England than they do to our own people, still making a profit by selling it there even without the additional tax of two cents a pound that we have to pay. Is there any question in your mind that the great bulk of the American people, almost to a man, are to be benefited by the removal of that tax, and that it is time that the wealthy owners of Calumet and Hecla, who sell their ores abroad without the tax and make a profit, should give the American people an equal chance with their buyers in foreign countries?

The Mills Bill provides for free flax. And who is benefited by that? Every industry that uses flax in its manufactured product, and every consumer in the land. Again I quote from an unfriendly source as authority for this statement. The "Evening Record" of July 16, 1888, printed a letter from J. R. Leeson & Co., the agents for the owners of the large flax-mills of North Grafton, Mass., and who also own flax-mills in Scotland. In that letter they state the disadvantages their industry here is under, as compared with their industry in Scotland. And what are those disadvantages? First, the duty that is now placed upon flax. And in that letter they say, "We would earnestly urge that our raw material be given to us free from all duty." And of the five disadvantages which they specifically enumerate that they are under, four will be relieved by the provisions of the Mills Bill.

I might go further into the provisions of this Bill if I did not feel that I had already exhausted your patience. Let me say briefly that on the great necessaries of life, like sugar and rice and others, the Bill makes a reduction of twenty or more per cent; and all the way through its provisions, its governing policy and idea have been, while making but an average reduction of five per cent in the tariff, — from forty-seven to forty-two per cent, — to make that reduction so as to cheapen what every man uses and needs, and to build up and develop the industries of this country. That is the Democratic programme; not as extreme, by any means, as the Republicans have heretofore advocated and now abandoned, but all of it wholly and solely in the interest of the people, and particularly in the interest of the wage-earners. In the light of these facts I have a right to say that the Democratic party is the party that to-day really advocates the advancement of American industries, not by throttling them, but by enlarging them, cheapening what they require, and opening vastly wider fields for them to enter.

A few words about the Republican position, and I have finished. In every vote of that party in Congress it has opposed free raw materials, and in almost every vote a reduction of taxation on the necessaries of life. I take, however, its programme from the official announcement of it in the Chicago platform. First, it advocates lavish expenditures, and proposes schemes to use up the surplus that are suggested and devised only for the purpose of spending it. It advocates forts and fortifications that may be useless and out of date before they are half finished. We believe, as has been said, that the defence of this Nation does not rest so much in millions and millions spent upon fortifications, as upon the three thousand miles of ocean before us, and the sixty million sturdy men and women behind, ready always successfully to resist any encroachment on our territory. There is not a nation that lives that dares to put a hostile foot upon our shores. Our opponents, however, feeling a little mistrust of their ability to use up the surplus, have undertaken to provide a plan to stop its accumulation; and that plan is free tobacco and free whiskey, and raising the tariff taxes to a prohibitory height, which innocent Mr. Long thought that "nobody advocated." I have shown you how contrary to its own past professions that programme of the Republican party is. I have quoted from Mr. Long and Mr. Lodge how bitterly they were opposed to that programme in 1884; and I would ask you, if those gentlemen happen to stray this way during this campaign, to put to them the question why it is there has come this change in their opinions.

Two other authorities let me cite from the Republican party to show the past and present opinion of that party upon its present policy. "These taxes" (the tobacco and whiskey taxes) said Mr. Sherman in 1882 in the Senate of the United States, "ought to be left as a part of our permanent system of taxation as long as any other taxes, internal or external, more oppressive remain on the statute book. This tobacco tax, of all others, is the easiest collected, the most certain, . . . and a tax which, by the judgment of all nations, is the best source of all taxation." And Mr.

Blaine, in his famous Paris message, said of the whiskey tax that it had been a powerful agent in the temperance reform; that to cheapen the price of whiskey is to increase its consumption enormously; that there would be no sense in urging the reform wrought by high license in many States if the National Government neutralizes the good effect by putting whiskey within the reach of every one at twenty cents a gallon; and finally he covers the whole question when he says that the removal of the whiskey tax would destroy high license at once in all the States. Not only that, but by removing government supervision over this production, it places the whiskey distillery by the side of your church and your school-house, and does this rather than cheapen for the people the great necessaries of life. The policy of the Republican party means, first, keeping the present burdens of over-taxation on sixty million consumers; second, restricting and crippling industries by failure to give them free raw material; third, raising tariff taxation to a prohibitory height in many instances; fourth, wild and wilful extravagance; fifth, free tobacco and free whiskey and the destruction of a powerful agent in temperance reform; sixth, the absolute abandonment of the prior declared policy of the Republican party. And who is benefited by this programme? A few already enormously enriched by the taxation of the whole people.

Is it not true that the Democratic party on this issue steps forth again as the party of the people, defending the people's interests, and that, as Jackson in his struggle for the people against a selfish monopoly swore by the Eternal that the people's will and the people's interests should be followed, so we, following in his footsteps, professing his faith, should also swear by the Eternal that the people should have the right of governing themselves, that their interests should rule, and that they who pay the taxes, and not the selfish few who gain by the taxes, should determine what the taxation should be, and that the money so raised should not be squandered by wild extravagance? Will you trust the Democratic party in this reform, or will you give your allegiance to the party which has become "the humble servant of these people who have been gathering their millions"?

When that quiet, brave, patriotic man, who faithfully and conscientiously has been administering the affairs of the government for the people against the selfish demands of clamorous interests, leads us in this battle, is he not leading us in the pleasant paths of Democracy, fighting as the people's champion, and making this in fact a government of the people, by the people, and for the people. God grant him strength in this fight, God grant that when the battle has been waged and the victory earned, there may be found no Democrat who has been faithless in the cause.

SPEECH

AT TREMONT TEMPLE, BOSTON, ON THE TARIFF, OCT. 27, 1888.

THIS greeting comes, I believe, from the heart. It is answered from the heart, not as a personal tribute, but as proof that we stand together to-day fighting the people's cause, serving the people's interest, loyal every one of us to a glorious President in his effort to lift a little the burden of unnecessary, unequal, and unjust taxation. I say unnecessary taxation. It has rolled up in the treasury vaults more than one hundred millions of idle dollars taken from trade, from business, from wages, lying there as a constant temptation to jobbery and corruption. Unequal taxation: it bears most heavily on the poor. It taxes consumption, not wealth; it taxes men, not according to their property, but according to their necessities. Unjust taxation: because it seeks to warp the power of government for the benefit of the few against the interests of all the people, — to build up the fortunes of the few, and then trust to their charity for a just and equal distribution. I know that this is neither the time nor the place for a long discussion of the tariff question. This is the time, and this is the place, to state what the issue is, and to expose the false issues of this campaign. Democracy takes its stand upon the issue of relieving the people from taxation. It maintains that the tariff is a tax that raises the cost of articles taxed, whether they come here or are produced here; and it cites for its evidence the confession of the protected industries in 1882, which then, through their Tariff Commission, admitted that the reduction of thirty-five million dollars of tariff duties would benefit consumers by hundreds of millions of dollars. Tell me the tariff does not raise prices. Let my Republican friends answer that confession of the protected industries. But to-day the Republican party boldly avows that it will uphold this high tariff, not to raise revenue, but for the declared purpose of raising prices. If it raises prices, then it raises the cost of living, then it enters every home, reducing its comforts, making less bright the humble fireside. That is the burden of high-tariff taxation. Show me an equal benefit, and I will consent to bear the burden. Where is the benefit that compensates for that burden placed on the people of the country? They say it benefits industries. My friends, I maintain, and have maintained on every stump in this State, that much of this high-tariff taxation stands as an actual burden on industries; and just where its burden is, the Mills Bill and the Democratic party propose to relieve it. Follow me for a moment in my pilgrimage through the State. I went to the little town of Bridgewater, and what did I find there? The Bridgewater iron works with their fires out, their industry killed. How? By a high-tariff tax on its pig iron and its coal; and hundreds of men out of employment in that little town can testify to the crushing effect of high-tariff taxation. I went to the little town of Sandwich, and what did I find? Its glass industries, thriving under a low tariff, declining under a high tariff, dead, to-day. Why? Because of high-tariff taxation on coal and on the raw material that enters into glass-making. I went to Gloucester, and what could I show to those fishermen of Gloucester? That high-tariff taxation had diminished the foreign shipping of this Nation from two million five hundred thousand to less than one million of tonnage since 1860. It is dying. Why? Because of the burden, the restrictive burden, of high-tariff legislation. Then I went to Fitchburg, to the iron industry, and what could I show there? One-third of the rolling-mills of Massachusetts killed since 1880, — in seven years dead; half of the rolling-mills of New England killed; the product of Massachusetts reduced from over one hundred thousand tons to less than fifty thousand, and now about one-fifth of what we once produced. What is the reason? High-tariff legislation. Their life has been taken by law to satisfy the State of Pennsylvania. And who has been benefited? Labor in Pennsylvania? There is not a State in the Union, there are no industries in the Union, where labor is more down-trodden and depressed, where wages are lower and men more often out of employment, than in the highly protected industries of the State of Pennsylvania. Then I spoke to the farmers of Greenfield, and what could I say to them? That their farms had been declining in value, that the products of their farming had been declining, that the value of their live stock had been declining, that their churches were becoming dependent, and the population of their towns being sapped, and all within twenty years. Why? Because they cannot compete with the great West while they struggle under this burden of high-tariff protection, with the cost of living increased by such protection. I went to Clinton, where there are woollen industries and carpet-mills, and what could I show there? That those carpet industries are burdened by a tariff tax on their raw materials, and that with the production of twenty-two million dollars worth of carpets in this country we export only ten thousand dollars worth. I went to Lowell, to Lawrence, to Fall River, to the great cotton cities, and what could I show there? That the cotton industries were sending abroad fifteen million dollars worth of goods, competing in open market with the labor of the world, but that the woollen industries were scarcely sending a pound of their product abroad. They never can till government lifts its hand and gives them the same chance that the cotton and the silk and other industries have. I went to the shoe cities, to Lynn, Marlborough, North Adams, and what could I show there? That the Republican party in 1872 made the raw material of that industry free, that no man called this free-trade, and that the export of their products rose from five hundred thousand dollars to more than ten million dollars, giving work and giving wages to our own employees. My friends, have I shown enough without taking you further in my pilgrimage to convince you of some of the evil effects which rise from high-tariff taxation? There are two burdens: first, upon the whole people in raising the cost of living; second, upon the industries of the land in taxing their raw material. And right here comes the Mills Bill, and has for its fundamental principles relief where we are in distress, cheaper cost of living, and free raw materials for the benefit of New England and of all our industries. Does the Republican party in this campaign meet the issue of that bill, or discuss the question I have touched upon? Does any Republican from any stump in Massachusetts argue whether it is wise, in reducing this surplus, also to reduce the cost of living? Does any Republican argue whether it is well for the industries of Massachusetts to have their raw material free? If he does, I have not yet seen his speech in print. My friends, they cannot meet us on those issues, and in their desperation, because they cannot, they have raised these false cries and false alarms. They cry "free-trade," and there rises up to confront them their broken promises, their unredeemed pledges, and their past record that, like Banquo's ghost, "will not down." Did not their last President advocate enlarging the free list and reducing the tariff on wool, woollen goods, iron, sugar, and molasses? Did not their last Secretary of the Treasury outline exactly the Mills Bill when he demanded that raw material should be free for our industries, and that the cost of living should be reduced by taking off some of the taxation on the necessaries of life? Did not the State Convention here in 1884 insist — that was their word — upon tariff reduction, and did not Mr. Lodge advocate in that Convention, as its mouthpiece, the freeing entirely of the necessaries of life, and the making of wise and discriminating reductions? Did not Mr. Long in that same Convention advocate enlarging the free list, and was he not pointed to as an "honest revenue reformer"? My friends, against the new Lodge and the new Long we place the old Lodge and the old Long. And we are not prepared to accept their excuses for their change of conviction. It is a poor excuse for Mr. Lodge to put his early sin, if it is a sin, on the back of his old Alma Mater thirteen years after he goes out from under her influence. It is a poor excuse for Mr. Long to protest that he has always been in favor of the protective system, when we, who advocate what he advocated in 1884, are denounced as free-traders and under British and Southern influence. My friends, the only British influence that has come into this campaign has been the forged, spurious extracts from English newspapers, known to be forged and spurious, and denounced as forgeries, yet still circulating with the sanction of the Republican party and of that group of gentlemen called the Home Market Club. Then there was the paid imported Englishman hired by the Republican party to instruct us in our political duties. They cry "Southern influence;" but when you test that by the main feature of our bill, that cry, too, is dissipated. Free wool is the main, the pivotal point of the Mills Bill. Who is injured, if any one, by that provision? Why, the State of Texas has three times as many sheep as all New England, and if any one is hurt, it is the constituents of Mr. Mills, and I think he deserves some credit for risking his political future, — if there is harm in the measure, — in order to give New England the benefit of free wool. Then there is the tax on sugar. They say we do not cut it deep enough because Louisiana is interested, and that is a Democratic and Southern State. Who fought the reduction of the tax on sugar in the House of Representatives, where there was the only live discussion and the only live bill that have come into this fight? Why, but thirty-seven Republicans — less than one fourth of their party — could be found to advocate a reduction in the tax on sugar. Who previously protested against it? The protest came from the Republican State of Kansas, and to-day Republican senators from that State are outspoken in their opposition to any reduction of the tax on sugar. My friends, so much for the false issues raised by their declarations. Three Republican senators have produced a still-born bill that never was meant to have life, and that bill they did not dare even to bring to a vote in the Senate. And what is the bill? The people have made two demands: first, for cheaper cost of living; second, for free raw material. And how does the Republican bill answer both demands? Outside of the reduction of sugar, eight million dollars taken off the tariff revenue, and seven-eighths of it comes by raising still higher tariff duties. They stop the surplus by burdening still more the people with taxation. And then comes their free list. And what a free list! Acorns and bristles,— to fatten and to save our hogs. Free tobacco and alcohol for the arts, — for the arts, mind you, of ruining men, and of bringing misery into many happy homes. I have said it was for the arts. If you ever get any of it, remember that you are to use it only for the arts, and do not make the mistake Mark Twain says he made; do not fall into his confusion, when he said, "I am an absolute teetotaller, but I must confess that a little whiskey for mechanical purposes tastes good."

My friends, I have spoken longer than I intended. This word let me say in closing. The issue is one of tax reduction; but that issue is founded on a principle broader than any principle of taxation: it is the principle of equality under the law. Other nations have had a contest something like ours. A hundred years ago almost to a day there came a great uprising of the people in France. For what? For equality under the law. They had been down-trodden and oppressed by the misuse of power that put its burdens on the many in order to give privileges to the few. I know that state of things was worse, vastly worse, than anything we have. But the same principle was there as here; and the people in their desperation rose in their might and swept away all laws, that they might have equality. Forty years ago and more there came a movement in England much like the movement here, but going further than we intend to go. What was it? It was of a people suffering from taxation on their food, their necessaries of life, their industries, on the raw material that entered into those industries. There came a great uprising of that people. It was the masses against the few; it was the people against the landlords; and there sprang forward to lead that movement such men as Cobden, Bright, O'Connell, and Peel. And when they had broken down those barriers, England stepped forward with new life. Her wealth and commerce grew as they had never grown before. Her population increased, and wages rose higher by fifty per cent. Convictions for crime diminished, and pauperism decreased. In closing the debate on the repeal of those laws, Sir Robert Peel uttered these memorable words: "I shall leave a name execrated by every monopolist who clamors for protection, because it conduces to his own individual benefit; but it may be that I shall leave a name sometimes remembered with expressions of good-will in the abodes of those whose lot it is to labor and to earn their bread by the sweat of their brow, when they shall recruit their exhausted strength with abundant and untaxed food, the sweeter because it is no longer leavened with a measure of injustice."

So might our glorious President say: "I, too, shall leave a name execrated by the monopolist who has gathered his millions in taxation of a whole people; execrated by every combination, monopoly, and trust in this land which is to-day contributing from its funds to control the government for its selfish purposes. But it may be I shall 'leave a name sometimes remembered with expressions of good-will in the abodes of those whose lot it is to labor, when they shall eat their abundant and untaxed food, the sweeter because it is no longer leavened with a measure of injustice.'"

SPEECH

AT THE YOUNG MEN'S DEMOCRATIC CLUB DINNER, BOSTON, DEC. 17, 1888, UPON THE LESSONS OF DEFEAT.

THE kindness of your introduction, Mr. President, is much more flattering than any service of mine has deserved. Your cordial welcome, gentlemen, is most generous to one who has not borne your banner to the victory it richly merited. But as I know this club was not organized for a single campaign, nor to fight a single battle, I am not surprised to find that your earnestness and enthusiasm are not dependent on the accident of victory or defeat. It was organized to declare, follow, and fight for the living faith of a great party; to love, honor, and cherish this bride of our choice, for better, for worse, in sickness and in health, until death, not defeat, us do part. So to-night we meet disappointed but not discouraged, defeated but not dead, to renew our loyalty to our party, to raise again its banner, and to write upon it the familiar principles of our faith, which we believe appeal to the conscience, patriotism, and unselfishness of a just and liberty-loving people. Our constitution requires that from time to time the club shall make a declaration of its principles upon pending issues. Most fitly to-day, in the soberness of defeat, it has made such a declaration as a creed under which we may rally with renewed vigor. Wisely it has written it so clear and definite that "he who runs may read." There is neither strength nor wisdom in hiding our belief under general phrases, nor in hesitating aggressively to uphold it. Again, and more emphatically, we demand a reform and reduction of the tariff on the lines marked out by our brave and glorious President. Behind our demand for free raw material stand languishing some industries of New England. A foreign shipping dead, a glass industry dead, an iron industry dying, a woollen industry stagnant, that, if unburdened, is ready and able vastly to extend its market, necessitate this demand; and the growth and prosperity of our cotton, silk, shoe, and leather industries, which are not so burdened, emphasize this necessity. If anything was proved in the last election, it was that the industrial centres of Massachusetts and New England favor such tariff reduction. For one, I believe that the life of some New England industries is now gradually being taken by law, and the aid they need of the government is that it should lift a little the heavy hand it lays upon them.

We demand reduction of taxation upon the necessaries of life, whose cost has been raised by this unjust discrimination of the law. And this we demand, not only as a great boon to the whole people in giving them cheaper clothing, food, and shelter, but as a simple measure of justice to those who have been taught to believe in the equality of the law, to obey and respect it as the people's mandate for the people's good, and not as the law of money makers, enacted solely for their money making.

If these demands were just and Democratic before election, they are made doubly so now by what seems to be the plan of our opponents. In every lull of clamor for office we hear the distant mutterings that portend a storm of unjust, extravagant, and burdensome legislation. Bounties, high taxation, and extravagant appropriations seem to be the only answer given to a conservative demand for free raw material and cheaper necessaries of life. At its recent meeting in New York the National Fishery Association, a stanch supporter of the Republican party, and so expecting its consideration, demands a bounty for its interest, and that fish now free be taxed, and fish now taxed be still higher taxed. They demand a gift from the people's taxes, while they raise the cost of the people's food. A Congressman-elect from this State insists that another share of the people's taxes shall be given to the shipping interests. Mr. Jarratt is urging in Washington a still higher tax on tin plates for the benefit of some possible industry that does not yet exist, and with a certainty that such legislation will burden many an existing industry, and raise the cost of living in every home in the land. Meanwhile, the Senate is seriously considering a tariff bill to raise by higher duties the cost of wool, clothing, hardware, glass, and many articles of universal use, as the best remedy for an overflowing treasury, and Congress is urged to make enormous appropriations of doubtful constitutionality and of certain inexpediency.

This club strongly protests against such legislation as unjust and un-Democratic in principle, and demoralizing in its results. We do not believe that a special industry should be allowed to stretch its hand into the treasury of the United States, or that this offence is excused by allowing others or all the same privilege. The people are watching with some anxiety and fear to see if it is possible that the guiding principles of the new administration are to be the pernicious doctrine that "to the victors belong the spoils," and the more pernicious doctrine, to campaign contributors belong the people's taxes. Both principles this club denounces.

In matters of State legislation also we have clearly defined our position. We believe there has been a steady drift away from the principle of local self-government, — too much government by State commissions, and too strong a tendency to manage cities from the State House, instead of from their own city halls.

We advocate home rule, not merely as a sentiment, but as a controlling power, and think there is virtue yet in the principle of the old town meeting. We would give to the individual the largest liberty consistent with the public welfare, and to every locality the right to control its affairs.

I am glad that our club has stated its position on a question that is not and never can be a party question, but one which of late has excited much interest and much unfair and violent discussion. I know I express your sentiment, and that of the whole Democratic party, when I declare our firm devotion to the public schools as one of the grandest, most useful, and most Democratic institutions of this old Commonwealth. They have been and are her special pride and glory. In these days, when there seems to be an evil tendency to break society into classes, to separate the rich and the poor, our public schools stand as a bulwark against such tendency. Open and free to all, they are constantly preaching the equality of all, and allowing the life of each one to blend with the lives of others. The best and most useful lesson that they teach is this lesson of Democracy, which may well be learned by every child. The Democratic party, in its professions and its practice, is a firm friend of the public-school system, and insists that that system must and shall be maintained. Thoughtful men may well consider whether he is not the real enemy of the public schools who breathes into the community a spirit of intolerance and proscription.

I have spoken, Mr. President, only of the present and the future. I believe there is no profit in mourning over the past. Bitterly disappointed, the Democratic party has accepted its defeat in a manly and patient spirit, following the example of its noble President, yet firm in its belief that the great reform it demands is not defeated, but opens now to us a field of splendid and useful activity. For a time we stand as critics to judge the new administration in a spirit of fairness and consideration, ready to accept and support all measures that accord with our belief.

Let us take, to encourage and strengthen us for the battles yet before us, the old inscription in the little chapel in the Tyrol, which to our greatest poet seemed in his hour of sorrow to be the footprint of an angel: "Look not mournfully into the past: it comes not back again. Wisely improve the present: it is thine. Go forth to meet the shadowy future without fear and with a manly heart." The past of disappointment and defeat I believe comes not back again. The present of glorious agitation in a just cause is ours; and if, in that cause, without fear we go forth to meet the future, it can have in store nothing but triumphant victory.

One phase only of our defeat seems to be irreparable, — the defeat of a brave, patriotic President, who knew his duty and dared to do it. It is his country's loss, not his. The high standard he set of official life entitled him to her confidence and support. Because his administration was not ever seeking votes, but the people's welfare, majorities unsought should have risen to uphold him. His faithful devotion to duty, his conscientious watchfulness, his manly bearing when stung by an unjust defeat, I confess have made of me something of a hero-worshipper. For one, I find it pleasant to apply to him those grand lines sent by Sir

Henry Taylor to Mr. Gladstone in 1874 in his hour of defeat: —

> "What makes a hero? An heroic mind
> Expressed in action, in endurance proved;
> And if there be pre-eminence of right
> Derived from pain well suffered, to the height
> Of rank heroic, 't is to bear unmoved,
> Not toil by day scarce known to human kind,
> Not watch by night when Fate is on the wind,
> But worse, — ingratitude, and poisonous darts
> Launched by the country he had served and loved.
> This, with a free, unclouded spirit pure,
> This, in the strength of silence to endure,
> A dignity to noble deeds imparts
> Beyond the gauds and pageants of renown;
> This is the hero's compliment and crown."

I propose a health to President Cleveland, — a brave, able, upright, and patriotic President. The people's cause he championed still lives; the saddest lesson of his defeat is that taught to his successors, — that it may be impolitic for a President to dare to do his full duty.

SPEECH

AT THE DEMOCRATIC CONVENTION, WORCESTER, OCT. 2, 1889, ON THE RECORD OF THE REPUBLICAN PARTY.

Mr. Chairman and Fellow-Democrats:

I FULLY appreciate the high honor tendered me by the Democracy of this State in the action of its Convention. I also appreciate the grave responsibility that comes with it. Unsolicited, you have placed in my hands the glorious standard of the party, have granted me the privilege of aggressively fighting its battle, and of rallying to its support all who believe with us in the principles that standard represents. The struggle must be no holiday pastime, but an honest, earnest, united effort to lift this old Commonwealth out of the rut in which it labors, to truer principles of government, to purer purposes in its administration. In these days of selfish, partisan abuse of power; of unjust and unequal laws; of reckless, extravagant, and irresponsible administration; of timidity, hypocrisy, and self-seeking that lower and degrade public life, — we confidently appeal to the people to turn from Republican misrule to our faith as the sign and the hope of progress and reform.

This is the proper place, not to discuss the issues of the campaign, but to state the principles of our faith. Starting with a firm, implicit belief in the people, in their integrity, intelligence, and patriotism, the Democratic faith demands that political power be given them, not as a privilege, but as a right; it asserts that their manhood, not the poll-tax, entitles them to a voice in the government which rules them. It declares the equality of all men in the affairs of State and before the altar of their God, and demands "equal and exact justice to all, of whatever State or persuasion, religious or political." It demands the freedom of the individual from unnecessary burdens and restrictions; that taxation, the greatest burden and power of government, shall not be used to enrich the few and oppress the many, but in its purpose be limited to the support of government for the benefit of all, rather than be made a gigantic instrument for distributing favors or paying political debts. Democracy stands beside the humblest individual to protect him from oppression, and to encourage him to make the most of himself. It would make him a partner in, not a dependent upon, government. That power which controls the lives, liberty, and property of the people our faith insists shall be kept closely within their reach. It therefore demands home rule, — the right of each community to govern itself, without interference in its local affairs by a power above and beyond it. In the administration of the people's government as a public trust Democracy demands honesty, efficiency, economy, and unselfishness.

This faith rests not on promise, but on service well and faithfully rendered. Much of the glorious history of our country rests on Democratic enforcement of these Democratic principles for nearly fifty years. More recently, under a wise, brave, and honest President, the people have felt the blessing of these principles vigorously and unselfishly administered. Seven months of Republican rule have but cast the shadow that brings into bright relief the virtues of the past administration. Cleveland and Harrison! They fitly represent the principles and purposes of their respective parties. Between them there is a difference as great as between courage and timidity, patriotism and policy, progress and stagnation, the living principles of a living party, and the lifeless faith of a party that dwells only in the past; between a people's President who fights for the people's cause, who serves them and them only, and a party President who hears the voice only of the politicians.

We charge the Republican party in State and Nation with repeated, constant, and deliberate violation of these principles, that are cardinal to our faith, and at the very foundation of Republican institutions.

It has debauched the public service in violation of its pledges and the plighted word of its President for partisan purposes, regardless of the capacity, fidelity, and honesty of the public servants it has brutally dismissed. To it reform of the civil service has become a byword and a jest.

It has surrendered its power in imperial States to irresponsible and discredited party bosses, to be used for politics only, and has tainted the administration of public affairs with the scandal of nepotism and jobbery.

It has repeatedly disregarded the right of local self-government in order to foist Republican rule upon Democratic communities, and now it demands national control of elections, coupled with the assuring declaration of one of its leaders that he has no objection to the presence of United States troops at the polls of a free and self-governing people! Faneuil Hall but a few years ago uttered its indignant and non-partisan protest against that principle applied to Louisiana. Faneuil Hall will be heard also against its application to the Commonwealth of Massachusetts.

It has maintained unjust and unnecessary burdens of taxation upon the people to enrich the few and to pay its political debts. It has substituted treasury made law for the will of the people by Congress declared.

It has left unheeded the demand to lift taxation, to cheapen a little the food, clothing, and shelter of the whole people, and to give our industries a chance to live; but has declared its purpose of increasing and extending this burden. No wonder that its own Governor in this Commonwealth breaks through all party allegiance and places himself with us on the side of the people and reform; or that languishing industries of Massachusetts cry out in distress that they be no longer throttled to satisfy the demand of Ohio and Pennsylvania. Our suffering woollen industry, our foreign commerce swept from the seas, and the unlighted fires of our glass and iron furnaces utter their emphatic and indignant protest against the Republican abuse of the power of taxation.

It has administered with reckless partiality a great department of government for the purpose of getting votes, rather than fairly, justly to all the veterans, and to uphold the pension list as "a roll of honor," and has made its scapegoat the man who did its will.

In State affairs we charge the Republican party with a thorough mistrust of the people, and with maintaining itself in power by taxing the right to vote.

It has violated the fundamental right of home-rule, and established State-House control of municipal government.

It has steadily increased the expenditures, taxes, commissions, burdens, and restrictions of the State, and been more anxious to raise salaries than to lower taxes, to increase the offices than to lessen the burdens on the people.

It has shown timidity, irresolution, and hypocrisy in dealing with the leading questions of the State. It has resolved to repeal the poll-tax one year, and defeated its own resolution the next. It has passed a prohibitory law, and repealed it; voted for and against constitutional prohibition; turned the question out of the Legislature to the people, and then back from the people to the Legislature. It has made a foot-ball of important matters, kicking them from year to year, or between the two branches of the Legislature it overwhelmingly controls.

It has not listened to the demands of labor for just and beneficent legislation, or only listened when compelled to by Democratic importunity.

It has used its power for partisan purposes in redistricting the State, so as to make its popular majority overwhelming in the legislative and congressional districts.

It has allowed an irresponsible third body to exist, that stands between the people and their Legislature, controlling legislation against the people's interests. It has defeated a law to limit the power of this body and give publicity to its acts.

It has not heeded the demand for purer, freer elections, uncontrolled by the corrupt use of money, but has defeated a law that would stop this vital evil by compelling the publication of campaign expenses.

Gentlemen, the issue this year is not between candidates, but between the principles and purposes of the two great parties in this State. The standard you have placed in my hands bears upon it, I believe, the principles I have stated. I know that you will declare those principles clearly, honestly, bravely. The people are in no mood to be satisfied with a platform built to mean anything or nothing, to hide rather than to declare a party's policy. "Party honesty is party expediency."

Grateful to you for the confidence you have placed in me, I accept the nomination you have tendered me.

I do not know whether I shall carry your standard to victory or defeat. The decision of that question rests with the people of this Commonwealth. But this much I can promise: it shall never be lowered, and shall be returned to you without a stain upon its folds. In such a cause "not failure, but low aim is crime."

SPEECH

AT THE BAY STATE CLUB DINNER, BOSTON, OCT. 12, 1889, UPON A COMPARISON OF THE DEMOCRATIC AND REPUBLICAN PLATFORMS.

FOR a second time it affords me great pleasure to acknowledge the generous hospitality of the Bay State Club, and through it to express my thanks to the Democratic party of this State for its confidence in me and in my Democracy in choosing me again to lead its campaign.

I recognize the fact that here at this board I sit in the presence of tried and trusted leaders of the party, who have led it gallantly in sunshine and darkness, who have unflinchingly kept the faith, and at whose feet we younger Democrats have gladly learned those principles for which now we are ready to make an earnest and an aggressive fight. The campaign this year is a fight between the principles and the purposes of the two great parties of this State. It is not, and cannot be made, a fight between candidates except as they represent those principles. As far as lies in my power, the fight shall be kept up to that standard, and shall not degenerate into personal criticism or personal abuse.

The questions for the people of this State to determine upon their conscience are: Has the administration of National affairs been so honest, faithful, patriotic, and unselfish, with a single eye to the people's interest and the people's good, that Massachusetts is ready by her vote to indorse and encourage that administration? For whatever our friends on the other side may say, every man of sense knows that the decision of Massachusetts in this election is of importance and weight in determining the course and policy of National affairs. Who believes that if Massachusetts on the fifth of November becomes Democratic, it is not going to determine largely what shall be done in the administration of National affairs?

Another question: Has the administration of State affairs been so honest, pure, unselfish, so free from irresponsible influences and beyond criticism that the people of this Commonwealth are ready to indorse its acts by voting to continue the Republican party still longer in power?

Another question: Has the Republican party so honestly and explicitly declared its policy, and in favor of measures that are for the people's interest, that the people are ready to support it by giving to it their votes?

I have taken pains at the outset of this campaign carefully to draw up the indictment that I think can honestly be made against the Republican party. That indictment shall be proved from the stump in Massachusetts by evidence that cannot be controverted. And if that indictment is proved, I have the right to call upon the conscience and patriotism of this State to support us in this fight.

I recognize the fact that here in this presence is not the place to enter into a detailed discussion of campaign issues, nor is it necessary; but it seems to me proper and pertinent at this time to point out one striking contrast between the parties as shown in the platforms of their conventions.

The Democratic party, true to its duty as the people's party, has stated that evils exist in administration and in unjust and unequal laws; and it has explicitly, bravely, and boldly told what the remedy should be. The Republican party has not had the courage to face those evils or to suggest a remedy. The Democratic platform outlines a policy that means something. The Republican platform was built to hide evils that exist, to evade disputed questions, and to avoid committing its party to any definite position or settled policy.

The Democratic platform is brave, bold, explicit, because of our consciousness that we are right. The Republican platform is non-committal, evasive, cowardly, because of their fear that they are wrong. And those platforms have been followed by the declination of their candidate officially to expound and explain his platform under the responsibility and criticism of a joint debate.

Now, if you will bear with me for a few minutes I propose to examine the Republican platform and to contrast it with the Democratic, but unfortunately in the absence of its official expounder, whom, as you suggest, Sir, we would gladly have entertained here to-day as the beginning of our joint discussion. The platform, after indulging in congratulations and a display of exuberant spirit over the Republican victory, — pardonable, perhaps, because of a pardonable pride one always has in a possession that costs a good deal, — proceeds to declare its position on the first great National question of the day, — the question of civil service reform. There are in this Commonwealth thousands of honest, disinterested men, men who have no other purpose to serve than to obtain good, honest, and unselfish government, who believe in that reform as vital to the safety of this Nation. I want to ask those gentlemen how well they are satisfied with the declaration of the Republican platform upon that question. Here it is: —

"We desire also to congratulate the President upon the practical wisdom and honest purpose" with which he has dealt with the offices.

Its framers might have added, without exaggeration: "And upon his wonderful celerity and easy conscience in forgetting his plighted word."

And then they add the request, or rather the threat, that in filling the offices in Massachusetts he shall take good care to satisfy "the great body of the Republican party." There is some moderation also in that. You will notice that they skip the head and tail of the party, and are satisfied if the offices satisfy the great body of the party. And then they go on to say: "We wish to commend most heartily the policy of the President in regard to civil service reform," as shown in various ways which they specify. What has been that policy? Thousands and thousands of faithful, upright public servants have been dismissed from the public service for political reasons only. Others of the President's own party, efficient and upright in office, who have lived through various administrations, and who have given their lives to their official work, have been dismissed in order to give place to the spoilsman, — thus making office part of the spoils of a victorious party.

Let us compare the policy with the pledges of the party. The National Republican party a year ago gave this pledge to the country: "That the existing law should be extended to all grades of service to which it is applicable, and the spirit and purpose of the reform should be observed in all executive departments." That was the pledge of the party to the people, and here is the President's personal pledge to them:

"That fitness, not party service, should be the essential test in appointment; that fidelity and efficiency should be the only sure tenure of office; and that only the interest of the public service should suggest removals from office."

Does any man believe that that pledge has not been violated? Does any man believe that the public interest only has been the test in determining removals from office? The record of fifteen thousand office-holders in one department dismissed in five short months proves that the acts of that party have been false to its professions.

On that issue will any man say that the platform, adopted this year, shows either courage or conviction? It commends the civil service policy of the President. Does it or does it not believe in civil service reform? That is the question which the people of this Commonwealth want answered. It cannot believe in that reform if it commends the practice of its President.

I will come to the next question dealt with in the Republican platform, and the most important question, either State or National, before the people of this country, — the question of tariff reform. As I read the plank on that question I ask you, not as Democrats, but as intelligent, reasoning men, to tell me, if you can, where the Republican party by its platform stands upon this issue. The Republicans commit themselves "to urge and support a thorough and equitable revision of the tariff so as to adapt the protection which it affords to changed business conditions affecting New England industries in common with those of the rest of the country." They fail to specify what are the changed business conditions. Is it a changed business condition that this tariff was adopted as a war measure, for war purposes to raise a war revenue, and that now for twenty-five years we have had peace, and still with increasing burdens a high tariff exists to raise a surplus revenue that is not needed? I want to ask my Republican friends if they recognize that as a changed business condition?

Is it a changed business condition that under the operation of that tariff great industries of Massachusetts have been declining and dying? Is it a changed business condition that under the operation of that tariff Pennsylvania is killing some industries of Massachusetts? Is it a changed business condition that in the highly protected industries under the operation of that tariff there have been the lowest wages? Is it a changed condition that under the operation of that tariff there has been an increase of cost of the food, shelter, and clothing of the whole people? Is it a changed condition that this tariff has caused overproduction which needs and must have wider and foreign markets? Can any man find in the platform what are the changed business conditions which it admits but does not dare to specify? You may search that platform long and far before you get an answer to those questions. You may search it farther and longer before you find a hint or a suggestion of any remedy to meet the difficulty. Does the platform mean free wool — that is what the people of this Commonwealth want to know — to satisfy the woollen industry? Does the platform mean free coal and iron? The Republican party does not dare to say, nor does it dare to take its position beside its own Governor in asking for free coal and iron. Does the platform mean free raw materials to give our industries a chance to live, and to give our people relief from the burdens that are oppressing them, and greater comfort in their homes and in their lives?

Now contrast that evasive platform with the declaration of Democracy upon the question. We do not hesitate to say, in answer to the demands of business interests and of the whole people, that we stand for free wool, for free coal to make more cheerful the fireside of the humblest home and to give our industries greater prosperity. Free iron we demand; free raw materials we demand, and cheaper necessaries of life. There is no evasion in the platform of the Democratic party.

Follow it down into State affairs, and see if my criticism on the Republican platform is not again true. It comes to the question of temperance, and begins with the declaration that "in State affairs the question deservedly most interesting to the people of the Commonwealth is that of temperance." Well, if it is, you would think that the Republican party would have some definite policy upon it. Let us see what that policy is. Here is its declaration as far as aggressive legislation is concerned: The Republicans pledge that "further legislation shall be had whenever and wherever it can secure further suppression of the terrible evil." Does that pledge them to anything? Does that commit the party to anything? I want to ask the Republican party and its candidate this question: Does your party or does it not believe in prohibition? Will you, Mr. Brackett, recommend in your message to the Legislature, if you have an opportunity of writing one, prohibition? Will you, if the Legislature passes a prohibitory law, sign it? That is the question the people want answered. Your platform commits you to nothing. It evades the question. The Republicans are praying still "Good Lord and good Devil" on the temperance issue in this State. If they do not favor a prohibitory law, does the Republican party or its candidate in this State practically favor prohibition by such stringent legislation as will accomplish it? Do they commit themselves to a single measure which was under discussion by the last Legislature, and was believed by many people to result in practical prohibition if adopted? No, gentlemen, no. They commit themselves to nothing. And though within a year they have been on both sides of the question of constitutional prohibition, though within twenty years they have hopped from side to side of the temperance question as easily and jauntily as if they were engaged in a pastime instead of discharging a solemn duty, yet notwithstanding that, or perhaps because of that, the Republican party finds it prudent this year to hide rather than to declare its policy.

So much for the courage of the Republicans in their acts of commission in their platform. Now a word or two for their acts of omission. There are great business interests in Boston and New England, and the interests of the people stand behind them, that demand freer commercial relations with Canada and with Mexico. There is not a word in the Republican platform as to their policy on that question. We do not know whether they believe or disbelieve in that demand of the people. There is also a strong public protest against traffic arrangements and restrictions of Canadian railroads that will operate to the detriment of business interests in Boston and New England and to the detriment of the whole people. The Republican platform has not a word to say upon that question. Why? They cannot take any position without hurting or stultifying themselves, and therefore they decline to be committed.

There is not a word in their platform of criticism or commendation upon the administration of a great department of this Nation that has attracted universal attention. They believe in a liberal policy in regard to pensions; but they do not care to say whether they support or oppose such administration of that department as has been given us under a Republican administration.

Passing then to State questions, notice there is not a word in their platform upon the two great public demands in this State for legislation. A large proportion of the people in Massachusetts and the whole Democratic party do not believe in the principle of the poll-tax as a qualification for voting. All know that in its effect it has been debasing and corrupting in public life. The Republican party has been on both sides of that question also, as on most questions in this Commonwealth. It has not a word now to say about it in its platform. So in reference to the demands of labor for just and wise legislation there is not one word in the whole platform. Nor has it taken any position upon a matter which perhaps more than anything else has attracted attention throughout the Commonwealth, particularly the attention of the Republican party as voiced in the Republican newspapers,— an irresponsible, secret lobby, acting upon legislation, and controlling it against the people's interests. There is not a word of condemnation of that in the platform or now from their party Press,— only this remark, that the Republicans "promise to give to the Commonwealth the same honest, economical, and progressive government which [they] have given to it for more than thirty years, and with which the people are familiar."

The people are becoming familiar with it, but are inclined to give it a different name.

I cannot help thinking, when one goes over that platform and sees how little it says that is explicit, honest, and straightforward, that it must have been written under instructions like those given by Hon. Preserved Doe in secret caucus, as reported in the "Biglow Papers."

With your permission, I should like to repeat those instructions, and ask you, in the light of this Republican platform, whether you do not think that they were also given by the chairman of the Committee on Resolutions. Says Mr. Lodge, if I may assume that he was the author of the platform, in secret caucus: —

> "The first thing for sound politicians to larn is
> Thet Truth, to dror kindly in all sorts o' harness,
> Mus' be kep' in the abstract,— for, come to apply it,
> You 're ept to hurt some folks' interest by it.
> Wal, these ere Republicans (some on 'em) ects
> Ez though gineral mexims 'ud suit speshle facts;
> An' there 's where we 'll nick 'em, there 's where they 'll be lost,
> For applyin' the princerple 's wut makes it cost.
> . . . .
> A ginooine statesman should be on his guard,
> Ef he must have beliefs, nut to b'lieve 'em too hard;
> For, ez sure ez he does, he 'll be blartin' 'em out,
> 'Thout regardin' the natur' o' a man more 'n a spout.
> Now, it don't ask much gumption to pick out a flaw
> In a party whose leaders are loose in the jaw;
> An' so, in our own case, I ventur' to hint
> That we 'd better not air our perceedin's in print,
> Nor pass resolutions ez long ez your arm,
> Thet may, ez things happen to turn, do us harm;
> For when you 've done all your real meanin' to smother,
> The derned things 'll up and mean sumthin' or 'nother.
> . . . .
> No, never say nothin' without you 're compelled tu,
> An' then don't say nothin' thet you can be held tu,
> Nor don't have no friction idees layin' loose
> For the ign'ant to put to incend'ary use."

And yet the same Convention which adopted that platform as its declaration of belief referred to itself as the party of Andrew, of Sumner, and of Wilson. Its members forgot that on what they call the "most interesting question" in this State to-day, Andrew stood pointedly against them, and with the Democrats in their belief in license and local option. They forgot that Sumner was read out of the Republican party because he dared to criticise the nepotism and personal politics which were controlling that party, for which act he came under the condemnation of a Republican Legislature of Massachusetts. Would not Sumner speak as bravely to-day against the nepotism and personal politics that are controlling the Republican party? They forgot that on the leading question, either State or National, Henry Wilson stood directly and emphatically against their present position, declaring over and over again his belief that free raw materials were necessary for the industries of Massachusetts and for the good of her people. They forgot that on the other great State issue Sumner and Wilson both lent their eloquent and emphatic voices in favor of the abolition of the poll-tax as a qualification for voting. Where would these men stand to-day? I believe if they could be brought back to life, and by strenuous efforts, through the storms and seas that surround the Republican ship, could get aboard that ship, that they would find a vessel without chart or compass, without a pilot or course, without a destination or safe anchorage, and under the control of an irresponsible and reckless crew. What assurance would they have that all was safe? Only the assurance given by the captain of a vessel to his reverend passenger, who, as the winds blew and the seas rolled, asked in alarm for some proof that they were to be saved. The captain tried to assure him, but failed. At last he took him forward, and asked him to look down the forecastle and see the sailors swearing and quarrelling. The captain said: "Do you think if this vessel were going to destruction, and those men into the presence of their Maker, that they would be swearing and quarrelling?" And after that the reverend gentleman every few minutes went to the forecastle, looked down, and lifting up his hands, thanked God that the crew were still swearing.

If those wise and able men referred to in the Republican Convention were on the Republican ship to-day, they would ask for some better assurance of its safety than the acts of an irresponsible and reckless crew. They would demand that the ship be sailed with chart and compass, with a pilot and a course and a fixed destination for its voyage.

Men may honestly differ in their positions on the issues of to-day. I do not believe that honest men differ in their belief that a party should take some position on those questions, and not be left to drift haphazard. Because the Democracy has been bold, aggressive, fearless in taking its position, it is attracting the young blood and life of this Commonwealth. The Democracy on these issues is engaged in a war in which there is no discharge till victory comes. I appeal with confidence to the sturdy people of this old Commonwealth to help us in that fight.

SPEECH

AT THE YOUNG MEN'S DEMOCRATIC CLUB DINNER, BOSTON, DEC. 14, 1889, UPON THE DIFFERENCE BETWEEN THE PARTIES.

I SHOULD indeed be ungrateful if I felt unmoved by the cordial welcome of this Democratic club. Were this an occasion for formal speech-making, remembering the able statement of the principles of our faith made here last week by distinguished Democrats of national reputation, I should doubt the necessity, and certainly my ability, to add anything to what was then so felicitously said. We have been especially glad to welcome among us our gallant ex-President, under whose banner we have proudly marched to victory, under whose administration we have felt the blessings of Democratic principles courageously enforced, and who now, though defeated, still exercises, through our party, a healthy influence upon the public opinion of this country. Stripped of all official power, he has proved how great and powerful a man can be who has unselfishly devoted himself to the people's interests, who consistently upholds a high standard of public duty and public life, and who breathes in every word encouragement, which inspires us to follow in the path of reform where he has blazed the way. But to-night we have come together at this annual meeting of the club, in an informal way, to talk over the past and plan for the future. We meet with a defeat behind us, yet, thank God, not a whit discouraged, but more loyal than ever to our party and its cause, and with a full and steadfast faith that defeat is behind, and victory ahead and near at hand. I never come to a meeting of this club without a feeling of proud satisfaction, mingled with much personal gratitude, for the splendid work the club has done, and for its aid in those campaigns in which I have taken an active part. Always in its presence I feel encouragement and hope for the future, and go forth from its meetings more determined than ever that the fight shall be kept up with renewed vigor, till the full triumph of those principles and reforms, for which the Democratic party stands, shall be written boldly and defiantly on its banner. There is no room for doubt or discouragement in a cause that appeals to the people, and day by day is gaining strength in public opinion. A victory is of little consequence in a failing cause, and in a growing cause defeat is only an incentive to harder work.

This club has to-night given its answer to Mr. Cleveland's wise and patriotic words by declaring its unfailing belief in these reforms, and its purpose to advocate and uphold them. I do not propose to discuss them in detail, but to say a single word of the fundamental principle upon which they are founded, — a principle at the very basis of our Democracy, and I honestly believe dividing the two great parties to-day in this country. Viewed broadly, the great principle of Democracy to-day is to regain for the people the right to govern themselves, and then to have the power of government used for their interests, and not for selfish purposes; that equal rights, privileges, burdens, and opportunities shall be extended to all citizens. What is ballot reform, to-day an accomplished success in Massachusetts? Only this in its spirit and purpose, that every citizen, unawed by intimidation, free from corrupt and improper influences, shall have the right to exercise a freeman's privilege in determining the policy of government and into whose hands power shall be intrusted. It is true that this reform has been carried by a union of both parties, and is to-day loyally supported by both parties. But the spirit and purpose of that reform to-day are and ever have been violated by the Republican party of this Commonwealth. What else is its declared purpose to uphold the law that taxes every man's right to vote? It is in its purpose and spirit an attempt to disfranchise men in this Commonwealth because of their poverty, and to limit the suffrage to that extent.

What is civil service reform? Only this in its fundamental principle, spirit, and purpose, — that the privileges and opportunities of government shall be open to all citizens, without distinction of race, religion, or party, or any distinction other than that of merit; and then that the great power of office shall be used for the benefit of all the people, and not for selfish and partisan purposes. The Democratic party in power, under the lead of President Cleveland, in spite of many objections, and notwithstanding an excusable spirit of revenge that was engendered by twenty-five years of merciless proscription, was loyal to that reform, and greatly advanced its progress; and to-day it stands as the just critic of a party which has violated its pledges, which has broken, or allowed its President to break, its plighted word, and which, outside of the narrow limits of law, has scattered that reform to the four winds of heaven.

What is tariff reform? Only a demand that taxation — the greatest power of government, and carrying its greatest burdens — shall be limited to public purposes, and shall not be used to enrich one at the expense of another, or to benefit a few at the expense of a whole people. I would not have believed until recently that any large proportion of our people would have boldly and seriously advocated that that power should be warped from its original purpose and made to divide our people into classes, — into those who get and those who give, into beneficiaries and taxpayers, — or that a great party would have boldly defended that policy upon the specious argument that those who got the benefits, somehow in their charity would distribute them to all, and that those who bore the burdens, somehow in God's providence would receive compensation for the taxes they were obliged to pay. Not only in this, but in the whole political programme of the Republican party, its conception of government is radically different from ours, and seems to be that its purpose is to distribute benefits at the discretion of the Republican party for the advantage of that party, blind to the fact that every bit of its power comes from the people, that every dollar of revenue is taken from their pockets, and can be rightfully used only for public purposes. A government of bounties and of benefits by the Republican party, for the use of that party and its beneficiaries, is in strange contrast to the old principle of a government "of the people, by the people, and for the people."

Yet you may take the Republican programme, as declared in the platform of the party in 1888 and followed by the declarations, the acts, and the professions of that party, and you will find this new principle underlying its policy. Take its position on the question of the tariff. For the first time, I venture to say, it advocates protection solely for protection's sake, regardless of any question of whether the government needs the revenue, or has any proper use for the revenue, or whether any public good is to be served by the taxes that are thus laid, but with the avowed declaration that it has a right to place a burden upon all for the benefit of a few.

Take its advocacy, now declared, of a system of bounties for a special interest. It is utterly regardless of the question of why that industry more than another, or more than all, has the right to tax the whole people for its special benefit. Take its advocacy of the expenditure of millions on education in doing the work that the States can and ought to and will do, and will be better and stronger States because of doing it. National gifts do not come without National control behind them I think that any State that is looking longingly to the Treasury of the United States to help it in education, might well quote the lines of the old poet, "I fear the Greeks, even when they come bearing gifts."

Take the policy of the Republican party in the matter of pensions. I have been often told that this was a delicate subject for any man to touch who ever had been or expected to be in public life. It is time that some man uttered what we believe to be the true principles with reference to the pension system of this country. No man of any party doubts that this country should be just and liberal to every veteran who has suffered in her behalf. But there is a wide difference between that policy and one which overlooks the fact whether a man has suffered or not, whether he is to-day suffering or not, whether he made sacrifices for his country, or whether he deserted her in her hour of peril. There is a wide difference between making the pension-roll a roll of honor which shall point out to all people and to all times that these were the men who bravely gave their blood that this country might live, and establishing the principle that patriotism is a commodity that can be bought, and that the call of this country to her citizens to stand forth and defend her in her hour of peril was a call to them when the peril was over to present bills for what they did in those dark and fateful days. We yield to no man and to no party in our unflinching patriotism, or in our gratitude to those brave men who answered bravely the call of their country. But we do believe that our President, the President of the whole people, was right when he said that the vast expenditures of this country should be carefully disbursed; that there should be a distinction made between a loyal veteran and a cowardly deserter, and between the man who suffered in war and the man who suffered by his own misfortunes or his own negligence.

Take, too, the Republican programme in reference to elections. The Republicans advocate now, in the message of their President and in the professed opinions of their leaders, that the National Government should step into the States and control their elections. As National gifts are never made without National control, so National control is never exercised without National power behind it. The people of this country who remember the dark days that followed the reconstruction period, who remember the days of '76, when National bayonets controlled the ballots of the people, have, I believe, no desire that that *régime* should be restored, or that the power of this Nation should undertake to influence our elections.

And what does it all mean? Study the President's message, study the Republican platforms, and tell me if there is not between the two parties a difference more fundamental than any question of revenue or of tariff reform, — if there is not that wide difference which exists between a party that believes the government is to use its power under partisan control for special and for selfish interests, and a party that believes the power of government springs from the people, and is to be limited to their purposes and to accomplish their wishes, and theirs only.

It is time that some party should stand forth to oppose what seems to be the tendency of these times. No party is so well fitted for that work, none can do it and still be so loyal to its history, its traditions, and its principles, as the Democratic party, which is and ever has been the people's party, which now serves and ever has served only the people's cause. I should be untrue to myself, and I know I should be untrue to the Democratic party of this State, if I took my seat without thanking the club for the useful, earnest, unselfish work it has done in the political battles that are past. It is a regiment of young men having no other purpose to serve than the good of the people and the enforcement, in law, of the Democratic faith. I do not believe that we are banded together to advance the interests of any man, except as that man can advance the interests of the Democratic party and enforce the faith of that party. I am sure, with our growing numbers and our great power, that we shall enter on the battles yet before us with renewed vigor, confident that an appeal to the conscience and patriotism of this old Commonwealth will at last turn Massachusetts from the error of her ways into the pleasant paths of Democracy.

SPEECH

AT NORWOOD, OCT. 11, 1890, UPON THE TARIFF AND THE LOBBY.

I THANK you for your hearty welcome. It is evidence of your sympathy with the party and the cause which it is my privilege to represent. It is your protest, too, against a party that has neglected the needs and wishes of our Commonwealth, that has not listened to her appeal nor considered her interests, but, cringing under party dictation, has dared to be disloyal to her.

I am glad to open this campaign here in Norfolk County, where sturdy sons, carrying their sovereignty each under his own hat, have not hesitated to break away from a party their conscience could not follow. I come to discuss serious questions, and, appealing to your intelligence and patriotism, to ask you to decide if this is not the time when the interests of Massachusetts and good government demand the defeat of the Republican party.

Let me point out some signs of its degeneracy. First, in the men who lead it. I know that in all parties there is an overwhelming proportion of upright, patriotic men; but parties are judged by the power that controls them, the way it leads them, and the policy that it dictates. At the head of the National organization of the Republican party to-day, by its assent and with its indorsement, stands a man denounced by his own party associates as a "branded criminal," convicted by public opinion.

At the head of one of the great departments of government is another man, placed there only because he passed the hat for the Republican corruption fund. High also in administration is still another, who gloried in the fact that more than thirty thousand times he had violated the pledge of his party and the plighted word of its President by removing faithful officials for politics only; and that man was feasted, applauded, and honored here in Boston by the Republican party. What, pray, is the moral condition of a party that submits to such leadership?

Next notice its utter indifference to the loss of thousands of men who gave it character, ability, and reputation. In every step of its downward career it has left behind a whole army of its supporters who could not and would not follow it further. Among them were many who had been its founders, leaders, members of Congress, presidents of its conventions, members of its committees in State and Nation, and others high in office abroad and at home. With them thousands of others, young men and old, and all men of character, guided only by their conscience, left it in utter disgust and despair at its evasion, hypocrisy, and lack of principle. Among these stands forth conspicuously a brave and brilliant young man, a son of Norfolk County, who has shown by his words and acts that he is a Democrat heart and soul. Democracy has honored him and itself by making him its candidate for Congress in this district. I am sure that, as he has stood by the people always, the people will now stand by him.

At each further revolt from the Republican party, leaving it more and more in the clutch of selfish and evil influences, there is heard no demand for reform within its ranks, but only mocking taunts and sneers. I want no better evidence of the decay of a great party than the action of the Republican Convention of this year. Speaking through its chairman, it confessed the loss of many men of character, conscience, and intelligence, but boasted its indifference to the loss, slammed the door upon their backs, and bolted it with the epithet of "Scribes and Pharisees." It did not add the word "hypocrite," as the Republican party still has the exclusive right to use that name.

Next notice its extravagant and reckless abuse of power, and its utter disregard of law and precedent. It has increased expenditures by tens and scores of millions; it has been ready to give everything to everybody who could give it votes, until Republican senators have been compelled to discuss how long it will be before a deficit in the National Treasury shall compel the levying of new taxes on a long-suffering people; it has passed important measures without giving an opportunity for discussion; it has stifled debate, unseated members elected by majorities of thousands, deprived a State of her chosen senators, violated the law and precedents of a hundred years, and turned the House of Representatives from a deliberative body to a bear-garden, absolutely controlled by the dominant will of a single man, who determines what shall and what shall not be law. I know the House of Reed is quick. It has unseated a member in three minutes and a half. Is it safe? Is it republican? Is it true to the laws and institutions of this country? The mills of God grind slowly.

Notice again the defeat in the Massachusetts Legislature by the Republican party of such important measures of reform as the law compelling a publication of campaign expenses, and the compulsory law to regulate the caucuses. These reforms were defeated because, though a benefit to the people, they would be an injury to the Republican party. Lastly, notice the evasion and hypocrisy of that party. I have time to give but one or two instances.

First consider its record on the liquor question. It has passed a prohibitory law and repealed it as a confessed failure. It has passed prohibitory measures in the Senate, and defeated them in the House, and has then reversed the operation. It has voted for constitutional prohibition in the Legislature, and then defeated it at the polls. It has nominated prohibitory candidates on license platforms, and, I believe, has reversed that operation also. And at last, on a platform that meant nothing, it nominated a candidate who would say nothing, but who now, as its Governor and leader, has proclaimed, as the climax of Republican thought and action on this question, the grand doctrine that a standing drink is sin, but a sitting drink is salvation. Meanwhile the Republican party sends its saints upon the stump to denounce the saloons, and its sinners around the corner to strike a bargain with them, by which it may retain its power in the State. I believe the people, no matter what their opinion on the liquor question may be, will all unite in crying shame upon such hypocrisy and deceit.

Take as another illustration the tariff question. It has been the question of supreme importance ever since the brave message of President Cleveland awoke the people to a sense of the heavy, unjust, and unnecessary burdens laid upon them for selfish purposes. It has been almost the only question debated in Congress for months, and now at last it comes before the people for their decision. What does the Republican party in this State say upon this question? Only a mere phrase, and that evasive, buried deep in a bottomless paragraph of a dreary platform; and yet how explicitly it might have spoken, and kept well within the line of past Republican professions! It might have declared, with every Republican President, from Lincoln to Harrison, in favor of a reduction of the tariff. It might have said, with its ex-President, that the McKinley Bill "is ruinous to all our best interests, and will do an infinite amount of harm." It might have declared, with its past Secretaries of the Treasury, and with Charles Sumner and Henry Wilson, in favor of free raw material and radical reductions of the tariff. Or it might have said, with its last Governor of this State, that the taxing of their raw material was tending "to wipe out the iron and steel industries, large and small, of New England," and had led to a "degradation of labor" here. It might have said, with Mr. Blaine, the Secretary of State, that there was not a line or section in the whole McKinley Bill that would open to Americans a market for another bushel of wheat or another barrel of pork. Or it might have said, with one of its Western senators, that the Bill increases duties for which there is no popular demand, that it consulted the interests of the manufacturers, and not of the consumers, and that it "was a shelter for trusts." And then it might have joined in his righteous indignation with the "greed of the manufacturers," "the Carnegies and Joneses of Pittsburg, and the Dolans and Dobsons of Philadelphia, who have prospered and grown rich beyond the dreams of avarice at the expense of the people of the United States." Or if it wanted the milder language of milder men, it might have declared, with the leaders of its State Convention of 1884, in favor of a reduction of the tariff, enlarging the free list, and freeing entirely "those great necessaries of life which enter into the consumption of every household." At least it might have followed its Convention of last year in demanding a revision of the tariff to meet the changed industrial conditions of New England.

But it said none of these things. Why? Because under the power of selfish interests it has repudiated its past declarations, forgotten its pledges, and passed a measure which it cannot and will not in this State defend; so it evades it and belittles it. I challenge the Republican party to go before the people of Massachusetts and show them that the McKinley Bill is in their interest.

I have spoken of the leadership, indifference, recklessness, and hypocrisy of the Republican party as evidence of its degeneracy. It has become a party of tactics rather than of principle, led by politicians rather than by statesmen, and controlled by wealth for its own purposes. From such a party it was as inevitable that the McKinley Bill should come forth as that a corrupt tree should bring forth evil fruit.

The Democratic party makes no demand, nor has it ever made any, for free-trade. There always has been and always will be a tariff in some form. But it does cry "Stop" to protection run mad, especially when its mad career means injury, if not death, to Massachusetts interests. I propose to-night to discuss but one phase of the tariff question,— What will best meet the needs and wishes of Massachusetts, and serve her interests? What did she want, and what did she get? A brief statement will be the strongest argument. She wanted, first, cheaper necessaries of life for the benefit of all her people. The Republican Convention in this State in 1884 demanded this, but since 1888 that party has lost its regard for the people in its greater regard for selfish interests which are hostile to them. Now it thinks it is a cheap man who wants a cheap coat.

How does the McKinley Bill meet this demand? By increasing taxation and raising the cost of almost every necessary of life; food, clothing, and shelter, all are raised. The day's wages will not bring as much comfort as they did. The Republicans have deliberately made it harder for the poor to live. The poor asked for bread, and were given a stone. For whose benefit was this? For the benefit of the few, to make money out of this burden upon all.

What next did Massachusetts want? A thorough revision of the tariff to meet "her changed business conditions." That was the Republican platform last year. What are her changed business conditions? Her foreign commerce is gone, her agriculture depressed, her iron industry dying, her glass industry dead, her carpet and woollen industries are suffering, her leather, boot, and shoe industries dependent for their prosperity upon untaxed hides, her new and growing electric industry needing free copper and mica, her canning industry free tin, and all her industries demanding that the hand of the law be lifted from them, that for their life and growth they be given free raw material, and that our ports be opened to give us an equal chance in the fierce competition with the West and South.

Nearly six hundred iron and steel industries of New England, including nearly all of any importance, without regard to party, petitioned for free coal and iron ore, and a reduction on iron, pig, and scrap. One half of the iron furnaces in New England have gone out in the last ten years, and many dependent iron industries, like nails and shovels and the foundries, have been suffering and have died. The facts are known to all. The industry itself says that but one thing can save it from death, and that is the granting of its petition. But the Republican party spurned the petition. Its Congressmen and its members of the Legislature refused their aid to a demand that is vital to this great industry. That party chose to stand with the mine-owners of Lake Superior and of Pennsylvania rather than with Massachusetts, and for selfish interests rather than for the public welfare.

Five hundred and thirty woollen manufacturers and dealers petitioned for free wool. More than once the woollen industry has stated its need of free wool. McKinley said there was no reason for free hides that did not apply with equal force to free wool. What answer was given to this demand and need of one of our greatest industries? A decided increase of duties upon wool was the only answer; and this injury to our industry, and this new burden on the whole people, was inflicted only because the wool-growers demanded it. Again the Republican Congress and our Republican Legislature stood with the few rather than with the whole people, with Ohio rather than with Massachusetts.

One hundred and fifty-eight builders, contractors, architects, masons, and others protested against any increase in the taxes on building material, especially on lime. That protest was unheeded, and taxes were again raised, and with them the cost of every home in the land, while an injury was also done to the whole building industry and its tens of thousands of laborers. The Republican party stood with the lime trust of Rockland rather than make it easier for the poor to get a home.

Take another industry, in which this town has a peculiar interest. Here are tanneries employing hundreds of men. It is a great and growing industry in

Massachusetts. In 1885 nearly 10,000 persons were employed in it, who made $28,000,000 worth of goods. In the boot and shoe industry, that is closely connected with it, there were employed 65,000 persons, — a larger number than in any other industry; and they manufactured $114,000,000 worth of product. In 1872 the Republican party took off the taxes upon hides, and immediately there followed a great growth of the leather and shoe industries. Our exports of leather made here, and giving employment to our own men, increased from $500,000 to nearly $10,000,000 a year, going into the markets of the world with a profit in competition with the labor of the world. Cities like Brockton and Lynn, and the shoe towns of the State, grew as they never had grown before under the impetus given them by free raw material for their industry.

What does the McKinley Bill do for this great industry? You remember well the agitation of last spring, and the intent then of the Republican party to put back the tax on hides. From every shoe centre, from boards of trade, from our Press, and from our whole people, there went up an indignant and unanimous protest. That tax meant injury, if not destruction, to one of our greatest industries. Yet in the heat of that agitation the Republican party in our Legislature deliberately and emphatically refused to make its protest against the wicked and fatal tax. But the voice of Massachusetts was heard in spite of the action of the Republican party. Hides were left on the free list. Still, we have by no means escaped the danger. There has been put into the McKinley Bill a provision that if the President is satisfied that any country from which we get our hides does not give us an equal advantage in trade by January, 1892, then "it shall be his duty," by proclamation, to put a tax of a cent and a half a pound upon hides. That is, if things remain as they are to-day between us and the Argentine Republic, the President is compelled to put a tax on hides.

The danger that threatens us is postponed, but not averted. Unless Massachusetts utters her protest now against the McKinley Bill, her vote will be taken as an indorsement of this, and of all its provisions. If she assents to that Bill now, she will have then no right to complain if in 1892 she finds a tax on the raw material of her greatest industry, and that industry suffering and declining as her iron industry is to-day. If free hides are so vital to the leather and shoe industry, why are not free coal and iron to the iron industry, and free wool to the woollen industry? If one industry has its raw material free, why not all?

Let me pass now to one or two other industries of Massachusetts. Take the tin and the canning industry. This has become one of the important industries of the country, existing here and in almost every State, giving employment in it and in its dependent industries to many persons. Its raw material, tin plate, has been taxed at one cent a pound, though not a pound of it has been produced in this country. Not a living soul in the country could possibly be injured by taking off that tax, and the whole canning industry would be greatly benefited, and every one of our people would get their tin and their canned goods cheaper. But ten or twelve capitalists of Pittsburg demanded of the Republican party that this tax should be raised. So the Republicans have raised it from one cent to two and two-tenths cents a pound, — an increase upon the amount used by us last year of from $7,000,000 to $15,000,000. That is, $15,000,000 are to be taken out of the pockets of the people, to the injury of an industry and its numerous employees, at the demand of these capitalists of Pittsburg to add to their already enormous fortunes. Again the Republican party has stood with the few and the wealthy against the manifest interest of Massachusetts and of the people of the whole country.

Our great electric industry is another that has not escaped a blow at the hands of the Republican party. Till the passage of this bill, mica, which is used by that industry, had been upon the free list. But there is a little mine in New Hampshire, employing thirty or forty men, that demands its share of the people's taxes in the grab and the divide which the Republican party is making. Notwithstanding that Senator Aldrich, in charge of the bill, said that this was "protection run mad," yet the Massachusetts senators voted in favor of putting a duty upon mica, and to-day that, too, is taxed.

I might go farther, and show you how the farmers, too, have been injured by high-tariff taxation, their farms and their products declining as the result. To them this bill gives a mock protection, and raises the cost of the necessaries of life. No wonder that all over the country farmers' alliances are protesting against such taxation. No wonder that the President of the National Farmers' Alliance, in speaking of the decline of agriculture and the distress of the farmers, uttered these words to the very committee that was framing the McKinley Bill: "We protest, and with all reverence, that it [their distress] is not God's fault. We protest that it is not the farmers' fault. We believe, and so charge solemnly and deliberately, that it is the fault of the financial system, — a system that has placed on agriculture an undue, unjust, and intolerable proportion of the burdens of taxation."

But I must stop. I have shown you the effect of this bill on some Massachusetts industries and interests. Is it not true that her wishes and needs have been utterly disregarded? She raises now no issue as between protection and free-trade, makes no war on a proper, just, and moderate tariff taxation, laid in the interest, not of a class, but of the whole people, but she does object to protection run mad, as in McKinley's "bill of abominations."

Surely she must often recall the words of Scripture: "And Joab said to Amasa, Art thou in health, my brother? And Joab took Amasa by the beard with the right hand to kiss him. But Amasa took no heed to the sword that was in Joab's hand: so he smote him therewith in the fifth rib." Protection said to Massachusetts, "Art thou in health?" And Protection took Massachusetts by the hand to kiss her: but Massachusetts took no heed to the sword that was in Protection's hand, and so Protection smote her therewith in the fifth rib. It is protection, which is a shelter for trusts and a cloak for selfish interests, that has smitten Massachusetts; and Massachusetts' sons, her Republican representatives, by their voice and their votes, have directed the blow.

The control of legislation by selfish interests exists in this State as well as in the Nation, and demands an immediate and thorough remedy.

A year ago I charged against the Republican party that it had allowed an irresponsible third body to exist which stood between the people and the Legislature, controlling legislation against the people's interest. I come to-night to repeat that charge, and to ask if any one now doubts the truth of what I said. I have no personal attack to make upon any one, but only an attack upon an evil system. That attack I shall not be deterred from making by any personal threats or sneers, as unjust and untrue as they are malicious. It is the right of every person, town, corporation, or interest to have its case heard publicly and fairly, either in a court of law or before the General Court of the people. It is the right and duty of any lawyer thus to act for a client. I have had the experience of every lawyer in active practice in this State. Sometimes I have had a corporation for a client; more often I have been against corporations. For no client have I ever done, or been asked to do, any act that was not strictly within the line of professional work. I had nothing whatever to do, directly or indirectly, with the legislation of last winter in reference to the West End or any elevated road, nor have I to-day any connection with any such road. The people of this Commonwealth have no fault to find with the public, proper advocacy of the cause of a client. They do object to the existence of a secret, irresponsible body that stands like a giant robber between the people and their Legislature, demanding money of every interest that comes within its reach. With this personal statement I repeat my charge against the Republican party. If the fire of personal attack and misrepresentation is to gather about my head, so be it. I will address myself and my cause to the justice of the people of this Commonwealth. But so long as God shall give me strength will I, in the people's name, denounce this irresponsible body that undertakes to control legislation for selfish purposes against the people's interest.

Does it exist? When I made this charge a year ago, my distinguished opponent denied that it existed; said that it was a false issue and a false pretence; averred that the talk of a State House ring was flippant; and called for specifications. I produced the report of a Republican committee of the Senate, another of a Republican committee of the House, the veto of a Republican Governor, and the confession of the leading Republican papers of Massachusetts, all admitting its existence, all regretting and denouncing it. In the light of the investigation of last spring, does any one now doubt its existence? Ask the farmers of this State how it happens that measures in which they are deeply interested are defeated year after year. Ask the working-men how it happens that labor bills which seem to have a strong popular support are defeated. Ask the people how it happens that a bill, supported almost unanimously by the Press, by boards of trade, and by the people, — a bill intended to relieve them from unnecessary railroad charges, — is defeated. If I am not mistaken, they will tell you that these measures have been assassinated by an unseen, irresponsible power.

It is due to every interest seeking legislation that it should obtain a fair and a full hearing, without paying tribute to the lobby. It is due to the Legislature that it should not be beset by such secret influences. It is due to the Commonwealth that this body, which has grown up and has thrived under Republican administration, — a body for which that administration is absolutely responsible, — should be eradicated.

What is the remedy? First, something more than to legalize the lobby. Measures should be adopted tending to limit or exterminate it. Next, let the Governor of the Commonwealth declare that any Act which comes to him tainted with improper influences cannot become a law with his approval. Speaking as the candidate of the people's party, charged with the duty of serving their interests only, I pledge myself, if elected, to use every power within my reach to apply these remedies to this evil.

My friends, I have detained you too long. I thank you for your kindness and your patience. In closing, let me impress upon you this one thing which underlies all that I have said. The one great evil in public life to-day is the selfish, grasping influence of wealth, that, seizing political power, uses it for its own purposes. It asserts the right to tax the whole people for its benefit. It creates a high tariff, and under this shelter greedy trusts prey upon the people's pockets. It turns the people's law against the people's interests. In the light of this growing evil, how impressive are these words of an early Democratic President: —

"I would persuade my countrymen that it is not in a splendid government, supported by powerful monopolies and aristocratic establishments, that they will find happiness, or their liberties protection, but in a plain system, void of pomp, protecting all, and granting favors to none, dispensing its blessings like the dews of heaven, unseen and unfelt, save in the freshness and beauty they contribute to produce. It is such a government that the genius of our people requires, such a one only under which our States may remain for ages to come united, prosperous, and free."

The time has come for this Commonwealth, which has led in many a glorious agitation, now to lead in demanding the right of the people to govern themselves, free from these selfish and money influences. Will Massachusetts indorse the Republican administration and the evils it has brought to her and the country, or, by her protest, now lead the country to better and to purer things?

SPEECH

AT LOWELL, OCT. 19, 1890, UPON THE TARIFF.

SOMEWHAT wearied by the labor of the campaign, your cordial greeting cheers and invigorates me, giving me new courage and strength to fight the people's battle. Before entering to-night into a discussion of the serious questions of this campaign, I wish to say a word about a little family scene in the Republican party as described in yesterday's "Herald." It occurred at one of those soul-inspiring, truth-provoking club dinners where the Republicans discuss the great questions of the day before a magnificent audience of a score or two of their stalwarts, and try to educate them into a belief in the old party, and if possible to arouse in them a little enthusiasm. Occasionally in their feast of reason and flow of soul they become frank, and speak right out in meeting. So it happened at the Middlesex Club on Saturday. The principal actors appear to have been Mr. Lodge and the chairman of the Republican State Committee. After the club had expressed its unanimous sentiment that it was a great mistake for the Republicans to talk tariff, Mr. Lodge repeated the "oft-told tale" of Southern outrages, and then he sprang something new. The report says:—

"He vigorously assailed the policy of the Republican State Committee in not putting more speakers in the field to meet the energetic campaign being prosecuted by the Democrats.

The chairman sharply replied that money was needed to do what Mr. Lodge required. 'Give me money enough,' he said, in conclusion, 'and I can do it. But even Mr. Lodge himself cannot do it by simply standing up and talking in his own district;' and he added, 'If these gentlemen who criticise would themselves address the meetings they say ought to be held, the result would be different.'"

The report closes by saying, —

"In spite of a request on the part of the chairman that Mr. Lodge would remain and hear him out, that gentleman abruptly left the room, and lost the concluding words of reply, and thus ended the speaking."

I should think it would have. It was a good stopping-place. They say they want more speakers and more money to meet the energetic campaign of the Democrats. We thank you, gentlemen. A week ago you thought the Democrats had to import their speakers to make a campaign. Now you think, with only home talent, they are making an energetic one. You jeered at imported Democratic speakers; but since then, with true Republican consistency, you have imported Reed and Hale and Frye and Dingley and Boutelle, and nearly the whole State of Maine. And now you want more money to get more speakers. Of course you do not pay your home talent. If you must hire outsiders, let me make a friendly suggestion to help you out of your trouble. Why don't you advertise?

WANTED. — Campaign speakers to help out the Republican party of Massachusetts; work light, and pay good; no special experience or knowledge of public questions required. Applicants must have a good voice, strong epithets, a few

Southern outrages, and a photograph of Tom Reed, or a tintype of Cabot Lodge. It is imperative that they should know nothing, and say less, on the tariff question. McKinley prices paid.

Such an advertisement inserted in the daily papers would be certain to get you what you want. Then, for money, why do you not take some of the manufacturers in Massachusetts who have benefited by the McKinley Bill, — if you can find one, — and fry the fat out of them? If you cannot find one, take some of the Pennsylvania manufacturers whom you have allowed to fatten on Massachusetts industries, and fry them. If these suggestions fail, why not draw again on your home market? You have not exhausted it yet. Where is his Excellency the Governor? 'Why don't you draft him? The people as well as the Middlesex Club would like to hear from him. They would like to know again his exact views on the liquor question; what he thinks of the success of his standing-sitting drink solution of this problem; whether he believes now there is a lobby at the State House; and his opinion on other real live questions, State and National. If you cannot conveniently arrange dates for him, I will agree to share my time with him any and all evenings, until the end of the campaign, for the discussion of these questions.

It is not the lack of speakers on the Republican side, but the lack of justice and right in their cause that makes their campaign drag. It is such stabs in their policy and in their McKinley Bill as have been given by their candidate in the third congressional district that takes the life out of their campaign; and the fact that the Republican party has refused to listen to the demands of Massachusetts especially for free raw material. No matter how great the benefit to the industries and to the people, the Republican party refuses to reduce or remove tariff taxes; and it insists that they shall be kept on and raised higher if any small selfish interest demands it. It does so either because it is bound hand and foot to such selfish interests and is under obligations to them, or because it is tied to a policy that it will follow, no matter if for a benefit to a few it burdens the whole people and crushes the industries of a whole section.

I want to show you a few of these burdens where the tariff tax has been raised by the McKinley Bill, and I will take articles that are within the description of the necessaries of life. Let us take first some articles that enter into the construction of a house. That bill increased the tariff tax upon lime and joists and boards and cedar posts and brick and tiles and glue and iron locks and handles and hinges and screws and window glass and cement, and many other articles that I might mention, the increase running all the way from five to twenty-five per cent upon these articles. Now, suppose that, notwithstanding this load of taxation, you have been able to build your house, and you come to the question of furnishing it. I have here a list of no fewer than twenty-four articles upon which the McKinley Bill has raised the tariff tax, — such articles, for example, as carpets and furniture and crockery and glass ware and blankets and linen and cutlery and oil-cloth and brushes and brooms, and so on.

Then, having succeeded in building and furnishing his house, if by good fortune the man of slender means has still anything left, his next thought will be properly to clothe his wife, his children, and himself. At this point he will find the McKinley Bill has increased the tariff taxes on dresses and stockings and cloaks and braids and collars and cuffs and buttons and corsets and shawls, and almost every article that enters into a person's clothing.

Now, what was to be the effect, and what has been the effect, of raising still higher all these tariff taxes upon the necessaries of life? Do you think these changes were made for the purpose of lowering prices? Well, how were they brought about? Did the people ask for them? No, those who had contributed to the Republican campaign demanded as a return for their contributions that these taxes should be raised. In every case you will find that the people who had goods to sell made this demand. It was the political shepherds of Ohio who had wool to sell that demanded the higher duties upon wool. It was the iron kings of Pennsylvania who had iron and steel to sell that wanted a higher tariff upon these articles. It was the Lime Trust with lime to sell, and the Glass Trust with glass to sell, and the owners of the coal mines of Pennsylvania with coal to sell, — these are the men who made the demand and who always stand behind high-tariff duties. Do you think that they wanted high or higher duties to make the goods cheaper which they had to sell? It is absurd on the face of it. They wanted higher duties to raise prices, and so they boldly proclaimed. And behind them stood a Republican President and the Republican party, who denounced cheapness as un-American and undesirable, and meant to prevent it if possible.

You cannot show behind one of these increases in the McKinley Bill a demand for it by the consumers or by the people. And why? Because they know well what is plain common-sense, that the whole purpose and object of the increase were to raise prices, and that the bill would fail of its object if it did not raise prices.

I might give you numerous instances to show the injury and selfishness and wrong of such taxes. I will give one other. Until the passage of this Republican McKinley Bill the silver ores of Mexico containing lead were admitted free. With these ores free, large smelting industries were built up in many of our States that use and depend upon these ores for fluxing. From 1881 to 1889, the Mexican ores being free, our imports of lead into the United States largely decreased, and the exports of lead from the United States largely increased. Evidently these ores were doing no harm to any home market. Seventeen smelting companies in Pennsylvania, Kansas, Illinois, New Jersey, and other States, employing thousands of men, protested against a duty on the Mexican ores, and said it meant injury, if not death, to them. Commercial clubs and boards of trade in Kansas City and other places also made their vigorous protests. Even our minister to Mexico sent in his protest. All declared that such a duty meant serious injury to American industries and the breaking down of a large and profitable trade with Mexico. In 1888 we exported to Mexico $14,500,000 worth of our goods, and imported about the same amount of her products and ores. These facts would seem to be sufficient to prevent this tariff tax; but they were not. On the contrary, the Republicans put on a tax of one and one-half cents on the lead in these ores. Now, let us see how they happened to do this. The St. Joseph Lead Company of Missouri, with a few others, demanded it, and of course got it. Perhaps they had contributed some "fat" to the Republican party. Of course they did not give that as the reason for wanting this duty, oh, no; they said they wanted it for the benefit of American labor. Here is their exact language: —

"What we demand is a fair and just protection which shall protect American labor and develop American resources, and render reasonable profits to the capital we have invested under promise of such policy."

And yet the fact is that the company making that false pretence in the year 1889 declared a stock and cash dividend of more than forty-one per cent on its capital, and was paying its laborers at its mines $1 a day in wages. I read from the local paper, the "Independent Register," which is published in the immediate vicinity of these mines. It says:—

"Upon a capital stock of $1,500,000 a total of forty-one and one-third per cent, or $620,000, has been made for this year, which is equal to a profit to the stockholders of $41.33 upon every $100. While this is so, the common laborers at their mines get $1 per day of ten hours' work, and the managers tell them that on account of the low price of lead they cannot pay more. Be it remembered, too, that the above is the net profit of a corporation whose president, J. Wyman Jones, last year at the beginning of the Presidential campaign, rushed into print, calling upon his employees to vote for the party which pledged protection to American homes, American working-men, and American industries. It seems to us that while the lead industry made under protection a profit of over forty per cent, that bonus goes into the pockets of investors, of employers, and not into those of the working-men."

Now who were injured, and who were benefited by this new tax?

First, all the smelting companies in the United States using these ores and their employees were injured. Already one company, the El Paso Smelting Company, is said to have moved its industry to Mexico, and another, the International Smelting Company, to be about to move to Mexico. In the next place, railroads built by American capital lose in freights directly and indirectly nearly $1,500,000 per year on these ores. Further, it is an injury to our trade with Mexico, and for that reason especially our minister there protested against it. And lastly, the whole people, as users of lead and other products, are injured. Now, who are benefited? The St. Joseph Lead Company, and perhaps a few Colorado miners. A Republican Senator from Kansas, in discussing this duty, said: "I know one excellent man in Colorado to whom this bill means probably an income of $750,000 or $1,000,000 a year more than he is getting now." He added: "There is nothing so soft as to have a good grip on the law-making power, so as thereby to make it tolerably certain that you shall not be subject to mutations which attach to the performance of ordinary business." And then he uttered these words of warning: "I confess that it seems to me that the building up of large fortunes by the direct operation of a law of the United States, made by representatives of all the people, and presumably for the benefit of all, is not wholesome, and ought to be justified only by exceptional circumstances. I can conceive that the accumulation of these fortunes would lead to very considerable discontent and feeling as to the benefits of legislation not equally conferred." He said further in the same debate: "We are coming to that point where the system of protection as applied is to result in the breaking down of certain industries for the benefit of others; where the large industries which have the most potential voice in Congress are to destroy the small ones."

I have given instance after instance during this campaign of just such tariff taxes, which not only are no benefit to labor or to our industries, but are a great injury to them, and a gross injustice to the whole people, and which bring enormous wealth to the few "who have a good grip on the law-making power." Under no principle of justice or equality of law can such taxes be defended for a minute.

SPEECH

AT FALL RIVER UPON LABOR LEGISLATION, AND THE TARIFF IN ITS RELATION TO WAGES AND TO THE COTTON INDUSTRY.

I APPRECIATE your cordial greeting, and the privilege of addressing this audience of working-men, who earn their bread by the sweat of their brow, and who are the backbone of the great industries here, bringing by their skill and labor prosperity to them, and building up this great manufacturing city. I have come to talk to you of the issues of this campaign, and to discuss with you which party, by its policy and its principles, is your truest friend, and which best advances your interests.

A sound public policy, just and equal laws, are more important to wage-earners than to any one else. Wealth can always protect itself. It does not need the strong arm of the law to save it from oppression; but the poor, for their rights, their liberty, and their safety, must look to the justice and equality of law. A hard law bears hardest on the poor; an unjust policy puts its burden upon them. Selfish control of legislation which makes fortunes for the rich inevitably filches that money from the pockets of the masses of the people.

Let us see now how the two great parties approach the questions of to-day, and which best and most unselfishly serves the people.

This is the season of the year when the Republican party goes about telling labor how much it has done for it. But labor is not often deceived by such talk. It knows that in its own party, the Democratic party, rest its hope and promise of wise and just legislation. In proof of this, examine the record of the two parties in this State on labor legislation.

A year ago I charged that the Republican party had not listened to the demands of labor for just and beneficial legislation, or had only listened when compelled to by Democratic importunity.

What is the first demand of labor?

If I am not mistaken, it is the abolition of the poll-tax as a qualification for voting, rightly believing that a man, because of his manhood, and not his property, should be allowed to vote. We know that this tax has served no good purpose, but has led to corrupt and evil influences in public life. For years and years the Democratic party has urged that it be abolished, but always the Republican party has refused to abolish it. Once or twice in the Legislature it has voted to abolish it; but as it is necessary that two successive Legislatures should vote for its abolition, the Republican party always manages the second year to defeat this measure. And this it does notwithstanding that, as far back as 1853, such Republicans as Sumner and Wilson, Boutwell and Burlingame, and many others I might mention, voted for its abolition. Why cannot the Republican party of to-day rise to the height of Wilson, who justly said that poverty was hard enough to bear, without adding to it the degradation of disfranchisement?

Let us see what labor legislation has been enacted in this State, and how it came to be enacted.

It is true that many just and wise laws have been passed in the interest of labor. It is also true that many others have been defeated by the Republican party. Every one that has been passed, I believe, without exception, has been suggested by a Democrat and fought for by the Democratic party; and almost all of them have finally passed only after the Republican party had repeatedly defeated them, but yielded at last to Democratic importunity.

Let me give you some instances of this. The weekly and fortnightly payment law was advocated by the Democratic party as early as 1882. In that year, and in 1884 and 1885, the Republican party defeated it; but it was finally passed in 1886 by the Democratic party, with the aid of some Republicans whom it was able to detach from their party.

The same is true of the Board of Arbitration Act. It was introduced by a Democrat, was defeated by the Republican party in 1881, and several times later, and was finally passed only because of its support by the Democratic party, with the aid of such Republicans as the Democrats could get to join them.

So, too, with the Employers' Liability Act. Year after year it was introduced by Democrats, supported by them, defeated by the Republicans, and finally passed because the Republican party could not withstand popular pressure and Democratic importunity. And since its passage the Republican party has refused so to amend it as to make it more useful and to broaden its scope.

So, too, with the Acts abolishing contract convict labor, incorporating labor societies, and making Labor Day a holiday. All were introduced by Democrats, supported by them, opposed by the Republicans, defeated for several years by them, and finally successful because of this urgent and unflinching support by the Democratic party.

I will not weary you with other instances. The same rule is true of all, that labor legislation has been suggested, supported, and fought for by the Democratic party, and always opposed by the Republican party, till finally it was compelled to yield.

On the other hand, I could give you a long list of labor laws that have been defeated by the Republican party against Democratic protest. I hold in my hand a list of some of them. The Republicans defeated five in 1885, five in 1886, five in 1887, five in 1888, eleven in 1889, and fifteen in 1890, all of them laws demanded in the interest of labor. Without attempting to mention all, let me refer to a few of them. They include a fifty-eight-hour law for women and children, otherwise known as a Saturday Half-Holiday Bill. This passed the House, but was defeated by a Republican Senate, though all the Democrats voted for it. A bill to regulate the hours of labor for railroad employees, demanded by such employees, was defeated in the Republican House by an overwhelming Republican vote, though supported almost unanimously by the Democratic party. So, too, a bill regulating the hours of tour workers and the Weavers' Fines Bill, and a bill to prevent discrimination by employers against members of labor societies, — all were introduced by Democrats, supported and urged by Democrats, and defeated by the Republican party. The same is true of the bill to extend the Employers' Liability Act, and to wipe out a distinction it makes which is thoroughly unjust. By the law to-day (1890), in case of his instant death the wife and children of an employee may recover damages; but if the death is not instantaneous, they cannot recover. The Democrats tried to amend this law, and allow recovery in either case; but the Republicans defeated it. So, too, the Republican party has defeated a law to forbid the employment of armed forces of Pinkerton detectives by private individuals. The Democrats believe that the public peace should be kept by the public authority, and that this grave duty and responsibility should be performed under official sanction, and not by private command for hire only. So, too, the Republican party has defeated an eight-hour law, a law requiring due notice of the reduction of wages, and numerous other labor measures that I might mention. It has defeated, also, great reform measures, in which you are all interested, — such measures as the Caucus Act, to secure fair and honest caucuses, and also the Act requiring the publication of all campaign expenses, for the purpose of preventing the corrupt use of money in elections.

Now, who have fought for these laws that have been enacted, and for the laws, too, that have been defeated? Always Democrats and the Democratic party.

To whom is credit due?

To the Republican party? Not a bit of it. It is due more to the Democratic party and to its faithful, loyal leaders; for the persons who have opposed these measures have been Republicans ever and always.

With this fact in mind, let us consider the most important National question of the day, — the question of the tariff. I propose to discuss it to-night especially from the side of labor; but I think you will see that all sides of it are labor, except where men are unjustly making money out of it.

When the glass industry died here in Massachusetts, and our iron furnaces went out, and great works like the Norway Iron and Steel Company and the South Boston Iron Company and the Fall River Iron Company, and many other foundries and iron industries of Massachusetts closed down, it meant loss of work to thousands of men in this State, and in their enforced idleness an injury to all labor. That loss to you was directly caused by tariff taxes on coal and iron. So the industry itself has said.

The "Boston Journal" does not believe that that industry is suffering. It does not believe, either, that the tax on hides would be of any consequence to the leather industry, or that free coal would be of any use to us. There are none so blind as those who will not see, and none so obstinate as those whom loyalty to party compels to close their eyes to facts that are evident to a whole people. It thinks I take a narrow view because I stand for Massachusetts rather than for Pennsylvania, and it says: "He does not recognize any community of interest between Pennsylvania and Massachusetts. If Pennsylvania prospers, it is nothing to him."

I recognize the right of no State in this Union to take by law the life of the industries of another State; and when, instead of community of interest, there is conflict of interest, and National legislation is controlled by the State of Pennsylvania, and she and her millionnaires, by abuse of the people's law, are killing the industries of our State, I stand every time for Massachusetts, and denounce the man or the party or the law that in such a fight is hostile to her. I think the most serious charge against the Republican party in Massachusetts to-day is that, with the "Journal," it stands for Pennsylvania, and has been disloyal to our old Commonwealth. I mistake the temper of the people of this State if they indorse such conduct, or if Massachusetts has not spirit enough left to assert her rights and defeat any unfaithful son who does not dare to defend her.

There is hardly an industry in Massachusetts at which the Republican party has not struck or threatens to strike a blow in its McKinley Bill and high-tariff policy. This is true of the shipping, the iron, the woollen, the canning, the electric, the leather, the boot-and-shoe industries, and the building industry, with their scores of thousands of employees; and the cotton industry only escapes because its principal raw material is beyond the reach of Republican tariff taxes, — unlike the necessaries of life, the taxes on which, as some one has said, reach everything, from the cradle to the grave, and would tax a man's eternal salvation if the Republicans could only get into the kingdom of Heaven.

I say the cotton industry only escapes because its principal raw material is untaxed. Let me emphasize this. I find by the census of 1890 that more than $32,000,000 is invested in the industry in this city, giving wages to over thirty-eight thousand hands, and making a product of nearly $25,000,000; that in Massachusetts the product of the cotton industry, with its principal raw material free, has increased, from 1880 to 1890, from $72,000,000 to $100,000,000, and the number of hands employed from 61,000 to nearly 76,000; that the product of the woollen industry in Massachusetts during the same period has increased only from $67,500,000 to $72,500,000, and the hands employed from 38,000 to 43,000.

The same census shows that while throughout the country there was an increase in the product of the woollen industry, and in the number of hands employed, yet the product of the silk industry, with its raw material free, during this period increased 112 per cent; of the cotton industry, with cotton free, 39 per cent; but of the woollen industry, with its raw material heavily taxed, but 26 per cent, and the average increase of the entire textile industry was 38 per cent. It also shows that though there was an increase of capital invested in the woollen industry, yet the number of woollen mills decreased, between 1880 and 1890, from 1990 to 1312, and that in the year 1890, of these 1312 mills 267 were idle. The census bulletin shows also that the raw material entering into cotton manufactures is equal to nearly 44 per cent, other materials nearly 14 per cent, making the total proportion of material 57.69 per cent of every dollar's worth of goods, while the cost of labor was but 25.93 per cent. I am told that 1891 and 1892 were most prosperous years in your cotton industry, and that five new mills were constructed in 1892.

Now, I ask what has been the reason of this? And I assert that any manufacturer here will tell you that more than anything else it is due to the fact of the low cost of this raw material of the cotton industry. I find that the cost of cotton in 1891 was about 8 cents per pound, in 1892 from 7 to 8 cents, or the lowest price in these two years that has been known since the war. In 1890 the price ran from $9\frac{3}{16}$ to $12\frac{3}{4}$; in 1889 from $9\frac{3}{4}$ to $11\frac{1}{2}$, and at about that average for many years previous.

Now, suppose the Republican party could do with your industry what it does with the woollen and iron industries, and tax this raw material? What would be the result? Suppose they should put a tax upon imported Egyptian cotton, — which is used to some extent here, — as they do upon wool; or suppose they were able to raise the price of other cotton by taxing it, as they do the price of the raw material of other industries?

There could result but one thing; that is, it would put an end to the great benefits you are now getting from the low cost of your raw material. If its price is raised either by natural causes or by Republican tariff taxation, it means an increased cost of the product (of whose cost it makes nearly one-half); and this means a less demand for goods; and with less demand comes less manufacture of them; and so less demand for labor, and necessarily lower wages.

Now, they say that all these high-tariff taxes, with their evident burdens, have been for the benefit of labor and to keep up wages. That is an absolutely false pretence.

In the first place, killing New England industries does not help labor or wages.

In the second place, the Republicans have claimed that high tariff makes lower prices. Of course this is not true; but if true, their theory must be: high tariff to make lower prices, so as to make higher wages. The whole thing is an utter absurdity. You may make any comparison you please, and you cannot show that a high tariff fixes or raises wages. You may compare free-trade England with the high-tariff countries of Europe, and you will find wages lower under protection on the Continent than in England. You may compare England under a high tariff and a low tariff, and the time when she had no protective tariff, and you will find that the wages were highest when the tariff was lowest.

In our own country you may compare the period from 1850 to 1860, when we had our lowest tariff, with the period from 1870 to 1880, when we had a very high tariff, and you will find that in manufacturing industries during the first period wages increased 60 per cent, and during the last period only 22 per cent.

You may compare the wages in highly protected industries and those in industries which are not protected, and you will find the highest wages in the industries where there is the least protection. Or you may go farther, and compare wages in the different

States in this country, between which there is absolute free trade, and you will find often a greater difference between the wages in different States than the difference between wages here and in England.

In the first place, let us compare what they call free-trade England with other countries that are highly protected, and notice their scale of wages.

The wages in the cotton industry in England are 50 per cent higher than those in Germany, and 30 per cent higher than those in France, while their hours are shorter. In the woollen industry wages are 50 per cent higher in England than in Germany, and from 20 per cent to 35 per cent higher than in France. Yet France and Germany are both highly protected countries, and England has a low tariff. Why are wages not highest in protected countries?

Next, England has had a high, a low, and no protective tariff; and the wages there have always been increased most when the tariff was lowest.

I read from a table of wages prepared by the great statistician, Robert Giffen, Nov. 20, 1883, making a comparison of wages in England under the high and low tariff; and he shows by this table that the wages of weavers and warpers and spinners, and all labor employed in cotton and woollen industries, were from 50 per cent to 150 per cent higher in England under free trade than when she had a high protective tariff.

At the same time there came to her the greatest growth in her commerce, her industries, and her exports that she had ever known. The condition of her people improved. The amount of provisions used by them and comforts of life greatly increased, crime diminished, and by every sign that marks prosperity she was wonderfully benefited.

Let me state one other fact, taken from Carroll D. Wright's statistics, bearing on this question of wages. In England, from 1872 to 1880, there was an increase in wages of 5 per cent, while in the same period there was a decrease in Massachusetts of 5½ per cent.

But let us come to our own country for comparisons. We have had here a high tariff and a low tariff. We had a low, a very low, tariff long before England had. Our lowest tariff was from 1850 to 1860. During that period wages increased in the United States 60 per cent, while under the high tariff, from 1870 to 1880, they increased only 22 per cent.

Carroll D. Wright's Annual Report for 1884 shows that in Massachusetts, in such highly protected industries as carpets, boots and shoes, furniture, leather, paper, silks and worsteds, the general average wages were lower in 1880 under high protection than they were in 1860 under a very low tariff, while the average wages in all industries were much higher in 1880 than in 1860. I have here, as further evidence, the report of the Labor Bureau of Illinois, which shows that wages in 1886 in 142 highly protected industries were, on an average, 18 per cent lower than in 1880, while in 12 unprotected industries there was an increase of 24 per cent in wages during the same period.

If high wages are due to a high tariff, we surely ought to find them highest in the industries that are protected, and lowest in those industries that are not protected. But the fact is exactly the reverse.

Taking the census of 1880, and dividing the total wages in an industry by the number of men employed in that industry, you will find that the wages are almost invariably less in the protected industry than in the one that has little or no protection. For instance, in the protected cotton industry the wages average $245, while the wages of carpenters, who are unprotected, average $454. In the manufacture of men's clothing (protected), wages average $286, but the wages of bakers (unprotected) $419. So in silk goods, $292, but meat packing, $385; machine making, $455, but printing and publishing, $522; iron and steel, $393, but stone work, $477. And many other instances could be given.

Senator Cameron, the Republican senator from the State of Pennsylvania, in the discussion in the Senate on the McKinley Bill, introduced a piece of evidence that will be found on page 8964 of the "Congressional Record," as follows: —

"The laborers working in the iron-ore mines in the little Lehigh district between Reading and Allentown are receiving but 80 cents a day. Mining operations were suspended during hay-making and harvesting because the miners were able to earn $1.25 among the farmers."

John Jarratt, the man who spoke in McKinley's district for the Republican party, testified in 1883, before the Senate Committee in reference to labor in the highly protected mining industries, as follows:

"Sixty thousand heads of families, to whom probably two hundred thousand women and children are looking for support, are in a pitiable and miserable condition, poorly paid, poorly clad, poorly fed, and poorly housed. From my experience among the miners in England, I may say that they are really better cared for than are the coal-miners in the United States."

Let us make one further comparison on this question of wages.

Between the different States of the Union there is absolute free trade; yet under it there has not been the least difficulty in each State developing its own industries. Why, in the South, after the terrible prostration of the war, and with all the poverty that came with it, there was a development of her industries to a greater extent than was ever known in a like period of our history in any section of the country; and this was accomplished notwithstanding the fierce competition of established industries in other States that had many advantages over her.

Now, often between the different States in this Union there is a greater difference in wages than between the United States and England. Let me give you a few facts to show this, taken from the census of 1880.

Taking the total amount paid for wages in the manufacturing industries, and dividing it by the number engaged in those industries, we find that the annual average wage earnings in the State of Maine in her manufacturing industries was $260, while in Massachusetts it was $364; in Connecticut, $385; in California, $483; in Oregon, $501. But in Georgia it was $211; in North Carolina, $155; in Tennessee, $234; in Pennsylvania, $349. And so I might go through the list, showing a vast difference in the wages paid in different States.

Have I shown you facts enough to prove that the tariff does not increase wages?

But you ask me, are not wages higher here than in England? Yes, measured in dollars, wages are higher; but measured in work, they are not higher. The reason labor is paid more in the United States is because it earns more. I do not believe that a single dollar is paid to our labor in comparison with the labor of any other country that is not fully earned by the work it does. But the Republicans insist that labor here, as compared with labor abroad, is paid more than it earns by its work. Let us see what the facts are.

I will take the cotton industry, in which many of you are interested. In his report made to the State Department in August, 1886, after a very careful examination, Consul Schoenhof made a comparison of the cost of labor in manufacturing certain yarns at Fall River and in Lancashire, England, and he found that the labor cost in making their yarn No. 18 was in Lancashire 52 cents, and in Massachusetts only 40 cents; No. 20 was in Lancashire 50 cents, and in Massachusetts 45 cents; No. 28 was in Lancashire 61 cents, and in Massachusetts 64 cents. And so on through the list, in almost every instance the labor cost being less in Fall River than in England.

Mr. Schoenhof reports that a weaver in America tends from six to eight looms, in England from three to four; that the number of yards a weaver turns out in America is 1350, and in England 857; that the number of yards of woollen dress-goods a weaver turns out in America is 300, and in England 105, and of cheviot cloth in America 120, and in England 80. I could show you that the same fact is true in other industries, for example carpets and boots and shoes; invariably our employees do more work, and so get more wages.

Mr. Schoenhof, in his official report, declares that in the cotton industry each weaver in America tends more looms and turns out more yards of cloth than in England, and that each spinner tends more spindles; so that the labor cost per 100 yards of print cloth in Fall River was 40 cents, and in Lancashire 51. These figures were confirmed by figures which were sent me in 1888 from one of our large cotton-mills. The letter accompanying them said: "They were collected by one of the best superintendents of one of the largest cotton-mills this year in England, for use, if possible, in this campaign. But they were not used, because they show that the labor cost in England, measured by work, was higher than here."

They are as follows: —

TABLE ON WEAVING AND SPINNING.

(Weaving about one-half the expense of the cloth.)

	Paid weavers in England, per cut.	In U. S. per cut.	England, higher per cent.
64 square (print cloth)	$0.26	$0.20	30
Argyle	0.27	0.20	25
Boott A. L.	0.35	0.27	29¼
Standard sheeting (China trade, etc.)	0.21	0.16½	27

SPINNING.

	Spindles.	A week.	Per spindle.
England, pay for tending	646	18s.	.0275s.
United States, pay for tending	1,120	19½s.	.0174s.

Or 57 per cent higher per spindle in England.

I have, too, in my hand an autograph letter from the president of the American Screw Company, giving in detail facts and figures to show that in his industry the labor cost of his product here is less than abroad, especially in wire drawing. He says also, in the Armington and Sims Engine Company, they employ here one man and two boys to do a certain class of work, while in England are employed five skilled workmen to do the same thing; and he gives further evidence to the same effect. Mr. Sargent, the great hardware manufacturer of Connecticut, gives evidence of a like nature, and shows that our labor, measured by the work it does, is the cheapest labor in the world, and that its high wages come from its great producing power.

Mr. Blaine, in 1881, in his report as Secretary of State, said: "The hours of labor in the Lancashire mills are 56, and in the Massachusetts 60 per week. The hours of labor in the mills in the other New England States, where the wages are generally less than in Massachusetts, are usually 66 to 69 per week.

Undoubtedly the inequalities in the wages of English and American operatives are more than equalized by the greater efficiency of the latter and their longer hours of labor."

Mr. Evarts, Secretary of State in 1878, in his report on the "State of Labor in Europe," made May 17 of that year, said: "The average American workman performs from one and a half to twice as much in a given time as the average European workman. This is so important a point in connection with our ability to compete with the cheap labor manufacturers of Europe, and it seems at first thought so strange, that I will trouble you with somewhat lengthy quotations from the reports in support thereof;" which quotations he proceeded to give.

That is the reason why we are able to send abroad and sell in competition with the whole world many articles in which labor is the principal item of cost, and the raw material is the least, — such articles as hardware goods, cutlery, machinery, watches, and furniture. We never could do it for a minute if it was not that our labor is more efficient than the foreign labor, and, though paid more in dollars, earns every cent that is paid to it.

We pay higher wages because our men earn more. Let me confirm this statement by Republican authority. Mr. Charles S. Hill, the statistician of the State Department, in his argument before the Tariff Commission, pointed out the fact that our manufactured product in 1882 was $8,000,000,000, made by 5,250,000 hands, and that for the same time the product of England was $4,000,000,000, made by 5,140,200 hands; and then he says: "Here is the positive proof that American mechanics, in the aggregate, accomplish exactly double the result of the same number of British mechanics. They are, therefore, very justly paid double in wages."

The Republicans say they need this high-tariff taxation because our wages are so high. I have shown you that this is not true; but, even if it were true, let us see how high a tariff tax would be necessary to pay the whole of the wages in our great industries.

In a report of the Bureau of Statistics, made Jan. 25, 1888, it is stated that the wages paid in the cotton industry are a little over 21 per cent of the cost of the product, and that the protective tariff is over 40 per cent, or more than double the whole labor cost in that industry. So, in iron and steel manufactures, the labor cost is a little over 18 per cent, and the tariff tax more than 40 per cent. In silk goods the labor cost is a little over 22 per cent, and the tariff tax over 50 per cent. In woollen goods the labor cost is about 17 per cent, and the tariff tax over 60 per cent.

Take as further evidence the report of our Labor Bureau in Massachusetts in 1885, which shows that while the wages here are higher than the average wages of the country, still they are not in these industries equal to one half the tariff tax that is put upon their products.

The tariff tax, the Republicans claim, is to equalize the difference between wages here and in England; but as it is more than double the whole wages paid in an industry, and many times more than any such difference, this claim is as absurd as their assertion that the tariff determines wages.

What, then, does determine wages? Demand and supply and the efficiency of labor. Labor is about the only thing in which there exists to-day free-trade. The manufacturer gets protection for his goods, and free-trade for his labor.

But these taxes, which permit him to burden every home in the land, are made in the name of labor by a party that never has any interest in labor until, on the eve of election, it tries to deceive it and to get its vote.

The truth is that these tariff taxes are all put on in the name of labor, but labor does not get them. You have heard of the cost of many of the necessaries of life increasing within the last few days since the McKinley Bill was passed, but you have not heard of any manufacturer here in Massachusetts suggesting an increase in the wages of his workmen. The protected industries are getting more by taxing the American people in the name of labor; but, I repeat, labor does not get it. It is not labor that has made this unjust McKinley Bill, but it is wealth and selfish interests, that, controlling the Republican party, have determined to add to their millions the taxes which they wring out of all the people.

It is wealth and monopoly and trusts that are getting the benefit of these high-tariff taxes; and behind many of these taxes that are burdening the people and hurting, instead of helping, the industries, you will find some selfish millionnaire extorting money by abuse of the people's law. That is why the Democracy fights this high and oppressive tariff. Never was it truer to its mission of serving the people's cause and fighting the people's battle than when it stands fighting organized wealth, and demanding that it shall not control the law of this country; when it stands, as it does, for the rights of the people against the privileges of the few, and demanding that unnecessary burdens shall not be laid upon them, but that all shall stand equal before the law.

SPEECH

AT GARDNER, MASS., OCT. 28, 1890, UPON THE TARIFF IN ITS RELATION TO THE FARMING INDUSTRY.

I WISH to-night to touch upon a phase of the tariff question about which I have not yet spoken, — its effect upon the farmers. Here in Gardner, and all about this section of the country, are many farmers who are thinking seriously of the tariff, now that the tariff is beginning to touch their pockets. They feel its burdens, and are asking what benefits they get as compensation. Finding none, they ask if the time has not come to break away from the Republican party that is inflicting on them taxes to their injury.

Now, the Republicans say that they make a home market for agricultural products by their tariff policy, that they indirectly give a benefit to agriculture by building up communities for farmers to feed.

But their tariff taxes now, instead of building up industries and communities, are, many of them, killing our industries and driving them out of the State, as in the case of the glass and iron and their dependent industries. Surely, that is no benefit to any one, at least here in Massachusetts.

But, in the next place, this cry of the Republicans is only another false pretence to get the farmer to submit quietly to the burden upon him, just as they say to labor — which always bears the heaviest burden of taxation — that the tariff is imposed for labor's benefit, because it will give benefits to the manufacturer, and then trusts to his charity to distribute them in wages,— which, by the way, he never does.

But let us state the account between the farmer and the tariff, and see how he comes out; what burdens and benefits he gets from it. In any scheme of taxation the interest of the farmer ought to be most carefully considered. Nearly one-half of the people in this country who are engaged in gainful occupations are farmers; far more are so engaged than in manufactures.

Now, the tariff taxes about four thousand articles of consumption in this country. I do not propose to give you a list, but I will show you some of the duties on articles which farmers must buy. There is a tax on earthen pipe, 25 cents on every dollar's worth; on linseed-oil, 75 cents; on wall-paper, 25 cents; on lime, 35 cents; on screws, 50 cents; on window-glass, $1.13; on slate, 25 cents; on nails, spikes, and tacks, 52 cents; on white lead, 58 cents; on cheapest crockery, 55 cents to 65 cents; on glass ware, 45 cents to 55 cents; on oil-cloth, 54 cents; on woollen blankets, $1.10; on woollen clothing, 84 cents; on hats, 81 cents; on cotton thread, 50 cents; on buttons, 25 cents, and ivory and bone buttons, 50 cents. And so I might go on showing you taxes on almost every article that enters into the construction and furnishing of your houses and barns, and upon your clothing and your food.

Now, most of these taxes raise the cost of the articles taxed, whether brought here from abroad or made here, — not always to the amount of the tax, but still to a large amount.

You know from your experience that the recent law, which raises tariff taxes 5 or 10 per cent. has raised the cost of many of the most common necessaries of life. If 5 or 10 per cent raises prices, as you know it does, what do you suppose is the effect of tariff taxes of 50 or 60 per cent, which is the average amount to-day of tariff taxation?

So, too, there are tariff taxes on agricultural implements of 45 cents on the dollar of their value; and yet we are sending abroad machinery and agricultural implements made here, and selling them to the foreigner for less than they are sold to our own people. I produced the other evening the evidence of one of the largest manufacturers of agricultural implements, and of manufacturers of saws and cutlery and many other articles, all admitting that they were selling their products cheaper abroad than they were selling them to our own people. Here then is a burden put upon the farmer absolutely without excuse, which exacts from him tribute in taxes without necessity, and which makes it more expensive for him to run his farm, and compete with the foreigner in the sale of his products.

Now, let us take the other side of the account, and see what benefit the farmer gets. Is his grain or potatoes or any farm produce raised in price by this taxation? The Republicans say it is, and declare that they give him a home market by establishing industries.

Well, there is no better place in which to test this home-market idea than Massachusetts and New England. Our State is one of the largest manufacturing States in the Nation. It has more large cities and towns in proportion to its population than any other State. Certainly here we ought to find agriculture growing, if the Republican argument is sound. Let us see what the facts are. From 1875 to 1885 there was a loss of nearly $6,000,000 in the value of farm lands in Massachusetts,— though, no doubt, much of this loss is due to a different standard of value; but we ought to have seen, with a high tariff, an enormous growth in the value of farm-lands.

Next take farm produce. From 1865 to 1885, the amount of beef produced in Massachusetts declined from 70,000,000 pounds to 10,000,000 pounds. Only one-tenth as much cheese was produced in 1885 as in 1865. The production of potatoes decreased from 4,767,000 bushels in 1845 to 3,584,000 bushels in 1885. Our wool product in the same time decreased from 1,015,000 pounds to 225,000 pounds. Yet during this whole period industries and manufactures were developing and growing in Massachusetts. The production also of barley, of buckwheat, of Indian corn, oats, rye, wheat, and hay has declined in 1885 as compared with 1850. So, too, with the number of working oxen and sheep and swine. Meanwhile the value of grains, meats, cattle, and other farm products has also declined. There was also from 1875 to 1885 a decrease in Massachusetts of the land under cultivation and in the value of farm lands per acre.

As a single but a striking piece of evidence that the farming communities in Massachusetts are becoming poorer, notice the report of the Home Missionary Society for June, 1888, which says that "in the western counties of Massachusetts the number of churches aided, not including mission churches in cities and large towns, has increased from 10 in 1860 to 32 in 1888."

Taking population as a test, what do we find? That since the war, up to 1885, the smaller towns of the State have lost 140,000 in their population, while the whole State has gained 18 per cent.

I know that Senator Hoar says that this is in the hillside towns, and is because the farmers on the hilltops have at last got over their fear of attacks from the Indians, and are beginning to slide down into the valleys; but the trouble with this explanation is that the farmers are not only sliding from the hilltops, but also out of the valleys.

Nor is this decline in the condition of our farmers confined to Massachusetts only. We know that in New Hampshire and Vermont there have recently been appointed those ill-omened officers known as commissioners of abandoned farms, appointed by the State to see what can be done to dispose of such farms.

The commissioner of New Hampshire advertises 1,442 abandoned farms in that State. He says, "Many of these farms can be purchased for less than what it would cost to replace the buildings, and for one-fifth of the cost of the permanent improvements upon them." Our poet Whittier has noticed this decline and been touched by it. In his pathetic letter to Judge Nott of Dec. 1, 1889, he says: "I thank thee for thy noble testimony in regard to the sad decline of New England agriculture. Every year when I go to the New Hampshire hill country I find more and more abandoned farms; and the sight takes away much of the pleasure of a sojourn in view of the mountains."

A like condition exists in Connecticut. The recent census shows that, taking the groups of towns described as agricultural, about her twelve manufacturing cities, there has been an actual decrease of population in them from 1880 to 1890. Evidently the farmers in New England have not been enjoying much benefit from the home market. And why not?

Well, the Republicans will say it is because of Western competition. Now, that is an important reason; but how do they explain the fact that in the West there is like distress in the condition of the farmer? And all over the country the wealth of the agricultural community does not begin to grow as does that of the manufacturing interests.

From 1850 to 1860, under our lowest tariff, the value of farms and property increased from $4,000,000,000 to nearly $8,000,000,000, — an increase, on the average, of $337,000,000 a year, or 10 per cent.

From 1860 to 1880 the increase averaged only $177,000,000, or $2\frac{1}{2}$ per cent. From 1870 to 1880 the increase was less than $1,000,000,000; and meanwhile the other half of our people, not farmers, from 1860 to 1880, increased their wealth nearly $23,000,000,000. In the six New England States the value of farms and farm property from 1870 to 1880 actually declined nearly $36,000,000, — though, no doubt, this in part is due to a different standard of money.

It is also true that there has been a decline in the value of such staples as corn, wheat, oats, and grain since we have had a high tariff. From 1850 to 1860 the price of corn averaged 72 cents a bushel, and of wheat, $1.36 per bushel. A recent bulletin of the Agricultural Department says that the present average value of corn is 29.1 cents, and of wheat 70.6 cents, and of oats 23.23 cents; though I believe since that bulletin was issued these prices have somewhat increased. It is a notorious fact that the price of corn has declined so in recent years that the Western farmers have actually used it for fuel.

The reason why farmers all over the country are suffering is, I think, a plain and simple one. By the Republican tariff policy, all that they buy is raised in price; but the price of most that they sell is fixed in competition with the labor of the world, and is not raised by tariff taxes. The price of farm products in New England, no doubt, is lowered by Western competition; but the price of Western products is fixed by the price they sell for in England in competition with the world. Our farms produce much more than our people consume, and the surplus must find a market abroad. Unless it did this, there would be a glut of the market here, and a still further lowering of prices. So each year we export enormous quantities of grains and breadstuffs, — last year nearly 70,000,000 bushels of corn, 46,000,000 bushels of wheat, nearly 10,000,000 barrels of flour, over 15,000,000 pounds of butter, — and great quantities of meats, cheese, tobacco, hops, etc.

Under the Republican tariff policy, which discourages foreign trade and looks upon commerce as a sin, our exports of these articles have been declining, while the exports of the same articles from India and other nations have increased. Our exports of breadstuffs declined from 1880 to 1889 to the extent of $165,000,000; of wheat, from 144,000,000 bushels to 46,000,000 bushels. In 1880 we furnished 69 per cent of all the foreign wheat consumed in European markets, and in 1889 but a little over 20 per cent. What is to become of the farmer of the West if the amount of his product is constantly increasing, but the foreign market for it constantly diminishing?

And if the farmer of the West suffers from this, in Heaven's name what is to become of the small farmer of New England, who suffers also from the Western competition?

Mr. Blaine appreciated this difficulty when he said that our great need was to extend our trade and get additional foreign markets, and showed that he was perfectly well aware of the enormous burden of this McKinley Tariff Bill on the farmer, and of the injury it inflicted on the whole country, when he said there was not a line or section in it which opened up a market for another bushel of wheat or barrel of pork.

Now let us see, with this well-known burden of the tariff on the farmer, and his present depressed condition, what the McKinley Bill does for him?

It gives him only a mock protection. For instance, it doubles the protective tariff duties on beef and pork, though we export about $100,000,000 worth of these articles, and import only about $500,000 worth. What possible good can the farmer get by a tariff on such articles under these circumstances?

It raises the tariff duties on butter and cheese, though we export 12 times as much cheese as we import, and 350 times as much butter as we import. It raises the tariff protection on wheat, though last year we exported 46,000,000 bushels, and imported less than 2,000 bushels; on corn, though last year we exported over 69,000,000 bushels, and imported a little over 2,000; on rye the tariff tax is left at 10 cents, though we exported 287,000 bushels, and imported 16 bushels.

Does any farmer believe that a high-tariff tax on these 16 bushels will affect the price of rye in this country?

So, too, we find a tariff tax on tallow, though we export nearly 80,000,000 pounds; on lard, though we export 318,000,000 pounds, and import 1,700 pounds. On flour they have raised the tariff tax, though we exported nearly 10,000,000 barrels, and imported 1,155.

And so I might go through the whole list. I say, without fear of contradiction, that such tariff taxes are the merest absurdity, and are a humbug and a mockery to the farmer for the purpose of deceiving him into a patient assent to his tariff burdens.

It is true, there are some articles of which we import larger quantities on which the Republicans have raised the tariff. For instance, they have put a duty of five cents a dozen on eggs, and the amount of eggs imported is 1 to every 100 used in this country. So, too, with potatoes, though we exported last year nearly 500,000 bushels, and almost as many as we imported. The tariff has been raised on these, though it is well known that the potatoes imported come at such a season and fill such a demand that they practically are not in competition with our home product.

No wonder, my friends, with tariff taxes bearing so heavily on the farmer, and little or nothing given him in return, we hear a cry of distress from him all over the country. We hear of a large increase through the whole West in the number and amount of mortgages on Western farms. Senator Hoar thinks that this is evidence of the prosperity of the farming class, — on the principle, I suppose, of the fellow who said he managed to live on his debts. No wonder the Farmers' Alliances are everywhere protesting against a high tariff. Here is a resolution adopted by a Farmers' Alliance in Indiana. It reads: —

"That the bill now before the United States Senate, which by its provisions increases tariff taxation, meets with our earnest protest. We scorn the increase of the tariff on agricultural products as a bit of hypocritical, vote-catching claptrap, well knowing that no amount of alleged protection on agricultural products, by any possibility, could have any effect on the price of the same as long as the home supply is greater than the demand."

Most properly, the President of the Farmers' Alliance enters his protest, too, in this indignant language. Speaking of the distress of the farmers, to the very committee that framed the bill, he said: —

"We protest, and with all reverence, that it is not God's fault; we protest that it is not the farmers' fault. We believe and so charge, solemnly and deliberately, that it is the fault of the financial system of the government, — a system that has placed on agriculture an undue, unjust, and intolerable proportion of the burdens of taxation."

I have shown you, first, that the burden of the tariff increases the cost of living, and falls heavily on the farming community, who are nearly one-half the people of the country. Second, that under a high-tariff policy the value of farms in New England and the United States has either actually decreased or not increased as much as under a low tariff. Third, that the value of farm products has declined. Fourth, that the selling price of those products is fixed in competition with the world, but that the farmers' purchases are raised by tariff taxation. To him the tariff is all outgo, and no income. Fifth, that the farming towns in Massachusetts and New England are growing poor and losing their population. Sixth, that throughout the West there is also suffering in this industry. Seventh, that what the farmers need more than anything are more markets abroad to prevent the home market from being glutted by over-production. Eighth, that this McKinley Bill absolutely fails to give them relief, but deliberately, defiantly increases the burdens on the farmer in his purchases.

I want to ask any farmer, with such facts staring him in the face, how he can on his conscience or for his interest give his vote to support the Republican party which has enacted such a policy, and done it, not for the good of the whole country or its industries, but because it is under the control of selfish interests that through it are determined to make money out of the people's law, and to force the people to contribute by taxation their dollars to roll up enormous fortunes for the few.

SPEECH

AT THE TARIFF REFORM LEAGUE DINNER, NEW YORK, DEC. 23, 1890.[1]

IT is a great pleasure to come to this gathering of patriotic and public-spirited men, and to rejoice with them in the success of principles for which they have gallantly fought through defeat to a great and deserved victory. It adds to my pleasure that I can bring to you the greeting and the sympathy of old Massachusetts and of all New England, except two States still in darkness, and perhaps one other which the experienced hand of an unscrupulous politician is trying to keep from the light.

New England has once more rebelled against unjust and unequal taxation. In her colonial days she uttered her first brave protest. In my own city it was ordered "to be recorded in the town books that the children yet unborn may see the desire that their ancestors had for their freedom and happiness;" and again it was there recorded, "We can no longer stand idle spectators," but will aid in any measure "to deliver ourselves and posterity from slavery." With the same spirit, and for the same purpose, New England has now severed old political ties to give emphasis again to her protest, and to declare to the country that she can no longer stand an idle spectator, but has buckled on her armor to deliver ourselves and posterity from the slavery of selfish control by selfish interests of the people's law.

[1] This speech was made to the toast: "The place of New England in the contest: once more she rebels against unjust and unequal taxation."

The issue was squarely made and fought out on the tariff question and the principles it necessarily involves. In Massachusetts, at least, no other question had sufficient weight to affect materially the result. That result was her deliberate conviction in favor of tariff reform upon the lines of making free the raw materials of industries, and cheapening — yes, cheapening — the cost of the necessaries of life.

I know that Senator Hoar has proclaimed in effect that the result was an accident due to misunderstanding and misrepresentation. If so, it was a misunderstanding of his arguments and misrepresentation that he was unable to refute. His explanations, opinions, and threats are by us taken with a liberal discount, as those of an honest man, no doubt, but one whose head requires a surgical operation to get into it public sentiment on the questions of the day, and out of it prejudices of thirty years ago. To himself and his policy might well be applied the remark of the wanderer in the old graveyard, who, finding on a moss-covered stone the words, "I still live," exclaimed, "Well, be jabbers, if I was dead I 'd acknowledge it."

No greater mistake can be made than to suppose the victory in Massachusetts was accidental, or personal to any man. It was her mature judgment upon the tariff after most thorough consideration. For three years the campaign of education had gone on with energy and ever-increasing confidence. It had for its primer and its bible the sound message of a brave President, who made the Nation listen, told it the truth, and marshalled its conscience to assert that justice, equality, and freedom should be with us, as with the fathers, the basis of all law. From 1887 on, through the public Press and public meetings, debates in Congress and our Legislature, in campaigns, and throughout the year, tariff reform was the one supreme subject of political thought and discussion.

Every opportunity was given the people to become informed of the facts and principles necessary for an intelligent opinion, and of the history, burdens, and benefits of a high tariff. Finally, the fatuity of our opponents gave the people a practical but expensive illustration of the whole system in its full development. Tariff reform with us at once made converts. It convinced the wage-earner that high-tariff taxation was to him a burden without adequate return. It awoke the farmer to the fact that to him such taxation was all outgo and no income; and even the manufacturer began to see that protection could take the life of an industry. With this, too, came a wholesome fear that an aroused public sentiment, unless satisfied and controlled by conservative concessions, might sweep away the whole system to get rid of its injustice and its burdens.

Two great influences controlled the action of Massachusetts on this question: first, her material interests; and, second, her moral sense of right and wrong. She remembered that under a low tariff her great industries were established and her manufacturing towns were founded; that in 1857 she, with the rest of New England, was in favor of the lowest tariff our country has had for generations; she recalled that in those days her agriculture thrived, her industries progressed by leaps and bounds, her commerce carried our flag into every part of the civilized world, and the New England coast rang with the music of anvil and of mallet, building the clipper ships that should win the carrying trade of the world.

Then she lived through thirty years of stringent protection. And sitting down at last to examine her condition after such careful "nursing," she found her agriculture declining, and new and ill-omened officers, commissioners of abandoned farms, created in some of the New England States. Her foreign commerce had been swept from the seas. Great industries, that for generations had been her glory and her strength, were folding "their tents, like the Arabs, and silently stealing away." Others were stagnant, others greatly prosperous; and the line of cleavage between stagnation and prosperity seemed to be free raw material. She felt the great and growing competition of the West and the South, with their natural advantages secured to them, while her own were destroyed by a policy which set aside a law of Nature and the will of God. Massachusetts, with her inherited aptitude for skilled industries, will take her chance in any fair competition. She does object to competing with her hands tied; she protests against law holding the knife that would cut the throat of her great industries.

But I love to think that a higher influence than her pocket controlled her action. I know that wrong which touches the pocket pricks the conscience. I also know that Massachusetts, God bless her! against her material interests, has been the fruitful field of many an agitation for human rights, equality, and freedom, meant to be the forerunner of law, and successful in their purpose. If the spirit of the olden time was still in her, it was inevitable that she, true to her history and her traditions, again should protest against unequal and unjust taxation. I rejoice that to make her protest she must walk in the pleasant paths of Democracy. Never was Democracy truer to its mission than when it made tariff reform the supreme question of the day. If Democracy means the rights of the many against the privileges of the few, the equality of all before the law, the freedom of the individual from unnecessary burdens and restrictions; if it really stands between the people and oppressive power, and beside the humblest individual to protect him in making the most of himself, — then it was bound to fight taxation that was enriching the few at the expense of the many, and under the control of selfish interests was being used for selfish purposes. I believe the victory of November was meant to be something more than the settlement of an economic question. I construe it to be the demand of the people that these principles shall control the policy and laws of the Nation.

So will there be a just and honest settlement of the tariff, not by compromises and log-rolling, not by stirring up antagonism of conflicting interests, but by applying to it sound Democratic principles, which define the proper power of government, and secure the rights of the people. Then, too, will they restore government to the purposes of its founders, and make equality, freedom, and economy its guiding principles, as they are the foundations of free and democratic institutions. This is the real significance and value of the victories in New England. They are not the mere assertion of a local position on an economic question. They are her pledge of loyalty to these principles vital to the welfare and happy union of all our people. Her political conversion, deliberate and well grounded, is not a fickle change of heart from which she may slip back to her old life, but a brave confession of her faith and her determined purpose, as long as Democracy shall keep that faith, to follow in its footsteps. Thus understood, it cannot but have an influence far beyond her borders. It shows that Democracy need have no fear of resolute leadership or of a fight for principle. It is New England's tribute to such leadership in the past; it is her trumpet-call for such leadership in the future.

SPEECH

AT THE DEMOCRATIC STATE CONVENTION, WORCESTER, SEPT. 29, 1891, UPON STATE ISSUES.

I AM deeply grateful for the honor conferred upon me by this Convention, representing a great political party, in whose principles I firmly believe.

Your renewed confidence in me is the more welcome because it is the indorsement of an administration which to the utmost of my ability and strength has tried to serve the people's interest and to promote the welfare of our beloved Commonwealth. I rejoice that at last the time has come when I am free to go before the public, who have confided to me an honorable and responsible trust, and to give an account to them of my stewardship.

I should have been glad if, in this aggressive campaign, this accounting to the people could have been made face to face with a valiant and responsible opponent. I cannot but believe that the plan of Lincoln and Douglass, of Campbell and McKinley, would have been a braver, fairer, truer contest on the real issues of the campaign than the irresponsible tactics of guerilla warfare.

However much politicians or platforms may seek to divert the public mind from the issues, the commonsense and honesty of our people can always be trusted to consider and determine the real merits of a campaign. There is, too, an intelligence and independence here which can decide each election on its own merits, and will not undertake in a State election of 1891 to settle a presidential election of 1892. While, no doubt, every State election involves National as well as State questions, and we gladly welcome the discussion of both, I believe that, under the frequent elections enjoined upon us by law, when a servant of the people comes before them for their indorsement, the question they deem most important is: Has he in the matters confided to his charge been honest, faithful, just, and patriotic?

I am confirmed in this belief by the oft-repeated question put to me in the past, What has the election of a Democratic Governor to do with the tariff question? To the test suggested I gladly submit the administration of the year, and to it I challenge the attention and criticism of our opponents. It is something in favor of the administration that a party which has often declared that State affairs only were involved in the election of State officers, which has followed it with keenest scrutiny and minute attack throughout the year, which has loudly proclaimed the need of what that party calls "the redemption of Massachusetts," yet, when it meets in solemn convention, in the responsible utterance of its platform, can find no word of objection or criticism upon that administration, and forthwith proclaims its policy to settle State affairs on National lines, and the election of 1892 in the fall of 1891. And then it leaves the duty of finding some kind of criticism, however specious or petty, to one whose only connection with State affairs during the year has been in the lobbies of the State House, trying to defeat the declared purpose of the Legislature, and to set aside the report of a Republican committee in favor of a fair and honest redistricting of the State, that he may substitute therefor his own purpose to have an unfair and dishonest gerrymander of the State for his own personal and partisan ends.

Four grounds of criticism this gentleman has discovered. First, two appointments made by me, he is informed, were bad. But he carefully omits to specify even the two. Will he now kindly specify them? What has he to say of the hundreds of other appointments made?

In the selection of judges, of new officers created by the Legislature, and of other important officials, there has been placed a responsibility upon the Governor greater than for many years. How has that responsibility been met? Is the proper test two possible mistakes, or hundreds of appointments confessedly good? Is it the one or the one hundred instances that mark the policy of an administration and give to it a character that explains and redeems a possible mistake?

I say without fear of contradiction that there never has been a Republican administration in the Nation, or in any of her States, that has made such a practical and thorough application of the spirit and purpose of civil service reform as this Democratic administration in the Commonwealth of Massachusetts; and this notwithstanding the fact that the precedents before me were a State administration with nearly every lucrative office filled by a Republican, and a National administration which, in violation of its own and its party's plighted words, had removed thousands and tens of thousands of Democrats for politics only, and, against the nearly unanimous protest of our whole people, had defiantly proclaimed that an honest, efficient Democrat, because he was a Democrat, was not fit to be postmaster of the city of Boston.

Second, my critic complains of two vetoes made by me. It is enough at present to say that both vetoes were unanimously sustained in a Senate evenly divided politically.

Third, he criticises the failure to reappoint a railroad commissioner, but of course neglects to say that scores of other Republican officials have been reappointed.

Reserving for another time a full discussion of this criticism, let me say now that when Massachusetts places so much of her administration in the hands of commissions which are beyond the control of the people, and to that extent irresponsible, and one of those commissions pointedly, defiantly, opposes the will of the people's Legislature twice expressed, and refuses to do its plain duty till compelled to by the peremptory and unanimous order of the Supreme Court,— I say that in my judgment the time has come when the people, exercising through their Governor the only power left to them over such a commission, should declare that at least he shall not reappoint a commissioner guilty of such an offence.

Fourth, my critic says that, though opposed to commissions, and having an opportunity to show his opposition, "yet this enemy of commissions has appointed not less than five, — rapid transit, World's Columbian Exposition, uniformity of legislation, manual industrial training, and Charles River improvement;" and he denounces my inconsistency.

He knows that my objection to commissions, as repeatedly expressed, was to those "whose work is wholly executive," and which make part of the State's "system of administrative and executive work." He knows that the commissions mentioned are for a different purpose; that they have nothing to do with State administration; that they are all for temporary objects; and that, with one exception, the service is entirely gratuitous. He knows that every one of them was created by an Act of the Legislature nearly, if not quite, unanimously passed, which compelled me to make the appointments, and my only power to object to them was to veto the Act of their creation.

Which one would he have had me veto? The one which is to plan and provide a proper exhibit for the World's Fair? Or the one which is to investigate the crying demand and need of our people for better transit facilities? Or the one which, in conference with other States, is to consider the question of uniform legislation on matters of marriage, divorce, etc.? Or the one which is to investigate the subject of manual training, in the hope of advancing the cause of labor and increasing the influence and value of our public schools? Or the one which is to investigate how best the Charles River basin can be improved for the benefit of all our people?

For such criticism from a party's apparent leader, which magnifies little things, purposely withholds necessary facts, and knowingly distorts an opponent's position, I am profoundly grateful. It is more significant as an indorsement, because of its labored effort, than the confession that comes from silence, or the pleasant compliments that mark a courteous and generous antagonist.

Something, however, may properly be said in behalf of the administration, not as personal to me, but as carrying out the aggressive policy and pledges repeatedly declared by the Democratic party. In the exercise of the appointive power it has been true to its party's promise, and has made efficiency, character, and ability the tests for public office. In the exercise of the power of removal it has sought to maintain a standard of honesty, decency, and unselfish purpose among public officials, and has been thwarted by a partisan Council. It has sought to make commissions responsible to the people, and has been met by a hostile Council which openly declared its power to confirm to be a power to dictate a nomination, and by its act sought to make nine men instead of one man the appointing power of the State.

It has abolished useless and expensive commissions. It has sought to eradicate the lobby by calling public attention to the evil, and suggesting more efficient restraints upon it. It has refused to allow the payment of $14,000, in violation of the good faith of the Commonwealth to Congress, for lobby services of a State agent. It has recommended and aided the constitutional amendment for the abolition of the poll-tax as a qualification for voting, which, having passed two Republican Legislatures, is now before the people; yet upon this measure the Republican party has nothing to say except in the silence of its platform and the known hostility of its candidate.

It has sought to reform the system of prison management, and to bring greater responsibility into administrative boards, but it has been met by a hostile or indifferent Legislature. It has sought to increase the usefulness of our public schools, and, as urged in my inaugural address, "not only to uphold this system in its full vigor, but also to provide for its progressive development," by suggesting new courses and methods of instruction, such as manual training and industrial education, and by better provision and more equal opportunity for the children in the poorer places. It has sought to abolish abuses connected with legislation, such as the giving of railroad passes and the entertainment of committees by interested parties, and has recommended more stringent laws to prevent improper influences at elections. It has sought to obtain the passage of general laws to do away with special legislation, and has urged that greater powers be given to municipalities and local governments. It has sought to obtain just and fair legislation in answer to the demands of labor, and has made a thorough investigation into the "sweating system," which has resulted in legislation to remedy its evils.

This is the proper time and place, I believe, to declare, if not to discuss, the real issues of the campaign, and to repudiate the false issues with which our opponents seek to divert public attention. They have declared that temperance and the public schools were the important State questions. Yet on the first they pointedly refused to declare their position, except by idle platitudes; and the second, thank God, is not, and cannot be made a political issue.

If the Republican party desires to make temperance an issue, let it first specifically declare its own, and but one, position. Does it or its candidate believe in legislative or constitutional prohibition? Will he recommend it, or the Republican party pass it? Does it or he believe in the legislation of this year upon the liquor question? Will he recommend repealing such legislation and re-enacting the public-bar clause of the statute?

An answer to these questions will be a plain declaration of his position far more honest, practical, and useful than idle platform expressions of sympathy, which are meant to hide a lack of courage and conviction. Until the Republican party finds and holds and declares some definite position on this question, it can hardly be an issue.

My distinguished opponent has seen fit to drag into this campaign an institution too glorious, too useful, and too sacred to be made a political issue. I yield to no man in my love for the public schools, or in my loyalty and earnest efforts to promote their interests. To me they have given an education, and, in return, to them I have given four years of earnest service.

Over and over again the Democratic party has declared its loyalty to them, and proved it by its acts. Every measure in this Commonwealth for increasing the usefulness and influence of the public schools has received its strongest support from the Democratic party, — such measures, for example, as free text-books, increasing the compulsory age for attendance, the establishment of evening schools and industrial training and manual education.

He is the enemy of the public schools who would breathe through a community the spirit of intolerance. He is disloyal to one of our greatest and noblest institutions who, placing party above patriotism, and politics above principle, seeks, for partisan ends, to excite prejudice and to divide a people politically over their public schools, when there is, or ought to be, a union in thought and word and act. How long can our public schools withstand such attacks of unscrupulous politicians?

But there are some real State issues in this campaign.

First, the Democratic administration to which I have referred. Let its every act be searched and criticised; but let it be judged in a spirit of justice and honesty, and not of petty partisanship.

Next, the issue of responsible executive government. By their acts and declarations the two parties on this are at issue. The Democratic party believes that, when the people elect their Governor, they mean he should in fact be Governor, that upon him should be placed the responsibility and power of control, for the exercise of which he is immediately answerable to them; that the power of government and administration is thus kept within control of the people, and the people's servant is responsible for every act. The Democratic party does not believe that commissions for administrative work should be beyond the control of the people, or that the responsibility for their efficiency should be divided among a Governor and Council, but that they should be made responsible to the Governor, and he to the people. It believes that the power of appointments rests with the Governor, and the power of the Council to confirm is not a power to dictate nominations. It believes in the principle that "power without responsibility is always dangerous, but power with responsibility to a constituency which can readily call it to account is not dangerous, — it is the first requisite of efficient administration."

Of National questions there are three of paramount importance, — the tariff, silver, and the civil service. On the last we gladly invite a comparison between the present National administration and its predecessor, or the Democratic administration in this State. For the first time in some years Federal officers are left free to take an active and offensive part in caucuses, conventions, and campaigns; and even Republican State officials, appointed by the Governor, do not hesitate to become active political partisans. The protests of the National Civil Service Commission against such conduct go unheeded, and the old abuses of compulsory contributions from officials have been revived. Officials by the thousand are removed for politics only, and even the protest of Republican senators and congressmen is unable to save the head of an efficient Democratic postmaster. In the civil service under

Republican administration there has been an utter and shameless abandonment of the spirit and purpose of the reform.

We unhesitatingly declare for a sound currency and an honest dollar, and we protest, not only against the free coinage of silver, but against the present Republican legislation, which is bringing us dangerously near to a silver basis and an unsound currency. I believe that in this Commonwealth both parties are honestly opposed to any legislation, present or prospective, which threatens these consequences. Then let the Republican party declare this conviction and repudiate such legislation, that the unanimous voice of the Commonwealth may be heard in protest against dangerous financial doctrines, with no discordant note except an honest rivalry as to the best means of carrying out her wish.

We believe that the revision and reduction of tariff taxation is the supreme political issue, and we again declare that it should be on the lines of free raw material and of cheapening the cost of the necessaries of life. We confidently believe that this will be a benefit, not only to all our people, but especially to New England industries. The demand of our industries for such reduction has not been heeded in the McKinley Bill. We declare our purpose, in behalf of our industries and the people, to fight for this reduction until the people get their burden of taxation lessened, and our industries the benefit of their location by receiving through our seaports their raw material free of taxation.

Fellow-Democrats, I go from you to the people to uphold and defend a Democratic administration and the principles of our party. We all begin here and now an earnest, vigorous, aggressive campaign. For nearly a year our opponents have been organizing their forces and preparing for the battle. They have searched for candidates, and advertised for issues. They have demanded harmony among their warring factions, and peace between their jealous leaders. They have raised false issues and evaded the real ones. Their aggressive leader, who prefers to fight alone, has blundered on the tariff, waved the bloody shirt, and endeavored to carry prejudice and politics into our public schools, — the glorious institution and the priceless heritage of all our people. They have demanded a revival of Republicanism, called the roll of their forces, and endeavored to gather all under a name, no matter what their convictions, or how much or little that name may mean to them. They will spare no effort to win a victory, whatever it may signify. Let us meet them with vigilance, perseverance, and unceasing effort, and, calmly, honestly discussing the real issues, trust to the common-sense, the conscience, and the patriotism of our people to decide aright between us.

SPEECH

AT MUSIC HALL, BOSTON, OCT. 5, 1891, UPON THE TARIFF AND ITS EFFECT UPON MASSACHUSETTS.

I THANK you most heartily for your cordial welcome. May I consider it not only a proof of your sympathy and support in the pending struggle, but also your indorsement of an administration which has honestly, earnestly tried to serve the people's interests, and promote the welfare of our beloved Commonwealth? As I believe it is the privilege and duty of every citizen carefully to examine the acts of a public servant, so it is the privilege and duty of such servant to account to the people for every act, and also to defend himself from unjust and malignant criticism. One such criticism to-night I propose to answer. The great honor has been given me by the people of the Commonwealth of presiding over her affairs. With that honor has come the grave responsibility faithfully and unselfishly to serve her interests, to defend her glorious institutions, and to uphold her honor. Any public servant of hers unfaithful in this is disloyal to his Commonwealth. Among the foolish, the false, and the wicked issues which the Republican party has endeavored to raise in this campaign to excite prejudice rather than to carry conviction, is the charge that in a public address delivered by me in New York on the tariff question I maligned the Commonwealth. With suspicious unanimity, as if suggested and forced by campaign managers, that charge has been echoed through the Republican Press, which refuses, however, to print the address. To-night, again, I challenge the "Boston Journal" and the Republican newspapers to print that speech, — the whole of it, not a single sentence. But you will look in vain for it there from now until election day, though these papers profess to rely upon it as a strong reason for my defeat. Then this charge has been caught up by my distinguished opponent, and after him have come Tray, Blanche, and Sweetheart, barking it at my heels. Let me read the charge as formulated by him in his speech at Haverhill, September 22. He then said: —

"We have in Massachusetts this year as our chief magistrate a Democrat. . . . Massachusetts had a right to expect that every son of hers, especially if endowed with the highest honors in her gift, would be a valiant defender of her honor wherever he went. And yet very soon after his inauguration, while the very plaudits of his friends were ringing in his ears, he took occasion to detract from our industries, to detract from this old Commonwealth. He spoke of our abandoned farms, and of our great industries 'folding their tents, like the Arabs, and silently stealing away.'"

Let me correct the first mistake of Mr. Allen — small, however, in comparison with the others — and remind him that I delivered that speech some time before I entered office, as a private citizen, and not as Governor of the Commonwealth. So much for the charge. Let us see upon what it is founded. The speech referred to was delivered by me, Dec. 23, 1890, before the Tariff Reform Club of New York at its celebration of the great tariff reform victory that had swept over the country, and in response to the toast, "The place of New England in that contest: once more she rebels against unequal and unjust taxation." A political revolution had broken Massachusetts away from her Republican moorings in the election of her congressmen and Governor. That result, after three years of thorough discussion, was due to the tariff question, — unless Mr. Lodge believes that he and his Force Bill were a potent influence in turning Massachusetts from Republicanism to the pleasant paths of Democracy. It was her protest, founded upon mature consideration, against the Republican policy on the tariff as embodied in the McKinley Bill. In that speech I spoke as follows of the influences that controlled her decision. I quote now every word that has been subject to adverse criticism: —

"Two great influences controlled the action of Massachusetts on this question: first, her material interests; and, second, her moral sense of right and wrong. She remembered that under a low tariff her great industries were established and her manufacturing towns were founded; that in 1857 she, with the rest of New England, was in favor of the lowest tariff our country has had for generations; she recalled that in those days her agriculture thrived, her industries progressed by leaps and bounds, her commerce carried our flag into every part of the civilized world, and the New England coast rang with the music of anvil and of mallet, building the clipper ships that should win the carrying trade of the world. Then she lived through thirty years of stringent protection. And sitting down at last to examine her condition after such careful 'nursing,' she found her agriculture declining, and new and ill-omened officers, commissioners of abandoned farms, created in some of the New England States. Her foreign commerce had been swept from the seas. Great industries, that for generations had been her glory and her strength, were 'folding their tents, like the Arabs, and silently stealing away.' Others were stagnant, others greatly prosperous; and the line of cleavage between stagnation and prosperity seemed to be free raw material. She felt the great and growing competition of the West and the South, with their natural advantages secured to them, while her own were destroyed by a policy which set aside a law of Nature and the will of God. Massachusetts, with her inherited aptitude for skilled industries, will take her chance in any fair competition. She does object to competing with her hands tied; she protests against law holding the knife that would cut the throat of her great industries. But I love to think that a higher influence than her pocket controlled her action. I know that wrong which touches the pocket pricks the conscience. I also know that Massachusetts — God bless her! — against her material interests, has been the fruitful field of many an agitation for human rights, equality, and freedom, meant to be the forerunner of law, and successful in their purpose. If the spirit of the olden time was still in her, it was inevitable that she, true to her history and her traditions, again should protest against unequal and unjust taxation."

Because of that opinion, expressed by me as a private citizen, and because of that only, have arisen the hue and cry that I have "detracted from this old Commonwealth." Let me answer this charge, not because I believe any unprejudiced man seriously thinks that the statement quoted is "detraction" of our Commonwealth, but because it gives me an opportunity to show what party and what policy are really injuring the Commonwealth and her industries. First, the argument and facts stated in that speech have been used over and over again in campaigns in Massachusetts, without the charge that such discussion of an economic question was maligning the Commonwealth. Is it maligning her to declare one's honest conviction that high-tariff taxation of the raw materials of our industries has injured and is injuring those industries? Has such taxation become so sacred that one cannot question it without being traduced as an enemy of the Commonwealth? Second, was not my statement of her condition, of her protest against unjust restrictions and unfair competition, and of the high moral purpose that guided her, and always has, far more complimentary to her than the graphic account given by my distinguished opponent of her agricultural and mineral resources? In his recent speech at Haverhill he said: "As an agricultural country Massachusetts cannot hope to excel. If Nature has endowed her with mineral resources, she has corked them up too safely in her bosom for our convenient inspection, and as a mineral community we are a dead failure." Was he, too, maligning the Commonwealth? Third. But my critics say, "No matter what your motive; no matter if you are patriotically trying to establish free raw materials for the benefit of our industries, and protesting against the selfish restrictions which Ohio and Pennsylvania have forced upon Massachusetts; no matter if Massachusetts has declared emphatically in favor of such change,— still, your facts are wrong, and so you have insulted the Commonwealth." Well, let us examine these facts. There are volumes of instruction on the tariff question in a fair and careful study of them.

Is it not true that under a low tariff our great industries were established and our manufacturing towns were founded? Turn to the history of Lowell, with such great manufacturing companies as the Hamilton, Appleton, Lowell, Middlesex, Lawrence, Boott, Massachusetts, Lowell bleachery and Lowell machine shop, all established before 1860; or to the history of Lawrence, with its Washington and Atlantic mills, built in 1846, its Pacific and Pemberton mills, incorporated in 1852, and its Everett mills, in 1860. Does not the founding of Holyoke's industries date from the building of her present dam in 1849? Were not great industries established in Fall River long before the high tariff; and through those industries did not Fall River grow to be a city in 1854? And is it not on record that after our great industries were established in these and other places, Massachusetts and New England, through their representatives in Congress, voted in 1857 for the lowest tariff our country had had for generations? Were her representatives then hostile to her industries? Were they in their official acts "detracting" from her interests and maligning their Commonwealth?

But it is said that I had no right to comment on her present condition after thirty years of stringent protection, or to say that some of her industries were "stagnant," some greatly prosperous, some were "silently stealing away," and that the "line of cleavage between them seemed to be free raw material," or to criticise the condition of her agriculture. If one honestly believes that an economic policy is injurious to his State, and that it is dictated by the selfish interests of competing States, I believe it is far more patriotic to protest against that policy than patiently to submit to it, or, worse still, to be an active agent in forcing it upon the State. The Democratic position on the tariff is a demand, not for free-trade, but for free raw materials,— free wool, coal, iron ore, copper, lumber, etc., and all in the interest and for the benefit of our great industries. Let us examine this position in the light of recorded facts and the statement of the industries themselves.

Some Massachusetts industries are, or have been, "silently stealing away." First, the copper-smelting industry. The time was when that industry thrived in Massachusetts, and great companies, like the Revere Copper Company of Boston and the Crocker Brothers of Taunton, did a prosperous business in smelting ores. But the demand was made upon the Republican party for a duty upon copper. In whose interest? In that of Massachusetts? No. It was bound to kill her smelting works, injure her ship-building and repairing industries, and burden the manufacture of copper and brass goods. Yet, in answer to the demand of the owners of the rich Lake Superior mines, against the protest of ship-owners and ship-builders, of smelting works and copper and brass manufacturers, and over the veto of a President, the Republican party in 1869 put a duty upon copper. What was the result? Let the treasurer of the Revere Copper Company answer the question. He says, on Feb. 10, 1888: "Our smelting works at Point Shirley were legislated out of existence." And, referring to this duty, he adds: "This killed our business. We ran for a short time longer, and then had to give up and sell out the property. The buildings and other evidences of the industry have wholly disappeared." That duty threw out of employment in Massachusetts some hundreds of men, and destroyed manufacturing property worth hundreds of thousands of dollars. But the Lake Superior mines, having the right by law and by the Republican policy to tax the whole people for their special benefit, have made enormous profits, and have been profitably selling our own American copper in foreign markets cheaper than to our own people; while our copper and brass industries were feeling the burden of this tax, and our vessels were being sent to foreign ports to be there repaired with American copper, because cheaper than in our own ports. So much for one industry that has been stolen away from Massachusetts by the Republican policy of taxing the raw materials of our industries. Second: let me now refer to another, the iron and steel industry; and here I quote from the printed statement and petition of the industry itself that was circulated in February, 1889, not as a political document, nor prepared for political purposes, but put forth by the industry itself, months after the election, as a fair statement of its condition, and its reason for tariff reduction. It is signed by five hundred and ninety-eight "proprietors or manufacturers of iron-working establishments in New England, being members of all political parties," as it recites, including Governor Ames and many other leading Republicans and the largest iron and steel industries in New England. Among the signers are the Taunton, Rhode Island, and Manchester locomotive works, the Albert Field Tack Company, the American Screw Company, Washburn & Moen, the Bay State, South Boston, Tremont, Plymouth, and Fairhaven foundries, the Armington & Sims Engine Company, the Boston Bridge Works, Cambridge rolling-mills, the American Axe & Tool Company, and hundreds of nail, machine, tack, boiler, locomotive, sewing-machine, and other manufactories and foundries. That statement declares that the duty on pig iron "is practically prohibitory;" that because of it "the tendency has been to wipe out the iron and steel industries, large and small, of New England. The surviving mills owe their continued existence in a small part to the fact that they have been able to pick up and rework a little old material (scrap iron, castings and turnings) in their own territory, but chiefly to the fact that they have, through the compulsion of circumstances, been systematically engaged in the degradation of American labor in New England. A skilled operative in a New England rolling-mill does not on the average receive one-half the pay that a man similarly employed in a Pittsburg mill receives for the same work." Then, after stating that the annual production of rolled iron and steel in New England has dwindled 40 per cent from 1880 to 1887, while during that time there has been an increase of 57 per cent in the production of rolled iron and steel throughout the country, this statement of the manufacturers adds: "The heavy mill-wrighting business hardly exists in New England. . . . Our iron and steel architectural beams, columns, roofing, gas pipes, water pipes, and sewer pipes are made in Pennsylvania." It states further: "It is then clearly the duty on coal and crude iron that is strangling in New England one of the largest of all the wonderful industries of our modern days." And with almost pathetic insistence it declares: "There is no necessity for letting it die; it is only the existing duties on coal, ore, and crude iron that are strangling it. The abolition of those duties will not only keep it alive, but will insure it a tremendous vitality and large increase, and will add more largely to the wealth and prosperity of New England than any possible legislation on any other subject." In a published interview about the same time, Governor Ames declared: "The iron trade of New England is gradually disappearing. The natural advantages of competitors plus the duty mean death to the New England iron industry." The facts show that the rolling-mills in New England have been reduced from 41 in 1880 to 24 in 1890; the cut-nail industries have been reduced from twelve to two or three since 1872. Governor Ames in the interview referred to says, after speaking of many of the shovel works that were in existence: "The Ames works at North Easton are now the only existing shovel works in New England of any importance." Such great works as the East Bridgewater Iron Company, the Fall River, Pembroke, Old Colony, and Tisdale iron works, the Weymouth and Providence and the Robinson Iron Company, Parker mills, and, more recently, the South Boston Iron Company, and the Norway Iron and Steel Works, have all gone out of existence, and others have removed, or are removing, from the Commonwealth.

Mr. Wadlin, the chief of the Bureau of Statistics, in his report on Massachusetts manufactures in 1890, says: "The total product of rolled iron was 109,252 tons in 1880, valued at $7,773,058, and 42,847 tons in 1889, valued at $1,887,062. The product of Bessemer and open hearth steel aggregated 22,342 tons in 1880, valued at $2,178,860, and 11,887 tons in 1889, valued at $461,419." And on page 391 he shows that the number of persons employed in the iron manufactures at Taunton have declined from 2,942 in the best days of that industry to 1,537 in 1890. Remember that this decline of the iron industry is of one of our earliest and strongest industries, and is wholly due, as itself says, to the present tariff policy, — that it is not the failure of a new industry, or of an attempt to create a new industry, but a struggle for life of an old and well-established one.

Third, let us now turn to another industry, — the glass industry.

What has become of it in Massachusetts? There used to be here great and prosperous companies, like the Sandwich, the New England, the Bay State, and the Suffolk, supplying not only our home market, but sending their goods into the markets of the world.

Mr. Wadlin, in his recent Report on the Growth of Manufactures, on page 372, states that from 1855 to 1885 the product of the glass industries declined from $2,648,125 to $1,091,949, and the number of men employed from 1,887 to 982; and since 1885 the two largest companies in that industry have finally closed their doors. What is the cause of this? Let me read a single extract from a statement of one thoroughly conversant with the industry, and formerly a director in the largest company: "Twenty years ago Massachusetts had two of the most famous glass manufactories in the United States. They had a large capital, paid handsome dividends, and produced as fine table glassware as was made in the world. They are now extinct. Neither one has produced glassware for several years. The duty on coal was the chief obstacle that discouraged the work." The failure of each of those industries threw from three hundred to four hundred men out of employment, and wrecked about half a million dollars of capital.

Fourth, let us pass to another industry, that of ship-building and ship-owning. The merchant marine of the United States in foreign trade has declined, from 1861 to 1890, from 2,486,894 tons to 928,062 tons. The tonnage of vessels built in New England has declined from 183,625 tons in 1857 to 39,983 tons in 1889. Mr. Wadlin, in his report, shows a decline in value in ship-building in Massachusetts from $4,435,323 in 1865, to $2,107,986 in 1885; and in the hands employed in that industry from 2,424 to 1,534; and this includes a large number of yachts and pleasure-boats that in recent times have been built.

Fifth. Next let us consider a few facts in reference to the woollen industry. In the first place, in 1889, 524 manufacturers and dealers in wool and woollen goods petitioned Congress for free wool, and 196 others for a reduction in duties. In those petitions they referred to "the present depression in the wool manufacturing industry," and added: "As the only civilized country in the world, so far as we are informed, which levies a duty on raw wool, we ask that American industry may be relieved of this unnatural burden, and that our domestic wool interests may now be put on the same wholesome basis as the cotton manufacturing industry, with free raw material." Among the signers were some of the most famous manufacturers and mills in the country engaged in that industry. Next, Bradstreet's report of Dec. 28, 1889, shows that in the year 1889 there were 72 wool and woollen goods failures against 57 in 1888, and that the liabilities were nearly three times as great. On June 14, 1890, the Wool Consumers' Association, in a petition to Congress signed by such well-known men as Arthur T. Lyman, Jesse Metcalf, and others, and by such famous companies as the Lowell Manufacturing Company, the Wanskuck, Weybosset, and others, said: "For the protection of the wool manufacture of the country, and for its rescue from a most hampered and depressed condition, we ask for a great reduction or a total abolition of the duty on wool." It added that such duties had been tried "at great cost to the consumer, with destructive restriction to the manufacturer, and without any compensating advantages to the wool-grower." Now let us turn to the statistics of the growth of the woollen industry in Massachusetts, and compare it with the growth of other industries in Massachusetts whose principal raw materials are free of duty. Mr. Wadlin, in the report referred to, states that the value of woollen goods made in Massachusetts in 1865 was $31,550,081, and in 1885 was $31,748,278, and the number of hands employed increased only from 18,965 to 18,970.

But during that period the boot and shoe industry, with hides free since 1872, increased in the value of its product from $35,741,393 to $114,729,533, and the number of hands employed from 52,821 to 64,858. The leather industry during the same time increased in its product from $12,062,046 to $28,008,851, and the number of hands employed from 5,321 to 9,228. In the silk industry during that period the increase in its product was from $751,146 to $3,501,240, and the number of hands employed from 503 to 2,126. In the paper industry during that period the product increased from $5,383,301 to $21,223,626, and the number of hands employed from 3,578 to 8,620. In the cotton industry the increase in the number of hands was from 24,151 to 60,132, and in the value of goods from $35,355,699 to $61,425,097. Even add to woollen goods the worsted goods, which are separately classified, and still there is a great difference shown in the growth of it and of these industries whose principal raw materials have, during most or all of this time, been free from duty. So great has been the prosperity in the cotton industry that last year six new mills were erected in Fall River, which have led to an over-production that at present is causing a reaction. In view of these facts does it not look as though some industries were "stagnant," some "greatly prosperous," and that the "line of cleavage" was free raw material? With justice, the woollen industry has demanded free raw material; it asked for bread, but it got a stone. Instead of free wool or lower duties, the duties were raised still higher, and with the full assent and aid of the Republican representatives from Massachusetts. What has been the result? Let me quote from the "American Wool Reporter," the journal of the woollen industry, whose editor is a pronounced Republican and protectionist. On July 23, 1891, he says editorially:—

"The wool industry in several departments shows greater depression to-day than before the passage of the McKinley Bill. . . . If the expected benefits from the tariff are to come, they are certainly a long time in materializing. At any rate, the next effort that is made for a general revision of import duties in an upward direction will be attended by the query of an increased number of manufacturers as to whether doubtful benefits that are to be enjoyed later on are worth the weary period of temporary depression which has followed nearly every application of higher tariff laws, except upon a few special articles."

On Aug. 6, 1891, he says editorially: —

"The woollen mills have had a long and exhausting period of depression. Their business was dull and unsatisfactory when the iron trade was active, when the shoe and leather interest was profitable, and when the cotton mills were enjoying the handsome dividends of the year 1889 and 1890."

Truly the opinion of its editor, expressed in his paper Oct. 23, 1890, has come true, when he said: "I arraign the tariff upon wool in the United States, because it is a tax on the consumer. Finally, I oppose the duties on wool because they are obstacles to the development of our manufactures."

A single word about agriculture. It is true that in some lines, such as truck-farming, dairy and greenhouse products, there has been an increase; but in staple agricultural products such as meats, cereals, wool, and tobacco, there has been an enormous decrease in the last thirty years. So it happens that places like Hadley, which in 1875 was the first agricultural town in our Commonwealth, have decreased in population,— Hadley has fallen to the sixth place, while Worcester stands first and Boston second as the leading agricultural towns of the Commonwealth. But there has been a marked decrease of the population in the genuine agricultural towns. Hampden County, with a gain of 20 per cent in population during the last ten years, shows a loss in over one-half of its towns; Berkshire, with an increase of $17\frac{1}{2}$ per cent, shows a loss in 24 of its 32 towns. In many counties of the Commonwealth more than one-half of the towns, and those agricultural, have lost in population. Commissioners of abandoned farms have been appointed in some New England States, and already there are reported in this Commonwealth 1,461 abandoned farms, and of these 772 have buildings upon them.

With this hurried review of our principal industries, noting the prosperity of some, and the lack of prosperity of others, I believe that it is true that Massachusetts asks and needs, and some day will have, free raw materials for the benefit of all her industries and all her people. I do not doubt, and never have doubted, that Massachusetts, with the skill, industry, and intelligence of her people, with their inherited aptitude for manufacturing, with the enterprise of her capitalists, is and always will be great and prosperous. I doubt as little that if the hand of the law should lift some of this burden of taxation and give to Massachusetts the benefit of her location, she and her industries would be greater and more prosperous. Is it not true, as I said in New York, that Massachusetts will take her chance in any fair competition? She does object to competing with her hands tied. She protests against law holding the knife that would cut the throat of her great industries. Who is the one that detracts from the interests and industries of our beloved Commonwealth? There came a demand from Pennsylvania that duties on iron and coal should remain. It was followed by another demand from the political shepherds of Ohio for higher duties on wool, and by another from Pennsylvania and the West for doubling the duties on tin plates, and for re-imposing a duty on hides, no matter how injurious these demands might be to Massachusetts industries. Against these demands went forth the indignant protests of our industries, declaring that such a policy would be injurious to them and to the welfare of our Commonwealth. Where were Massachusetts' sons in that struggle? Her Democratic representatives were listening to her appeal and fighting for free raw materials to build up her industries. Her Republican representatives were bending the knee to Ohio and Pennsylvania, and, deaf to her protests, gave their aid to let her burdens remain, or to make them heavier still. I charged them then from every stump in Massachusetts, as I charge them now, with being recreant to her interests, and yielding for partisan purposes to demands from other sections that were hostile to the welfare of our State. I said Massachusetts had an accounting to make with them; and hardly were the words spoken when Massachusetts made her accounting, and, with emphatic voice, declared that not those who denounced this policy, but those who were responsible for it, were the sons who had been disloyal to her. I have no fear of trying this question over again in Massachusetts, nor shall my voice be hushed by the unjust and silly criticism that he who points out the injurious effects to his Commonwealth of an economic policy is maligning her name and interests. Malign my old Commonwealth, where I was born and have passed my life, whose glorious public schools have given to me an education, whose people have confided to me a high and honorable trust, whose brilliant history and sturdy virtues, whose great institutions and blessed charities I have praised from a hundred platforms, and to whose service I have given the utmost of my strength and ability? My friends, there is some criticism that cuts to the heart, and yet is almost too contemptible to answer.

SPEECH

AT LYNN, OCT. 29, 1891. STATE ISSUES.—THE TARIFF IN ITS RELATION TO THE LEATHER INDUSTRY.

IT is a little late now to discuss the issues of the campaign, but it is not too late to sum them up, and to show you what sort of a campaign the Republicans have been waging. They started long ago with a search for a candidate and an advertisement for issues. They demanded peace between their jealous leaders, and harmony among their warring factions, and called upon all their forces to rally under the name "Republican," however little that name might now mean to them.

They demanded an aggressive candidate, but nominated one who has declined to meet his opponent in fair and manly debate, and who absolutely refuses to define his position, or to declare any conviction on the great questions of State policy over which he asks the people to give him a controlling influence.

In his speech last night at Worcester, Mr. Allen remarked to his audience: "You and I have alike reason to rejoice that this campaign is so near its end. You, because, having performed the political duties enjoined on American citizens, you will be free to pursue your usual business and employment undisturbed by politics; I, because the exacting requirements nowadays imposed upon a candidate will be at an end."

Mr. Allen, your duty is not over, nor have you ever begun it. There is time left to do it, and this platform and to-morrow night, when you speak here, are the time and place for it. You owe a duty to the people of the Commonwealth. You come before them as the candidate of a great party, seeking election to a high and responsible office. Your first and obvious duty is to declare to them your views on the great questions of the day in which they are vitally interested. That duty you cannot escape, except by evasion or silence. Let me tell you our people recognize and will tolerate differences of opinion; but they will not tolerate the absence of all opinion, and they condemn a lack of courage or conviction in any political leader.

I propose to-night, as I have done repeatedly, to point out to you this obvious duty by demanding your attention to some matters upon which you have failed to express an opinion.

First, there has been an attempt, Mr. Allen, by the leader of your party, supported by four-fifths of it in the Legislature, to gerrymander the State in the congressional districts. That attempt thus far has been defeated. Your leader has refused, however, to repudiate his purpose. The present law is within the control of the Legislature and the Governor of next year, and can be repealed or amended to carry out his purpose. Do you, Mr. Allen, repudiate that purpose? Will you agree, if elected, to veto any attempt to change that law; or do you stand, with Mr. Lodge and four-fifths of your party, in favor of gerrymandering this State?

Second, there is before the people a great constitutional amendment to abolish the poll-tax as a qualification for voting, and to give to our people the great blessing of free manhood suffrage. Mr. Beard said last night: "It has been favored by Republican governors and Republican leaders all the way down."

I know that ever since the birth of the Republican party the Democratic party has demanded the abolition of this tax, but that in this it has always been defeated by the Republican party. I know that the justice of our demand has been recognized and admitted over and over again by Republican leaders like Sumner, Wilson, Dana, Boutwell, and Banks, and by many of its leaders of to-day; but our demand has always failed because the Republican party feared, when it ceased to tax the right to vote, that its power in Massachusetts was ended.

I know that your party has refused this year to declare its position upon this question. I know that upon every opportunity you had, Mr. Allen, you voted against the abolition of this tax, yet, notwithstanding your opposition, this amendment is now before the people. I demand, in their name, to know your present position. Are you still in favor of this tax qualification, and opposed to its abolition, or have you changed your mind? If you have changed your mind, why have you not announced the fact? Is it conversion under the stress of a losing campaign? If even at this late day you will declare in favor of its abolition, we can probably secure this desirable result. Your first duty to the people is to state your position.

Third. Your party professes to believe in temperance, and yet refuses to declare specifically its position. We know it has been on all sides of that question. We know that upon a platform which means nothing, and is meant to mean nothing, it has nominated this year one who will say nothing, but who has voted both for and against a prohibitory law, and later even found a third position on the question,— a straddle where, on a tie vote on the passage of such a law, he refused to vote at all.

I do not believe in a prohibitory law. Do you, Mr. Allen? Will you, if elected, recommend or approve a prohibitory law? Do you or do you not believe in the legislation of this year on the liquor question? Would you recommend or approve of the repeal of such legislation? Would you recommend or approve putting back the public-bar clause in the statute? Are you with the majority or the minority of your party on this question? Do you believe that a standing drink is a sin, and a sitting drink salvation?

I demand, in the name of the people of the Commonwealth, whose votes you are seeking, that you declare your position on all of these questions. An eager and unsatisfied public will get from you an answer, or go to the polls with a knowledge that you have not the courage to answer.

Fourth, there is, Mr. Allen, here in this, as in other communities of Massachusetts, a large body of our fellow-citizens vitally interested in the enactment of wise, just, and conservative laws to promote the interests of the masses of our people, and to elevate the cause of labor. You have had an opportunity to act in the Legislature on many of these laws. You have opposed and voted against weekly and fortnightly payment Acts, against the Employers' Liability Act, against free text-books for our public schools, and against other such measures. Many of these, notwithstanding your opposition, have since become laws, recognized and upheld by all as wise and just, and in the interests of our people. Are you still of the opinion that these laws are unwise? Does your unbroken record of opposition to them correctly define your position to-day towards legislation of this character?

Fifth, there is and has been, Mr. Allen, for many years a demand of the people that elections should be made the honest, free, and independent expression of the voters' opinion, clear of all attempts at coercion, corruption, or undue influence. You had an opportunity to act upon these matters in the Legislature. Besides voting to tax the suffrage, you voted against a bill to prevent intimidation and interference with voters at the polls. You also voted against a bill to prohibit the improper use of money or other consideration for election purposes. Do these votes express your present opinion, or outline your policy if elected Governor of our State?

Your views upon all these matters, as a candidate for the highest office in the State, where, if elected, you can exert a powerful influence, are far more important than your opinion upon the silver, the tariff, or any other National question. It is time, then, for you to declare your position. While your past delay may raise a doubt as to your sincerity now, it is far better in this to be late than never.

The Republicans had not the courage in their platform to declare any position for their party on the constitutional amendment to abolish the poll-tax, or any definite position on temperance and other great questions of interest to our people; but they nominated as their candidate one who has voted in favor of taxing the right to vote, and who has been on all sides of the temperance question, and who now refuses to state his position on either question. They have talked of free and fair and pure elections, but rallied under the leadership of Mr. Lodge, the author, sponsor, and promoter of a scheme to gerrymander our Commonwealth vehemently denounced by some of his own party leaders, though supported by four-fifths of his party. Neither he nor his candidate, nor his party, though often challenged to do so, will now repudiate this scheme. Only the defeat of the Republican party will prevent this outrage to our Commonwealth. The candidate of this party of professed purity voted also against laws to prevent the intimidation of voters, and the corrupt use of money at the polls.

Their hypocrisy to the cause of civil service reform is made obvious by the turning loose of their Federal and State officials, who appear as a fighting force for the Republican party, and by such gross violation of the spirit of that reform as our Commonwealth has not seen for many years.

Their hypocrisy to the cause of labor is consummated in the nomination of a candidate who has an unbroken record of opposition to every measure in the interest of labor upon which he could lay his hands.

They arrogantly profess to be the sole guardians of our glorious public schools, and wickedly strive to divide a people politically over this great and sacred institution who are and ought to be one in love and loyalty to it; but they nominated as their candidate a man who voted against free text-books,— a great measure in the interest of our public schools, — and the Republican party has been constantly opposed to laws that would increase the influence and usefulness of such schools. The strongest support for every measure in their interest — such as free text-books, evening schools, greater public school facilities in manufacturing towns, raising the compulsory age of attendance, industrial education, etc. — has always come from the Democratic party; and our leaders, unlike theirs, have experienced the great benefits of education in the public schools, and later given their services to them.

Then the Republicans have sought to make the character and intelligence of a majority of the people of this Commonwealth an issue in this campaign. Their candidate, has referred to the Democratic party as an ignorant lower stratum of society, with a fringe of respectability; a Republican ex-Governor has referred to Democrats as mud and dirt. Other speakers have spoken of them as the "slums." A Republican congressman calls them "a combination of Harvard College and the slums;" and at last comes Mr. Lodge, undertaking to prove by statistics that the Democratic party — a majority of the people of the Commonwealth — comes from the criminal classes! I do not believe that in any campaign in this Commonwealth so gross and false a libel has ever been uttered against her people. I believe, too, that the people will remember this insult, and indignantly resent it upon election day.

Next, let me show you the sort of criticism that the Republicans have made upon me and my administration. From every speaker, big and little, on their side, at the instigation of their campaign managers, has come an attack upon me because in public speech I stated the injurious effect that their tariff policy had wrought to some of our Massachusetts industries, and demanded relief for them by freeing from taxation their raw materials. Yet that speech no Republican paper, though challenged to do it, has dared to print; and their State Committee has deliberately mutilated and garbled it, in violation of every principle of honesty and decency; until at last the indignation of the people compelled the Republicans to suppress their wretched and contemptible work. The facts stated by me in that speech in reference to the injury to our iron, steel, and glass industries have been admitted in public speech by Mr. Allen to be true; yet for his slander of me, based upon my statement of those facts, he has uttered not one word of retraction or apology. The Republican campaign has sunk below the level where conscience and a sense of honor seem to have any influence upon it.

. . . .

Then on National questions we find their campaign has been on the same line of hypocrisy. The Republicans undertake to criticise the Democratic party for its position on the silver question when their own party stands responsible for the present silver legislation, which would not have been enacted except for the votes of the Republican members from Massachusetts, given "for politics only;" and against that legislation as well as against free coinage stood the Democratic members of Congress from Massachusetts.

Not content with that record, the Republican party has repeatedly in State Conventions indorsed the present silver legislation, against which our great commercial bodies have protested, and even in this State the Republicans defend that legislation; and the only party in Massachusetts which stands absolutely committed to carry out the real sentiment of our people in favor of sound currency and a repeal of present dangerous silver legislation is the Democratic party. Yet the Republicans have the audacity to say that victory for their party in this State will be a victory for sound and honest money!

It is easy enough to see why the Republicans have run their campaign on this low level. They have entirely underrated the intelligence of our people. They profess to believe that the verdict of last year, after three years of thorough discussion, was due to ignorance, and was based upon misrepresentation. They forget that no question since the agitation against slavery has had a more thorough consideration than the tariff question, nor has the decision on any political issue ever been given with more deliberation and intelligence. But starting on this false assumption that our people could be deceived, they determined that their campaign this year should be run upon that basis; and from beginning to end it has, therefore, had the ring of utter insincerity and hypocrisy.

Now, let us sum up briefly what has been shown in reference to the tariff question and the McKinley Bill. We have shown that the influence behind the increase of taxation in that bill was the influence of men who had goods to sell, and not of people who had goods to buy; that the object and purpose of that increase of the tariff was to check imports, as Republicans declared, so as to check competition, and so to raise prices; that last year the Republicans confessed that that was its purpose, and, from their President down, derided any one as a cheap man who wanted a cheap coat, and said they were "sick of this cry of 'cheap, cheap, cheap;' that it was undesirable and un-American."

We have shown that immediately after the passage of the McKinley Bill, and because of it, the various trades — and I have here in my hand the circulars of many of them — sent word to their customers of an increase of the price of their goods, on account of the increase of duties in the McKinley Bill. These are not advertisements, but trade circulars.

We have shown that our leading firms of Boston are paying their duties under protest, in the hope of upsetting the McKinley Bill in court, because they feel the additional burdens of that bill, as they pay its taxes, and will be relieved by the lesser taxes of the old law. If they pay these taxes and find them an additional burden, it is you and I, my friends, their customers, who will finally pay them.

We have shown by price-lists taken from trade journals, from Republican papers like the "Commercial Bulletin" and the "Daily Advertiser," from well-known and responsible firms, that already on six hundred articles where duties have been raised, prices have been raised also; and these articles, almost without exception, are the common necessaries of life. We are quite willing that this question of prices should be submitted, as it must have been already, to the test of every man's experience in making his purchases.

We have also shown that these high and increased duties are many of them a grievous burden to the industries of Massachusetts, and against them those industries have protested. We have shown that against the increased duty upon lime and tin plate and other articles there came the formal protest of some of our industries; that when under this bill it was threatened to put back the tax on hides, from every leather and boot and shoe centre in Massachusetts there came an indignant protest because such tax would be a grievous injury to those industries. And yet, notwithstanding their protest, that tax still hangs over that industry, and may be imposed on Jan. 1, 1892, unless some unforeseen relief appears.

We have shown, as facts admitted now by our opponents upon the stump, that our iron and steel industry has declined, that our glass industry has declined, that our ship-building has declined, that our foreign shipping has declined, that our copper-smelting industry has gone, and that other industries have been injured by this taxation of raw material.

We have also shown that since the high-tariff policy our great industries, whose principal raw material has been free from duty, have grown much more than our industries whose raw material is taxed; that our silk, our paper, our cotton, our leather and boot and shoe industries, largely free from this burden of taxation, show a larger growth than our woollen industry, which is hampered and embarrassed by such taxation.

In the light of these facts it is evident that some of our great industries have declined by this tariff taxation, that some have been stagnant, that some have greatly prospered, and that the line of cleavage seems to be free raw material. We have, therefore, a right to say that those sons of Massachusetts who gave their voices and their votes to put this burden of the McKinley Bill upon our people and our industries were false to the interests both of our people and the industries of our Commonwealth; that they permitted other sections of the country to reap benefits by such taxation at the expense of Massachusetts and New England.

We have further shown that though such taxation is claimed by the Republicans to be for the benefit of labor, yet in no protected industry has any one pointed out any benefit that has come to labor in that industry, or any rise in wages since the passage of the McKinley Bill; but, on the contrary, we have proved that upon the working-man, as upon all our people, has come the additional burden of higher taxation.

A few words only about the boot and shoe industry, which is so important in this part of our State. That is the greatest industry in Massachusetts, measured by the number of persons employed in it. An injury to that branch of manufacture would affect more people than any other in our State. The product of that industry in 1885 was $115,000,000. The value of the stock used was over $70,000,000. Much of that stock is leather, the raw material of which, hides, is free from these tariff taxes; but a large proportion of it is made up of articles upon which there is tariff taxation. I have here a list, that has already been published, of forty of these articles which go into the manufacture of boots and shoes, upon all of which the McKinley Bill raised the tariff, and upon twenty-seven of which the price has since been raised.

Do you think that that higher price is any benefit to your boot and shoe industry? Does it not make the cost of its product greater, and with a higher cost will there not be less demand? Will not this less demand mean that fewer goods will be made, and so a less demand for labor, which can only result either in a shut down of work or a cut down of wages?

Is it not true that when its principal raw material, hides, was threatened directly with a tariff tax, there came a unanimous protest from all the boot and shoe manufacturers in the country against that tax as a burden to their industry? And yet, by the terms of the McKinley Bill, the President is compelled, on Jan. 1, 1892, to declare a duty of $1\frac{1}{2}$ cent per pound on hides, unless by that time reciprocal relations are established with the countries from which hides come. From such countries, where no reciprocity treaty has yet been made, we imported last year $24,000,000 worth of hides and skins. The fact that with some smaller countries reciprocity treaties have been made, compels the President in good faith to them, as well as by peremptory provision of the law, to enforce these taxes against the other countries, so that it seems inevitable that on Jan. 1, 1892, the tax on hides will be put back.

There is one thing that will prevent the imposition of this tax,—another sweeping Democratic victory for tariff reform. That will quickly lead Congress to relieve the boot and shoe industry from this injury which now hangs threateningly over its head. I do not see how any manufacturer of boots and shoes, I do not see how any employee in that industry, who is vitally interested, as all must be, in its growth and prosperity, can hesitate to cast his vote for the Democratic party and tariff reform, which means relieving his industry from present taxation, and also preventing this grievous and threatened tax on hides from being again established.

The leather and boot and shoe industries certainly cannot have forgotten the great impetus and growth that came to them when in 1872 the tax upon hides was removed, nor can they have forgotten the fact that every year since then we have been exporting millions of dollars worth of finished leather and boots and shoes made here by our workmen, and sold in foreign markets in competition with the labor of the world.

SPEECH

AT DEDHAM, OCT. 9, 1892. STATE ISSUES: THE MEANING OF TARIFF FOR REVENUE. — THE EFFECT OF TARIFF UPON PRICES.

I THANK you for your welcome. I am glad to come here to open the campaign. Here is a sturdy Democracy, which year in and year out has seen the light and followed it.

Here through this whole community, too, is a body of independent men, who, seeking only the truth and good government, have broken from their old party associations to follow where their conscience and convictions led them. We welcome them to our ranks, and recognize in their support an unselfish and unprejudiced indorsement of the principles, the policy, the truth, and the justice of our party's cause.

I am glad to be here with the distinguished representative from this district [Mr. Williams]. His conspicuous ability, undaunted courage, loyalty to Massachusetts, her interests and her beliefs, have made him render her that faithful service which a grateful State is glad to recognize and indorse.

Our numbers and enthusiasm are proof that there is no apathy within the Democratic ranks, but confidently, with a firm belief in the justice of its cause, our party means to renew the fight and repeat the victory of 1890. It believes that victory was the deliberate, emphatic judgment of Massachusetts, that the time has come when war taxation on the consumption of the people should be reduced; that special selfish interests should not stand in the way of this benefit to both her people and her industries, nor shall they control for their sole benefit the taxing power of the Nation. There is a question of morals as well as of markets involved in the issue. There is a question, too, of self-government as well as of self-interest dependent upon its decision. I believe the conscience of Massachusetts, as well as her pocket, sustains the Democratic policy.

Her judgment of 1890 was equally emphatic that the time had not come to impose upon her other burdens through Federal law, and to take from her the right she has exercised from the foundation of her government to control her own elections.

McKinley bills and Lodge bills were both condemned in her decision. So, too, she declared, in that Democratic victory, for sound and honest money, which was to be upheld and fought for by her representatives, no matter what the exigency of personal or party necessity.

Upon this point she has already reaped a just reward, which ought to be a source of pride to all her people. In place of Republican representatives from this State, who, against her convictions and their own, at their party's dictation, gave their votes for the dangerous silver legislation of 1890, and actually the votes necessary to carry it, she found Democratic representatives true to her and their own convictions, exercising an equally potent influence for the defeat of legislation of a like character and equally dangerous. As Massachusetts appreciates faithful services rendered her, admires ability, pluck, and patriotism in public life, so I think she will reward with her indorsement her faithful Democratic representatives, especially the member from this district, who bore so honorable and conspicuous a part in the contest.

The issues upon which Massachusetts passed judgment in 1890 are again the principal National issues between the parties in 1892, and so it becomes necessary to re-argue them.

I am aware that there are also certain State issues in this election which it will be my pleasure and duty to discuss, especially those issues necessarily involved in the nomination of my distinguished opponent.

The work and character of the administration of the last two years are submitted to the people for their indorsement. I gladly invite their fullest scrutiny and criticism, and especially the attention of the Republican party, which a year ago was so free and petty in its attacks.

The administration, in its suggestion of many reforms, in its exercise of the veto and appointing powers, in its conflicts with a Republican Legislature and a Republican Council, and in many other executive acts, gives ample grounds upon which to test its work and character.

It has vetoed nine bills of a Republican Legislature, many of which involved important principles and reforms, such as the right of local self-government, responsibility in executive office, the defence of the game-laws of the Commonwealth against special legislation for a special interest, reform in the building of State institutions, and the sale of stock by railroad corporations at public auction. Were these vetoes right?

What says the Republican party?

Thus far, only silence.

The administration has made hundreds of important executive appointments, — more in number and importance, I believe, than in any like period since the war. How has it exercised this, perhaps the greatest power of the Governor?

What says the Republican party?

Thus far, only silence.

It has suggested many reforms, some of which have become law. It has recommended measures to guard the purity of elections, of the ballot, and of legislation; other measures in the interest of the great masses of the people, such as the abolition of the poll-tax qualification, of the sweating system, reducing the hours of labor for women and children, and other labor measures; and has suggested legislation for exterminating the lobby, abolishing free passes on railroads and the sale of franchises, for extension of local self-government, and the passage of general laws in place of special legislation.

What says the Republican party about these suggestions?

Thus far, only silence.

It has suggested reforms in our system of prison management and in other executive departments, and its suggestions have been defeated by a Republican Legislature. Were these reforms right?

What now says the Republican party?

Thus far, only silence.

It has abolished some useless and incompetent commissions, and sought to abolish others. Was it right in this?

What says the Republican party?

Thus far, only silence.

It has sought to uphold a proper standard of official duty, by attempting to remove an important officer who was charged with using his office for personal and partisan ends. The attempt was thwarted by the opposition of the Republican candidate for Governor and of the Republican Executive Council.

Does the Republican party and its candidate still

rally to his support? Will they do in the State what they have done in the Nation, — demand partisan service of a public official, and reward such service with public office?

What says the Republican party on this issue?

Thus far, only silence.

I have asserted, still assert, and will assert, that full responsibility for nominations rests with the Governor.

I have resisted the attempt of the Republican candidate for Governor and the Republican Executive Council to usurp this power, and to dictate nominations; and I have denounced their rejection of nominees admitted by them to be fully qualified, but rejected because I would not nominate others at their dictation. I believe that the Constitution makes one, and not ten, supreme executive magistrates.

What says the Republican party and its candidate upon this issue?

Thus far, only silence.

I am content to rest upon their silence. Until broken, it is the forced confession of an opponent, more emphatic in its commendation than the praise of any friend. It is, too, our opponents' condemnation of their own candidate and their own acts.

But more important than the election of any State officer or the settlement of any State question are the National issues and the National campaign in which we are engaged. If you believe in Democratic principles and a Democratic administration, you can best give voice and emphasis to that belief by support of our National candidates.

The upright, able, patriotic, and economic administration of a Democratic President for four years has given the country not only confidence in him and his party, but full assurance of what his election will mean, and what will be the policy of his administration.

It means lifting at last the burden of taxation by reform and reduction of the tariff.

It means honest and sound money, without compromise or equivocation.

It means death to Force Bills, and new life to the just and deserving, but abandoned, cause of civil service reform. I verily believe it means to Massachusetts relief to her people, growth to her industries, and the administration of government upon the principles of equality, liberty, and economy, which she has ever upheld.

It certainly means rebuke to the dangerous combination of wealth with a political party to control elections, and to use the people's law for payment of its contributions and the profit of its contributors.

I propose to-night to discuss one issue of the campaign, — the tariff question. It is, and has been, the most important issue since the brave message of President Cleveland, and it will be until it is settled right.

How has the Republican party met this question in the past?

In its early history up to the time of the war, it advocated a tariff for revenue only, and gave its support to the lowest tariff the country had had for generations. Sumner and Wilson, and substantially the whole New England delegation, voted for this tariff of 1857. That was a time when industries were being founded, were infants, and needed, if ever, the right of taxation of the people for their support.

Then came the war and the necessity for larger revenue; so the Morrill tariff. Then came higher internal taxes, and, to offset their burden, the higher tariff laws of 1862 and 1864.

The author of these tariffs, and all the Republican leaders, distinctly declared that they were revenue tariffs, and should be reduced when the necessity for the greater revenue of the war was ended. Mr. Morrill, the author of a higher tariff, said on May 8, 1860:

"There are no duties proposed on any article for the simple purpose of protection alone. The highest duties in the bill are proposed for the purpose of revenue. The manufacturers might get along with lower duties, but we require the revenue."

On June 2, 1864, he said of the high protection of that year: —

"This is intended as a war measure, and we must as such give it our support. In making an estimate of the effect of such a war tariff as is now proposed, it is important that we should bear in mind that as we increase taxes on any article, we diminish the number of those who will be able to consume it."

In 1870 this author of high tariff again said: —

"It is a mistake of the friends of sound tariff to insist on the extreme rates imposed during the war, if less will raise the necessary revenue."

Senator Allison, another Republican leader, on March 24, 1870, said: —

"The tariff of 1846 (a very low tariff), though confessedly and professedly a tariff for revenue, was, so far as regards all the great industries of the country, as perfect a tariff as any that we have ever had."

Here are the authors of high tariff laws and Republican leaders distinctly and positively declaring in favor of tariffs for revenue only, stating that their own high tariffs were for this purpose, and averring that they were ample to protect all interests. Yet now they denounce unsparingly such doctrine when uttered by Democratic lips. Next, the Republican party in its platforms and the declarations of its leaders said that the high tariff should be reduced. That was its direct declaration in the platform of 1868, and its indirect declaration in the platform of 1884. That is what Mr. Lodge meant and said when, speaking for his Convention in 1884, he declared in favor of "freeing entirely those great necessaries of life which enter into the consumption of every household." He calls that free-trade now, and denounces it. The Republican Tariff Commission of 1882, made up entirely of the representatives of the highly protected industries, after a most thorough examination of the whole question made a report in which it spoke of the "excessively protective period of the late war," declared that "a substantial reduction of tariff duties is demanded, not by a mere indiscriminate popular clamor, and is necessary not only as a due recognition of public sentiment, but as a measure of justice to consumers, and one conducive to the general industrial prosperity," and recommended a reduction of from 20 to 25 per cent. That was the time when the Republican party was talking tariff reform and tariff reduction.

Next came the breaking by the Republicans of their pledges by opposing every attempt to reduce the tariff, and their defeat of the recommendations of their Tariff Commission and of their own leaders. Instead of the reduction recommended in 1882, we got the higher tariff of 1883. Instead of reducing the tariff 20 or 25 per cent, they opposed the reduction of 10 per cent in the Morrison Bill. Then they opposed the reduction of half that amount in the Mills Bill. Then they opposed every effort to get free wool and free raw materials, or to put the tariff on a revenue basis.

They demanded that the tariff should be revised and reduced at the hands of its friends. It got into the hands of its friends in 1882, and came out higher in 1883. It got into the hands of its friends again in 1888, and came out with the McKinley Bill of 1890, — the highest tariff we have ever had.

Then, having satisfied the demands of selfish interests, the Republican party declared the tariff question was settled, that New England's demand for free raw materials must go unanswered, and that she must be content if Ohio and Pennsylvania are.

Its record, then, is, first, cordial approval and support of the lowest tariff almost we have ever had, and a tariff for revenue only; second, raising the tariff during the war confessedly for revenue only; third, repeated promises and pledges to reduce it; fourth, opposition to every attempt at reduction, and the constant raising of it still higher; fifth, demand that the question be considered settled; and now at last that party, with broken pledges and forgotten principles, unmindful of the rebuke of 1890, boldly declares that the taxing power through the tariff can and shall be used, not for revenue, but for protection only, to the annihilation of revenue; not for public purposes, but private interests; not for the benefit of the people, but to enrich the few.

The issue becomes, then, not merely an economic question, but one as to the rightful use, the scope, and the power of government.

The United States Supreme Court on this very question in the famous Topeka case declared that "to lay with one hand the power of the government on the property of citizens, and with the other to bestow it on favored individuals to aid private enterprise and build up private fortunes, is none the less a robbery because it is done under the forms of law and is called taxation." It added, "There can be no lawful tax which is not laid for a public purpose."

Judge Cooley, the leading authority in the country on constitutional law, declares: "Constitutionally, a tax can have no other basis than the raising of revenue. A tax on imports, therefore, the purpose of which is not to raise revenue, but to discourage and indirectly prohibit some particular import for the benefit of some home manufacture, may well be questioned as being merely colorable, and therefore not warranted by constitutional principles."

I see that Mr. McKinley, who takes exactly the opposite view, in all his speeches in Massachusetts has cited Webster as an authority for his position, and has repeated this question: "Is Governor Russell a safer expounder of the Constitution than Daniel Webster?"

I cite the great authority of Webster for my position.

Edward Everett, who ought to have known Webster's views, in his memoir of him in his published Works of Daniel Webster, says: "In 1820, in discussing the subject [protection] in Faneuil Hall, he [Webster] argued that if the right of laying duties for protection were derived from the revenue power, it was of necessity incidental, and on that assumption, as the incident cannot go beyond that to which it is incidental, duties avowedly for protection, and not having any reference to revenue, could not be constitutionally made."

That I understand to be the Democratic doctrine.

Every effort to reduce the tariff has met not only opposition from the Republican party, but has led to its raising false alarms and false issues. The Republicans denounce the Democratic attempt to reduce the tariff 10 per cent as free-trade, notwithstanding the Report of their Commission in favor of its reduction of from 20 to 25 per cent. They denounce the Mills Bill, with its 5 per cent reduction, as free-trade. Every attempt of the Democratic party to give the manufacturers of the country the great boon of free raw materials they call free-trade. And now, when our party repeats the demand it has made for twenty years, that the tariff shall be for revenue and for public purposes, again the demand is called free-trade, though the ablest Republican statesman and leader, Senator Sherman, once declared that such revenue tariff could not fail to give all the protection necessary.

But the people are used to these false alarms. They answered them in 1890, and will answer them again in 1892.

Never yet has the Democratic party in power attempted to reduce the tariff without the most conservative regard for all the interests of the country. Over and over again it has shown by its acts and votes and declarations its policy of tariff reduction, and declared that it was to be upon the line of free raw materials and cheaper necessaries of life.

This was shown in Mr. Cleveland's message of 1887, in the Mills Bill, in repeated votes in the Senate for amendments to the McKinley Bill, and again in the Democratic platform of 1892, where it indorsed the effort of the Democratic party to modify the tariff "in the direction of free raw material and cheaper manufactured goods that enter into general consumption."

That, too, is the position taken by our party in the last House, which was overwhelmingly Democratic. No effort was made to establish free-trade, but every suggestion of legislation was on the basis of free raw materials and cheaper necessaries of life. If reducing tariff taxes on the necessaries of life is free-trade, where, in Heaven's name, stood Mr. Lodge and his party in 1884, when he declared in favor of "freeing entirely the necessaries of life"? If giving free wool, coal, ore, copper, and tin to our great industries, with a protective tariff on their finished products, is free-trade, I mistake the sentiment of New England if it does not demand this benefit, under whatever name it comes.

To-day the Republican party stands just where it placed itself in 1888. It declares the basis of the government to be privileges, not rights. It has substituted selfish interests for its character and its conscience; it stands for them rather than the people. It wins the enthusiastic support of the wealthy few, who control it for their profit, but it has turned against the many, who demand equality before the law, and the use of the people's power only in the people's interest.

The first effect of the present high protective policy of the Republican party is to raise prices and make the cost of living higher than it would be but for such tariff. This is its purpose and object. It is intended to shut out competition, to protect from competition by law as a trust does by mutual agreement, and to prevent people buying where they could buy the cheapest. Either protection is useless, or it must work through higher prices.

John Sherman declared in 1867: "I said it, and I stand by it, that as a general rule the duties paid on imports operate as a tax upon the consumer."

Mr. Blaine, in his "Twenty Years in Congress," says, speaking of the increase of duties on imports by the Tariff Act of July 14, 1862, that it "shut out still more conclusively all competition from foreign fabrics. The increased cost was charged to the consumer."

John Quincy Adams long ago declared: "The duty

constitutes the price of the whole mass of the article in the market. It is substantially paid on the article of domestic manufacture, as well as on that of foreign production."

Mr. McKinley himself, in the report introducing this very bill, said it was not the intent of the bill "to further cut down prices," that the people were "already suffering from low prices," and would not be satisfied "with legislation which will result in lower prices."

President Harrison, knowing that the effect of the bill would be to raise prices higher than they otherwise would be, tried to discount it by saying it was a cheap man who wanted a cheap coat.

What a striking contrast is this to that glorious inscription put by the working-men of England on the monument of Peel, who had given to the country the great blessing of a reduction of tariff taxation! They said in that inscription, as the crowning glory of his life, "he gave the people cheap bread."

Let me say of the recent report of the Senate on this question of prices that I believe the report is perfectly fair and reliable, because it was made after a thorough examination of witnesses who could be cross-examined, and was not founded, as many State reports are, on facts furnished by interested persons, without opportunity for any cross-examination. It certainly is more reliable than any Peck report, made by an officer who in the space of three months absolutely contradicts his own earlier report, and then destroys the official data upon which it is based, and finally turns up in court charged with crime in connection with it.

The conclusion of the Senate report is that at the end of three years, the average price of the 214 articles investigated was a fraction of 1 per cent lower than in 1889, but during three-quarters of that period these prices have been higher, ranging from .61 per cent to 3.57 per cent. These articles the committee chose as a fair average of general consumption, and a fair test of prices generally.

Assuming such general consumption to be, as statisticians agree, about $10,000,000,000, the net increase of prices during the period examined (which was the period of the McKinley Bill and tariff agitation) amounted to $285,000,000. This was part of the burden on the people of McKinley tariff taxation.

No one doubts that all the forces of civilization, with every improvement in machinery and skill and transportation, are constantly fighting for lower prices. No one doubts that they can in course of time reduce prices, notwithstanding the protective tariff. No one claims that the tariff tax can wholly offset and defeat the progressive reduction of prices which these forces accomplish; but just as surely as they fight for lower prices, a protective tariff tax stands in their way, fighting for higher prices.

This is strikingly shown in a detailed examination of the prices of these very articles examined and reported on by the Senate committee. Such examination of these 214 articles discloses that the majority have risen in price in those cases where the McKinley Bill increased the duty, that the majority have declined in those cases where the duty was left unchanged or was lowered, and that the general tendency of prices of all the articles was towards a lower level prior to the enactment of the bill.

In proof of this tendency, Senator Carlisle, in his speech of July 29, 1892, said: —

"Mr. Grosvenor, a gentleman whom this committee must indorse, because it had him employed for some time to assist in collecting prices, made an investigation, June 1st, 1889, which showed that prices of commodities in this country had declined 14 per cent during the eighteen months next preceding the beginning of this investigation. Fortunately it so happened that our investigation began the day that his investigation closed; and while his investigation showed that during the eighteen months covered by it the prices of commodities declined in this country 14 per cent, all the senator from Rhode Island can now show is that after twenty-four months of unnecessarily high prices, the cost of living had declined .64 of 1 per cent."

The direct effect of this bill upon retail prices can be seen with great distinctness in a table of these 214 articles, the very ones selected and investigated by the Senate committee, showing the fact of increased or diminished price of each article side by side with the increased, unchanged, or lower tariff of the McKinley Bill. An examination of this table shows that 75 of the 214 articles embraced within it increased in price, while 139 articles decreased in price. Of the 75 increasing in price, 54, or 72 per cent, had their duties increased by the McKinley Bill, while of the 139 articles decreasing in price, 92, or 66 per cent, had their duties unaltered or reduced by that bill.

This table when analyzed further shows emphatically that prices of commodities were still tending towards a lower level, as Mr. Grosvenor had shown they were prior to the Senate investigation. To observe this tendency, an examination of those articles upon which there has been no change of tariff duty by the McKinley Bill should be made. The number of these articles is 82; and 65, or 79 per cent, of them fell in price, while only 17, or 21 per cent, increased in price. There were 31 articles upon which the tariff duties were decreased. Of these, 27, or 89 per cent, fell in price, and 4, or 11 per cent, increased in price. There were 101 articles upon which tariff duties were increased. Of these, 54, or 53 per cent, increased in price, and 47, or 47 per cent, decreased in price.

Here, then, is presented in the clearest possible manner the effect which the McKinley Bill has had upon prices. The tendency of prices has been towards a lower level, as an examination of the articles unchanged in duty by the McKinley Bill shows. This tendency is emphasized in a marked manner in those cases where the duty has been decreased, 90 per cent of these articles decreasing in price. But in the cases where the duty was increased, the tendency of prices towards a lower level is entirely overthrown, and it is found that a majority have increased in price.

This exhibit is of prices at the end of the period it investigated. The Senate report shows they were even higher at every other time covered by the investigation.

SPEECH

AT MALDEN, OCT. 10, 1892, THE FORCE BILL.

MANY times during the past few weeks it has been my privilege to represent and to speak for the Commonwealth, and to receive the cordial greeting which loyal citizens ever give to her. But to-night I come here representing a great political party, to plead its cause, and to fight its battle; and your hearty welcome is gratefully received as evidence of your unflinching loyalty to Democracy, your earnest interest in its work and principles, and your firm determination to carry them to victory.

I reciprocate your welcome, and join in your enthusiasm for our party. May I express the earnest hope that that enthusiasm means the triumph of your brilliant candidate for Congress [Dr. William Everett], who, answering the call of duty and of principle, has turned from the rest and peace of a scholar's life to enter the turmoil of political struggle that he might serve the people's interests, the cause of truth and justice. He brings to the contest character, conscience, and convictions, with learning, undaunted courage, and unselfish purpose. His ability, pluck, and vigor carried our party against heaviest odds almost to victory two years ago. Confidently, now, Democracy, honored by his candidacy, expects the further honor of his service as her representative.

I am glad to come to the district represented by Mr. Lodge to discuss to-night a question in which he and his party have shown the keenest interest until very recently, — a question which is one of the most important issues of the campaign, but of which the Republican party to-day is very shy.

The issue is presented in the bill framed by the notorious Davenport of New York, fathered by Mr. Lodge, and known as the Force Bill. As that bill interferes largely with the control Massachusetts for one hundred years has had over her elections, as it proposes to hand this control over to the National Government, but really means to hand it over to the Republican party, the question is important.

It seems to me a proper place to discuss it in the district of its nominal author and its uncompromising and constant defender, — constant until this year; but now he is silent.

We remember that two years ago he claimed that this was the most important issue and measure before the country. Speaking in this very town on October 27, 1890, Mr. Lodge declared: "I am proud of my connection with the bill, and I ask for your votes, not merely for myself or my party, but for the cause in which I am engaged, which is righteous work, more important than the tariff, or the Silver Bill, or anything else before Congress." He declared that the tariff question was settled; and as it had been settled in his way, evidently he was anxious to have elections so controlled by his party through his Force Bill that the tariff could not be disturbed.

Mr. Watterson graphically described the connection between the McKinley Bill and the Lodge Force Bill when he said: "With one the Republican party ties the hands of the Nation, while with the other it skins it."

Mr. Wilson, the Chairman of the Democratic National Convention, rightly declared: —

"We are not deceived as to the temper of the Republican party. We are not in doubt as to its principles. Having taxed us for years without excuse and without mercy, it now proposes to disarm us of all powers of resistance.

"Republican success in this campaign, whether we look to the party platform, the party candidates, or the utterances of the party leaders, means that the people are to be stripped of their franchise through force bills, in order that they may be stripped of their subsistence through tariff bills."

I believe that the people are as anxious now as they were two years ago to know the position of Mr. Lodge and his party upon this question.

An examination of his bill shows that it practically gives to Republican Federal officers control of elections, including the registration of voters, conduct of the election, and the count of the vote; and finally provides for Republican canvassing boards to revise the returns and to issue election certificates.

It deals nominally with National elections; but as the State election comes at the same time, its power necessarily covers both. I do not believe that Massachusetts needs or wants this Federal control of her elections. She certainly does not want it in partisan hands for partisan purposes. Let us see how this is accomplished.

First, a chief supervisor is appointed for life, by the judge of the United States Circuit Court. As almost without exception these judges are Republicans, it is altogether likely that the chief supervisors would be of the same party. The chief supervisor then presents to the Circuit Court lists of persons for appointment as subordinate supervisors, and double the number required for the district. From the list so appointed he selects three for each precinct, two of them of the same political party.

A Republican judge appoints a Republican chief supervisor. A Republican chief supervisor prepares lists of subordinates, and then selects two out of three of such subordinates Republicans. The supervisors so chosen are given power to guard, scrutinize, and supervise elections, including naturalization and registration.

In cities of over twenty thousand inhabitants they are to make a house-to-house canvass, on the order of the Republican chief supervisor. Here would begin the Republican campaign, to be conducted by employees paid from the public treasury. Then follow provisions for the control of the conduct of the election, including the challenging of voters, and the count of the vote by a partisan board, — provisions, too, which interfere with the secrecy of the ballot, with our Australian ballot law, and are almost certain to lead to a conflict between National and State authority. They are just as certain to give an opportunity for the partisan abuse of power.

Then comes the appointment of canvassing boards of three, two of the same political party, and of course of the Republican party. Those boards decide who is elected to Congress; and upon their decision the clerk makes up the roll of the House, without regard to the certificates sent by State officers.

Then provision is made for the trial by partisan juries of all offences against the law. The juries are drawn by three jury commissioners selected by the court, but care is taken not to provide that even one of the commissioners should belong to some party other than the Republican party, or that they should select the juries without regard to politics. This gives an opportunity for just such partisan abuse of power as was practised in the northern district of Florida in

1889 by the Republican United States marshal, who issued the following order:—

JACKSONVILLE, FLA., July 5, 1889.

C. C. KIRK, Esq., De Land, Fla.,

SIR,—You will at once confer with McBulby and make out a list of fifty or sixty names of true and tried Republicans from your county registration list for jurors of the United States Court, and forward same to H. P. Walter, clerk of the United States Court; and it is necessary to have them at once, as you can see. Please acknowledge this.

I am, yours truly,
JOHN R. MIZELL,
United States Marshal.

The bill further provides that the United States marshals (Republicans), in conference with the chief supervisor (Republican), shall appoint as many deputy marshals as the chief supervisor thinks necessary to enforce the election laws. Then, if this force is not sufficient for Republican purposes, Federal troops may be placed at the polls. That is what Mr. Lodge anticipated when he said in debate on the bill that he had no objection to the use of soldiers if necessary at every polling precinct of his district.

Another leading Republican from Pennsylvania, Mr. Brosius, said in debate on the bill, June 28, 1890: "When passed, I am for its enforcement North and South, if need be, with firmness and effectiveness." And he added: "Every sword, every bayonet, every cannon, and every dollar of the Nation's wealth are pledged to the enforcement of every one of its provisions."

Senator Frye, in the debate, Dec. 11, 1890, expressed an equal willingness, if necessary, "to put a bayonet behind every ballot." The necessity would easily be found if the Republican party controlled the power and needed the votes.

Then the bill, in order that no hostile House of Representatives may interfere with it, makes permanent the appropriations for carrying it out. Now note some of the objections to it.

First, it provides for an army of office-holders at an enormous expense. Over two hundred and fifty thousand is a moderate estimate of the number of officers provided for by the bill, and the expense would be many millions of dollars.

Second, it leads as certainly to corruption as it does to gross partisanship. All the "floaters" could be made deputy marshals at five dollars per day, and the chief could assign them to nominal duties.

Third, it surrounds the polls with paid agents of the Republican party, and authorizes the use of the army at the polls. We have had some experience of this in the Southern States. We have seen there United States troops at the polls and in the halls of legislation. Massachusetts has uttered her indignant and non-partisan protest against such action. She felt the danger from it to her as well as to Louisiana. "The Cradle of Liberty" rang out the warning that Federal interference with elections in a State, and Federal soldiers directing the functions of a State, were a menace to self-government and to free institutions; and to that meeting of protest in 1876 Mr. Lodge, I believe, gave the influence of his name and assistance.

Fourth, it interferes necessarily with the conduct of State elections, and leads to conflict, as I have said, between State and National authority.

Fifth, it drags the judiciary into politics, and may make it part of the Republican machine, and under the control of a Republican chief supervisor of elections. We have had some experience of this, too, with the electoral commission of 1876, with the partisan orders of Republican judges in the South, and with the judicial release of the chief manipulator of the Republican corruption fund of 1888. The confidence of the people in their judiciary ought not to be impaired by asking judges to become partisans, and to be made responsible for the partisan acts of partisan officers.

Sixth, it may interfere with the secrecy of the ballot and the reforms accomplished by our Australian ballot law.

Seventh, it practically hands over to the Republican party, backed by Federal power, the right to canvass voters, register them, challenge them, count their votes, and certify the result of the election. The people prefer to do this themselves. They have not entire confidence in the Republican party, since it by gross fraud, and through just such agencies as the Lodge Bill creates, seized the Presidency in 1876. Recent events, too, in Montana, New Hampshire, and Connecticut remind us of their abuse of political power and their willingness to override the will and votes of the people in order to get and retain office.

The crime in the election of 1876 was followed by the scandals in the election of 1888. At last the Republican party, facing the fact that the people have lost confidence in them, their methods, and their selfish policy, seek to devise some means to override the people's will and defeat their free choice.

Eighth. Lastly, the Force Bill, changing the practice of one hundred years, tells the States that they cannot be trusted to regulate and control their elections, and so this power must be taken from them. That bill says to Massachusetts: "The Republican party mistrusts your fairness and honesty in elections. You must surrender the right you have always had to control them, and give over this right to the National Government, to be exercised by Republican officials aided by Federal soldiers."

The bill is an insult to the State and a blow at self-government. I do not wonder that the Republican senator, Teller, whose vote was influential in defeating the measure after it had passed the House, thus described it: —

"Two years nearly have elapsed. I have read that bill with care and attention more than twenty times. I have read it again in the light of calm consideration, and I repeat, that if it were presented to me now, with the question of my support or party dismissal, I should not vote for the bill. A more infamous bill, in my judgment, never passed the threshold of the Senate. Avowedly in the interest of good government, it was instigated, in my judgment, by men whose interest was in preventing a free expression of the voters at the polls."

The people are always jealous of their right of self-government. They know the further political power is removed, the less control they have of it. To be self-government, it must be kept within their reach. The control they exercise must be through their elections. When deprived of the right to control them, or when this right is put into partisan hands, self-government is put beyond their reach.

The Republican party stands thoroughly committed to this Force Bill. Not only by the declarations and acts of men like Mr. Lodge and Speaker Reed, who declared, "We must cut loose from State elections and do our own registration, our own counting, and our own certification," but it stands committed by the recommendation of its President, and by repeated declarations in its National and State platforms.

Its National Convention this year again committed the party thoroughly to the support of the Force Bill; and almost without exception its State Conventions have pledged the party to its support.

But Republican advocacy does not rest on pledge and declaration alone. Under the leadership of Mr. Lodge, by the coercion of Speaker Reed, and through the urgency of a Republican President, the law passed a Republican House, and was defeated in the Senate only because the conscience of a few Republicans rebelled against it.

Just as emphatically the Democrats stand opposed to this measure, and have shown their opposition by declaration and pledge, and by their united votes in Congress.

SPEECH

AT NEWBURYPORT, OCT. 14, 1892, UPON THE TARIFF, ESPECIALLY IN ITS RELATION TO TRUSTS.

I PROPOSE to-night to consider with you the tariff question, and to begin by pointing out some of the evils of a high-tariff protection. I maintain, first, that it raises prices and the cost of living higher than they otherwise would be, and to that extent it is a burden which enters into every home and is felt by every individual. This is clearly shown by the official declaration of Mr. McKinley, the author of the bill, in his report submitting it to Congress. Speaking for his committee, he said: "We have not been so much concerned about the prices of the articles we consume as we have been to encourage a system of home production," etc.

No, sir, you were not concerned about prices to consumers, but you were concerned about privileges and profits to special interests. He further said in that report: "We have not believed that our people, already suffering from low prices—" Mark that expression, "suffering from low prices!" He speaks of it as a calamity, like the cholera or the yellow fever. Do people suffer from low prices? Does the head of a family, earning his $1.50 per day, with a half-dozen little ones to support, suffer when coal is $1 a ton less, or flour $1 a barrel cheaper? I say that that phrase is an insult to the people of this country.

Now notice how he continues: "We have not believed that our people, already suffering from low prices, can or will be satisfied with legislation which will result in lower prices." That is to say, the McKinley Bill was not concerned about high prices. It believed the people were suffering already from the calamity of low prices, and that they would not be satisfied with legislation which would lower them; and so this "great" and "beneficent" measure of Mr. McKinley is made the law of the land to remedy this evil, to stop this calamity, and to stand as a permanent obstacle in the way of lower prices.

Speaking again after the passage of his bill, and practically admitting increase of prices as one of its effects, but trying to avoid its consequences, Mr. McKinley said, Oct. 14, 1890, in his speech at Kalamazoo: "Well, now, they say you would have things cheaper if you only had a Democratic revenue tariff. Cheap! I never liked the word. 'Cheap' and 'nasty' go together. This whole system of cheap things is a badge of poverty; for cheap merchandise means cheap men, and cheap men a cheap country; and that is not the kind our fathers builded."

It no doubt is true that other influences are constantly working for cheap prices, and may accomplish this result, notwithstanding the opposition of a high tariff. This truth has often been recognized. For example, Senator Plumb of Kansas, in the debate on the McKinley Bill, Aug. 1, 1890, said: "The whole tendency of civilization is [towards] the reduction of the prices of everything which results from human labor; and to claim that the tariff has been the sole or the main factor in the reduction of prices of manufactured goods is to ignore all the forces of civilization. The American people are entitled to have cheap goods if competition can bring that about." He adds: "When is the time coming when the people at large can get some of the benefit out of the establishment of these industries? Just as fast as we get to that point where we may expect that natural competition will do its work, and prices will go down to the consumer, these people come in and say we need more duties; and up the duties go, whereby the progress of prices downward is arrested. I say that the people of the United States ought to have their innings some time, and I think that time has come now."

He was right. In three months the people had their innings, and gave his party the most stinging and deserved defeat ever given a party in this country. The people still hold their innings, and mean to make some more base-hits and home-runs in this election. No wonder an indignant people, finding the declaration of the author of this bill to be true, and that its purpose was not for their interests, but for the interest of the few and the wealthy, rose in their wrath at the first opportunity, and condemned Mr. McKinley, his bill, and his party.

I propose to-night to turn to another phase of the tariff question, and show you how it has surely led to the formation of trusts, which are raising prices, reducing production, and lessening the amount of work and wages.

The tariff accomplishes this, first, by excluding competition from without. It is meant to do this.

Senator Hawley in debate declared its purpose when he said he wanted a Chinese wall a hundred cubits high built around this country. The Republican platform of 1888 officially declared the policy of the Republican party to be to check imports; and the McKinley Bill afterwards was framed for the purpose of excluding anything which was produced here, or whose production could be forced here.

The tariff, having excluded competition from without, gives the opportunity to the trust to come and shut out competition from within. That is what Senator Plumb meant when he declared it to be the "shelter of trusts," and "in a very large measure of great impositions upon the American people in the matter of the price of manufactured goods." And later, with an honest indignation at the injustice it was working, he declared: "The manufacturer insists that he will not take any chances; and so the Carnegies and Joneses of Pittsburg, and the Dolans and Dobsons of Philadelphia, have prospered and grown rich beyond the dreams of avarice, at the expense of the people of the United States."

And another shining light of the Republican party, Congressman Butterworth, of Ohio, declared on May 14, 1890, that "the manufacturers and the trusts get the protection and the profits of the tariff. The farmers get the husks and the humbug."

The opportunity for the trust is the exclusion of competition from without. The excuse or the incentive for the trust is over-production, caused by a limited market; and both these evils are dependent upon the high-tariff policy of the Republican party. That policy tends to shut out our goods from the markets of the world. First, by discouraging trade with other countries. One would think such trade almost a crime, from the Republican denunciation of imports and importers, whose offence is giving the people a chance to buy where they wish, and on the cheapest terms, and whose efforts must result in an increase of trade, with greater exchange of products, which opens to us new and larger markets abroad. Next, by taxing the raw material of our industries, which places us at a disadvantage in the markets of the world, when we compete with other countries which have free raw material.

So, while bountiful crops here and short crops abroad have led to a large increase of our exports of food, we are not surprised to find that this Republican policy, which discourages trade, and so burdens our manufacturers, is leading to a reduction of our exports of manufactured goods. The United States Bureau of Statistics shows that the exports of manufactured articles from the United States for August last were $12,583,000, as against $14,814,000 in August, 1891; that for the first eight months of 1892 these exports were $99,131,000, as against $113,717,000 in 1891.

Yet, notwithstanding this burden, we can and do export many manufactured products, and the very products where labor is the largest item of the cost, and the taxed raw materials not an important part; for instance, watches, sewing-machines, agricultural implements and machinery, and the smaller hardware.

So, too, where the raw material is free, we can and do export to the markets of the world. With hides free, we export leather; with rags free, paper; with cotton free, millions of dollars worth of cotton goods, all in competition with the labor of the world. But with wool heavily taxed, we hardly export a pound of carpets or of woollen goods.

It is not high wages, but high cost of the raw material which handicaps us in the world's competition. Our high wages are more than made up by the efficiency and skill of our labor. Many a manufacturer has so contended, agreeing with Mr. Farquhar, president of one of the largest manufactories of farming implements in the country, who declares: "We do manufacture and sell in Canada, South America, and Europe many agricultural implements and machines; and could we have free raw material and the commercial advantages which free-trade would give us, America would become the great manufacturing emporium of the world."

But the Republican party adopts the opposite policy. Instead of giving free raw material, it puts a high tariff tax upon it, and then gives the manufacturer whatever amount of tariff protection he wishes for his finished product. So we find such duties as those on copper and tin plates, which a Republican Congressman, Butterworth, in the debate on the McKinley Bill, declared to be "a mere gratuity and extortion."

Let us consider the facts about this duty on copper. From 1850 to 1860 copper ore was free, with a slight duty on copper pigs; and all were free from 1857 to 1860. From 1850 to 1860 the ore produced here increased tenfold, and our export of manufactured goods of copper and brass fourteenfold. Meanwhile our imports of these goods decreased from $330,000 to $23,000. This industry then was one of those healthy infants described by Colonel Ingersoll, which was six feet tall, weighed two hundred pounds, and which did not need to have its cradle rocked, especially when it threatened to get up and knock you down if you stopped rocking its cradle.

Still, it demanded of the Republican party and got tariff protection. In 1868 a bill was passed putting a tariff protection of three cents per pound upon copper, though against the protest of smelting companies, of ship-builders and ship-owners, and of the manufacturers of copper and brass goods. It met the veto of the President, who declared that "the bill will prove detrimental to the shipping interest of the Nation, and at the same time destroy the business, for many years so successfully established, of smelting home ores," etc. It was passed over his veto. And there resulted just what he predicted, — the death of smelting companies on the seaboard, great injury to shipping and all its dependent industries, and the sending of our vessels abroad to be coppered with our own copper, which there could be bought cheaper than in our own country.

While the duty has since been lowered, for years we have seen our copper sold to the foreigner cheaper than it was sold to our own people. There was, and is, no need of tariff protection on such an article. It can and does lead only to one result, — a burden to industries and the people, and a great profit to the few and the wealthy.

Let us consider as another example the tariff tax upon tin plates. This tax used to be 1 cent a pound; but it was raised by the McKinley Bill to 2.2 cents. The amount at 1 cent was a burden of from $6,000,000 to $7,000,000 a year upon the people, and at 2.2 cents it amounts to over $15,000,000.

Against the imposition of this tax came a protest from our canning industries, of which there are nineteen hundred, employing, directly or indirectly, hundreds of thousands of people, from our manufacturers of tin, and, if their voice could be heard, a protest also from the 65,000,000 of people who were to pay this tax and feel its burdens. In its favor was the demand of a few capitalists of Pittsburg, who wished the privilege of law to increase their profits at the expense of the people. Two years have elapsed since the passage of the McKinley Bill; and the industry which the Republican party promised should grow up under its fostering care has been able to make but 2 or 3 per cent of our total consumption of tin plate, and, meanwhile, the people have been paying millions of dollars as their contribution to the burden.

I assert and have shown that a high tariff is a burden to the people by increasing the cost of living, and a burden to our industries by limiting our market to a home market, and there even limiting the sales more than they would be with free raw material, because it raises the cost, and so lessens the demand for the product.

Let us now see what next follows. Inevitably the trust. With no outlet abroad for over-production, and a lessened demand at home by high cost, the manufacturer turns to the trust to remedy his trouble. Through the trust he controls and raises prices, and through it he controls and limits production. With lessened production comes less work; and then men out of employment, and necessarily less wages.

Instead of urging the manufacturer to enter the markets of the world, and giving him as the means to do it free raw material, the Republican policy compels him to stay at home, and invites him to form a trust. Protection from competition from without gives him his opportunity. Over-production at home or desire for enormous profit furnishes the incentive.

Take one instance of such a trust, — the steel rail trust. Notice a few facts in reference to it.

First, a protective tariff tax of $13.44 per ton. This is a higher tax than the total labor cost of the steel rail from the mining of the ore to the time of the finished product. It is four times higher than the difference in wages here and abroad as claimed by the Republican party to exist in that industry. Here, then, is a protective duty, placed in the name of labor, which is more than the total wages of labor in the industry.

Now note the next fact. This duty accomplishes its real purpose, and absolutely excludes all competition from without. Having done that, the next step inevitably follows, — the formation of a trust to exclude competition from within. So we find the six largest companies, headed by the Illinois Steel Company and Mr. Carnegie, with an annual capacity of nearly three millions of tons, formed into such a trust.

Having effectually disposed of competition, this trust then determines how much profit it will extort from the people. For the year 1891, from February through December, they fixed the price of steel rails absolutely at $30 a ton. Yet Mr. Carroll D. Wright, the United States Commissioner of Labor, in his report declares that the department has been positively informed relative to the cost of making rails in several of the very largest establishments in the United States; and there is no shadow of a doubt in his mind that in these establishments the actual cost of standard rails is and has been for some time within a few cents of $22 per ton at the works. This report was on facts gathered in 1889 and 1890, since which time the cost has probably fallen still further.

Here, then, is $8 per ton profit on a capacity of nearly 3,000,000 tons fixed by a trust under shelter of a Republican protective tariff.

How much do you think this steel trust can afford to give to the Republican campaign fund in return for the $24,000,000 per year profit and protection which that party is giving to this trust?

The sheltering influence of a protective tariff upon trusts was recognized by John Sherman when he declared that the remedy for the trust was to reduce the tariff duty. He said on Oct. 15, 1889: —

"The primary object of a protective tariff is to invite the fullest competition by individuals and corporations in domestic production. If such individuals or corporations combine to advance the price of the domestic product and to prevent the free result of open and fair competition, I would without a moment's hesitation reduce the duties on foreign goods competing with them, in order to break down the combination. . . . Whenever this free competition is evaded or avoided by combination of individuals or corporations, the duties should be reduced, and foreign competition promptly invited."

If reducing the duty can remedy the evil, then a high tariff stands responsible for its existence.

Let us see, then, if trusts exist in highly protected industries. I hold here in my hand a list of one hundred and thirty-nine of such trusts, "combines," and monopolies, every one of them in a protected industry; and in fifty-eight of them additional protection was given under the McKinley law.

Is it not about time to apply John Sherman's remedy to these trusts? And if it was applied, how much of the protective tariff do you think there would be left? As we read this list of trusts and monopolies, it seems almost as if we were back in the days of the Tudors, and were reviving the practice which then led to the indignant remonstrance of a burdened people.

The historian Hume, referring to those days, said of the granting of monopolies in the reign of Elizabeth:

"She granted her servants and courtiers patents for monopolies, and these patents they sold to others, who were thereby enabled to raise commodities to what prices they pleased, and to put invincible restraints upon all commerce, industry, and emulation in the arts.

"It is astounding to consider the number and importance of those commodities which were thus assigned over to the patentees, — currants, salt, iron, powder, cords, calf-skins, pelts, oils, cloth, potash, vinegar, sea-coal, steel, lead, tin, pots, bottles, glass, paper, starch, and sulphur. These are but a part of the commodities which had been appropriated to monopolies. When this list was read, a member of the House cried, 'Is not bread in the number?'

"'Bread?' said every one, in astonishment.

"'Yes; I assure you,' replied he, 'if affairs go on at this rate, we shall have bread reduced to a monopoly before the next Parliament.'"

Then we read further that these monopolies were frequently granted, without consideration, to political or personal favorites, that they might grow rich out of the proceeds; and that little public revenue was reaped from them; that of £210,000 thereby levied upon the people, scarcely £1,500 came into the king's coffers; but still that the owners of the monopolies demanded that they should be upheld, because "they did give much employment to the king's lieges, and did pay much wages to his Majesty's subjects for their labor and in the patent operations." As we read all these things it sounds as if the historian were speaking of to-day, and of the cause, result, and excuse for McKinley high protection.

It has been given to political favorites of the Republican party in return for favors rendered, that they might grow rich out of the proceeds. It has turned little into the public treasury of the enormous sums levied upon the people. And its excuse for its enormous profits to the few has been the pretence that it is a benefit to labor.

But the Democratic policy, on the other hand, offers our industries a field of legitimate growth and profit, with certain benefit to all our people. It would give them free raw material, with a certainty that this would reduce the cost of their product, increase its demand at home, and open new and broader markets. Then there will be no necessity or excuse for the trust, with its burdens to the people, and especially to labor.

Mr. Blaine, in a speech at Waterville in August, 1890, declared that "the United States has reached the point where one of its highest duties is to enlarge the area of its foreign trade." He added: "Our great demand is expansion. I mean expansion of trade with countries where we can find profitable exchanges;" and "we should be unwisely content if we did not seek to engage in what the younger Pitt so well termed ' the annexation of trade.' "

The Democratic policy is exactly in line with this declaration, while high protection is absolutely at variance with it.

A McKinley high tariff discourages trade, raises the cost of our products, taxes their material, limits the demand, and fosters trusts. It substitutes enormous profits in a limited market for a legitimate and healthy growth. It causes over-production, but furnishes no outlet for it. It burdens the people through abuse of the power of taxation, and makes the basis of law privileges instead of rights, and its controlling influences selfish interests instead of justice, equality, and the public welfare.

SPEECH

AT LAWRENCE, OCT. 26, 1892, UPON STATE ISSUES AND UPON THE TARIFF IN ITS RELATION TO THE WOOLLEN INDUSTRY.

I AM glad to get back to our old Commonwealth, and, may I add, glad to get back to the campaign in which the Democracy is fighting so vigorously and hopefully.

Let me to-night first consider some State matters. In many of my executive acts I have been at variance with a Republican Legislature and a Republican Council. I have requested my distinguished opponent to meet me in man fashion, face to face, to discuss these issues. When he failed to do this, I urged him and his party, who are seeking to supplant a Democratic administration, to point out wherein it has erred, and to step forth and defend their partisan opposition to its measures and its acts.

Thus far there has been only silence from any responsible source. The silence of the Republican Convention and platform and candidate and leader I have a right to construe as a most emphatic indorsement of my administration. If so, it is equally a condemnation of my opponent and his party in their partisan opposition. Is it not about time that this ominous silence was broken, and some attempt at least made by my opponent to defend or explain his position?

I remember in 1890, when I was a candidate for Governor, the "Boston Journal," late in the campaign, in an editorial said that National questions had nothing to do with the governorship of Massachusetts, and that "the questions which should be answered by those who urge the people of Massachusetts to make Mr. Russell Governor" were, "What kind of a Governor would he make? What are his qualifications for the high office to which the Democratic party has nominated him? What knowledge has he of questions of State policy?" It said the burden of proof rested upon those who sought to make the change. I now respectfully request it to apply its own test to its own candidate, and to beseech him, with its characteristic vehemence, to address himself to some questions "which have to do with the governorship of Massachusetts." Let me call his attention to a few.

. . . .

When, in 1891, the first vacancy occurred on the Savings Bank Commission in this State, I reappointed a Republican whose term had expired, though every member of the board belonged to the Republican party. When the second vacancy occurred, in 1892, I nominated for the office a man of experience and of superior qualifications, who was indorsed by the presidents of banks, by Mr. Getchell, the United States Bank Examiner, and by many men of high position in financial circles. You admitted, Mr. Haile, in answer to my demand for information to be used before the people of this Commonwealth, that there was no objection to my nominee on the ground of character, fitness, or qualifications for the office, and that you and your Republican associates in the Executive Council rejected him solely for the purpose of holding in office the member whose term had expired. And he was an active Republican politician, who, while holding the office of Bank Commissioner, had been at the head of an influential Republican organization.

I said then, as I say now, that when the power to confirm is used to reject nominees admitted to be fit, in order to compel the nomination or holding in office after the expiration of his term of some one else, I said that this was a gross usurpation of power, which proper respect for the dignity and privileges of my office demanded should be resisted.

This issue was raised and discussed before the people in the campaign of last year, and by their votes the people sustained the position of the Executive, declaring in effect that when they elected a Governor they meant he should assume full executive responsibility, and that this should not be divided and lost between him and an Executive Council.

As my administration has been faithful to the spirit and purpose of civil service reform, as it has, in contrast with Republican precedents, appointed a very large proportion of men to office who were not of its political faith, notwithstanding that there was scarcely a Democrat on a salaried commission in the State at the time of my election, the rejection, for partisan reasons only, by a Republican Council of nominees admitted to be fit, is the more unjust and inexcusable.

You, Mr. Haile, were one of the Republican Executive Council that repeatedly rejected a nominee for Savings Bank Commissioner admitted by you to be fully qualified. I ask you to discuss this question before the people. It involves an important principle of executive responsibility. Will you, if elected, submit to the dictation of nominees by the Executive Council? Will you agree that they have the right to reject a proper nomination simply because they prefer some one else?

Let me direct your attention to one other State question which is always with us, and which your party has declared over and over again to be a most important question. I mean the control of the sale of intoxicating liquor.

I have tried for four successive years to get from the candidates of your party their views and their position on this question, but always without success. I have pointed out the shifting, contradictory, and hypocritical position which your party has constantly taken upon this question. There seems to be some clearing up necessary to make the people understand what is the position of your party. Your platform this year has only its usual perfunctory generalities. You can make it mean something. As head of your party, if elected, you must deal with this question. You are declared publicly by a leading minister of this State to be an ardent prohibitionist, and as such he gives you his support. Is this correct? Do you, or do you not, believe in a prohibitory law? Will you, or will you not, if elected Governor, either recommend or approve of a prohibitory law? I believe that the people have a right to know from a candidate for Governor his views upon such public questions. As a candidate and an official I have given my own repeatedly upon this question. In this Commonwealth a party cannot expect the support of the people when it hides its opinion on an important question, and forces its candidate to maintain silence upon it.

All these questions that I have asked of my distinguished opponent are about official acts and public matters with which he may have to deal. I have no wish or reason to indulge in any personal criticism. I share with the people of the Commonwealth a high opinion of his character as a man and his courtesy as a gentleman, and I value the pleasant friendship which exists between us. But these considerations should not, and will not, deter me from demanding in behalf of the people of this Commonwealth his opinion on these important State matters.

I propose next to discuss the tariff especially with reference to one great industry in this city, — the woollen industry. What is the exact position of the two parties on the tariff in relation to this industry? Their position is easily ascertained, not only from platforms and conventions, but by their acts and votes and bills. The Democratic party stands for free wool and a reduction of the tariff tax on the manufactured product as an equivalent for free wool. This position was declared in the message of President Cleveland in 1887, in platforms and conventions since, but better still in the Mills Bill of 1888, in suggested amendments to the McKinley Bill, and in the Free Wool Bill framed by the able Democratic congressman from this district, which passed the last Democratic House.

There is no possibility of misunderstanding the Democratic position on this question, and the false cry of free-trade is answered by the measures which the Democratic party has attempted to make law.

The Republican position is equally clear. It is shown in the McKinley law, which the Republicans enacted. Instead of free wool, they placed a higher duty on wool, and to meet this additional burden to the manufacturer gave him a still higher duty upon his woollen goods.

Because the tariff tax on wool is a burden to the industry, the manufacturer claims and gets additional duty on his goods, exactly equivalent to and measured by the tax on the amount of wool which enters into their manufacture, and even called a compensatory duty.

The Democratic policy in removing entirely the tariff

on wool reduces the tariff on the goods, still leaving a duty of 35 to 40 per cent, which is almost double the total labor cost of the manufactured product, as may be observed from the following table.[1] This table shows that the total labor cost is about 20 per cent of the cost of the manufactured article, and that the duty proposed by the Democratic bill is double this amount.

The Republicans say that the tariff tax is necessary to make up the difference of cost of labor here and abroad. I ask, in the name of common-sense, if twice the labor cost and many times any possible difference in labor cost here and abroad is not sufficient protection?

Let us go a step farther in the Republican policy. Not only did the McKinley Bill greatly increase the tariff duties on woollen goods, but it discriminated most unjustly in raising these duties highest on the cheapest goods used by the masses of the people, and least on the finer goods used by the few and the wealthy.

Now, which policy is the wiser and more for the interest of the people and our industries? First, note that ours is about the only civilized country which taxes wool. France and Germany, with high protection, as well as free-trade England, admit wool free. Even here there was but a light tax on wool until the war.

In 1866 the woollen manufacturers asked for free wool and 25 per cent protection on their goods; but in 1867 they entered into a bargain with the wool-grower for increased duties on wool and woollen goods, justly described as a bargain for the double skinning of the people. The wool-grower got a higher tax on wool, and because of it the manufacturer asked and got a higher

[1] Table omitted.

tax on his goods. If this coalition had not been made, and the manufacturer had insisted upon free wool, which every one knows his industry needs, that industry would have been placed on the same footing as the silk and the leather, the cotton and the paper industries now are, and would have reaped the same benefits.

Mr. Robert Bleakie, one of our leading woollen manufacturers, expressed this when he declared that he was an ardent admirer of the Mills Bill, "because it proposed to give our industry free wool and open to it the same chances for development that were enjoyed by the silk, cotton, and leather industries, which, getting their material at the world's market price, have expanded and grown until they are a credit to our country, and do a profitable exporting business. All that has been possible for them is possible for the woollen industry under similar conditions."

But the manufacturer then, as now, bending to the political influence of the political shepherds of Ohio, was afraid to assert his independence, and assented to raising higher and higher these tariff taxes upon wool and woollen goods, until they culminated in the McKinley Bill, with duties so high that the Boston "Commercial Bulletin," a Republican paper, declared, Sept. 6, 1890, that they were "simply indefensible."

Now, what has been the result? We produce less than one half the wool we use in manufacture and in imported goods. The wool clip of 1891 is less than it was seven, eight, and nine years ago. There are fewer sheep in this country than there were ten years ago. So much for the wool-raising industry, which this tax has undertaken to foster. Meanwhile our imports of wool are constantly increasing, until in

1891 they amounted to over $18,000,000, or in amount more than in any year since 1880.

Our import of woollen goods has been steadily increasing, until in 1890 they amounted in value to $54,000,000, or more than any year since the war; and in 1891, notwithstanding the severe restrictions of the McKinley Bill, and its avowed object to check imports and destroy competition, they were in amount nearly $42,000,000, or more than they have been in any year, with five exceptions, since 1875. All these imports of wool and woollen goods since the McKinley Bill have had to pay a much higher tax, which burden falls upon the people as consumers.

Meanwhile this tax upon wool has been a heavy burden on the manufacturer as well as on the consumer. So Mr. Whitman, the President of the Woollen Manufacturers' Association, declared in 1885, in his official letter to the Secretary of the Treasury, when he said, "The European manufacturer possesses the advantage which would be overwhelming, if not counteracted by special legislation, of having the raw material of his manufacture free from duty."

He adds: "Our European competitors are exempt from the direct enhancement by a duty of the cost of wool." Again he declares: "They are able from the lower cost of their raw material to relieve themselves from over-production by consigning their surplus stocks at comparatively slight sacrifice to foreign markets, to which their cheapness has already introduced them;" and, finally, he insists: "It needs to be better known that the admittedly high duties, and, on a cursory view, unduly high duties, on woollens are made necessary by the assumed necessity of protecting the domestic wool-growers and providing for them a profitable home market; and that the manufacturers, exempted from the wool duties, would be amply content with the much lower range of duties provided for other branches of the textile industry." On this ground over seven hundred woollen manufacturers and dealers petitioned Congress in 1890 to be relieved from this duty.

Let me point out one important effect of this duty. The manufacturer, shut out from getting the wool of the world, or compelled to pay a high price, has been forced to use adulterants more than ever before in the manufacture of his goods, and so the people are getting more and more shoddy, and less and less of woollen clothing and other goods.

Observe a few significant facts which show this. Note the remarkable increase in the shoddy mills, especially since 1890, as seen in the appended table,[1] which gives the mills by States, and shows an increase of 44 per cent in them since that time.

First, the census of 1890 shows a remarkable increase in the use of such materials as shoddy and animal hair and other substitutes for wool to lessen the cost to the manufacturer of woollen goods. That is seen from the appended tables[2] in the woollen, worsted, and carpet industries.

Second, in view of the increase of 44 per cent in the shoddy mills since 1890, it is fair to assume that since these tables were compiled, the use of adulterants in woollen manufactures has greatly increased.

Third. One further fact. There has been a noticeable increase also of the import of these wool substitutes, as appears from the following table.[3]

So that in place of pure wool, our manufacturers are being steadily compelled, because of this high duty on foreign wools, to substitute for it old rags, castoff clothing, animal hair, and cotton extracts. The

[1] Table omitted.   [2] Tables omitted.   [3] Table omitted.

inevitable result of such duty must be either higher prices or poorer quality, or both.

The wool consumers' petition of 1890, signed by such men as Lyman and Metcalf, and by the proprietors of the Weybosset and Worumbo mills, and other large woollen industries, declared that "the high cost of foreign wools forced the manufacturers to resort to shoddy, hair, and cotton to make so-called wools of. The importation of goods made by foreign manufacturers who have the overwhelming advantage of free selection of free material has been enormous." Now, what has been the result of this duty upon the industry? In 1888 the failures in the wool or woollen business were fifty-seven, with liabilities of $3,600,000; but in 1889 the failures had increased to seventy-two, and the liabilities to nearly $10,500,000.

On June 14, 1890, in the petition of the wool consumers which I have just mentioned, they declared: "For the protection of the woollen manufacture of the country, and for its rescue from a most hampered and depressed condition, we ask for a great reduction or the total abolition of the duty on wool." In their opinion the woollen industry was not thriving at that time. On Dec. 31, 1891, the "American Wool and Cotton Reporter" declared, "Unfortunately for the woollen goods industry, that which has been predicted [referring to the alleged benefits of the McKinley Bill] did not materialize, and 1891 goes down into history as a year of depression probably equally as intense as that which prevailed the two years previous."

I do not say that special industries like your Arlington mills, which have been given the privilege of framing a tariff schedule to suit themselves, and to tax at their pleasure a whole people, cannot make exceptional profits. I believe they can and do. But I assert that such profits, made out of the taxation of the whole people, are burdensome on the people, and are not distributed to their employees, in whose name these taxes are laid, and that they involve a gross abuse of the power of taxation.

Over and over again manufacturers and Republican authorities have protested against these high taxes in the woollen schedule. Sept. 6, 1890, the "Boston Commercial Bulletin," thoroughly familiar with this industry, speaking of the increase of these duties, said: "There is small wonder that the importers protest, and that the consumer begins to talk about monopolies."

It added: "The men responsible for the increase in the duties in woollens are Mr. Harpster and Mr. Delano, who have forced upon a weak-kneed Congress duties on a raw material that are simply indefensible."

On Oct. 25, 1890, the same paper declared, "The wool schedule of the new tariff is about as absurd a bit of political jobbery as ever was botched." And over and over again that paper has repeated this opinion.

What the woollen industry needs, and what it has repeatedly said it needed, is free raw material. One hundred manufacturers said so in 1888, and nearly seven hundred in 1890. Instead of this the Republican party has given them higher duties, with the result of higher prices and poorer goods, and all at the expense of the people. Why has this been done?

Senator Allison explained it in his speech on the McKinley Bill, Aug. 31, 1890, when he declared that the woollen schedule had been made up by "experts familiar with the trade, and by agricultural interests engaged in the growing of wool." He said that the schedule was higher than it ought to be, but that he, with his colleagues, assented to it "because this question has become a party question to a certain extent." Yes, politics had got into it. The Republican party had heard the crack of the whip in Ohio, and Massachusetts Republicans yielded to that domination. The party saw an opportunity to bind to itself a selfish interest, exact from it contributions, and give it in return the right to tax the people at its own sweet will.

What would be the effect of free wool? Let me quote a few words from manufacturers. Mr. Beach, a leading manufacturer of cloths and blankets in Hartford, declares, "Free wool would be a great advantage to us, because we could then compete with foreign manufacturers who get their wool free."

Mr. Bleakie declares, "We could sell our surplus in foreign markets profitably if wool and all necessary dyes and chemicals were free, just as well as cotton and shoe manufacturers who both sell their surplus that way."

Mr. Ayres, of Philadelphia, a leading manufacturer of blankets, declares, "Free wool means to the people cheap, good clothes, better food, and happier homes."

Mr. Metcalf, of Providence, the head of large woollen mills, said: "With free wool we have not half enough machinery in this country to supply the demands for goods." And he added that he had promised to erect a new mill in case of the passage of the Mills Bill.

Mr. Houston, the head of the Hartford Carpet Company, said that the duties on carpet wools "protect no one, and they do of course handicap the carpet manufacturers in competing with foreign products of that variety. Their removal would widen our markets, and without doubt tend to increase our exports of all kinds."

Mr. S. S. Terry, speaking for the hat and cap industry, declares, "With cheap raw materials we should take away a large part of the hat export trade, not only of England, but also of Germany, France, and other hat-making countries."

Mr. Sanford, of the well-known firm of Glover, Sanford & Co., says: "Let us buy our wool as cheaply as the English manufacturer, and we take the Englishman's market away, build up a foreign trade, give steady employment to our labor, run the year through on full time, and give our working-men three hundred days' work in the year."

And such well-known manufacturers in this vicinity as Mr. Arthur P. Lyman and Congressman Stevens have strongly urged free wool as a great benefit to their industries.

And so I might go on indefinitely, quoting from manufacturers. What is true of the woollen industry, and of the benefit of free wool to it, is also true of the benefit that would come from free coal and iron and tin and other raw material to our other industries.

Why have not we got reduction of these duties and free raw material? Because the few and the wealthy are controlling legislation and using it for their profit, no matter what the burden to the people or injury to their industries. Behind these taxes on coal and iron and lumber and wool and tin stands always some selfish interest, making profits out of the people's law. These selfish interests control and dominate the Republican party, giving their money to get that party power, and exacting in return legislation for their benefit. They compel it to violate its pledges, to break its promises, and, raising taxes higher and higher, to lay down as its fixed principle and policy the right to use the power of government, not for public purposes, but for selfish interests, and the power of taxation, not for revenue, but for private gain.

The saddest of all this is that the Republican party of Massachusetts, which used to be led by its Andrews and Sumners and Wilsons, to be devoted to high purposes and governed by conscience and patriotism, is now kneeling with the rest, and has surrendered itself body and soul to selfish interests. No wonder day by day there step out of it men of character and conscience. No wonder we hear of its MacVeaghs and Greshams and Cooleys and Coxes and Amherst professors, and thousands of others, who are influenced by their high character and motives, abandoning this party. It is fast losing its character as it attempts to subvert the proper purposes and power of government, to carry elections by money, and to pay for its success by taxing a people.

The time has come when the people are going to say, in a voice that cannot be mistaken, that no such interests with such a purpose and such results shall usurp a people's government and control a people's law.

SPEECH

AT FITCHBURG, OCT. 31, 1892, UPON THE TARIFF IN ITS RELATION TO THE IRON INDUSTRY.

LET us consider the effect of the tariff upon the iron and steel industry. Here is an industry which is one of the oldest in New England, and used to be one of the greatest and most prosperous. I am not speaking now of the manufacture of metallic goods and machinery, where fifty-six per cent of the capital invested is covered by United States patents, and where the raw material makes but a small proportion of the cost. The manufacturers of patented machinery and specialties no doubt can get along under the shelter of their patents, where the burden of the tariff tax on their raw material is comparatively slight. But I am speaking of the great industry which used to be represented by many blast and puddling furnaces, iron and steel rolling-mills, nail works, and shovel factories, and by heavy millwrighting, and the rolling, casting, and finishing of iron, and the various forms of iron and steel industries, where the raw material is an important element of their cost.

How does this great industry stand to-day under high protective tariff taxation? Let me turn to Republican authorities for a statement of the facts, and let the usual Republican answer, that he who states these facts is "calamity shrieking," be given by that party to its own utterances.

First, I quote from the Census Bulletin No. 156, of Jan. 18, 1892, on the manufactures of iron and steel in the New England States, issued by Mr. Porter, the Superintendent of the Census, and prepared by his special agents. It shows, in the first place, that iron and steel establishments in New England from 1880 to 1890 decreased from 61 to 35, and the number of working-men employed from 8,654 to 6,645.

Mr. Porter, in speaking of this decline, says that "it is due principally to local causes affecting the supply of raw material." After referring to the fact of an increase in the value of the products made, it says, "This is due mainly to the development of a single concern engaged in the manufacture of more highly finished products of iron and steel. While the value of the products of this establishment has more than doubled during the past decade, there has been a decline of almost one-half in the aggregate business of the other works during the same period." I believe the concern referred to is the Washburn & Moen Works of Worcester, which has recently transferred a portion of its plant to the West, because of the burdens here and the greater advantages there.

The census report further shows that the blast furnaces in New England were reduced between 1880 and 1890 from 14 to 10; that of the blast furnaces reported in 1890 three were idle during the entire year, and that the number of rolling-mills and steel works from 1880 to 1890 diminished from 44 to 25. It adds: "During the period covered by the 10th census the establishments, since abandoned, represent an invested capital of $2,932,000, giving employment to 2,262 hands." It further says: "Several works that have continued in operation have abandoned portions of their plant, and are now running on a smaller scale than formerly."

It still further shows that of the machinery in the rolling and steel works during this period there has been a decrease in single puddling furnaces from 220 to 48, of heating furnaces from 302 to 162, of open-hearth furnaces from 7 to 3, of crucible pots per heat from 202 to 188, of hammers from 49 to 39, and of cut-nail machines from 801 to 311. Speaking of the 48 puddling furnaces still remaining, it adds: "It should be explained that the greater number of these furnaces were idle during the census of 1890, and very few of them are likely ever to be used again for the purpose for which they were built." It further states that "the re-rolling of Norway and Swedish iron was formerly an important branch of the iron industry in New England, but within the past decade it has dwindled to small proportions." It speaks of the "considerable decrease in the quantity of pig iron used," and so it goes on giving innumerable facts as to the decline of this industry.

It states the reason for the decline as follows: "The decline in the iron rolling-mill industry of New England has been due chiefly to conditions peculiar to locality rather than to causes affecting the industry at large. The rapid growth of the iron and steel industry in other sections of the country, where pig iron and fuel can be obtained at much lower cost, has gradually narrowed the market of most of the New England iron mills to the limits of local demand, and even much of this trade has been absorbed by manufacturers in more favored localities." It adds, "There is no local supply of either fuel or pig iron."

Now, the only reason why other sections obtain their raw material at much lower cost is that their natural advantages are secured, and more than secured, to them by law, while our natural advantages of sea-coast location are neutralized by the same law which prevents, through tariff taxation, our getting our raw material through our ports. Remember, I have been quoting from the report of the political Superintendent of the Census, who is always trying to use his office for service to the Republican party.

Let us now turn to another authority, — the industry itself; speaking through the principal iron and steel concerns in New England, and pleading for its life in its petition to the New England congressmen in 1889. It pointed out in that petition the distress in its industry, but most emphatically the remedy, declaring, — let me quote, —

"There is no necessity for letting it die; it is only the existing duties on coal, ore, and crude iron that are strangling these industries; and the abolition of these duties will not only keep it alive, but will insure it a renewed vitality, a large increase, and will add more largely to the wealth and population of New England than any possible legislation upon any other subject."

Governor Ames, with his large practical experience in this industry, and still a staunch Republican, has over and over again publicly declared the same facts. Feb. 15, 1892, he said that "the old law [1883] was, and the new law [McKinley] is, in its effect, hostile to some of the interests of New England,— notably our iron industries, — in preventing her from enjoying those advantages she ought to have from our proximity to the sea, thus depriving her of the opportunity to compete on equal terms in many ways with other sections of the country." Speaking of this petition, which he had signed, he declared, on March 31, 1892, "It would save to New England her iron manufactures, and I signed to save them." On June 20, 1892, referring to the decadence of the great iron industries, he said: "No candid man can deny that these works are closed, never to be reopened, and others now running must be closed, unless the tariff laws are speedily so changed that raw material for them can be obtained at a price which will enable their proprietors to run them at a profit."

Now, what has been the cause of this disaster to the iron and steel industry? Just the cause stated by the industry itself, — the taxation of its raw material, the heavy tariff duties upon coal, iron ore, and pig and scrap iron. How came these heavy duties to be laid? I assert that they were laid for special and selfish interests, for the benefit of the few without regard to the rights of the many, and for the benefit of other sections of the country, with no regard to the interests or the rights of New England industries.

Take, for example, the tax upon iron ore of seventy-five cents a ton. The Tariff Commission of 1882, made up wholly of representatives of protected industries, recommended that that duty be reduced to fifty cents. A bill with such reduction passed the House and the Senate; but the bill went into a conference committee on other points, and when it came out, this tax was found to be seventy-five cents a ton, as at present.

What was the reason for this? Let me quote the facts and the reason from the leading Republican authority on the tariff, Senator Aldrich. In the debate on Aug. 7, 1890, in the United States Senate, he said: "The facts were these: It is true that the bill introduced by the senator from Ohio in this body, and the member from Pennsylvania [Mr. Kelley] in the other house, which was identically the Tariff Commission's report, contained a provision fixing a rate of duty of fifty cents per ton upon iron ore. It is also true that the bill as it passed the Senate fixed the rate of duty upon iron ore at fifty cents a ton." And then he adds: "I think I may say without any violation of the secrets of the committee [the conference committee] — because in a certain sense it is an open secret — that the rate was increased on account of the urgent solicitation and great array of facts which were presented to members of the conference by one of its members, the then senator from Virginia, Mr. Mahone." And he further adds, " Upon his urgent request and suggestion the rate was increased to seventy-five cents a ton."

This was about the time of the infamous coalition between the Republican party and the readjuster senator and repudiating Republican faction in Virginia, to carry out which coalition, you remember, the junior senator from this State threatened to hold the Senate " until the crack of doom." The first fruit of that coalition was the appointment of Mr. Riddleberger of Virginia to an important office in the Senate. And the second fruit of that coalition was the higher tariff duty upon iron ore, which was higher than that recommended by the Tariff Commission or by either house, and which, with its kindred duties, is killing a great New England industry.

The urgent demand of a single Republican senator, to which the Republican party yielded, gave us this infliction. Yielded! It was bound to yield. Is not its whole tariff policy founded on the principle and pledge that all protected interests must stand united for the tariff taxation each demands, and that it is not safe to lower a single duty, however exorbitant or unjust, for fear that their coalition may break, and their system be endangered? New England may thank this coalition and this unjust policy for the putting out of the fires in her great industry, for the throwing out of employment of thousands of her working-men, and for the closing up of the great concerns which I have mentioned.

What injury has flowed from these taxes? Why, look about you. All can recall the death or migration of such great works as the Norway Iron & Steel Company, the South Boston Iron Works, the Hinckley Locomotive Works, the National Tube Works, and rolling-mills and foundries and iron works by the score.

I have quoted in this campaign the words of John Roach and Mr. Cramp, the great ship-builders, who have said that with free iron ore on the banks of the Delaware River they could build ships as cheaply as ships could be built on the Clyde; the words of Mr. Bent, president of one of the largest iron and steel companies of Pennsylvania, who said that with free raw material he could lay down pig iron in Liverpool, and send steel rails to London; the assertions of great manufacturers like Mr. Sargent of Connecticut, and many others to the same effect; and nearly the whole of our iron and steel industry of New England has uttered the same opinion as to the great benefit that free raw material would be to it.

Now, who would be injured by reducing or removing these duties? I assert that no one who has a right to complain or who is supplying a market which rightly belongs to him. The removal of these duties means that here in New England we shall supply our own market from our own industries, and that that market shall not be seized by Pennsylvania, who gets it only by the privilege of an unjust law which permits her to destroy our industry. Never before has protection been carried to that extreme. It never was understood to give the right to one industry to take the life of another, — and that, too, not that the first might live, but fatten with inordinate profits on the victims it has killed.

Let me call your attention now to those who are benefited by this tariff taxation, which is such an injury to this New England industry. The "Iron Age" of Jan. 30, 1890, referring to the beneficiaries of this tariff protection, said: "The iron ore mining companies of the Lake

Superior region are now reaping enormous profits." It spoke of the dividend of twenty-five per cent just declared by the Metropolitan Iron & Land Company. On April 30, 1890, it said : " The dividends declared in fifteen months by the Pittsburg & Lake Angeline Company have amounted to $710,000, which, it will be observed, is considerably more than the entire capital."

An editorial in the " Boston Herald " on Jan. 18, 1891, gives the carefully prepared figures of Mr. N. Dale, of Pittsburg, showing the enormous profits earned during the year 1890 by some of the iron firms of Pittsburg. Thirty-one firms are given, whose aggregate profits amount to from $20,000,000 to $21,000,000. The Lake Superior mines and the Pittsburg manufacturers, sheltered under these high protective duties, are both reaping enormous profits, which come from taxation of the people, and at the same time are at the expense of the great iron and steel industries of New England.

But our Republican friends say that the Democratic party does not propose to reduce or remove these duties, and so help our own industries. Over and over again the Democratic party has declared, in National and State conventions, in favor of free raw materials, — free wool, coal, iron, and the other raw materials which are the basis of our industries. Time and again it has attempted by legislation to put its declaration into law, starting always with free wool as the cardinal point of its policy.

But Republicans ask, " When have you ever voted to reduce the duties on coal and iron ? " I will tell them when. The only time the Democratic party had any fair chance to discuss or amend the McKinley Bill, that party by its united action in the United States Senate moved and voted for amendments reducing these high duties. We never had a chance in the House; for

Speaker Reed drove that bill through the House with a coach-and-four, with scores of amendments, and many on this very line, pending, not reached, and not acted upon. But in the United States Senate, where there was opportunity for discussion, Massachusetts saw Democratic senators like Morgan of Alabama and Kenna of West Virginia, from great iron and coal producing States, voting and speaking for reduction of duties upon coal and iron for the benefit of New England industries, while our own Republican senators from New England were humbly bowing to the will of Pennsylvania, and turning a deaf ear to the demands of New England, — were giving their votes and their influence against the reduction of these very duties.

No wonder New England, and especially Massachusetts, uttered her protest in 1890 against the neglect and betrayal of her interests. I said then that she had a score to settle with these her recreant sons and representatives; and hardly were the words spoken when Massachusetts settled that score with them, and told them that their first duty was to her rather than to Pennsylvania. And she repudiated those who had forgotten her, not only in their support of this high McKinley tariff, but in their support of such dangerous financial measures as the Silver Act of 1890, and such revolutionary measures as the Lodge Force Bill. In all of these the Republican representatives from Massachusetts have been untrue to her interests and her beliefs.

Feeling the sting of this rebuke, we see them now apologizing for and repudiating their action on silver legislation, and maintaining a cowardly silence on their Force Bill. It is time they began to repent, too, for their action on the tariff question, for just as surely as the conscience and the interests of this Commonwealth, her love of justice and liberty, repudiated Lodge Force

Bills and Sherman Silver Bills, so do they also repudiate the McKinley Tariff Bill, which was conceived in selfishness, bought and paid for by the campaign fund of its beneficiaries, which has given to them profits wrung from the taxation of a people, and which distinctly and emphatically threatens the institutions of our country and the liberties of our people.

SPEECH

AT HAVERHILL, OCT. 24, 1893, UPON THE POLITICAL CAUSES OF THE BUSINESS DEPRESSION OF 1893.

YOUR welcome makes me feel almost as if again I were a candidate whom you were cheering on to victory; but though not a candidate, I rejoice that at last relief from official engagements permits me to go into the thick of the fight and to raise my voice for our party, its principles, its honored candidates, and its brave and steadfast President.

Gladly I thank the Democracy for the united, earnest support which for years they have given me, and I urge upon them to give a like support to our able leader, who, year in and year out, has fought the good fight and kept the faith. We are honored by his candidacy, and Massachusetts will be honored by his election.

To-night I propose especially to deal with National matters. We are in the midst of prevailing distress which all deplore, but out of which one party is striving to make political capital. It is well for us, therefore, to consider its cause, its remedy, where rests the responsibility for both, and the influence of our election upon the decision of these questions.

I readily agree that the vote of Massachusetts will have a National influence, — at least upon that brave and patriotic man who, as President of the whole country and of all the people, stands firm in the midst of storm, dissensions, and partisanship as the bulwark of the people's rights and interests, and voicing their demand for legislation and relief. He is listening to the voice of Massachusetts. He knows that the Democratic party here in its candidate, its platform, and its united ranks is behind him heart and soul in the fight. He is watching and waiting to hear in its success that word of good cheer and godspeed which he has a right to expect from this loyal Commonwealth to nerve him to the courageous discharge of his patriotic duty.

What sort of encouragement will it be to him and the cause of repeal if Massachusetts, by the election of Mr. Greenhalge,[1] supports, forgives, or forgets the man who by his vote, given for politics and not for patriotism, is largely responsible for the ills we have? Is a bad law to be repealed by honoring its sponsor or supporter? No, a thousand times no. Rather let the righteous, indignant demand of our people spend at least a part of its force in the punishment of such sponsor or supporter, not only for present good, but for future warning. I repeat that the ills we have are caused by laws for which Mr. Greenhalge and the Republican party are responsible. I understand the issue to be whether our admitted distress is due to existing Republican legislation or impending Democratic legislation. Let us see what the situation is.

We are still living under the laws and policy of the Republican party. Its policy upon tariff and finance is still the law of the land. Our revenue is raised under Republican taxation; our money is spent under Republican appropriations. If mills are closed, remember that the Republican McKinley Bill is still in force. If honest and sound money is threatened, remember that the Republican Sherman Bill is still unrepealed. If there is an accumulating deficit of $50,000,000 a year in the treasury, remember that President Cleveland left to

[1] The Republican candidate for Governor.

his successor a surplus of over a hundred millions, and that our income and expenses since have been determined by the Republican party.

These causes, many and still existing, gave us four years of reckless, extravagant Republican legislation, with the inevitable result of panic and distress. We find ourselves to-day suffering from diminished revenue, increasing expenses, reduced gold reserve, and a flood of useless silver. No wonder confidence is shaken and business stagnant. Yes, but the Republican party, through its McKinley Bill, declared its purpose to shut off imports, and so reduce revenue. Then it set the precedent of the extravagant billion-dollar Congress, and by its laws fastened these expenses on the future. Then, for politics, and politics only, protection and silver made their coalition for taxing and skinning the people, and, against the unanimous protest of the Democratic party, passed the Sherman Bill.

We know the excuse of the Republican party, that the Sherman Bill was necessary to defeat free coinage. We deny it, and no intelligent man believes this. The House had already defeated free coinage. The President, it was known, would veto it. The excuse of the Republicans means that this measure could pass by a two-thirds vote of the Senate and the House, though a majority of the House had already declared against it. No, the Sherman Bill was not passed from patriotism to avert a danger, but from politics to risk a danger, in order to save the mining States to the Republican party and to secure the passage of the McKinley Bill. And so Republicans themselves have confessed. Senator Teller, a Republican, said in the Senate recently that Senator Sherman, when he reported his bill, "stated in the most emphatic manner that the House of Representatives had determined in a very positive way that no free coinage bill could pass that body." Mr. Teller added that, "keeping as closely within the rules of senatorial decency and courtesy as the circumstances will admit," the excuse of Senator Sherman "was an afterthought," and that the real purpose of the passage of that bill was "to maintain intact in the Northwest the Republican column of States."

Senator Sherman, on July 8, 1890, in reporting his bill, used the language which I have quoted, and a Congressman from this State, in the discussion in the House, declared : ." We Republicans want to come back. That is all there is in this silver bill, — pure politics. Being a Republican and voting politically, I am for this bill."

I admit that neither party is united upon this question. But the difference between them is that at the critical moment the Republican party yields to financial heresy in its ranks, and the Democratic party conquers it.

Let us look at the record. In 1884, notwithstanding a difference of opinion in the Democratic party, Mr. Cleveland announced his firm opposition to free coinage and all unsound silver legislation, and for the four following years there was no talk or hope of such legislation. Contrast his course with the action of the Republican party in 1888, which, instead of supporting him in his course, by the solemn action of its National Convention denounced him and his party for their hostility to silver. Then the Republican party followed this by the admission of silver Territories with scarcely enough population to be entitled to a member of Congress, and did this to strengthen the Republican party in the Senate for years to come, with the inevitable result of financial heresy, no matter what the injury might be to the country. Then it followed this action by the passage of the Sherman Bill; and Mr. McKinley, its leader, was sent through the country advocating silver, and denouncing Mr. Cleveland and his party for their opposition to it. An ominous silence followed in the Republican platforms in State and Nation while the dangers and evils of the Sherman Bill were becoming more and more manifest. Contrast such action with the record of the Democratic party in 1892 in Congress and in its National Convention. There it met and fought and defeated the spirit of financial unsoundness within its party, denounced the Sherman Bill, demanded its repeal, and nominated for President the man who stands to-day, and always has stood, as a pillar of strength for sound and honest money; and Democratic Conventions since have sustained him in his course. Within a few weeks, in Nebraska, the Democratic party in convention, by a vote of three to one, indorsed his policy. And now the country turns with confidence to the Democratic party to cure this distress by undoing Republican legislation. It knows the cause of its trouble, and the cure.

From boards of trade and business centres throughout the country there has come a unanimous demand for what? To let the tariff alone? No; but, without a dissenting voice, to repeal the Sherman Bill. Patiently and hopefully, business watches every move at Washington, as if its very life depended upon the action of the Senate. No barometer ever more truly indicated change of weather than business indicates from day to day the ups and downs of the movement for repeal. It knows and says through its representatives that the one predominant cause of our trouble is the financial legislation of a Republican Congress, and the one remedy for the evil is its repeal by a Democratic Congress.

But the Republican party, anxious to shirk this responsibility, pretends that our troubles are due, not to existing laws, but to laws which the Democrats mean to pass; that we are not reaping the whirlwind which the Republicans have sown, but are suffering because an overwhelming majority of the people have thrust them from power and condemned their financial and tariff policies. They tell the laborer out of work that his suffering is due to the Democratic victory. They forget to tell him that no law has yet been changed, that he is still enjoying the blessings of McKinleyism, of high protection and Republican laws and policy.

Let us examine briefly their claim. What is the legislation the Democrats intend to pass? First, the repeal of the Sherman Bill. To this they are pledged; for this their President has called Congress together in special session; already the Democratic House has passed repeal by an overwhelming vote; and a Democratic Senate, in spite of all obstruction, is bound to follow, without compromise or concession.

The Democratic party has no thought of avoiding the full responsibility which rests upon it now; but if the country is impatient of delay, let it remember that it takes time to exhaust Stewart and Teller and Jones and Peffer and Allen and Du Bois and Wolcott, — not one of them a Democrat, and all permitted by foolish rules to talk to their heart's content. Let it be remembered, also, that it takes time to change the rules which a Republican Senate for a generation has established and upheld. But just as sure as the rising sun, the right of a majority to rule and of a legislative body to vote will be asserted, and, with or without rules, the demand of the country for legislation will be enforced. It is no time now to talk of compromise, but, under a Democratic President, it is our duty to fight this battle to a finish, and in the repeal of the Sherman Bill to establish once and for all the right of a majority to rule.

Is this the impending legislation which causes trouble? No; but in the unanimous opinion at least of the people of this State it is the sole and necessary remedy.

But the Republicans say it is fear of reduction of the tariff which is injuring business, and that the Democratic party means to repeal the McKinley Bill and to reduce the tariff. It is true the Democratic party has, by the deliberate, repeated judgment of the country, been charged with the duty of reducing tariff taxation and repealing the McKinley Bill. It is true it means faithfully to discharge this duty and to enforce the will of the country. No vote in Massachusetts or elsewhere can change its purpose or swerve it from this duty; but the vote and support of Massachusetts can give her influence in such legislation, and make her as potent a factor in Democratic tariff reform as Pennsylvania or Ohio has been in Republican high protection.

But I assert emphatically that the fear of tariff reduction has not caused present distress, and will be when accomplished only a blessing to our people and their industries.

Let us look a little into the past, and see how far the fear or promise of tariff reduction has been an injury to business or caused distress. There has scarcely been a year since the close of the war until the surrender of the Republican party to McKinleyism when there has not been promised and impending tariff reduction. Even the war tariff was passed under a distinct pledge that it should be reduced when the war was over. Presidents Grant and Arthur and their Secretaries of the Treasury frequently urged such reduction. The Tariff Commission of 1882, made up wholly of protectionists, and almost wholly of Republicans, after thorough examination recommended a reduction of from 20 to 25 per cent. In 1884 the Republican party generally, and notably in this State in its Convention, and speaking through Mr. Long and Mr. Lodge, recommended such reduction, and largely on the line of the present Democratic policy. Then, in 1887, came the vigorous message of President Cleveland, followed by the Mills Bill, that proposed reduction, but not so large as had before been advocated by Republicans themselves. Through all these years there were promise and hope of tariff reduction through both the Republican and the Democratic parties; and though these efforts failed, some of them unexpectedly, nowhere did the expectation of tariff reduction cause panic or business distress. There came then three years more of agitation for tariff reduction; then the emphatic verdict of the country in 1890, with its condemnation of the McKinley Bill, and its overwhelming demand for tariff reduction; and in that verdict Massachusetts joined, and sent a majority of Democratic Congressmen to carry out her will.

It was perfectly certain then that tariff reduction had got to come. True, Republican control could still thwart the will of the country; but its unmistakable judgment had been rendered, and it was certain that it must soon prevail. The timid manufacturer who believed that this would be an injury to him might well have shortened sail; tariff reduction on Democratic lines was then impending. Was there business depression? The Republicans say that after the McKinley Bill had been emphatically repudiated there followed years of prosperity; but, whether prosperity or not, was our condition due to the McKinley Bill, or to its repudiation by the country?

Then came the election of 1892, and the country again and more emphatically repeated its verdict, demanded tariff reduction, and, for the first time since the war, restored Democracy to power in all branches of the government, to make its will law. It was certainly known then that McKinleyism had got to go, and that tariff reform was to be a settled fact. Yet prosperity continued. Not for months afterwards did we have depression.

Did Massachusetts fear tariff reduction? Why, no longer ago than April of this year, in one of her most important manufacturing districts, she reversed a large Republican majority, and sent a Democrat to Congress to aid in the good work of tariff reform.

The McKinley law is still in force. If it brought good times, it has also brought hard times. Twice it has been repudiated by the country, yet for months and years after, prosperity continued. Not until our revenue fell off and gold was exported, our gold reserve impaired and silver purchases had enormously increased, — all acts directly chargeable to Republican legislation, — not until then was confidence destroyed. Then business became stagnant and mills idle. If ever a party was responsible for public evils, the Republican party is to-day for its legislation, which has led to this certain result. No wonder it is trying to shift the responsibility on to other shoulders, and to deceive the people by declaring that it is Democratic victory and tariff reform which cause distress. No honest, intelligent man believes that to be the true cause, not even Republican leaders and protectionists.

Listen for a minute to their evidence. Mr. Thomas Dolan, the president, I believe, of the Manufacturers' Club of Philadelphia, the most important protective organization in the country, says,—

"I believe that the depression is almost wholly due to the silver policy. If the alarm was due to the victory of the Democrats, why was it not manifested last November?

The people knew then as well as they know now that it was within the power of the new administration to repeal the tariff laws, yet no uneasiness was felt."

And then, having in mind the repeal of Republican legislation, he adds : —

"As soon as Congress enacts the proper laws, I look for a complete restoration of confidence, which will cause the tide of prosperity again to sweep over the land."

Senator Sherman no longer ago than October 17 declared in the Senate, —

"If we would repeal the Silver Act to-morrow, after the long debate that has been had, and dispose of this question as we think best for the people of the United States while you are assuming your responsibility, we would gladden the hearts of millions of laboring men who are now being turned out of employment, we would relieve the business cares of thousands of men whose whole fortunes are embarked in trade. We would relieve the farmer of his product for free transportation to foreign countries, now clogged for the want of money."

And he adds : —

"In ten days from this time the skies will brighten, business will resume its ordinary course, and 'the clouds that lower upon our house will be in the deep bosom of the ocean buried.'"

These leading Republicans and protectionists point out the true cause of our trouble; and for that cause the Republican party is solely responsible, and no man in it more so than the Republican candidate for Governor in this State.

Now let us go one step farther. I assert that the fear of tariff reform not only is not the cause of our distress, but that the Democratic policy, when accomplished, will be a help to our industries. Massachusetts said so in 1890. Even in the presidential year of 1892 she gave the smallest majority for Republican congressmen that she has ever given in a presidential year; and she certainly said so again in one district at least in April, 1893, in the election of Dr. Everett.

What is the Democratic policy? It is to reduce tariff taxation so as to cheapen the necessaries of life and give free raw materials to our industries. This is the policy of the Democratic party as declared in its National Conventions and State Conventions over and over again, in bills which it has formulated, and in votes which it has given.

Just as certain as that the McKinley Bill has got to go, it is also certain that in its place will come a Democratic bill, with free wool, coal, iron ore, and other raw materials for our industries, and still raising the revenue necessary for public purposes.

Is such a policy, or the fear of such a policy, an injury to our industries, or the cause of our depression and idleness? I say no, emphatically no.

Every large iron and steel industry, almost without exception, in New England declared over its signature that free raw materials not only would bring prosperity to that industry, but are necessary for its very life. Republican tariff duties on its raw material, they said in exact terms, were "wiping out," "strangling" this industry, and that the "abolition of those duties will not only keep it alive, but will insure it a tremendous vitality and large increase."

So the woollen industry, speaking through such great manufacturers as Stevens, Lyman, Blaikie, and seven hundred other manufacturers and dealers, declared that free wool would be a great benefit to it. Every civilized nation except ours has said the same thing, and given to its woollen industry the great boon of free wool. The whole industry here was in favor of this policy in 1866, and petitioned for free wool, and twenty-five per cent only of protection on its finished product. Then came the "trade" in 1867 between the woollen manufacturer and the wool-grower, by which they, leaving the people wholly out of account, agreed that the grower should have a high tariff tax on wool, and because of this burden to the manufacturer that he too was to have a higher tariff tax on woollen goods.

It was one of those "trades" of which we have seen so many since, — sometimes one industry with another, sometimes the protectionist with the silver-mine owner, sometimes the Republican party with all protected interests; all seeking the interest of the producer only, neglecting that of the whole people as consumers, and using their law to tax them, not for public purposes, but for private benefits.

What do these tariff taxes on wool, high, and made still higher by the McKinley Bill, mean to you and to me? I will tell you what they are intended to mean: A higher price for wool; a higher cost of woollen goods; a burden on all of us as consumers; a burden also on the manufacturer. Because of it he asked and got a further tariff tax on his finished goods, called "compensatory," because to make up for the burden to him of taxing wool.

That is what the McKinley Bill meant, that is what Mr. McKinley himself meant when, in reporting it, he declared that he did not believe "that our people, already suffering from low prices, can or will be satisfied with legislation which will result in lower prices."

That is what Mr. Greenhalge meant when in his speech here, October 16, he declared that these articles taxed were luxuries, — having in mind, I suppose, the fact that they were made expensive, and so luxuries, under Republican high protection. Let me quote his words: —

"'I will make and advance this principle in economic laws as adapted to our nation of producers: that any man who wants to buy as against a native product the product of another nation is in effect trying to buy a luxury, and, therefore, that luxury should be treated as a proper subject of taxation, in order to equalize the taxation of our people here."

You notice he says he "makes" that principle. He seems to have a remarkable faculty for making off-hand new tariff principles which the wisdom and discussion of one hundred years have quite overlooked.

"Luxuries," he calls them. Are coal and wool, are food and clothing, luxuries? Are they made so because you can buy them cheaper in another market? Is coal made a luxury to you because you can get it seventy-five cents a ton less if the Republican tariff tax is lifted?

Against his novel principle of economics I will advance this plain principle of common-sense: That where a tariff tax is laid upon a necessary of life which is the raw material of a great industry, and such tax is not needed for revenue, then the tax is unjust, unnecessary, and injurious, because a burden on the people and a burden on their industries. Such are these taxes on coal and wool and crude iron and the raw materials of our industries.

Which principle, his or this, do you believe is best for the working-man?

Well, let us see what the effect would be of removing these taxes, as the Democratic party proposes to do.

They were laid, as Mr. McKinley confessed and protection declares, for the purpose of making these materials higher in price. Remove the taxes, and you make these materials cheaper. If wool is cheaper, clothing is cheaper; if clothing is cheaper, there is a greater demand for it. You and I might buy two suits, perhaps, where now we buy one. If there is a greater demand, then more clothes must be made. Then comes more work, a greater demand for labor. Then come the two jobs looking for the one man, instead of the two men for the one job, and then necessarily come higher wages.

Take as another illustration the cotton industry. Suppose the government should put an internal tax on cotton as it does a tariff tax on wool, or that a short crop or other cause should raise its price: what would be the effect on this industry? Well, cotton goods would be higher, people would then buy less, and you would manufacture less. Then mills would become idle, wages would be reduced, and men would be out of work. You remember when Mr. McKinley planned to put back the tariff tax on hides, the raw material of the leather and boot and shoe industries, there came a vigorous protest from Massachusetts and throughout the country. Did not the manufacturers say it would be a serious injury to that industry? Mr. McKinley said there was just as much reason for taxing hides as for taxing wool. He was right; but he did not dare to put back that tax. The Democratic party says there is just as much reason for free wool as free hides, and it means to remove that tax.

Working-men, — I address you especially now, — if your employer tells you that tariff reduction is going to hurt your industry, ask him how free wool is going to hurt it? Ask him if free silk has been an injury to the silk industry, or free hides to the boot and shoe industry, or free rags to the paper industry. If so, why did the Republican party remove the duties on those raw materials? If he says free wool means free woollen goods, ask him how he knows it. Tell him the Democratic party has twice put its tariff policy into bills which it has tried to make law; that those bills gave free wool and a tariff on woollen goods higher than the whole labor cost of the goods, and much higher than the twenty-five per cent which in 1866 the woollen manufacturers said was all that was necessary; and then tell him that your representative, Mr. Stevens, who is more largely interested in the woollen industry than any other man in the country, says there can be a reduction of these taxes with benefit to the people and the industry, and add that he is an influential member of the committee which is to fix these tariff schedules.

If your employer tells you that high tariff makes high wages, ask him how he proves it. Remind him that in free-trade England wages are higher than in the protected countries of Europe; that average wages here are lower in protected industries than in the unprotected; that they increased more under a low tariff than they have under a high tariff; and that the Democratic policy of free raw materials means greater demand for goods, and so for labor. Then say to him quietly — very quietly, for he is sensitive on this point — that we have now a high tariff in the McKinley Bill, the highest tariff the country has ever known; that under it wages have been cut down, mills are idle, and men out of work.

If he says you get higher wages than men do in England, tell him yes, because you earn them, and do more work. Measured in dollars, they are higher; measured by your work, they are not. Not one dollar is paid you which you have not fully earned in comparison with labor anywhere. Remind him that the leaders of his party, Evarts and Blaine, both so declared when they were Republican Secretaries of State.

If your Republican employer then turns and threatens you, and tries to coerce your vote, keep your peace,— your bread may be lost by a hasty word,— but go to the polls and vote as your conscience and convictions dictate; for there is no meaner or more unjust man than the one who, having the power to take the bread from the mouth of another, tries through this power to coerce his conscience and control his vote. In the secrecy of the polling-booth you can resent intimidation, you can remember that the Democratic party is and always has been your friend and champion.

Working-men, the Democratic party, of which you are the backbone, and which has always fought for your interests, has no policy on the tariff which will not bring to you cheaper necessaries of life, greater comfort and happiness to your homes, and increased prosperity to your industries. If you are suffering to-day, remember you are still under the laws and policy of the Republican party, still reaping what they have sown, and that they are to blame for present evils. The country, disgusted and indignant at Republican misrule, placed Democracy in power to undo Republican work and to remedy its mischief. The Democratic party is now beginning this duty. As it proceeds with its good work, I believe there will come to our country, North and South, East and West, greater prosperity and happiness.

THE END.

www.ingramcontent.com/pod-product-compliance
Lightning Source LLC
Chambersburg PA
CBHW020834020526
44114CB00040B/749